RELEASED

AMERICAN ANTHROPOLOGIST

The Human Element in Industrialization

A Hypothetical Case Study of Ecuadorean Indians

6

By

BEATE R. SALZ

HD
8316
S3

ST. JOSEPH'S UNIVERSITY   STX
HD8316.S3
The human element in industrialization;

3 9353 00088 3338

107880

AMERICAN ANTHROPOLOGICAL ASSOCIATION

VOL. 57 · NO. 6 · PART 2 · MEMOIR NO. 85 · DECEMBER 1955

This is published jointly with the Research Center in Economic Development and Cultural Change, University of Chicago, and appears as Volume IV, Number 1, Part 2 (October, 1955) of *Economic Development and Cultural Change*. Financial assistance toward publication has been contributed by the Wenner-Gren Foundation for Anthropological Research, Inc., and the Department of Anthropology, University of Chicago.

The *American Anthropologist* is published six times a year in the months of February, April, June, August, October, and December by the American Anthropological Association. Subscription is by membership in the Association, which includes the issues of the *American Anthropologist* and the *Memoirs* as published. Entered as second-class matter in the post office in Menasha, Wisconsin. Accorded the special rate of postage provided for in paragraph 4, section 538, P.L. & R., authorized August 22, 1922.

TO

ARTHUR SALZ

Father   Friend   Scholar

PREFACE

The case developed in this book is essentially a construct or model designed to illuminate in some manner the immediate reactions and effects which the introduction of a deliberate course of industrialization is likely to elicit among a specific geographical and population segment of Ecuador. The latter, similarly, constitutes a reality that is inferred and, as it were, synthetized from extant literary materials rather than known directly. Whether the experiment presented in the pages that follow is convincing, whether the case is a realistic one, and the reality on which it is based a substantial one, are questions that remain open. A three-weeks' visit of Ecuador in the Fall of 1950, after the completion of the first version of this study, gave me an opportunity to compare actual reality with my inferred and constructed one. The comparison, although based on necessarily superficial impressions, yielded amplifications and confirmations, but no corrections to my case.

This study was begun toward the end of 1944 and owes its inception to a combination of interests: one, of long standing, in Latin America, its distinctive societies and time-layered cultures; others were provoked by the questions raised by, and the very contemporary concern with, the expansion of forms typical of mid-twentieth century and industrial civilization across the globe. In addition, a certain insensitivity toward the boundaries conventionally drawn among the various disciplines of the social sciences, and between them and the humanities, accounts for the general conception, design and approach underlying this study. As now presented, it is a revision[1] of a dissertation submitted in 1950 to the Graduate Faculty of Political and Social Science of the New School for Social Research in partial fulfillment of the requirements for the degree of doctor of philosophy. I wish to express my cordial thanks to Professors Adolph Lowe, Carl Mayer, and Hans Staudinger, members of the dissertation committee, for their active interest in this work. Professor Staudinger, by virtue of his chairmanship of the Council of Research of the then Institute of World Affairs of the New School, has particularly stimulated some of the ideas developed in this study.

Research and completion of the dissertation, as well as the present revision, were made possible by grants awarded by the Wenner-Gren Foundation for Anthropological Research, Incorporated (formerly The Viking Fund, Inc.) for study of "The Human Factor in the Industrialization of Some Latin American Countries." The Foundation has also provided other facilities materially furthering this project which included orientation in the field in Mexico, Ecuador, and Peru during 1950-1952. This aid is hereby gratefully acknowledged. I am deeply indebted to Dr. Paul Fejos, Director of Research of the Foundation, for many a stimulating conversation, for encouragement and patient interest.

---

1. The revision incorporates materials which had not been available up to 1950 and consists, among others, in the elimination of certain notes on the history of manufacture in Ecuador, on immigration and on natural increase, and in a condensation of footnotes and documentation which was somewhat ampler and more detailed in the original version.

This volume is inscribed to Professor Arthur Salz, the economist who does not stop at the borders of his discipline nor limit his council to that of a father. He gave the first completed draft a searching reading and did me the honor of treating it in the spirit of a colleague. It has benefited from the abundance of his insights and suggestions.

The greater part of this revision was carried out at the University of Chicago and concluded at the University of Puerto Rico. I wish to express to the former institution my warm thanks for its hospitality, and to the latter my appreciation for facilitating a reduced teaching schedule.

A number of friends and colleagues have read all or parts of this study previous to or during its revision, and have contributed much needed suggestions and criticisms. For this I thank Professor David E. Basile, Department of Geography, the University of North Carolina, Chapel Hill, who added to my largely indirect knowledge of Ecuador from the store of his long and direct knowledge of that country and who was good enough to permit use of an unpublished manuscript of his; to Edward C. Banfield, Peter Gregory, Bernice Kaplan, Sol Tax, Arthur Vidich, Alvin Wartel, R. Richard Wohl for helpful comments and editorial advice; to John Collier, Jr. for various points of information. For much other verbal information and hospitality shown me during my sojourn in Ecuador I am beholden to Aníbal and Barbara Buitrón and to the Buitrón family in Otavalo; to Miss Lilo Linke in Quito; and to Father Leonidas Rodríguez Sandoval.

The maps were drawn according to my specification by Mr. José Valledor of San Juan, Puerto Rico.

None of the institutions and individuals here named are responsible for any statements made, or views expressed, by me in this work. For all of these I hold myself responsible as well as for all translations which are mine except as otherwise indicated.

Beate R. Salz

Facultad de Ciencias Sociales
Universidad de Puerto Rico
Río Piedras, P. R.

June 20, 1955

TABLE OF CONTENTS

THE PROBLEM AND SOME ISSUES: AN INTRODUCTION

I

Industrialization has come to be the watchword of the era which opened with the second World War. It expresses hopes, intentions, programs, plans--and also apprehensions--as well as incipient developments, all centering in countries and areas of the world whose people up to now have remained largely unaffected by the methods and organization of production that were ushered in by the Industrial Revolution some one hundred and fifty years ago. To extend this "revolution" within and, indeed, beyond the confines of the Western world and to transform the economies of "backward" or "underdeveloped" countries by introducing modern, rationalized, power-mechanized mass-production methods in combination with modern factory organization--that is the meaning of industrialization.

Industrialization, so understood, is only one, though very important, phase in economic development. In seeking to increase, improve, and diversify productive capacities and to raise levels and standards of living, industrialization and economic development have many aspects in common. Yet, considered by itself, industrialization is the more radical process. It is not only an "increase of manufacturing and other 'secondary' production," nor is it limited to introducing "better techniques," "installing more and better capital equipment," or to merely "raising...the particular skills of labor" (Staley 1944:6). Industrialization also means a qualitative change of an economy, a frequently fundamental alteration of existing skills, and the introduction of entirely new techniques in, and organization of, productive work. If industrialism is understood as that state of affairs under which a sizable part of a given population derives its living mainly and directly from employment in manufacturing industry, industrialization means transformation of nonindustrial people into industrial workers.

The present study is concerned with the implications of this process of transforming peasants and herders, traders and carriers, craftsmen and servants, the "hewers of wood and the drawers of water," into industrial employables and with their induction into the industrial production system. It intends to furnish a systematic statement of the specifically human problems arising in the early stages of industrialization and a conspectus of the interpersonal and cultural problems faced by incipient industrialism; to lay down a schema of inquiry of what--and particularly who--is involved in industrialization and to point out factors facilitating or inhibiting this process among nonindustrial peoples; and to present a system of orientation toward the study of industrialization prospects and possibilities. The topic of inquiry, broadly stated, is the confrontation of the human factor with the first concrete beginning of industrialization.

During and immediately following World War II, the propositions for industrialization became increasingly articulate. There is now hardly a country or area for which at least a measure of industrialization has not been slated. The proposals for industrialization as part of economic

1

development are informed by a variety of motives, ranging from sheer necessity for survival to the affirmation in Charters, Recommendations, Resolutions, Conventions, Declarations, Plans, and Points of the most idealistic sentiments. Imperative economic, political, diplomatic, and strategic considerations, as well as national prestige and vanity, insist on industrialization as a means toward the attainment of so many ends: greater economic self-sufficiency and political independence, political power, military security, internal stability, and, last but not least, "freedom from want" and a higher level of living than is enjoyed by most of the world.

Regardless of the interests which prompt support of industrialization, there are some aspects which distinguish this new "industrial revolution" on a global scale from its earlier prototypes of the Western world. Among such aspects are the emphasis on international co-operation rather than on competition; on bringing about a state of general welfare directly rather than leaving it to result gradually from individual benefits; and, above all, reliance on planned and peaceful penetration of the nonindustrial or underdeveloped economies rather than on dictatorial methods.

Yet despite the enunciations which profess regard for the well-being of people and peoples, and despite all economic development and industrialization programs, the problems of implementing such projects are largely posed in economic, hence impersonal, terms. Surveys of the possibilities for industrialization in various areas point to rich natural resources and untapped raw-material deposits. Trade areas, trade balances, and trade relations and volumes are considered, and questions of financing developments are studied. Yet what is conspicuously lacking is the mention of man. There is, as it appears, "a deep-seated tendency to separate the consideration of economic development from the human factor."[1]

There are, of course, exceptions to this tendency to consider economic development processes in nonhuman terms. The human element finds mention in passing references or explicit statements affirming the importance of human resources and registering concern over problems such as lack or scarcity of skilled labor and technical personnel, and unproductiveness of labor. The establishment, safeguarding, or expansion of labor standards and work and living conditions are certainly matters of concern to special associations and organizations. The necessity of taking into account the attitudes and reactions of a population to the irruptive and possibly disruptive effects of industrialization and its carriers and instigators is occasionally pointed out, and attention may be drawn to the significance of furnishing specially trained personnel for development work in nonindustrial countries. The question of incentives and motivations among nonindustrial populations is posed far more rarely (it may be implied in discussions on consumption and the necessity of raising its level first), while empirical studies of these matters, though occasionally urged and even theoretically outlined, are practically nonexistent.[2]

There is, admittedly, little doubt that the actual decisions for or against industrialization of a region will be guided primarily by the availability of capital and capital equipment, raw materials, and domestic and foreign markets. Sheer abundance of manpower may constitute an additional basis for a decision in favor of industrialization. Yet once industrialization has been decided upon, no matter on what scale, the question of the quality of the prospective manpower presents itself at once and forcibly. Recruitment, training, education, rehabilitation, prevailing or emerging labor relations, old customs and established habits pose substantial problems from the very beginning. In the actual situation these may consist of nothing more than petty and irritating disturbances; yet they are apt to snowball and assume crucial importance. In the last resort, it is daily frictions and upsets of this kind which determine the success and even the form of a newly implanted industrialism. Labor may be docile, and wages may be low; but indirect expenditures on labor, including costs occasioned by its fundamental intractability, may be unexpectedly high. As a general proposition it may be said that these kinds of "costs" are likely to be in direct proportion to the capacity and willingness of a given population to answer the stringent requirements of industrialism. These are some of the important aspects of the role of the human factor in industrialization.

The present study is conceived as a pilot analysis of an essentially non- or preindustrial Latin American country and its population. By concentrating on the social bases of, or the cultural factor in, the process of industrialization, it intends to supplement the more orthodox, "objective" type of surveys and estimates of the possibilities for industrialization. As an outline for a systematic study of the role of the human element in industrialization, it offers a selective description of conditions pertinent for the implantation of industrialism. This description includes, above all, the people with whom and, if such be the case, for whom industrialization is to be initiated. In focusing on this aspect of industrialization, rather than on the impersonal and relatively "external" factors favoring or inhibiting this process, the orientation of this study is fundamentally toward prognosis regarding the behavior of people in the face of a process, proposed or actuated, the essence of which is change. The study means to suggest that the day-by-day implementation of an industrialization program, of getting a single factory organized and started and of keeping it in operation, can be materially aided by some advance information on questions of crucial importance, such as: Who are the people, how many of them and what kind, and how far are they both willing and able to man the machines? What will they give up and what do they stand to gain by reorienting their lives, as they necessarily must to varying degrees, to become a sustaining force of industrialization? What, in short, are the potential resources of manpower in quantitative and, especially, in qualitative terms as required for a system of production of the mass, by the mass, and for the mass through the techniques of machine and deliberate organization?

These and other detail questions are to be tested with reference to the Indians of the highlands of Ecuador. These people have been selected because they are culturally most remote from the modern sector of Ecuador and because they seem to constitute numerically the most solid core of potential industrial manpower in that country. Concentrating upon this concrete case, the scope of this study is twofold: first, it means to suggest a scheme of systematic inquiry into the possibilities for industrialization in nonindustrial countries, with central attention to a country's human resources and the technical and organizational problems which are incidental to the process of industrialization; second, in supporting this scheme of inquiry by concrete illustrations, this study provides a conspectus of information on Ecuadorean conditions, with emphasis on the size and kind of its human resources, relevant to the promoters, if any, of industrialization.

II

Industrialization is easily viewed as a panacea for the sickly, the lanquid, the underdeveloped, as well as the overstuffed economic organisms. If not immediately effective in imparting new growth and vigor to them, it is still tempting to think that, once administered, the tonic will do its stuff. But industrialization is neither a panacea nor a prophylactic. It is above all a problem pregnant with dilemmas. Some of these may be made explicit.

Industrialization may be invited, accepted, or fostered for a variety of interconnected reasons. This does not mean that it is desired with equal intensity in all quarters or that the proposition of developing or diversifying an economy by industrialization is pressed forward everywhere. For one thing, the proposition itself is not of that type which captures popular imagination and enthusiasm, except under very special conditions. Some countries, or their spokesmen, hold back for a variety of reasons which render industrialization in their eyes either impossible of realization at the time or altogether unnecessary. Arguments centering on slow versus rapid industrialization tend to reveal such fundamental reluctances and touch on the question of the ultimate desirability of industrialization. What are some of the specific features of industrialism or, by extension, of industrial civilization or of economic development in general that appear so undesirable in so many quarters and are apt to raise such severe doubts and misgivings?

In presenting, first of all, two very general types of argument against industrialization, it is intended not to allay all apprehensions, but rather to provide convenient starting points from which to state some of the premises, assumptions, and conceptions which inform this study.

One such stock objection against industrialization is guided by doubt regarding the benefits of industrialism as such and by a fundamentally negative evaluation of present-day features of modern industrial civilization itself.[3] The idea of industrializing primitive, colonial, peasant peoples or those peoples generally whose cultures differ from standard-type Western civilization is most distasteful in those quarters. Nothing but dismal consequences is expected from a process which subjects "healthy," "natural," "organic," self-sufficient cultures to modernizing schemes: rampant materialism; alienation; cultural displacement and social disintegration; a tedious sameness of looks, behavior, institutions, and values; a snuffing out of native arts, originality, and distinctiveness in exchange for a mess of shoddy mass fabrications, tinned foods and vitamin pills, slums and neuroses. Industrialism, in this view, can breed but a single type of man, all others being doomed to extinction.

Another position considers industrialization, irrespective of the means by which it is brought about, an out-and-out fraud, its avowed ends a pretense, a hypocrisy, and both means and ends simply another form of exploitation. Industrialism, being an offshoot of capitalism, will benefit only the investors and, combining forces with "imperialism," "colonialism," and other disreputable systems considered as inherently exploitative, will aid their perpetuation and, at any rate, work the abuse of the peoples by subjecting them to a new dependence to the machine and all its works.[4]

It is easy to consider both views irrelevant once industrialization has been decreed in any one specific instance, or to dismiss them as doctrinaire. Yet such objections have to be taken seriously, not only because they contain much that is indisputably true on the basis of historical experience, or because industrialization may indeed entail "cultural losses," but also because, on the face of it, they evince human interests in the fate of people and peoples--interests which are conspicuously absent in "sober" nonromantic discussions on industrialization and its instrumental value in the attainment of given ends. This type of objections presents several challenges, some of which ought to be taken up here.

It seems very necessary to distinguish in principle between two aspects of industrialism: one, defined by a body of requirements, or characteristics, by which industrialism is set apart from other systems of production and ways of deriving incomes (such as farming, commerce, transportation, handicraft, financing, domestic service, piracy, etc.). Under the other aspect, modern industrialism may be considered a historically and culturally unique phenomenon, an integral part of Western economy and, by extension, an essential element of Western ways of life in general. The historical features attached to the "invention" and growth of industrialism in a particular part of the world must not be confused with the functionally constitutive elements of industrialism.

If this distinction be accepted, it follows that industrialism is functionally independent of, and neutral with regard to, a particular economic system, specific forms of enterprise, or even the sources of entrepreneurial initiative. The broadly technical and organizational requirements of industrialism remain the same regardless of who or what entities own, finance, and manage a given industrial plant or the totality of industrial plants, and regardless of the wider aims which industrialism is to serve. Individuals and corporate bodies (an army, a cooperative, a political party, a monastery, a business corporation, a government bureau, a trade union), once they are "in business," encounter the same order of problems in setting up and running an industry. The problems remain the same no matter whether industrial enterprises are undertaken for private profit, for social welfare, for eleemosynary purposes, for the subsistence of its participant members, for national defense, or for the waging of wars.

As a method by which to produce goods, and as a means of deriving incomes, industrialism is neither "good" nor "bad." The aims for which it is called into being, or the specific means employed to staff a plant or to distribute the derivates of industrial production, may be "good" or "bad" in a social, legal, or in an absolute ethical sense. These means may also be efficient or inefficient, economical or wasteful. And as a way of obtaining a living, industrial work may be congenial or uncongenial. But these are not questions that are relevant to industrialism specifically. What is specific to industrialism are certain minimal requirements, such as sizable numbers of workers, their concentration at fixed times and places, and others which do not need to be spelled out at this point. Industrial work has its own conditions, distinct from other types of work, and demands specific human qualities and specific behavior.[5] However, the question how workers are recruited and concentrated into industry and how the behavior and deportment appropriate to industrial work are elicited is determined not by industrialism as such but by those who direct it and so are in position to elect the particular modus operandi of industrial work. Thus the shaping of industrial workers may be left to "necessity," "natural selection," and the "law of the survival of the fittest." Direct and indirect coercion may be employed to bring man to the machine, and brute force, intimidation, or other forms of threatened or actual violence to keep him in the factory. Finally, industrial labor may be deliberately "cultivated" by suasion and by creating conditions under which human waste and attrition can be dispensed with.

The present study, being animated by the idea that human beings are not things, is concerned precisely with the problem of implementing industrialization by methods which are in principle noncoercive and which are geared to minimize waste.

It is true that industrialization exacts its price from nonindustrial people--the price of change. In the so-called backward countries there are advocates of change as such; they see in "modernization" of their countries an end in itself, and in this vision industrialization is included. Others are not quite so willing to pay the price for innovations that entail sudden, rapid, and possibly thoroughgoing changes massively and directly affecting old habits, cherished customs, traditional skills and crafts, and many comfortable because familiar arrangements and features of life which are at once a matter of pride and national and cultural distinctiveness. Such apprehensions regarding cultural losses are paralleled by fears of political disruptions, economic dislocations, foreign interference in national affairs, and exploitation in all spheres.

Even a casual look at expressions of Latin American opinion on economic matters provides good illustrations of these points. Fear and mistrust of change reverberate in many Latin American discussions on economic development and/or industrialization. In Mexico, for instance, the proposition itself tends to be associated not only with the conditions of industrialism's earlier developments in Western Europe and North America but also with an antithetical culture--both suspect because of their very dynamism. Thus even discussions which are eminently receptive to the idea of industrialization and whose general tenor is one of hopeful and sanguine expectation with regard to its potential achievements nevertheless exhibit a tendency to equate industrialization with the specifically alien, namely, (North) Americanization.[6] Realistic assessments of the need for, or desirability of, industrialization and sober discussions regarding its realization and technical difficulties are often tempered with unmistakable expressions of caution, of qualifications, of warding off those effects of industrialization which forebode a conquest of Hispano-Indo-American by Anglo-American culture by virtue of the latter's proximity, economic supremacy, and near-indispensability.[7] There is little doubt that such ambivalent attitudes are typical for practically all of Latin America.

There are other dilemmas. The status quo of a people and the palpably evident deterioration of an economy as a whole may be as "costly" or as "exploitative" as the change and the painful accommodation to the exigencies of industrial work. The attrition of a population by sheer poverty exacts a senseless toll. And certain things are definitely wanted, with or without industrialization: higher levels of living for more people; checks on morbidity and mortality; more and better schooling. In many respects, and in many instances, the standards are already set. In some cases, they exist only as aspirations, in others they have received institutional forms consisting in advanced social welfare and labor legislations, social security systems, health services, even housing developments. These things may be premature with regard to a given economy or viewed from a historical-comparative perspective, or they may be ill-fitted to a given culture, but they bespeak needs felt by at least certain segments of a population. And although, from an economic point of view, any one of these institutionalized standards may be an encumbrance on the whole political and economic organism, together they may press in the direction of change, of economic modernization, though not necessarily toward industrialization--as the example of Ecuador seems to show. At first sight, a modern public-health improvement program appears a dead weight on other developments, but such a program may be a precondition of improvement in a situation where there are too many to feed, too few to produce.

Some further aspects of the problem of industrialization remain to be considered. One relates to industrialization at a particular historical

moment, the middle of the twentieth century. The other refers to industrialization as one problem in a general class of perennial problems.

In the face of the pessimistic and critical assessments of our own
industrial heritage and the uneasiness felt in making over to nonindustrial
peoples so dubious a complex of "goods," it may be pointed out that
present-day industrialization (neoindustrialism) has certain palpable
advantages not enjoyed by early industrialization in the old countries (now
mature industrialism). Present-day, i.e., late, industrialization reaps
where it has not sown. To the accumulation of technical perfection and
technological knowledge, acquired piecemeal over some two centuries and
now ready to be handed on in bulk, belong also ideas and notions such as
"planning," "multipurpose development," "scientific management," "human
engineering," and others--a body of practices, experiences, rational
techniques, as well as certain conceptions and ideals. And although this
equipment is by no means perfect, nor applicable to all situations, it exists
and must be considered an integral part of late industrialization. Some
principles of planning are available and may aid in obviating the step-by-
step, trial-and-error procedure which developed the old models of
industrialism.

The present study may be considered a part of this tendency inherent in neoindustrialism and, indeed, starts from some premises implied in the above remarks: that investments made blindly and in
ignorance of existing conditions or according to historically derived
standard patterns only are wastes; that procedures in organizing and
mobilizing people for industry are likely to prove inefficient if undertaken in ignorance or disregard of the conditions peculiar to a given country or region; and that the dissipation of money, efforts, and resources,
including human resources, through inertia and failure to accommodate to
novel conditions, are undesirable from the economic as well as from the
social point of view. It is assumed, furthermore, that substantial control
of such wastage is possible, since it is possible rationally to anticipate
potential ill effects and dislocations due to industrialization among nonindustrial peoples and to devise, accordingly, measures by which to avoid
or at least modify such effects. Studies contributing toward the clarifi-
cation of a specific social and cultural reality would be one of the measures by which to outline, for instance, a path of least resistance toward
the habituation of nonindustrial people to industrial work.

The present study thus intends to perform the type of scouting which
today tends to precede, as a matter of systematic procedure, the initiation of actual development projects. It is addressed, in the first place,
to the planners and initiators of industrialization--on whatever scale--and
offers an analysis of the human resources specific to one country. In
addition, it means to alert the technical personnel in actual charge of industrial operations among nonindustrial people to the specific problems
presented by the meeting of different traditions. In this respect, the
matter to be illuminated is one of "education" for industry, the character
of "teacher" and, particularly, of "pupil," the relations between both,
and the conditions and nature of the process of "learning."

This analogy is by no means far-fetched. Nor is the type or
"class" of problems here posed at all a novel or advanced one either in
terms of practice or in terms of science for application. On the contrary, it is as old and as universal as any problem of statecraft. The
broader frame of reference underlying this study is derived from those
precedent cases in recorded history which have involved deliberate,
conscious, systematic endeavors on the part of one people or of specific

groups to impose substantial changes upon another people by a minimum of direct coercion. Every "empire," be it Persian, Roman, Inca, Spanish, or British, is practically defined by the fact that it sought its own integration by "civilizing" its "barbaric" components. Whatever the specific content, the means, and the ultimate ends, changes in specific directions are the immediate aim of such endeavors. Colonial problems of administration and development, today as yesterday, are eminently of this order. So are problems of recruiting and training "natives" as army auxiliaries or regular soldiers in the service of affairs that are of little concern to them. The conversion of pagans or gentiles to Christianity belongs in this class of problems. The ideologically aggressive and organizationally and technically advanced power exacts a change of heart or of habits, or both, from the less advanced and may do so for its own interest or for the real or imagined good of the latter. It is also relevant to recall that the formulation of the detail policies as well as their execution "in the field" is generally entrusted to a corps of hierarchically ordered specialists and experts, and it is particularly "in the field" that the tangible problems arise. It is in the sphere of direct, intimate, face-to-face contacts between a native population, on the one hand, and the agents of change (administrators, officials, overseers, officers, traders, missionaries, etc.), on the other, that the actual frictions and bottlenecks occur, the mistakes are made, good-will lost, and misunderstandings perpetuated. And yet it is also at this precise point that the insinuation of advanced institutions, the better creed, and industrialism into the integument of a culture, into daily life, begins. It is not only specific political organisms, territories, or creeds that confront the novel; it is also distinct ways of life, attitudes, values, and expectations--it is distinct cultures--which industrialization faces.

Needless to say, the introduction of comparatively isolated complexes, such as formal education and technical training, public health and modern medicine, improvement in agricultural methods, or a body of laws and legal procedures, encounters the same problem of establishing congruence between different cultural systems or systems of values in the service of given ends.

III

In this light, the selection of one of the Andean countries, Ecuador, to test the process of industrialization among nonindustrial people, is particularly appropriate. For this "tiny, far away" country straddles the outer rim of an area in which two great civilizations, two regimes of imperial dimensions, have wrested with precisely the problems that go with the endeavors of incorporating diverse small populations into comprehensive political, religious, and economic systems. Both regimes, the Inca and the Spanish, brought advanced methods of statecraft to bear upon the task of integrating a mass of native nuclei, once they were subjected by force or allied by diplomatic means, into the body politic, into a new religion, and of rendering them effective within an economic fabric designed to assure a continuous yield of surpluses. These processes are well documented for both the Inca and the Spanish regimes, although for the latter the documentation is more direct. In pursuit of their civilizatory aims, the Spanish seem to have sought systematically for pragmatic information on the institutions, beliefs, and details of life of the natives over whom they exercised both power and tutelage. In effect, a large part of the Spanish so-called "Chronicles" of the sixteenth and earlier part of the seventeenth centuries can be considered as nothing less than research reports with or without recommendations, compiled at the behest of the Spanish and Spanish-colonial governments. They furnished the basic data necessary for purposes of administration, development, and deliberate, rational change in all spheres of native life.[8] Whether these chronicles be considered as historiographies or as field reports, they contain ample evidence as to where resistance to Spanish policies and measures was encountered. It is a moot question whether the Inca or the Spanish succeeded in completing their conquests or in realizing their aims. Both were faced not only with intermittent open rebellions and wholesale defections but with the continuous passive resistance, the tenacious traditionalism and peasant conservatism that still seem to be the outstanding characteristics of contemporary Andean Indians.

Today, the problem of "incorporating the Indian into the life of the modern nation" remains. And in some of the Latin American countries a systematic approach toward the problem is being re-elaborated under a philosophy which emphasizes deliberate changes of the conditions surrounding the Indians rather than changing the Indians themselves.

The entire conception of the present study has been considerably stimulated and influenced by this ancient problem of reconciling the Indian sector with the European-derived sector of Latin America, or with modern occidental twentieth-century civilization in general. The approach toward the specific problem of industrialization among populations so largely Indian is in many ways that of the more temperate and scientific among "pro-Indian" students of Latin America or, more precisely, of "Indo-American" realities. That approach includes a new respect for the value of existing cultures and excludes advocacy of forcefully breaking or eliminating habits, customs, and institutions that happen to differ from the norms of modern life, or of stampeding Indian into "white" culture for the sake of creating a uniform cultural milieu. Obviously, what remains is the problem of judging what in Indian "culture" is valuable, useful, indifferent, or innocuous with regard to modern culture, or what is irreconcilable with its demands. The present study does not seek to solve this problem. It might, at best, suggest realistic aspects of this problem as they emerge within the complex of questions incident to industrialization.

As will be seen, Ecuador is not predisposed at the present time to change its economic face. From the point of view of population, industrialization is not a vital necessity for Ecuador as it is for some of those countries where overpopulation is a far more pressing problem. In a way, Ecuador is in a very fortunate position: it is able, so to speak, to choose between industrialization and nonindustrial economic development. Its over-all manpower potential is such as to enable any one individual to choose, as it were, among alternative ways of making a living. This circumstance again makes the selection of Ecuador for our inquiry particularly significant: it enables us to pose questions regarding motivations and incentives to work in industry in a more realistic manner, i.e., by indicating preferences.

In any case, the data for Ecuador are meant primarily to illustrate the problems of industrialization from the point of view of so universal and ubiquitous a factor as the human one. Because of this function, and because it is anticipatory to industrialization, this "case study" should be termed a "hypothetical" case study. It is hypothetical also in that it constitutes an imaginative experiment which inquires into the probable reactions and behavior of real people if they were to find themselves plunked down in an industrial situation, as they are and with their whole background still adhering to them. It has been termed hypothetical, finally, in consideration of the material on which this "case" rests.

IV

Our study is divided into two major questions: one concerns the quantity, the other the quality, of the prospective industrial labor force.

Part I is therefore devoted mainly to an attempt to establish an order of magnitude of the number of persons dispensable for industry from agriculture and other nonindustrial pursuits. In addition, two other matters are treated as incidental to this main question but of some importance in their own right: the "external" conditions ("external" from the point of view of the human factor at any one moment) faced by incipient industry are summarized, and this background summary includes some trends on the level of economic development plans and programs. Thus particular attention has been paid to assessing the "climate of opinion" in regard to industrialization, not only because this by itself is a datum of first importance but also because the receptivity or non-receptivity of the proposition of industrialization as over against other methods of economic development has direct bearing on the availability of labor for industry and is likely to influence materially the future distribution of manpower in general.

Part II deals with qualitative aspects of the human, industrially "raw" material. The disposition of the problems raised chapter by chapter follows at first the set of questions which an employer might ask of a job applicant: previous experience (skills and education) and health would presumably be the first "qualities" inquired into. Work and other habits relevant to industrial work are usually revealed on the job, as are the goals for the sake of which work is engaged in. Here, an attempt is made to preview them in terms of predispositions to work in a manner required by and in industry. Thus, human relations within industry have been the object of major analysis.[9] For this purpose they have been conceived as an approximate reflection of social and interpersonal relations as they obtain in Ecuador in general, that is between the Indian and the modern sector, and among Indians.

The concept of the Indian, the element of the Ecuadorean population with which this study is mainly concerned, is a deceptive and elusive one. The matter will be discussed at some length in the second part and need not be anticipated at this point.

It may be emphasized at this point, however, that "opinions" have been very widely treated as data throughout the entire study. In the first place, "prejudices" with regard to Indians or "stereotypical" portrayals of "the" Indian are an inseparable part of the reality into which industrialism is to be injected. Under the supposition that industrialization were to acquire actuality, the initiative to industrialize might come from Ecuadoreans, and the process might be carried out by them. In that case they would need to be aware of their own "prejudices"--if such they be-- in so far as relations between Indian workers and non-Indian managerial personnel would be colored by "images," expectations, or other preconceived notions held by one with respect to the other. If, on the other hand, industrialization in Ecuador were to implicate non-Ecuadoreans, awareness of the existing "climate of opinion," of Latin-American "mentality," of values and judgment systems, would be even more forcefully necessary. Non-Ecuadoreans would have to deal not only with Ecuadorean "prejudices" (to stick to this example of one type of "opinions") with regard to non-Ecuadoreans but also with Ecuadorean prejudices with regard to the Indians and, lastly, with their own regarding Ecuador and "natives." It is

for this reason that "facts" and "opinions"--often so difficult to distinguish from one another--have been treated as a continuous reality throughout this study.

In view of the dearth of information on many points regarding
Indian life in Ecuador, the temptation was great to fill such gaps by drawing on ampler and more comprehensive materials on Indians elsewhere
in the Andean area. Such an expedient might have been entirely defensible
in consideration of the cultural and historic background which Andean
Indians have so largely in common, their ethnic affinities, and the many
obvious geographical and institutional similarities of the South American
west-coast countries. In fact, the more general literature on Ecuadorean
Indians shows much evidence of such procedure, providing data by analogy,
as it were, derived from Peruvian or Bolivian field studies and other
research. However, such procedure suffers from the disregard of at
least three facts: First, the area roughly coinciding with that of modern
Ecuador was the latest to be incorporated into the Inca Empire, with only
a few decades left for the integration of its numerous scattered tribes and
little kingdoms into this relatively new all-Andean system. The consolida-
tion of Ecuador with Inca Peru was never completed (and would perhaps
never have been completed even if the Spaniards had not come at the crucial moment). Second, under Spanish colonial rule Ecuador constituted a
unit of its own: from 1563 as Audiencia or Presidency of Quito and, beginning with the early eighteenth century, forming part of the Viceroyalty of
New Granada (comprising today's Ecuador, Colombia, Panama, and
Venezuela) as distinguished from the Viceroyalty of Lima or New Castile
(Peru). Third, the modern Andean republics have gone their own sovereign
ways for some one hundred and twenty years. In consideration of these
facts, there is no good reason to treat of the Indians of Ecuador other
than as a people sui generis. Hence the selection of the materials pertinent to their study has on the whole been rigorously confined to the
Indians of the politically defined area of modern Ecuador.[10] For illus-
trative purposes, data pertaining to Indians outside Ecuador have occasionally been drawn upon.

V

A full discussion of the material on which this study is based and
the manner in which it has been used will be found in the Appendix. Meanwhile, the main reservation to be made cannot be better formulated than
in the caution of the historiographer: "My duty is to report all that is
said, but I am not obliged to believe it all alike" (Herodotus, Persian Wars,
vii).

The picture presented in the following is pieced together from very
heterogeneous literary materials: the few extant reports on Ecuadorean
economy and surveys of natural resources and passing references tucked
away in general accounts on Latin America; what is known in the book trade
as "travel books" and a few socioeconomic investigations and sample
studies; and less than two dozen ethnographic and other descriptive monographs and articles having specific reference to Ecuadorean Indians or
specific aspects of Indian life. In this sense, the present study is a
"synthetic" case study, based on relatively meager and qualitatively uneven materials.

Whatever seemed even remotely pertinent for assessing the possibilities of industrialization in Ecuador, with the human element as central
focus of interest, has been recorded and fully documented, from the anec-
dotal to the weighty field result methodically obtained. Analysis was

pressed to the utmost by judiciously weighing the data, such as they are, for their relevance to the problem, rather than by discriminating against a mass of live impressions in favor of one irrelevant but impeccably established fact. Such as the material is, it has been taken generally at its face value. And the interpretation as to what it forebodes, if and when industrialization should come, ought to be understood strictly as following the "if thus...then so" formula--reasoned judgments based on limited data.

VI

The first part of this study, entitled "On Resources and the Quantitative Labor Potential," is devoted primarily to an attempt to determine the size of Ecuador's industrial labor potential, at the same time indicating some factors that are likely to influence its availability and mobility at any one time. This main question is to be dealt with against the background of some conditions, considered here as given, which comprise matters such as the totality of natural resources, their exploitation and utilization, as well as the relative importance which the proposition "industrialization" occupies in present-day Ecuadorean thinking.

No attempt is being made to provide an exhaustive description and analysis of each of these interconnected conditions. Rather, the intention is to highlight a few of them; to establish, incidentally, the relationship of the economic orientation or current economic policies to certain felt economic and social problems; and to indicate the prospects for ready availability of industrial labor. This does not mean that a number of problems will not be at least touched upon which, under more orthodox and perhaps more orderly economic or historical analyses, could be marshaled with more emphasis; they are the well-known features of economically underdeveloped countries, any one of which could be singled out and made the pivot on which all other problems articulated. Thus we shall not dwell on such matters as the undeniable fact that incomes in Ecuador are low and their distribution uneven.[11] The question of consumptive capacity or of effective and potential demand for goods and services is equally remote from the starting point here decided upon.

The descriptions and analyses that follow are largely confined to developments that have occurred during the last two decades. It is natural that, in taking such a short period under consideration, a certain distortion or disproportion of the magnitude of any developments is inevitable; estimates regarding the chances for industrialization are thereby slanted. But since industrialization itself is here also considered on a short-run basis, the estimates, such as they are, are probably realistic within these limitations.

Under a longer, historical perspective, the particular assessment and evaluation of changes and developments that have taken place during the last twenty years or so would be different, even if one were to make allowance for a quickening of the rate of change in these decades. Nevertheless, reference may be made to descriptions and accounts of the Ecuadorean economy of the 1850's and 1860's:[12] it is remarkable how minor the changes appear to be in the structure of the whole economy, the location of industry, the composition of production or of export trade. The problems are approximately the same and as besetting then as they are now, though they are, in part, stated somewhat differently today.

Omitted are, in particular, long-range demographic considerations, not only because there are no adequate data by which to arrive at more than the most general conclusions, or rather guesses, and not only because of the gearing of our inquiries to short-run considerations and to more or less immediate problems that would arise for an incipient industry, but also because the question of industrialization is here approached as a process independent of population growth.[13]

The paucity of generally adequate information on Ecuador must be kept in mind in the assessments of the various states of affairs which are dealt with in the following and which relate to some features of the Ecuadorean geography and economy and to economic orientation, the raw quantity of potential industrial labor supply, and the outlook for its mobilization into industry.

NOTES

1. Paraphrase of a statement by Hernan Santa Cruz of Chile, in which he criticized the studies attached to the United Nations' Secretary-General's report, during the debates of the United Nations Economic and Social Council on economic development of underdeveloped countries, in Geneva, July, 1949 (reported in United Nations Bulletin, VII, No. 5 [Sept. 1, 1949] : 271-84).

2. Reference may be made to Aubrey (1951) and Moore (1951), both of which contain valuable bibliographies. A rising awareness of the problems here indicated finds expression in Hoselitz 1952 (see esp. Part II, "The Cultural Aspect of Economic Growth") and in various contributions to the periodical Economic Development and Cultural Change (Vol. 1, 1952, ff.) and to the collection of lectures, Formulation and Economic Appraisal of Development Projects (1951).

3. Ordinary, nontechnical discussion on industrialization, as well as much of the literature in and out of industrial sociology, reflects this profound unease and sense of inability to overcome the domination of man by machine and mass society or to master the degree of "rationality" which industrial civilization ideally presupposes. See, for examples, Garrett 1944, Mumford 1934, Meadows 1950.

4. Social scientists, abetting this and similar schemes by bringing their "techniques" in the field of human relations to bear upon the solution of problems involved in planned or deliberate social and cultural change, are occasionally subjected to the same type of censure. For example, cultural anthropologists "are useful to administrators. They can make exploitation palatable. And no doubt, if one is to be exploited, it is pleasanter to be exploited anthropologically, that is, politely and understandingly, than brusquely by hard-boiled administrators" (Bernard 1949).

5. See, e.g., Balchin 1947, Baumgarten 1947, Dietze 1946, Mace 1948, Mayo 1945, Meadows 1950: 11-16, Merton 1947, Moore 1946: 60-61 and passim, Salz 1933 and 1934, Seashore 1946, Tiffin 1944.

6. Cf. Northrop 1946: chap. ii and his happy phrasing describing this dilemma on p. 7. See also Blanksten 1954.

7. The following provides a sampling of the various opinions: Behrendt 1948, Enriquez 1945, Marquez 1946a and 1946b, Mosk 1945, Neumann 1948, Polit 1946, Robles 1944.

8. The practical purpose behind the compilations of these materials (now historical and ethnological sources) is clearly suggested by, for instance, Gibson (1948), Hanke (1946), and Kubler (1947: 331-32).

9. The treatment of this class of problems has been materially influenced by the lines of approach of that branch of sociology called "industrial sociology," as developed during recent years, particularly in the United States. Much of the literature in this field has been of heuristic value for this study as, for instance, in the formulation of the questions raised. On the other hand, some of the premises with which much of American industrial sociology operates are either irrelevant to specific, i.e., non-U.S.A. situations, or are not tenable on empirical grounds.

10. This restriction does not deny that much of what is said in the following pages does not apply to the "folk" in the Andean countries or even in Latin America generally, or to what Gillin calls "criollo" culture, i.e., Spanish peninsular sixteenth to nineteenth century culture plus Indian ingredients, plus twentieth century general elaborations (Gillin 1947: 151 ff.; 1949; 1952).

11. Estimates on per capita annual incomes in Ecuador and distribution by income classes, largely for the early and middle forties, will be found in Population Index 13, No. 2 (1947):96 ff.; Behrendt 1948:2; Benites 1950: 262; CEPAL 1954: 34; OCIAA 1945: 26; Ecuadorian Commission n.d.:79; Laso 1942-43; Linke 1954:9.

12. Cevallos 1873 (the manuscript for this edition was substantially completed between 1858 and 1868); Hassaurek 1868; Orton 1875 (3d ed.).

13. Cf. Kingsley Davis (1946), who observes that "socio-economic modernization is seemingly proceeding faster than population growth" in certain Latin American countries; he has in mind literacy and urbanism. See also chap. iv and n. 1.

PART I

ON RESOURCES AND THE QUANTITATIVE LABOR POTENTIAL

I / SOME FEATURES OF ECUADOREAN GEOGRAPHY AND ECONOMY

Ecuador, like some of the other countries of the Latin-American Pacific Coast, is conventionally divided into three distinct natural regions or zones called "Costa" or "Litoral" (the Pacific coastal region to the west), "Sierra" (the inter-Andine, or Andean mountain region), and the "Oriente" (the eastern lowland region of the Amazon headwaters). These three zones are sharply differentiated from each other in terms of topography, climate, vegetation, and other concomitant geographical features. They and their subregions have, however, been described often enough and sufficiently well to make lengthy descriptions here unnecessary.[1]

It is not amiss to point out, however, that Ecuador's geographical features, taken singly or conjointly, constitute conditions which do not permit ready comparison with the conditions and developments of other countries, least of all with any of the older industrial countries.

Differences between the major and minor zones are accentuated by the paucity of communication and transportation facilities; indeed, their state is in part a direct result of the nature of Ecuador's geography. The sharply differentiated distribution of crops and other natural resources is, of course, another consequence of geographical differentiation. From this follows, also in part, the differential distribution of industries.

A. Communications[2]

Since communication and transportation are particularly pertinent to industrialization and to the location of any one industry, a somewhat detailed discussion is devoted to this subject. Development in this regard has been hampered not only by lack of funds but especially by topographic and climatic factors and has been slow, halting, and sporadic until recent years. By the same tokens, maintenance of existing roads and railroads is difficult, and complete interruptions for more or less extended periods of the year are frequent.

At the present time, Ecuador's communication network consists of one important railroad line which connects the port city of Guayaquil with highland Quito and a few points north up to and a little beyond Ibarra, about halfway between Quito and the Colombian border, which section constitutes a part of the projected Quito-Ibarra-San Lorenzo (formerly Quito-Esmeraldas) line which is under construction. This line is to link the highlands with the northern coastal lowlands, the railhead being located at a potential deep-water port at San Lorenzo, a point some 400 to 500 miles nearer the Panama Canal than Guayaquil. This ambitious project is now scheduled for completion in 1955 and will open up a rich and so far unexploited agricultural region in the lowlands. Other existing railroad lines are very short transcoastal lines by which ports are connected with points within the immediate hinterland; hence their importance is largely local. A trans-Amazonic line has also been projected; it is to link a maritime port, Puerto Bolívar, on the southern coast, via the two southern Sierra provinces, with the Zamora region in the Oriente, but so far only a fraction of this line has been completed, nor is it likely to be continued within the foreseeable future.

Among highways and routes suitable for wheeled traffic, the Ecuadorean section of the Pan American Highway is the most important of the country's road system. It is open from Tulcan, on the Colombian-Ecuadorean border, to about Loja in the southern highlands; the remaining section to the Peruvian border consists of gravel and dirt roads ending in mule trails (as of 1953), a definitive route as between two alternative branches being still under discussion. Among the lateral routes, that is, highways linking coastal with highland points, is the Manta-Quevedo-Latacunga highway, under construction for almost fifteen years, but apparently nearing completion. The construction of that highway, as well as one paralleling it to the south and linking Guayaquil to the southern inter-Andine region (Durán-Tambo), was practically completed in 1953. Another road linking Guayaquil to the more northern Manta-Quevedo coastal system is also largely completed. Under construction and nearing completion are a northern lateral highway (Quito-Santo Domingo-Esmeraldas) and a southern lateral connecting Cuenca in the southern highlands with the port of Puerto Bolívar.

But if lateral coast-Sierra highway connections are so far few and incomplete, Sierra-Oriente highways are virtually nonexistent. Of three major routes there is but one road suitable for motorized traffic, an extension of the Ambato-Banos road to Mera in the Upper Pastaza region.

The rest of land communications within and between regions and subregions consist of trails and mule tracks, unusable for wheeled traffic and much of it impassable for man or beast for more or less extended periods of the year.

Within the Litoral a good deal of transportation and travel is carried on by river. This applies especially to forest-exploiting industries which send balsa rafts and other lumber and forest products to ports. Hence Guayaquil is a center of sawmills and, ever since colonial times, of shipbuilding, today limited to the construction of small river and coastal fishing craft.

Barring air service, which connects the larger towns and cities with each other, Ecuador's present-day communication and transportation network has wide and irregular meshes. It does not reach into the Oriente for all practical modern purposes, and it fails to cover many and large parts of the Litoral and highlands. Conditions of travel and transportation, except between highway-, railroad-, and aviation-connected points, do not show substantial improvement from those obtaining in the 1850's and 1860's.[3] Hence large-scale interchange of products among major regions hardly exists or is, at least, extremely difficult and costly.

B. Crops and Raw Material Resources

The distribution of crops[4] and of some other natural resources runs largely along regional lines. Warm-climate, mostly plantation products (cacao, coffee, rice, cotton, bananas, and other fruits and sugar), forest products, and some of the minerals belong to the coast, its hinterland, and in part also to the foothills and deeper valleys of the Andes. It is the Litoral which furnishes Ecuador's all-important export crops. Various indigenous and European cereals, potatoes, vegetables, beans, etc., sheep wool, beef and dairy products, and most of the minerals derive from the western slopes of the Andes and, particularly, from the inter-Andine proper.

Unlike some of its sister-republics, Ecuador is not an exploiter of minerals[5] on the large scale, and exploitation of these resources has been sporadic and generally minor. It still remains for a future mineral survey to indicate whether some processing and manufacturing industries based on such materials could not be developed. Deposits of a number of minerals of varying size are known to exist, and some of these are being worked or have been worked in the past, such as copper, silver, lead. Iron-ore mining was carried out on a small scale in 1942 and 1943 in some provinces, such as in Imbabura and Pichincha, and coal mining in Cañar. But, so far, major exploitation of mineral resources has been limited to gold (lode and placer) and, generally on a marginal basis, to copper, silver, zinc, lead, sulphur, salt, lime and gypsum, clay, marble. Only in a few of these cases does exploitation seem to have been systematic and sustained for a period of time, as during the war years. Among the minerals further known to exist are antimony, asbestos, graphite, magnesite, manganese, mercury, saltpeter, quartz, jasper, alabaster, kaolin, corundum. Of late, the sulphur deposits of Tixán (Chimborazo) and the coal deposits of Biblián (Cañar) have risen into prominence and, at least the former, beyond the discussion stage.

Petroleum is the most important mineral resource at the present time, although the high expectations of the forties regarding this resource were disappointed when, in 1951, Shell-Mera abandoned its survey operations in the Oriente after some ten years of exploration in that region. Nevertheless, petroleum (and its products), derived from the central coast, used to be among the more important export products of Ecuador and is now steadily gaining in importance as a domestic fuel.

The war brought to the foreground a number of forest products[6] which should be counted among those resources having potentialities as industrial raw materials. Among these are tagua or ivory nut (vegetable ivory), used mainly for buttons; cinchona bark, for quinine; various species of bamboo, for structural material, furniture, etc., and possibly pulp; balsa wood, for airplanes; kapok; and other woods and plants yielding construction, furniture, and pulp materials, fibers, edible fruits, latex, gums, dyes, tannins, oils, flavorings, and a variety of chemical and pharmaceutical base materials. A great many of these plants are considered suitable for systematic cultivation. Because of their dispersed stands and the general transportation situation, exploitation of timber and other wild forest resources has been, and is, difficult. Still, Ecuador enjoys some advantage over its neighbor countries in this respect in that much of her timber resources are located in the western lowlands, hence are of somewhat easier access than the other countries' trans-Andean forests. Guayaquil owed its erstwhile prominence as shipbuilding center to its comparative proximity to timber stands.

As for industrial motor power,[7] hydroelectricity, though little developed at present, is eminently the power of the highlands. During the middle forties the government was reported to be contemplating a ten-year program of hydroelectric development up to 100,000 horsepower.

Liquid fuel, on the other hand, at present sustains a considerable part of industry and will probably continue to do so for some time to come, particularly in the lowlands. Data on the power situation are scant but do indicate shortages and uncertainties in the supply of motor power, however derived.

C. Industry - Present Stand and Prospects[8]

Industry, on the whole, occupies a very minor place in the total economy of Ecuador, the mainstay of which is agriculture. Yet a glance at the list of manufacturing industries shows that this field of economic activity, for all its small size, is more varied and in certain respects more highly developed than might be expected in a country of the size and conditions of Ecuador. To be sure, there is no heavy industry, either in metals or in chemicals. All machinery, all raw materials for the few metal-working and chemical-pharmaceutical plants, and much of the raw materials of practically all other industries have to be imported.

In number of establishments, the foodstuffs and beverages industries are the largest. Among them are the agricultural products industries which work largely on the basis of domestic raw materials: the lowland sugar mills and rice-hulling plants, and the highland flour mills and cotton gins, both of which, however, require additional imported wheat and cotton.

In terms of their total capitalization, the mineral-extracting and processing establishments represented almost 40 per cent of the total capital invested in the about 990 establishments for which data were available in 1944. These were also among the largest labor-consuming industries, but this situation has changed considerably in the last three or four years.

Of the consumer-goods industries proper, the textile industry, operating on the basis largely of cotton and secondarily of wool and imported rayon and silk, is the oldest and most important. Now consisting of about two dozen major plants, it is credited with an employment of 3,500 to 7,000 and even 9,000 workers and employees, according to various estimates. The textile plants are located in the highlands (Quito, Atuntaqui, Otavalo, Latacunga, Ambato, Riobamba, Cuenca) and away from the cotton-producing regions, since the highlands furnished and still furnish water and hydroelectric power and a labor supply that not only is ampler and cheaper than lowland labor but also has been engaged in textile handicraft for centuries.

The leather industry (tanning, manufacture of shoes and other leather products), though it does not figure in recent surveys, appears to be another of the more important and fully developed industries. It operates to an appreciable extent on the basis of domestic raw materials and produces a small surplus for export, as do some of the beverage industries. The only modern manufacturing industry which exports finished products on any scale, however, is the young chemical-pharmaceutical industry, which imports a large part of its raw materials but does not fully satisfy the domestic market.

Other industries of relative importance in number of establishments or capitalization are the woodworking and nonmetallic minerals industries. Most of the industries belonging to other groups are of the small-shop type.

During and since World War II, a number of processing and manufacturing industries have been mentioned as likely to expand or as requiring improvement; needs and possibilities have been stated to exist for yet others. Among a lengthy list of these was named the textile industry, which, since the war, has increased by about six units but leads an uneasy existence (see UN, ECLA 1951). A second cement factory is in process of construction in the highlands and is expected to fill the growing need for cement. A cellulose plant, also in the highlands, was to begin operations first in the summer of 1953, then early in 1955. Two fishing and fish-processing units were mentioned as being organized in 1951 and 1952. A fertilizer factory has long been under discussion, and food-processing plants such as sugar and flour mills and a malt factory have come in for expressions of interest. Power development, whether hydro-electric or fuel, appears to be a constant matter of concern. The pro-duction of refined petroleum products has sharply increased since 1947.

Lest this enumerative treatment leave the impression that Ecuador is well on its way to industrialization, it must be stressed at this point that such is by no means the case. The areas in which economic activities are concentrated, those to which plans, programs, and projects refer, and those on which articulate opinion pronounces all tend to show that it is agricultural and closely related production and development that hold first place in interest. That agriculture is, in fact, a main occupation of Ecuadoreans is not difficult to show and is, moreover, to be expected, given the historical antecedents. That industry, industrialism, or indus-trialization is not, by and large, a major preoccupation can be shown from various indications, briefly to be summarized below. They tend to be revealing of a socioeconomic orientation and even of explicit policy which by themselves amount to being among the conditions that influence the chances of industrialization.

D. Orientation

Literature on Ecuador and literature emanating from Ecuador, in so far as it relates to the state and development of the economy and to specific social problems, is strikingly devoid of mention of industrializa-tion and, specifically, of manufacturing industry development. This contrasts with the space given over to discussion of development, en-largement, and improvement of agriculture and to raising the levels of living and purchasing power of the rural and agricultural population on the basis of this established branch of economic activity.[9]

The terms industria and industrialización are, of course, en-countered, but in Ecuadorean usage they do not usually connote de-liberate organization and concentration of a number of people for mechanized large-scale production of specialized lines of finished articles. Rather, they refer to processing of agricultural, livestock, or forest products, such as banana flour, yuca starch, pig lard, etc.,[10] or else to cottage industries or hand manufacture and repair in individual small shops, possibly associating such activities with co-operative marketing of products. More often than not such "industries" are thought of as supplementary to farming and as offering opportunities for the realization of the artistic and manual abilities of the people. Very often, industria means merely a single specific plant. There is no lack of opinion that pronounces itself in favor of industrialización in either of these senses or in no defined sense whatsoever.[11] Others, certainly, attach to the term the more specific meaning employed here, but it may be noted that in such cases a well-reasoned skepticism with regard to this mode of economic development as premature and "a luxury" for Ecuador is apparent (Bustamente 1942; Laso 1942-43).

Analysis of public statements amounting to economic policy and planning statements made by responsible Ecuadorean officials shows quite clearly that Ecuadorean thinking is directed toward agriculture, somewhat and variously toward mining, but not toward more advanced processing and manufacturing industry as such.

Very revealing in this respect is the 1945-46 Report of the Minister of Economy to the Legislature, consisting of 107 printed pages not a single section of which is devoted to industry. The largest section, about one-third of the report, deals with agriculture and livestock, detailing problems connected with them and discussing plans related to their development. The section includes mention only of the textile industry, and that in relation to cotton-growing, of sugar mills, and of flour mills. Smaller sections deal with import and trade controls, mining, banking, the Grand-Colombian Merchant Fleet, Bretton Woods, and other organizational matters. Three other industries are mentioned in the context of mining: a fertilizer factory to be set up by the government on the basis of guano deposits and of phosphate-containing limestone on the Santa Elena Peninsula; the exploitation of a sulphur mine and sulphur processing; and an oil-refining plant for aviation gasoline planned by the Bureau of Mines for the indefinite future. In reference to the first two, there is one brief statement, no more than a vague hint, to the effect that economic activities other than agriculture and mining are being given official consideration.[12]

The presidential reports and addresses of 1949 and 1950, in so far as they deal with economic matters, differ from the above-mentioned report in some details only: except for placer mining, there is no other positive reference to mining. Industries mentioned as new possibilities include malting (in relation to domestically grown barley), fishing and fish-canning, and cellulose and cement plants. Practically all other projects considered in these addresses relate to agricultural production, including mechanization, livestock raising, food storage or processing, irrigation, reforestation, transportation, the tourist industry, and small manual crafts industries.[13]

Earlier, an address by the Delegate of the Ecuadorean Commission of Inter-American Development, delivered at a luncheon tendered to the Commission by the United States National Association of Manufacturers on the occasion of the 1944 Conference of Commissions of Inter-American Development in New York City, revealed a similar pattern of orientation, the more significant in view of an audience of potential exporters of machinery and equipment and containing, as it did, an open bid for United States capital investment in Ecuador. The delegate spoke of the expansion of existing industries (mining, oil extraction and refining, textiles, shoemaking) and of the expansion of power, communication, and transportation facilities. But among the items required under a development program he enumerated none that would signify any wholesale industrialization plans. Instead, the items needed for the development of agriculture and transportation figured large.[14]

In line with these requirements are the estimates[15] made during the first half of the forties regarding the needs for machinery and equipment following the termination of World War II. In one of these estimates, of the ten types of equipment and material listed for Ecuador, that for manufacturing industry figured in ninth place in terms of dollar values and constituted barely 5 per cent of the total estimated dollar value for all types of machinery and equipment. Calculated on a per capita basis, prospective Ecuadorean requirements for manufacturing equipment were the lowest of all Latin American countries: U.S. $1.56. The item for agriculture, on the other hand, was the second largest in size, with an estimated value of 19 per cent of the total. The other estimate, made by means of a questionnaire circulated among Latin American machine-tool and metal-working importers, indicated for Ecuador that lathes and drill presses constituted 81 per cent of all requirements, i.e., predominantly small-shop installations.

Also of interest is the composition of credits which were granted in the latter half of 1944, and in 1945, by the Ecuadorean National Development Bank and the Provincial Banks for the Expansion of Agriculture, Industry, and Commerce.[16] Thus, in 1945, agriculture obtained about 64 per cent of the total credits granted in the amount of around 146 million sucres; commerce obtained 20 per cent, and industry 16 per cent. The largest slice of agricultural credits went to ricegrowers. But since other agricultural credits were granted for projects such as purchases of farms, irrigation, the building of stables for livestock, the purchase of agricultural tools and machinery, it is evident that all credits were not granted on a short-term (sowing-to-harvest) basis--a fact which might have explained the low investment rate of industry as far as credits are concerned. It should be added that figures for bank credits of all banks show a strong emphasis in favor of commerce as over against agriculture, but with industry still markedly tailing behind (CEPAL 1954:149, Table 108, for the period 1946-50).

If development activities since 1942 were surveyed in detail, the emphasis on agricultural development would become more apparent still. The projects of the Ecuadorean Development Corporation (Corporación Ecuatoriana de Fomento, 1942-46) and those sponsored since then by the Instituto de Fomento through its Corporación de Fomento and the Development Banks are practically all in the nature of agricultural and livestock improvement and diversification projects or consist in other projects of a basic nature such as public health, certain public works, colonization and rehabilitation in rural life, home craft industries.[17]

In brief, the general orientation of Ecuadorean economic and social concern is toward agriculture. It thereby offers a contrast to some other Latin American countries where industrialism and industrialization are extensively discussed as a desideratum and real possibility, as economic activity that is definitely distinct from the traditional ones, and in a literature, moreover, that is properly economic literature.

E. An Assessment

In summarizing, the trend of Ecuadorean economic development in the foreseeable future is fairly clear: it is evident from the agricultural orientation of the country considered historically[18] as well as from those of current practices and explicit intentions; it is based on chronic scarcities of staple food items and a long-standing awareness of nutritional and other insufficiencies among large parts of the population, and constitutes, in that respect, a part of the efforts made to raise the general level of living; it is based, finally, on the country's need to insure imports of items not produced domestically, such as machinery and various consumer goods, and to obtain a degree of independence from the fluctuations in world demand for such export commodities as oil, minerals, and forest products and the vulnerable monocultural products such as cacao, coffee, rice.

The policy, as evinced by such recent trends as have been discussed, of retaining agriculture as the mainstay of Ecuadorean economy by increasing and diversifying its production serves two ends. The first is to insure the domestic supply of staple foodstuffs, to obviate the necessity for imports and to improve native diet by new food crops. This applies to a number of basic food crops, particularly of the highlands, and it applies also to crops such as sugar, rice, soya, and cotton and to livestock production. The second end aimed at is the increase and improvement of agricultural production of export crops, some of which are also domestic staples. In all these respects, the government evinces its interest by various protective policies and by direct support in the forms of subsidies and credits for the importation of, for instance, agricultural tools, machinery, and certain livestock.

The mining industry, despite its present decline, is likely to be given some attention, partly as a valuable source of direct government revenue and partly for its contribution to the development of communication and transportation facilities (sometimes stipulated in the concession contract) and of other tangible investments which foreign concessionaires make.[19]

In comparison, manufacturing industry seems destined to play a role subsidiary and supplementary to agriculture and, in yet smaller part, to mining--to stay confined largely to the processing of agricultural and mining products. Hence the existence of industry as well as its further development seems to be entirely contingent on the development of those two fields. (This is apart from the consideration--curiously enough not found anywhere in the literature here surveyed--that industrialization would have to await the development of a broader basis of domestic food supply.) Although manufacturing industry proper exists, there is nothing to indicate any special support for it with the exception of the textile and, perhaps, the leather industries.

Industry, then, may fit into the interstices of a predominantly agricultural pattern. It is not, or not yet, admitted as a potential equal or near-equal partner within the economy. It is in this that Ecuador differs strikingly from its neighbor countries, also basically agricultural but where everything indicates a deliberate redesigning of the economy with a strong emphasis on industry and industrialization.

On the other hand, while industry at present constitutes but a small sector within the total economy, some industrial enterprises and some branches of industry are conspicuously developed and may go on developing; other existing ones, or even new ones, may follow suit by circumventing some of the limitations such as those regarding transportation and other "given" factors. In practice this would mean a tendency for industrialization to occur on a small scale and, above all, on a regional or even local level. This form of limited industrialization by regionalized or localized units would constitute an accommodation to retarded developments in transportation facilities and raw-material exploitation. It would secondarily appear that new industrial plants would have to be geared more emphatically than elsewhere to multipurpose production rather than to specialized production, namely, in those cases where a variety of raw materials is regionally or locally available and given the generally small size of consumers' markets.

With these conditions and limitations in mind, attention will be turned now to the question of Ecuador's manpower resources. Focus will be exclusively on the number of people that might be available for industry, supposing it were to expand rapidly for whatever reason, and on certain aspects of the mobility of an industrial labor potential.

NOTES

1. Omitting mention of such classical works as that of Wolf (1892) and others mostly by non-Ecuadorean writers, the following will be found useful: Enock 1914; Ferdon 1950 (esp. on the coastal area, pp. 8-34);

James 1950:110-25 (includes three good maps on surface configuration, land use, and population distribution); Orton 1875; Romero 1947; Sauer 1950. A great deal of the literature cited throughout this volume contains more or less extensive descriptions of the geography of Ecuador; none is technical.

2. Linke (1954: chap. xiii) has an up-to-date account on communications and includes a useful map. Other materials drawn upon are Ecuadorian Commission n.d.:24, 64-5; IRS IV, 52 (Oct., 1947), V, 74 (Oct., 1948), and Supplement No. 11 to VI (Aug., 1949), VIII, 24 (May, 1950); WTiC VI, 1, 3 (Jan., 1948), VII, 1, 9 (July, 1949), VIII, 1, 4 (March, 1950); American Embassy Reports, No. 16 (Jan. 28, 1949); Bol. Trim. Info. Econ. III, Nos. 20-21 (Jul.-Dic., 1953):56.

A series of journeys along existing and projected railroad lines and highland-lowland roads, undertaken by a number of Ecuadorean journalists in 1945, are described in UNP 1946:199-279.

References on roads and road construction are scattered among a number of items used throughout the present volume. Some of these are purely descriptive of travel conditions over given roads or trails, others provide data on the current state of roads, road construction, and projected roads.

The Peruvian Times and West Coast Leader occasionally has notes on developments in this field. National and provincial newspapers not only contain data but currently give space to innumerable complaints on the existing state of roads and requests for maintenance and for the construction of specific highways and feeder roads and other roads vital to a given locality. A certain amount of information has been gleaned from such sources.

3. Compare, e.g., Hassaurek (1868) and Orton (1875) with recent travel descriptions by Bemelmans (1941), Franklin (1943), and Rainey (1946).

4. Detailed and critical accounts, especially of lowland crops and their economy, as also on livestock raising, in CEPAL 1954, particularly pp. 41-94 and 153-213, but very little on Sierra crops; Linke 1954:117-26.

5. CEPAL 1954:95-101; Ecuadorian Commission n.d.:44-52; IRS IV, 52 (Feb., 1947) and V, 74 (Oct., 1948) and Supplement No. 11 to VI (Aug., 1949); Lasso 1944:238-55; Linke 1954:126-31; Mosquera 1952; Pan American Associates 1945:282-83; Peruvian Times XI, No. 532 (March 2, 1951); Polit 1947; Tucker 1946:276,296; United Nations Reporter 24, No. 9 (July, 1952):3.

On the recent expansion and development of sulphur mining and processing in Tixán: Hanson and Platt 1945:37-38; Hitchcock 1953; Peruvian Times XI, No. 557-58 (Aug., 24-31, 1951) and XII, No. 582 (Feb., 1952) and XIII, No. 661-62 (Aug. 21-28, 1953); Ruess 1951; Zevallos Menendez 1946:52.

6. It seems significant that the latest comprehensive works on Ecuador (CEPAL 1954; Linke 1954) make no mention, or only the barest, of such products. These omissions well reflect the changes in hopes, expectations, and orientations which can occur in less than a decade. The war and immediate postwar period found these forest products highly interesting. On them and other wild-semiwild and cultivable products, current stand of exploitation, and actual and potential uses, see: Acosta Solis 1947; Anon. 1948; W. C. Davis 1944; Ecuadorian Commission n.d.:23-27, 35-43; Ferdon 1950:9-34; Horn 1947; Hughlett 1946:382; Little 1948; McCann 1947; McClure 1945, 1946; Pan American Union n.d.; (Plaza) 1950:62-74 and distribution map; OCIAA 1943; Popenoe 1924; Roller 1947; Schreiber 1946; WTiC VI, 2, 6 (Feb., 1948) and VI, 19, 22 (June, 1948). A new project, the cultivation of abaca in the lowland zone of Quevedo, was recently under discussion,

on which see Peruvian Times XII, No. 582 (Feb. 15, 1952); El Comercio (Quito, May 5, 1952).

7. CEPAL 1954:130-32; Ecuadorian Commission n.d.:53,60,71,72; Hughlett 1946:50,335; The Inter-American IV, No. 11 (Nov., 1944):45; Inter-American Development Commission n.d.:151; IRS IV, 52 (Oct., 1947) and V, 74 (Oct., 1948); U.S. Tariff Commission 1949:9,18-19; WTiC VII, 21, 19 (Aug., 1949); Wythe 1945:238.

8. The most recent surveys and statements on processing and manufacturing industry will be found in CEPAL 1954:103-32 and passim; this work is quite detailed regarding six major industries, but fails to cover a number of minor yet potentially important branches. UN, ECLA (1949) surveys Latin American economies by topics; mentions of Ecuador are scattered and scant. Linke 1954:131-40.

The present summary has drawn particularly upon the following: Davies 1945:543-59 and 1950:495-511; Ecuadorian Commission n.d.:52-74; Hughlett 1946: passim; IRS VII, 24 (May, 1950); Pan American Union 1944:18 and 1954:32-3; U.S. Tariff Commission 1940 and 1949; Wythe 1945: 235-39.

References for distinct branches of industry: Textile--UN, ECLA (1951) is a very illuminating document not only with regard to "Labour Productivity in the Cotton Textile Industry. . ." but also, indirectly, with regard to industry in general; WTiC VII, 19, 9 (March, 1949). Leather--Wolff 1946:187. Pulp and paper--WTiC VII, 10, 1 (Jan., 1949); El Comercio (Quito, Sept. 26 and Oct. 2, 1950); Peruvian Times XIII, No. 661-62 (Aug. 21-28, 1953) and XIV, No. 725 (Nov. 12, 1954). Glass containers and flat ware--WTiC VI, 18, 8 (Sept., 1948) and VII, 18, 2 (Jan., 1949). Cement--El Comercio (Quito, Sept. 24 and 26, Oct. 11, 1950); Hanson and Platt 1945: 37-8; IRS V, 74 (Oct., 1948); Suarez D. 1950. Chemical--Agriculture in the Americas V, No. 10 (Oct., 1945):196; El Comercio (Quito, Oct. 2, 1950); IRS IV, 52 (Oct., 1947); Andrade Marín 1951; see also n.5, above, on sulphur processing (sulphuric acid). Fishing and fish processing--Peruvian Times XI, No. 527 (Jan. 26, 1951) and XII, No. 599-600 (June 13-20, 1952). Addresses and reports by public officials were found instructive, e.g., Navarro, in Inter-American Development Commission (n.d.); Plaza May 1949, June 1949, Jan. 1950, and May 1950; Zevallos Menendez 1946.

9. The literature cited in this chapter as well as much of the literature used throughout this work are the sources on the basis of which these statements are made.

10. Bruzzone, then Director of the Banco de Credito (1946:150-57); El Comercio (Quito, Nov. 20, 1952), with a proposal by Ing. Octavio Alvarez to "industrialize" the production of banana and other tropical crops in Santo Domingo de los Colorados (dehydrated banana flakes and flour, banana pulp and fibers, banana alcoholic beverages, yuca flour, starch, and tapioca), thus to obviate the difficulty in transporting the raw produce out of this area.

11. E.g., Benites 1950:269-70; and an address by Dr. Antonio J. Quevado, U. N. delegate, before the Ecuadorean-American Association in New York, as reported in El Comercio (Quito, April 3, 1951).

12. Zevallos Menendez 1946 (relevant passages on pp. 23, 19-22, 29, 45-46, 52, 37).

13. Plaza May 1949, June 1949, Jan. 1950, May 1950.

14. Inter-American Development Commission n.d.:149-51. See also Ecuadorian Commission n.d.; The Inter-American IV, No. 11 (Nov., 1944): 45; Pan American Associates 1945:282 ff.

15. OCIAA 1945:26-27 (note also the assumptions, p. 1 ff., 51 ff.); McCain and Loinaz 1946:207-9. With these advance estimates, compare the findings of CEPAL 1954:135-39, especially for the years 1945-50. However, the bases for comparison are not entirely congruent.

16. El Trimestre Estadístico I, No. 3-4 (July-Dec., 1945):121, also pp. 119, 120; I, No. 1 (May, 1945):73 and No. 2 (April-June, 1945):112-13. There are minor discrepancies in these official figures, but the data are sufficient for an over-all statement. CEPAL (1954:149-51) has recent, entirely comparable, data as far as the Development Banks are concerned; see especially Table 110 for the period 1944-51. Dorfman (1953) also remarks on the preponderance of agricultural credits as over against those granted to manufacture.

17. Material on these entities and their activities is scattered: Foreign Agriculture XIII, No. 11 (Nov., 1949):263; The Inter-American III, No. 10 (Oct., 1944):42; IV, No. 3 (March, 1945):39-40; V, No. 7 (July, 1946): 9; IRS IV, 52 (Oct., 1947); CEPAL 1954:145-46; Ecuadorian Commission n.d.: 28-29, 32-33, 34; Executive Committee, Pan American Union 1943:26-27; Franklin 1943:312-13, 316; International Labour Office 1946:285-87; Oreamuno n.d.; Plaza June 1949, Jan. 1950; Zevallos Menendez 1946: 30-35, 87-93.
　　On an agricultural experiment station at Hacienda Pichilingue and other developments in agriculture and livestock farming up to about 1950, see Leonard 1947; Long 1944; Soule, Efron and Ness 1945:247, 279-80; Troncoso 1946:259-74.
　　On the rehabilitation work in El Oro Province: Clark 1943a, 1943b; Loomis 1943; Pan American Union 1944:14, 18, 21.
　　See also the assessment of the emphasis placed on agriculture by the 1948-50 administration, New York Times, Jan. 7, 1953.

18. With a qualification: colonial Ecuador was a not inconsiderable manufacturer of a number of products, not only in the food line (hams, sausages), but also textiles, gunpowder, and watercraft, among others.

19. See, for instance, Zevallos Menendez (1946:35, 36, 46, 48, also 51-52), mainly on the improvements, such as road-building and other installations, made by mining companies, and their leaving of fully equipped mining towns to the state after abandonment of operations. Mining concession contracts usually provide for the construction of roads and other facilities (housing, schools, hospitals, etc) by holders of mining concessions, according to law, on which see Serrano Moscoso 1946:34, 35.

II / THE QUANTITY OF A POTENTIAL LABOR SUPPLY FOR INDUSTRY: AN ESTIMATE

This part of the study is concerned mainly with the conditions of and possibilities for industrialization from the point of view of labor supply, and with the factors influencing that supply. The present chapter is therefore devoted to a discussion of the Ecuadorean population with a view to arriving at an approximate estimate of the quantity of its potential labor resources. Previous to the 1950 census, Ecuador's first population figures consisted in estimates or "informed guesses." The following is based in part on such estimates and in part on such census data as are available so far.

A. The Ecuadorean Population

The total population of Ecuador, including the Colón Archipelago (Galapagos Islands), was variously estimated during the forties to be between 3.2 and 3.5 million, and even more.[1] The 1950 Census[2] gives the country an enumerated population of 3,202,757 persons inhabiting a territory of more or less 300,000 square kilometers,[3] including the Colón Archipelago with its less than 1,500 inhabitants.

The concentration of the population follows roughly geographical-regional lines. Less than 2 per cent of the population inhabit somewhat more than half the total territory of Ecuador, namely, the Oriente provinces (Napo-Pastaza and Santiago-Zamora) and the Colón Archipelago. Hence these areas may be ignored as potential labor suppliers. The other half of Ecuadorean territory is approximately equally divided into the ten highland, or Sierra, provinces and the five western lowland, or Litoral, provinces. Of this total population, about 59 per cent live in the highlands, 41 per cent in the lowlands.

Of the population of these two regions, about 24 per cent live in urban centers of 5,000 or more inhabitants.[4] But the difference in urban-rural distribution between the two major zones is appreciable: of the lowland's population, 71 per cent are rural, the number of towns of 5,000 or more inhabitants being eleven, as compared with the 78 per cent rural population in the highlands with its fourteen urban centers of equivalent size.[5] It is, therefore, in the highlands that the densest population is encountered: an average of about 30 persons per square kilometer. Comparative figures for the Litoral provinces are about 19.[6]

New industry would presumably look first for its labor supply toward those areas in which the population is relatively dense, other conditions being equal. It would look secondarily toward the rural population if the urban were not found to be sufficient, which would be the case if industrialization were to occur at a rate exceeding that of urban population growth. Industry would look thirdly toward those of the rural population who do not find a sufficient income, by prevailing standards of living, from land and farming. It is on the basis of these considerations and assumptions that everything points to the rural population of the highlands as the industrial labor reservoir.

28

B. Ethnic Composition

The ethnic elements composing the Ecuadorean population are dis-
tingusished in Ecuador by the terms Indios or, more generally, Indígenas
("Natives"), Mestizos or Cholos, Blancos ("Whites"), Negros, Mulatos,
and, occasionally, by terms such as Orientales ("Orientals," i.e., Chinese,
Japanese, etc), Afro-Indios, Indo-Mestizos, Blanco-Mestizos, and others
denoting indeterminate and intermediate ethnic statuses.

Estimates[7] regarding the ethnic composition of the population
differ widely not only because of lack of adequate statistics but mainly,
in this case, because of disagreement concerning the classification of
persons or groups, particularly in the case of "Indian" and "Mestizo."
The general tendency is to define these on the basis of external tokens,
such as dress, habitat (urban and rural), occupation, income, relative
amount of formal education, and, comparatively speaking, physical features. The single characteristic by which persons could be assigned to
one or the other group, namely language, is unreliable in view of a certain
amount of bilingualism (Spanish and Quechua) and because of the absence
of linguistically specific enumerations anywhere, even in sample studies.
Hence the numerous sets of data on ethnic or "racial" composition must
be considered as indicative of the fact that the population of Ecuador is
an ethnic continuum without sharp and convenient demarcations. Percentage figures are thus purely heuristic and must be treated as resting
on the subjective impressions and predilections of the compilers and on
the conscious or unconscious emphasis which they give to one or more
of the obvious external characteristics just mentioned.[8]

Examination of over twenty sets of data on Ecuadorean population
composition,[9] some derived from single estimates, others made independently during the last twenty years, shows that estimates regarding
the Negroid element[10] and "Others" (i.e., lowland "savage" Indians,
particularly of the Oriente, and a few Asiatics) range from 3 to 23 per
cent of the population; Mestizos from 15 to 45 per cent; Whites from 1
to 28 per cent; and "civilized" (i.e., highland) Indians from 20 to 80 per
cent. An official Ecuadorean estimate[11] assigns to the Negroid and
"other" elements 10 per cent, to Mestizos 41, to Whites 10, and to the
Indian 39 per cent; another, apparently more recent, assigns 56 per cent
to the Indians alone.[12]

It is probably safe to say that the Mestizo and Indian elements
together constitute in excess of 80 per cent of the total population, and
that, in the highland provinces, Indians--almost exclusively rural--
make up at least 55 per cent, rural Mestizos and Whites 10 per cent,
urban Mestizos 25 per cent, and urban Whites 10 per cent of the total
highland population.[13]

C. The Present Labor Force

Of the total population of Ecuador, 1,236,590, or 38.61 per cent,
were found to be actively or gainfully employed in 1950.[14] The female
contingent of this labor force constitutes almost 29 per cent. The incidence of economic activity varies considerably regionally, sectionally,
locally, and, sometimes, as between village or hamlet and large estate
populations. Thus in the Litoral the rate is a little over 35 per cent,
whereas in the Sierra region it averages an ample 40 per cent and in some
localities reaches almost 60 per cent.[15]

Most of the estimates of the earlier forties assumed that about
80 per cent of the actively or gainfully occupied are engaged directly in

agriculture (including livestock raising), and this would apply to practically all the population identified by the 1950 Census as "Rural" and a large part of that enumerated as "Suburban."[16] An indeterminate number of this farming population supplement agricultural pursuits by the manufacture of various articles for home consumption or for the market, by construction work, and by various service activities such as trade and transportation. Few of the rural population engage full-time in these craft and service occupations. Other employment opportunities, either seasonal or full-time, are offered in public works, particularly road-building and maintenance, and other activities requiring only unskilled labor. Small numbers, especially in the lowlands and western foothills, are engaged in the exploitation of forest products, as also in gold washing.

This largely agricultural but somewhat mixed occupational pattern applies particularly to the highland rural population, including the so-called Indian element. The great majority of these Indians work the land as dependent or independent workers, or both, and some of them engage in supplementary activities. But even among those who engage in trading, crafts, or other specialized or skilled trades as main occupations there are many who are occupied with farming at the same time. The proportion of those who live in rural areas but engage exclusively in nonfarming pursuits is small in most regions and even in most localities. Table I summarizes the data compiled by us from the very few extant sample studies, made in recent years, of the rural highland population; it should be noted, however, that the figures for Pichincha Province and, to a lesser extent, those for the canton of Otavalo (Imbabura Province) are probably not representative for most of the highlands, which is generally less accessible, less urbanized, and less industrialized than these northern provinces.

Estimates of the number of workers employed in mining, refining and processing, and manufacturing industries vary, but within not too wide limits. Mining, during the early and middle forties, was supposed to have employed between 5,500 and 10,000 workers.[17] With the abandonment of operations by major mining and petroleum companies since then, these figures have today probably shrunk to a fraction. The latest available total number of industrially employed workers registered with the Caja de Seguro is 20,000, but the real total employment in industry, excluding artisans, is estimated at 40,000 to 50,000. At the most, and taking "industry in its widest sense, i.e., including artisan occupations, it does not employ over 5 per cent of the active population " (CEPAL 1954:105, 107; Linke 1954:66).

Again, by way of illustration, two estimates applying to the highland province of Pichincha are presented. The first is the result of a survey made in the early thirties which included the then twenty-one industrial establishments of the province, according to which only 0.7 per cent of its population were industrially employed. The sample study of the rural population by the Buitróns, made some fifteen years later, indicates that 1.7 per cent of that population were industrially employed. Of the economically active population, less than 5 per cent were employed in factories, the majority being concentrated in one textile plant, the others in glass- and cigarette-manufacturing establishments.[18] It should be noted that Pichincha is one of the two provinces (the other being lowland Guayas) in which most of Ecuadorean industrial enterprise is concentrated.

TABLE I

Farming and Nonfarming Occupations among the Rural Highland Population

(in per cent of working population)

Class of Occupations	I. Rural Highlands	II. Otavalo Canton (Imbabura Province) — All Groups	II. — Indians & Mestizos	III. Quiroga (Province) — Men	III. — Women	III. — All	IV. Pichincha Province — Wage Workers Only	IV. — Wage & Independent Workers	V. Four Pichincha Parishes — Total	V. — a	V. — b	V. — c	V. — d
Farmers	75	46	56				78.3	76.8	44.19	35.65	35.92	73.23	52.74
Farmers, Owners	40								40.57	43.35	18.47	30.49	74.00
Farm Laborers, nonowners	35								59.43	56.65	81.53	69.51	26.00
Nonfarmers	25	54	44				21.7	22.2	55.81	64.35	64.08	26.77	47.26
Craftsmen, artisans	10	(38)*	(36)*	36*	90*	63*		(27.1)*	29.56	35.75	39.16	17.34	8.44
Service (trade, commerce, transport, domestic service)	8			30	10	20			14.52	13.53	11.81	5.55	36.08
Professionals, Civil Service	3								11.73	16.07	13.11	3.88	2.74
Mendicants	(4												
Factory Workers	(			34	---	17							

* Wholly or almost wholly supplementary to farming

Sources:

I. Suárez 1934:38. Data are based on estimates, apply to the entire highland rural population, but exclude the huasipungeros, i.e., hacienda debt-bound peons.

II. Buitrón and Buitrón 1945. Data have been compiled from the marriage registrations of one year, and apply to (a) 331 men of all ethnic groups, (b) 258 Indian and Mestizo males. The canton is noted for the textile industry, a typically Indian cottage industry.

III. B. S. Buitrón 1947. Data apply to the main activities, practically all supplementary to farming, of the 360 Mestizo men and women who are economically active. Quiroga, Canton Cotacachi, had an enumerated population of 1,186, exclusive of less than 10 per cent Indians whose main supplementary occupations are working as peons (men) and wool spinning (women).

IV. Buitrón and Buitrón 1947, Tables V-VIII. Data apply to an estimated 8 per cent sample of the rural population of the 5 cantons of the province and cover 3,555 gainfully employed or active persons, including independent self-earners, "free" wage workers, and huasipungeros.

V. Buitrón 1951b. Data are for the year 1948-49 and are based on complete enumeration of the population of 4 parishes in the canton of Quito. Over 75 per cent of the populations of parishes a and d are identified as Indian.

D. Land Tenure in the Highlands and the Labor Potential

For purposes of the present inquiry it is assumed that fast-growing industry would draw its labor from those groups among which one might ordinarily expect the greatest mobility or readiness to shift to new opportunities by which to make a living. Hence attention is turned now to those highland rural groups of people who do not own land or do not possess it permanently, or who own land but not in sufficient amount to make them economically independent within the prevailing levels and standards and traditional modes of living. The object is to arrive at a tentative conclusion regarding the number of those who, under the stated assumptions and barring direct compulsion, would be first available to industry. Despite the fact that statistical data pertaining to the subject are few, fragmentary, and deficient, an order of magnitude can be established with such material as is at hand.

All the surveyed data,[19] heterogeneous and uncertain as they are, point in one direction, namely, that there is available among the Sierra population a labor reservoir the size of which lies somewhere between 100,000 and 200,000 adult men. (For the sake of simplicity, no allowance is made here for industrially employable women.) This, the "industrial reserve army," is the potential yield of that part of the Sierra rural population which is wholly without land resources of its own, lives under various systems of land tenancy, or has but fractional holdings for its free disposal.

For instance, CEPAL surveyed the situation in eight of the ten highland provinces and found the number of tax-paying farm properties to be 23,941, of which 81.4 per cent, or 19,470, consisted of farms of one to twenty hectares. In addition, there were 32,740 holdings so small as to be tax-exempt. Hence the total number of properties that can be considered small-scale would be 52,210. The rural (including the so-called "suburban"), i.e., eminently agricultural, population of the eight provinces amounts to around 983,000, as calculated from the 1950 Census. The figures suggest a landless or land-poor, underemployed male adult population likely to be in excess of 100,000 (on an assumed ratio of one adult male for every five persons). This suggestion is entirely congruent with the figures of the much-discussed 1943 tabulation of farmholdings by cataster-values, according to which the number of small properties in the ten Sierra provinces valued between 200 and 10,000 sucres was estimated at 68,894 and the then-estimated rural highland population close to 1,271 million. The resulting manpower surplus appears to be closer to 200,000 than to 100,000.

Careful inspection of the other materials, consisting of statistics as in the above cases, estimates based on statistics as well as on assumed proportions of population groups relative to each other, or blanket statements regarding the size of the landless or land-poor population, does not materially affect the general conclusion that the highland rural population should be able to furnish contingents from a "pool" of between 100,000 and 200,000 men to nonfarming occupations and, of course, does so to some extent if part-time nonagricultural pursuits and minimal rural trades and services are considered. A figure of 100,000 men, and up, would thus seem to be a likely one, and may be compared with the "almost half a million" Sierra population which CEPAL (1954:31) believes should be absorbed by the underpopulated coast so as to balance population densities in the two regions.

It must be stressed at this point that the size of such "reserves" or "pools" of potential nonagricultural labor is not uniform throughout the highlands. Rather, their proportion to any given local population will vary considerably in various parts of the rural Sierra. For example, the situation with regard to land tenure is quite favorable from the point of view of the independent small farmer in the case of the canton of Otavalo (Imbabura Province). There, a large proportion of the rural population represents a largely Indian, small-owner peasantry, regarding which a survey of 8,160 homes or farmsteads, made in 1946,[20] indicates only about 31 per cent of all households to be not wholly independent farmers but dependent or semidependent to varying degrees on farm work on other than their own holdings or on work away from their households. If this proportion were to hold for all of the Sierra--which is far from the case--an occupationally mobile maximum reserve of considerably under 100,000 could be expected.

Actually, the average landless or land-poor population for the Sierra region appears to be higher, province by province. Hence the estimate of over 100,000 potential industrial workers that could be expected from the ten Sierra provinces in general would appear to be conservative.

Even the largest estimated number of properly industrial workers in Ecuador, 40,000 to 50,000, is small if measured against a presumptive and conservatively estimated potential of the size indicated. Hence the conclusion might easily be drawn that conditions for industrialization in Ecuador are most auspicious on the score of labor resources. Indeed, there are quite a few statements, referring to an abundant, readily available supply of unskilled and semiskilled labor for employment in occupations other than agriculture,[21] so much so, in fact, as to prevent a higher degree of mechanization and rationalization in existing industries, such as the highland cotton textile mills.[22] When it comes to numbers, such an impression seems justified.

But if rural labor seems abundant, does that mean that it would be actually forthcoming in quantities if it were sought by industry? Can it be taken for granted that large numbers of men and their families who do not own land in sufficient quantities to make them dispense with taking employment are actually readily available for occupations other than agricultural ones? Do sporadic and perhaps ephemeral movements into nonagricultural occupations (such as in times of economic boom or during the war years) constitute good grounds for believing that massive movements into industry would occur at the given moment? There are no such grounds.

On the contrary, there are indications that semiskilled and skilled labor in Ecuador is scarce at all times and that unskilled labor, such as might be expected from the rural population at large, is by no means always at hand.[23] It behooves us, therefore, to look for lasting and systematic factors which may, or may not, impede the flow of labor into industry.

NOTES

1. Carrera Andrade 1946; Cisneros Cisneros 1948:117, 118 and passim; Garcés 1941; Lasso 1944; Paz y Miño 1936; Maes 1941; United Nations 1949. Ecuador's total area and population size approximate that of Norway;

areawise it is comparable to the State of New Mexico, but with a population approximating that of the State of Alabama in 1950.

2. Dir. Gen. Est. Censos, Census 1950 (1952).

3. The 1950 Census does not provide data on the size of the territory of Ecuador. An estimated, but generally accepted, figure is 270,670 square kilometers (104,510 square miles) for the area left as the result of the Protocol of Rio de Janeiro of 1942 by which a large part of the disputed Oriente region was adjudicated to Peru. Linke (1954:1 and 158) gives 111,168 square miles (288,000 sq. kms.) as a "semi-official figure, provisional and approximate only," and CEPAL (1954:37) uses the figure of 300,398 square kilometers.

4. CEPAL (1954:2) has an over-all rural incidence of 78 per cent. These figures were calculated from Table 2, Dir. Gen. Est. Censos, Census 1950 (1952). The census classifies the population under three ecological rubrics--"Urban," "Suburban," and "Rural"--the first two corresponding, respectively, to the area within the periphery of the capital and of the cantonal capitals, and to those without that periphery but under the jurisdiction of an "urban parish" (p. 17). The figures corresponding to these rubrics are as follows: 20, 15, and 56 per cent. For most of our purposes the so-called "suburban" population may be counted as equivalent to the rural (total, therefore, 71 per cent), for others to the urban (hence, 44 per cent).

Previous estimates of the urban-rural distribution cannot be reconciled with the present data because of divergencies in the concepts "urban" and "rural."

5. Calculated from Table 5, Dir. Gen. Est. Censos, Census 1950 (1952). There, the "urban" population is listed for the "Provincial Capitals and Cantonal Seat" (Cabeceras Cantonales), of which 30 are located in the lowlands, 47 in the highlands.

6. Cisneros Cisneros 1948:115; Maes 1941; OIAA 1945; Saenz 1933:18; IRS V, No. 11 (Feb., 1948). CEPAL (1954:2, 31) and Linke (1954: 11-12, 120) differ greatly as regards the highland density: 26.3 and 32.6 per square kilometer. The above figures are gross densities. In the highlands, actual densities must be appreciably higher, considering the area's broken topography. Cf. Bennett 1946:30 ff.; CEPAL 1954:31; Linke 1954: 11-12; Romero 1947:46-47, 154-56; and especially Cárdenas (1954), who advances densities of, respectively, 46 and 16 inhabitants per square kilometer by considering Sierra-Costa distinctions from the geographical point of view instead of from that of political divisions.

7. So far, no publications of the 1950 Census are available which include linguistic or other data indicating the ethnic composition of the population. Available information on the scope of the census in this respect is conflicting. See Linke 1954:10 and CEPAL 1954:35.

8. For example, there is a tendency to equate "Indians" with the entire rural population, particularly of the highlands. This becomes evident on comparing estimates of the rural population with estimates of the proportion of Indians in the total Ecuadorean population. Data on the distribution of incomes exhibit the same tendency; see, e.g., Behrendt 1948:2 and Laso 1942-43.

9. Brand 1948, Tables 2 and 3; Cámara Barbachano 1954; Carlson 1943: 291-305; Cisneros Cisneros 1948:92 ff.; CIAA 1944:78-79; Davies 1945; J. Davis 1946:16 and 32; Ecuadorian Commission n.d.:74 (note printing

error in the total population figure, which should read 3,011,153 instead of 5,011,153); Garcés 1941:16-17; Gillin 1949:161; Henry 1946:85; IRS V, 11 (Feb., 1948); James 1950:112; Jaramillo Alvarado 1936; Lasso 1944:45-47; Maes 1941; Pan American Associates 1945:276; Paz y Miño 1936:37-40; Romero 1947:52; Rubio Orbe 1953; Saenz 1933a:18-22, 186; Santiana 1952a: 44-46; Steward 1949:666. Some of the cited estimates are based on that by Paviolo (1927).

10. The Negroid element is largely concentrated in the coastal province of Esmeraldas and in some of the western foothills and river valleys of northern Ecuador.

11. Dir. Nac. Est. 1944:55; Pearl 1943.

12. Cited in International Labour Organisation 1949.

13. Though they may be arbitrary, these are the figures with which the present study will operate on a compromise basis. Cf. Angel Rosenblat's 1930 estimate, cited by Bennett (1947:6). CEPAL (1954:35) advances the following interesting figures as "generally accepted" in Ecuador: 90 per cent of the rural population of the Sierra, or 1,140,000, are "Indígenas" (i.e., Indians and Mestizos leading the life of the Indian); of the urban population of the Sierra, 15 per cent, or 110,000, are also Indian, a total of 1,250,000 "Indomestizos" for the Sierra.

14. Dir. Gen. Est. Censos, Census 1950 (1952, Table 12). This publication provides no breakdowns of occupations. It considers the "economically active" population as consisting of employers, employees, self-employed, workers, and peons; armed forces, nonremunerated employment within the family, and students and housewives who have also remunerated occupations. It excludes persons under twelve years of age, rentiers, unemployed, permanently institutionalized persons, prisoners, members of religious associations under clausure, and persons without occupations. Estimates of the economically active population for the forties were 28 and 32 per cent (Ecuadorian Commission n.d.:75, 79-80; IRS V, 11 /Feb., 1948/).

15. Computed from Table 12, Dir. Gen. Est. Censos, Census 1950 (1952). For other differential rates see the studies of the Buitróns of a sample of the rural population of Pichincha Province whose rate of 37 per cent compares well with that of the census (38 per cent); those show the rates for village or hamlet populations as 34.4 per cent and hacienda populations as 44 per cent of their respective totals (Buitrón and Buitrón 1947, Tables I and II). Ample data on four parishes in Pichincha Province show that the average incidence of the working population is 42 per cent, with a range from 39 to 59 per cent; almost 72 per cent of this population is considered Indian (Buitrón 1951b). Rates for a small, mainly Mestizo, community in Imbabura Province are 27.5 per cent: Mestizos, 31 per cent; Indians, 23 per cent (B. S. Buitrón 1947).

16. Linke (1954:9) and CEPAL (1954:34) cite a 1946 estimate to the effect that 63 per cent of the working population are engaged in agriculture and forest exploitation, a figure which CEPAL cites with hesitancy, evidently considering it too low. We believe that the higher figure is justified, considering the supplementary and part-time pursuits, a share of which may have been ascribed to the "construction and repairs" (5 per cent) and "services" (26 per cent) of the 1946 estimate.

17. Ecuadorian Commission n.d.:79-81; Garcés 1941:38; Linke 1954:9.

18. Suárez 1934:23-24; Buitrón and Buitrón 1947 (compiled from Tables VII and VIII).

19. Carrera Andrade 1946; CEPAL 1954:75; Cisneros Cisneros 1950; Ecuadorian Commission n.d.:27; Garcés 1941:17, 18, 25; Maes 1941; Moomaw 1946:165-66; Rycroft 1946:281. Most of this material relates to tenure and distribution of land by size or, more often, by assessed value. Cisneros Cisneros 1948:128 and El Trimestre Estadístico, Año I, No. 1, 1945:55 contain the official tabulation of Sierra and Litoral farm holdings (predios) in use, classified according to cataster (land tax rolls) value for the year 1943, by provinces. Discussion of these and other such surveys will be found in Benites 1950:257-58; Gomezjurado 1945, especially with regard to the minifundia (fractional and small holdings); this category would comprise farms between 0.5 and 10 hectares (1.2 to 25 acres) and the majority are considered not to exceed 2 hectares. On various details, statistical data, and other observations on property tax laws before and since 1944, see Ferdon 1945; Parsons 1945:11, 18, 20, 185-86, 189; Saenz 1933a:50ff.; Serrano Moscoso 1946:68 ff.; Suárez 1934:38, 84. The latest available study on the subject is that of Cárdenas (1954), which discusses the results particularly of a sample agricultural and livestock census of the province of Pichincha, conducted in 1952.

20. Buitrón 1947a. The households of the 37 surveyed parcialidades (Indian settlements) had been approximately enumerated and the total population estimated on the basis of an average of 4 persons per household (which to the present writer appears as a somewhat too low estimate).

21. Ecuadorian Commission n.d.:57, 70; Franklin 1943, passim; Wythe 1945:239.

22. See the findings and conclusions of UN, ECLA 1951.

23. E.g., IRS V, 11 (Feb., 1948); WTiC VIII, 1, 4 (March, 1950).

In addition to the size and distribution of a population, its "mobility"
is a matter of primary consideration in any attempt at industrilization.
How free--or how impeded--is the laborer to move out of one locality
to seek or obtain remunerative employment, as in industry, in another
locality? It is here suggested that the existence of latifundia tends to
obstruct such mobility by virtue of the system of tenancy which is associated with latifundism. A development directly opposing latifundism, that
toward minifundism,[1] may also act as a mobility-obstructing factor.

A. Latifundism as a Block

As in other Andean countries, latifundism is discussed whenever
the Indian is discussed. It constitutes the heart of the "agrarian problem"
which, in turn, is held to be at the base of the "Indian problem" (cf.
Salz 1944).

Latifundism is differentially marked in the various parts of Ecuador.
Given the "underpopulation" of the coast, it is not felt there to be a problem as it is in the highlands. There, it is declared to be particularly
severe in the provinces of Carchi, Chimborazo, and Cotopaxi, as well as
in several cantons of the northern provinces of Imbabura and Pichincha
and the central province of Bolívar. It is present in sporadic form in
Tungurahua, though especially during the last few decades it seems it is
minifundism which has come to prevail in that province. Information
regarding the situation in Cañar and Azuay is scant, while Loja, the south-
ernmost province, is unanimously asserted to be almost free of latifundism and on that score is classed with sections of Imbabura, such as the
canton of Otavalo.[2] In sum, the greater part of the central Sierra and
parts of the northern Sierra are identified as the regions in which latifundism prevails, while medium and small property are characteristic
of the south.

It has been suggested that high population density, especially of the
rural Indian population, is functionally correlated with latifundism, and
this has been shown to be the case regarding the province of Chimborazo
(Buitrón 1948a). It is probably true also for Cotopazi. Elsewhere, this
correlation cannot be substantiated. The most densely populated province,
Tungurahua, is marked by prevalence of minifundia, and the case of Cañar
seems similar. In those parts of Imbabura where there are large Indian
populations, minifundism is also marked. On the other hand, population
density is comparatively low in Carchi Province, where latifundism is
accentuated. In the case of the other provinces, Buitrón's thesis remains
very much in doubt.[3]

Extensive holdings of land are concentrated not only in private
hands but also in those of corporate bodies. In the case of Ecuador, the
state owns extensive lands, most of which are unused (tierras baldías)
and some of which are let to hacienda management. In former times it
was the Church which was the conspicuous landowner, but such former

church lands are now controlled by the government or by the beneficencias or asistencias públicas by virtue of which hospitals, public assistance, and other welfare activities are financed. Other corporate bodies such as parishes, municipalities, and universities also own lands, though to a lesser extent.[4] Finally, a number of communities throughout the Sierra own lands in collectivity.[5] Here attention is given to latifundism as private landownership on the large and concentrated scale and as extensive exploitation of such lands by agriculture and livestock raising.

As a social institution, latifundism in highland Ecuador is frequently likened to, or treated synonymously with, "feudalism" because of the nature of the tenant system or systems that go with latifundism and because of the relatively heavy dependence of a great number of people on the large haciendas for their livelihood. These are largely the people discussed previously as landless, in the sense of being nonowners. The various tenant or peonage systems under which they live have been the main butt of the attacks by progressive elements in Ecuador (as well as in those of the Latin American countries where such systems prevail). A vast body of literature has grown up around the feudalistic-latifundia theme, much of it one-sided and militant. The bulk of the more sober and descriptive accounts picture substantially the same basic facts, and differences in them concern local details or changes as they have occurred over the last ten or twenty years.[6] A number of classes of tenants or tenant-laborers--predominantly Indians or Indianized Mestizos--may accordingly be distinguished, given here in a rough order of relative advantage of the tenancy arrangements' conditions.

There are, first, those who rent land from the haciendas for cash; generally, no other commitments accrue to the tenant under this arrangement. Second, there is a group of share croppers (partidarios, aparceros, medieros) who receive land and/or tools and seed from the landlord against a share, usually one-half, of their crops. The third class of tenants rents certain use-rights, such as in water and irrigation, pasture lands, forests and their resources of fuel or timber, or rights of trespass, collectively or individually, paying for such rights in labor of one, two, or more days for the benefit of the hacienda. This system is called yanape (yanapa, ayuda, hence yanaperos, ayudas) and is quite common. The last class, representing perhaps the largest single class of the tenant groups, consists in properly debt-bound labor tenants called huasipungeros, from huasipungo (sometimes ración), the plot of land given them for their own use and for their homesteads (also conciertos, from concertaje, the labor-tenant contract and the term by which the system is known; also indios propios, "owned Indians"). This plot of land and the advances initiating this labor-tenancy, consisting in seed, tools, and often building materials or the house, are paid off by personal work in farming, herding, and in the landlord's household (huasicamía service) at the hacienda or in the town house. The whole family of the huasipungero or peón concierto is implicated in this arrangement, and the number of labor days per week traditionally need not be specified but may, at times, include the entire week. The tenant-laborer may or may not have to furnish his own animals for hacienda work, and he may or may not receive food rations and/or cash wages in addition to his plot of land. His hut may be furnished by the landlord or he may have to build it himself. At any rate, the race between the debt accruing from the initial advance and other subsequent ones or fines incurred because of failure to perform stipulated work or assessments made against the tenant for loss of animals or tools is said to end but rarely in his favor. The accumulated and never-canceled debt may be made over to his sons and thus handed down from generation to generation.

The details of the system[7] are subject to local variations; the system also allows for combination with the other forms of tenure mentioned above. But the main outline of the concertaje system is the one here sketched. The term glebe adscripti is occasionally used in reference to this class of tenants to characterize their actual situation, although it is now a debtor-creditor nexus that determines their status.

There is a fourth group, apparently also large,[8] the members of which, though not necessarily tenants, are in a measure dependent on work in the haciendas. These are the "free" laborers (peones, peones sueltos, peones asalariados, jornaleros), who may or may not own some land but who are largely dependent on work paid for by the day or week or longer stipulated period of time, or by a unit of work performed (destajeros, "pieceworkers"). Their cash wages are generally higher than those, if any, paid to conciertos, but their actual income is probably not higher. However, they constitute a more mobile group than any of the others mentioned.

While the institution of concertaje, or (debt-)peonage, has been that part of the agrarian system, and of the "Indian problem" with which it is closely associated, against which progressive Ecuadorean elements have most militantly and consistently spoken out, and while various legislative measures have sought to improve matters, examples of its de facto existence are constantly brought forward. Moreover, its spread into quite modern economic situations has been observed. For instance, it was charged that an oil company operating in the eastern lowlands tried to hire local Indians, but succeeded only after paying the hacendado in that region five sucres per day per head, of which sum only one sucre was paid to the Indian worker.

In so far as the main basis of this system is constituted by the tenant-workers' indebtedness, it is no longer supported by law. But it is rooted in custom and tradition--understandably enough, if it is seen as a derivation from the Spanish colonial encomienda system, which entrusted the encomendero, by way of royal grants, with the land and the Indians on it as a work force, while at the same time charging him with their Christianization.[9] Bearing in mind the force of custom, lack of communication, and isolation, one can easily take the continued existence of the institution for granted, sanctioned by tradition and relative absence of alternatives, both for hacendados and conciertos.

There are instances which bespeak the power of haciendas to immobilize their workers effectively. For, as will be shown in greater detail below, the haciendas tend to be short of labor, and their efforts to retain their labor forces do not, therefore, spring merely from "feudalistic" sentiments. The means employed to retain their laborers are not, however, money inducements or other rewards.

In one case that has come to attention, such an indio propio had found his way into mining work, had become a good worker, and drew good wages. When he returned to his home community for a visit, the hacienda to which he had belonged prevented his return to the mine on the ground that he had debts which he had to work off (Franklin 1943:82). Elsewhere, free peons are made to work on haciendas at lower than prevailing wages under threat of being put off the hacienda lands where they have their homes, or under threat of their huasipungero-parents' being dispossessed (Buitrón and Buitrón 1947:68-70, 80). Legally substantiable debts and intimidation are the means employed to keep labor on the haciendas.

There is every reason to believe that such instances, although they rarely find their way into the literature, are not isolated but are, in one form or another, common practice. What latifundism effects by virtue of the conditions under and in which it has operated up to now is a blocking off of labor flow into off-hacienda occupations.

There are no data on the numerical composition of these hacienda-dependent agricultural workers' groups. It is estimated that one-third or more of the highland Indians are hacienda peons (J. M. Davis 1946:38), i.e., predominantly conciertos. This would indicate a total hacienda-dependent population of around 350,000 to 400,000, or a male working population of 60,000 to 80,000.

Sample studies of the five cantons of the province of Pichincha, which covered 24 villages and hamlets (anejos) and 36 haciendas and their resident and working populations, show that the proportion of working population to the total population is appreciably higher on the haciendas (almost one-half) than in the villages and hamlets (almost one-third). Other compilations from the Buitróns' raw statistical data show, furthermore, that of the total surveyed population about 24 per cent were definitely committed to hacienda work, at least half of that as huasipungeros, the others as women helpers or by virtue of their being residents of haciendas. At least another 18 to 19 per cent work on haciendas as free peons. The proportion of specifically huasipungero to all hacienda-employed personnel (hacienda peons) varies. It is said that in the four northern cantons of the province of Chimborazo, 93 per cent of all hacienda peons are huasi-pungeros, in the southern two cantons 24 per cent. Table II summarizes this information for Chimborazo, the five surveyed Pichincha cantons, and four parishes in one of these cantons (males only).[10]

Table II

Proportion of Huasipungeros to All Hacienda Workers

Chimborazo Province, north	93 per cent
south	24
Pichincha Province, average	34
Canton I	33
Canton II	42
Canton III	17
Four Parishes, average	34
Parish a	29
Parish b	46
Parish c	32
Parish d	41
Canton IV	46
Canton V	40

These sample data seem to warrant the conclusion that at least one-third of the rural highland population is locked up in haciendas by virtue of residence and work commitments and that latifundism at least impedes the mobility of a male labor force of some 65,000.

The next question is whether a development opposing latifundism is conducive to such free flow, that is, whether a mere mitigation or even liquidation of latifundism is sufficient to unloose a stream of free labor into industry.

B. Small-Farm System and Minifundism as Blocks

There is, indeed, ample evidence of a development which is taking place at the present time that points toward a gradual weakening of large-scale property-holding. True, a strong tendency is still seen--and feared in many quarters--toward the continued increase of latifundism at the expense of the small landholder.[11] But reverse trends were observed at least as early as the thirties, and they appear to have grown in recent years: that is, the trend toward small holdings by private, individual owner-workers and toward minifundism--at the expense of large estates.

This trend toward the formation of small and diminutive holdings is not, of course, wholly a function of the "liquidation" of latifundism. It certainly consists in part, as everywhere else in such cases, of the results of population increase and consequent subdivision and fragmentation of holdings; and this autonomous process is accentuated by absolute losses of land due to erosion and exhaustion of soil which has been cultivated, often on steep hillsides, often without rotation of crops, for as much as two hundred and fifty consecutive years.[12] The rate at which this process of "natural" fragmentation through dividing inheritance occurs is graphically presented for the village of Nayón, a community a little north of Quito, for which a sample calculation indicates that the amount of land held by individual families is reduced by 84 per cent in the fourth generation, even if additions such as dowry lands are figured in (Beals 1952).

But this "natural" fragmentation must be distinguished from the new fragmentation by "accretion" or "recuperation" of land from latifundia, the incipient breaking up of large estates through voluntary sales or by way of expropriations and distributions of such lands to new small-owners. This development is not confined entirely to those regions in which small-scale property has been dominant or has been in some balance with large-scale latifundism. Thus the province of Tungurahua, said once to have been a stronghold of latifundism, was reported to offer a far healthier picture after some large haciendas had been bought up by a government social security agency and sold in small lots to Indians.[13] Today, small holdings or minifundia are considered to be characteristic of the province.

Elsewhere, particularly where latifundism was not so prevalent to begin with, Indians have bought up land either individually or, as has been said, in concerted action, whenever it was offered for sale. It seems, however, that in the majority of such cases no conciertos were involved (their chances for obtaining cash wages or other cash incomes being almost nil due to their status and condition), although a few exceptional cases are on record. Rather, it seems that most of these land purchases were made by persons who owned some land already, though in small and unproductive lots, and who had derived some cash incomes from craft work or from day-labor during a few seasons in the lowlands where plantation wages are relatively higher than those paid peons in the highland haciendas.[14]

In some cases, such purchases seem to be made spontaneously as the occasion arises, that is, without an agency intervening between selling hacienda and buying Indians. In others, they are facilitated through government action, by means of the laws concerning land settlement including settlement on vacant state lands; through the intermediacy of public or semipublic agencies, such as one of the units of the social security ministry; and also through bank credits. In the early forties "some 60,500 hectares" were reported to have been "taken from various estates, mostly by purchase. This land was resold to small farmers, being divided into 2,000 or more different holdings."[15]

The cataster rolls 1939-45, too, seem to tell a story, though it may not be conclusive. It is worth noting, however, that the four registers show a steady increase in the number of registered farm properties. The increase is especially marked in comparing the years 1941 and 1943, and the upward trend is most pronounced in the Sierra, in which the net increase of all such properties was 64 per cent. It also seems remarkable that the greatest increase in the number of properties occurred in the category of those valued at 3,000 sucres or less, namely 69 per cent.[16] But it is impossible to tell whether all these increases result from more comprehensive registrations or to what degree they bespeak an actual trend. The trend, nevertheless, exists, even though it may be considerably smaller than appears from the sources.[17]

Such newly acquired lands are no doubt in the majority of cases real minifundia, that is, lots too small to furnish the owner-worker with more than bare subsistence. Hence it is likely that he still has to rely for any cash income on supplementary work, either as self-employed craftsman or artisan, as day-laborer at neighboring haciendas, at larger holdings, or in public works, or as seasonal worker in the neighborhood or elsewhere, all of which would be in conformity with old patterns in most regions.

The trend toward such fractional holdings is, incidentally, feared in some quarters as much as that toward latifundism, and is especially pointed out for those communities in which all or some of the land is communally owned.[18] The trend, in other words, does not seem to halt before this communal type of properties either.

It is not altogether clear what, precisely, impels haciendas to offer their lands for sale. In point of fact, it is declared that "the majority of farmers /i.e., haciendas/ are not disposed to sell their lands, even less willing to divide their farms into lots," and other opinions are cited according to which much of the land is not for sale since the estates have been in the same families for many years (Ecuadorian Commission n.d.:7; Moomaw 1946:174). Nevertheless, the same factors which render land dear[19] seem to operate also to bring it occasionally upon the market: low agricultural profitability, especially in the Sierra, due to high costs of transportation and irrigation, hazardous production, and, not least, scarcity of labor. For instance, it seems that land sales were favored when haciendas changed from livestock raising to corngrowing following the abrogation of a trade treaty in 1930 under which cattle had been exported to Columbia; and again, in 1942, when corn rose in price while meat and dairy products were subject to price control. Hence there occurred "a constant change of extensive pastures and meadowland formerly used for livestock into cultivated areas,"[20] and it might be this point which induced some haciendas to sell some of their land. Other reasons are suggested, such as the desire of the hacendado, as one informant put it, "to have a Chevrolet and to live in Quito," and the knowledge that Indians will pay any price to obtain land.[21]

The existence of a development toward small-scale agriculture suggests the nature of the block against the mobilization of a substantially indeterminate number of people into steady industrial employment. The development seems to parallel and to reinforce another circumstance which has been hinted at several times and which shall now be dealt with more explicitly: that is, a chronic, and periodically and regionally acute, scarcity of labor, particularly agricultural labor. The point may appear paradoxical in light of an estimated industrial labor pool of between 100,000 and 200,000 and the undoubted scarcity of land in the Sierra in face of an increasing population. The paradox is resolved in taking into consideration the effects of latifundism and minifundism on the mobility of labor.

C. Supply and Mobility of Agricultural Manpower

The evidence for this scarcity is scattered and has not, so far as can be ascertained, found systematic treatment. But there is no doubt that it is felt, and at times acutely so, for scarcity or high costs of domestic food items are too often blamed specifically on lack of agricultural manpower. Certainly, shortages in general agricultural production or deficiencies in specific crops can be more readily explained by a host of long-run as well as immediately operative factors, such as lack of transportation and distribution facilities; weather and other crop damages; speculative investments in and development of exportable crops; soil erosion and agricultural malpractices, etc. It would also be proper to refer underproduction to a change in standards of production, population growth, and changes in the demands of foreign markets, and thus treat it as a relative matter. Yet among all these palpable factors (which in part do operate) and all these considerations, one fact stands out: both Litoral plantation and Sierra hacienda agriculture are shorthanded and tend to desire an increase in their labor forces, or at least to maintain what they have.[22]

The indications of this state of affairs appear in many different contexts, especially in discussions on agrarian reform and colonization and on agricultural production. For instance, the article by Carrera Andrade (1946), in itself an argument for agrarian reform and against large-scale landed property and its undercultivation, purports to show that colonization of the vast Oriente region by internal migration is superfluous if not impossible. He points out that, on the one hand, both coastal and Sierra lands are far from being utilized; on the other hand, there are not enough workers to cultivate the five hectares of cultivable land that could be made available to each under agrarian land reform and distribution, particularly in view of the population's low level of health and the poor agricultural techniques. "The absolute absence of labor," states the Report of the Ecuadorian Commission, impedes the development of new, i.e., hitherto not cultivated lands, and a leading newspaper, in commenting on a new set of agrarian reform plans which contemplate colonization of the western foothills of the Andes by internal migration, states flatly that "the number of inhabitants of the Republic is still insufficient for the amount of land it has."[23]

Scarcity of labor is, of course, more pronounced in the coastal zone, with its low population density, its emphasis on the production of export crops under fluctuating world-market conditions, and with a population that is rather more mobile than that of the highlands.[24] Thus, particularly during the war years, did shortages develop in certain lowland crops, such as coffee and sugar, because of manpower shortages. During that period the exploitation of forest resources in the western lowlands and in the Andean foothills (balsa wood, rubber, cinchona) had engaged apparently increasing numbers of rural workers, a proportion at any rate important enough to be commented upon in the 1946 Report of the then Minister of the National Economy as having appreciably detracted from the agricultural labor force, thus adding to those factors which had caused lowered yields in various crops.[25] After the war, the output of these products and others was reduced not only because of the expected falling-off of demand abroad but also and precisely because of the re-diversion of labor to rice production. It is interesting to note in this context that the Ecuadorian Commission took a dim view of the possibility of further extending rice cultivation beyond the Litoral into the Oriente, one of the two reasons given being again scarcity of labor.[26]

In the inter-Andean region, such as in the area around Cuenca (Azuay Province), there was noted a "marked labor shortage on the haciendas" because the making of "Panama" (toquilla straw) hats had diverted many people there from farming (Bennett 1946:13-14) during the war years. Shortages of panela (unrefined brown sugar), staple of the poorer classes, were due not only to the diversion of sugar cane to alcohol making but also to a decline of sugar cultivation in the lower valleys of Imbabura Province owing to manpower shortage. A high-ranking official is quoted as saying that "farm labor is coming to be our chief agricultural problem" in the inter-Andine, and the need for a larger and better-qualified supply of labor on the land is expressed by a number of persons in public and private life. In all, large-scale agriculture seems to operate on a very slim margin of labor supply, so much so that the situation is characterized as a "crisis de 'mano de obra' agricola."[27]

Various reasons are given for such surprising agricultural labor shortages in the highland region. In some cases, as in certain of the lower valleys, the prevalence of malaria was decisive and might still be so. Differences in wage rates, such as the higher wages paid for road-building work, seem to be effective among free laborers, including free Indian agricultural workers. With wages higher in road building, "the workers desert haciendas, production decreases, and manpower shortages develop on the large estates. This is the case at the present time in Ecuador" (Garcés 1946a:10). Oppressive conditions on the haciendas, lack of sufficient land and irregular employment opportunities, and nearness to urban centers are most often cited in explanation of an urbanward trend, especially among the younger people, who engage in domestic service, municipal service (such as street cleaning), petty retail and street hawking, and unskilled labor.[28] Consequently, urban migration is often singled out for special comment in explaining agricultural labor shortages, and measures to put the peón back on the land are felt to be necessary.

In many cases, however, such migrations to the city by individuals seem to be accidental rather than intentional and are occasioned by military service in the city barracks or by the fact that children of hacienda peons were taken to the city by their masters for domestic service. In other cases, urban employment is clearly supplementary to subsistence farming and seasonal. In the absence of precise data and figures, a solid, large-scale migration from the country into the cities is hard to establish. In the province of Pichincha (in which Quito, the country's capital, is located) it has been observed that men prefer to seek employment within the immediate vicinity rather than to venture farther afield. Moreover, a study made in the Litoral contains data which suggest that it is the young women rather than the men who go to the cities and, furthermore, that there is an appreciable amount of out-migration from the Litoral cities into the country.[29]

The sex-ratio data of the 1950 Census,[30] although they permit of other interpretations as well, provide interesting suggestions regarding geographical mobility and, especially, urban migration. The over-all gross excess of females over males for the whole country is on the order of 33,000 (sex ratio: 99.18) and is accounted for in the age-groups 15-49 and 60 years and upward. Moreover, men are in absolute short supply in all but one of the ten Sierra provinces, or in thirty of the forty-three cantons making up these provinces. By contrast, all the provinces of the Litoral as well as the two Oriente provinces and the Colón Archipelago have an excess of males over females, with the exception of four Litoral cantons, among them Guayaquil; in a few cases, this excess seems considerable, with sex ratios of 120 and over. As for the male-female composition in urban centers of 5,000 or more inhabitants, females exceed males in all of the fourteen Sierra cities and in seven of the ten Litoral cities of that class, and in all these cases sex ratios are below the national average. Settlements of lesser size (cantonal seats, called "urban" in the Census), seem to reflect the sex ratios of their respective cantons. The data seem to de-emphasize other possible factors making for the prevailing sex ratios, such as immigration from abroad,[31] or highly differential vital rates which may be operative. They do suggest, however, first, a net movement from the Sierra, mainly, into the western lowlands, the volume of which is on the order of between 7,000 and 10,000 males; second, a net movement within the Sierra, into a few inter-Andean low valley regions with tropical crops, on the order of perhaps 3,000 males (Baños in Tungurahua Province; Pangua in Cotopaxi; and six of the eight cantons of Loja); and, third, more females than males go to the larger urban centers.

In other words, a truly mobile male labor force in and from the Sierra does not seem to exceed 13,000 at most. These apparently "excess" males among the Litoral and Oriente populations do not indicate that they are permanent settlers. Rather, this group seems to be composed of, first and largely, seasonal labor on tropical plantations and may include some, but very few, "commuters" between their own small Sierra and new Litoral farms (of which Nayón in Pichincha Province and the Santo Domingo de los Colorados in the littoral part of that province may be one instance), and, second, individuals engaged in transport and trade, including wholesale (agricultural products) and retail (huckster-style) and even barter trade, as described in a few detail studies,[32] in sum, a "transient" population caught outside their permanent homes during the time of the census-taking.[33] At any rate, the size of a "floating" population in general, and the size and quality of urban migration in particular, is insignificant in itself; it does not seem that it is urban migration that accounts for a scarcity of agricultural labor to any significant extent.

Other tendencies, on different levels of analysis, remain to be summarily considered, for they help in apprehending the possibilities and limitations, the orientations and trends, of Ecuadorean social economy; they reinforce those features which have already been noted.

D. Agrarian Reform Pressure and the Trend toward Rural-Agricultural Stabilization

Much of Ecuadorean thinking on matters of social and economic concern is characterized by antilatifundism and takes the form of pressure for agrarian reform.[34] This is quite evident from the tone of much of the literature here used and the indictments of latifundism by many writers. On the whole, their proposals do not go beyond demands for effective legislation calling for the breakup of the large estates, including state-owned lands, and making these lands available to small farmers. The formulation of more concrete proposals is evidently hampered by the lack of sufficient information regarding the extent of cultivated and cultivable lands in the highlands and, in fact, lack of agreement as to what constitutes usable land. A perusal of the literature shows so little congruence among the data that have been advanced on these questions that even a guess at the amount of available and usable land is impossible.

In the main, proponents of agrarian reform envisage land distribution to landless or land-poor agricultural workers at the expense of the large estates. Such proposals are treated as eminently matters of social justice and in terms of protest against the social and economic ("feudal-istic") conditions associated with the latifundist exploitation of land. The advocacy of medium- and small-scale landownership is furthermore informed by an attitude sympathetic to the Indians not only as underdogs but also as culturally valuable elements. The viability of this element, and hence its potential contribution to national life, depends upon land and the individual and communal security that goes with it.

Beside and within this broadly framed goal, more specific arguments, phrased in terms of an agrarian policy, are advanced.[35] The level of living of the rural population has to be raised (else it remains a constant drag on the national economy), and rural-agricultural living conditions have to be improved by raising agricultural production and rural consumption. Besides raising agricultural production by modernization of agricultural techniques, diversification of crops, provision for irrigation, rural credits, producers' and marketing co-operatives, etc., the cultivated area needs to be expanded by distribution of privately and publicly owned large holdings to small-scale owner-workers. This demand of agrarian reformists has been bolstered for a long time with the significant technical reason that small-farm owner-workers, particularly the Indians, cultivate their small holdings most intensively,[36] while the productivity of the latifundia (not to mention idle state lands), because of the underutilization of their lands, generally compares unfavorably with that of these small farmers.[37]

One important alternative to the distribution of land, whether private or public, is also discussed as part of agrarian policy proposals, that is, the redistribution of the rural population by internal colonization and settlement on new lands in the western and eastern foothills and lowlands. This alternative arises with the doubt that redistribution of cultivable lands in the highlands would provide nothing but ephemeral solutions in view of the highlands' dense population. It is particularly non-Ecuadorean observers who hold agrarian reform measures through the breakup of the latifundia only to be futile unless accompanied by substantial colonization of vacant new lands, and these are no longer found in the highlands (Saenz 1933a:115-16; Romero 1947:48). A further variant on the virgin-land-colonization-theme is colonization by immigration, preferably by Europeans. Past attempts in this direction have not been successful, but the matter is given serious consideration from time to time.[38]

The features, then, on which these concerns, proposals, and pressures for action turn are, summarily, these: low agricultural yields due to antiquated methods of cultivation, underutilization of land by haciendas, and chronic and sporadic and felt shortages of agricultural labor; population pressure on available land resources or, to put it in different terms, the known and demonstrated desire of the rural, specifically the Indian, population for land, and the concatenation of the agrarian with the Indian problem together with modern humanitarian considerations; and the urging of progressive elements within and without government for small landholdings, on economic no less than on social and moral grounds. To a certain extent these concerns are reflected in governmental policy programs as well as in legislation: they have engendered legislative schemes of internal settlement and colonization and of land distribution by the state through its agencies, as well as provisions designed to raise the level of living of the rural populations as a whole, of the rural agricultural workers in particular. Together, these efforts constitute a long-term trend which ought to be taken into account as one of the basic features of the Ecuadorean reality. In so far as they should become effective, they would tend to immobilize a population that would otherwise be available for nonagricultural pursuits.

The main elements of what amounts to a "rural-agricultural stabilization legislation" consist in certain constitutional and other provisions[39] relating to concertaje, to property rights in land and other natural resources, to expropriation and distribution of land, and to the reversion of vacant or unused lands to the state and their disposal (Ley de Tierras Baldías y Colonización, of 1936). There are supplementary provisions regarding settlement colonization on new or practically new lands in the eastern and western lowlands and public aid to prospective settlers.

An attempt to contribute to the stabilization of the rural population may be seen in the Ley de Comunas (Law of Organization and Regulation of Communal Lands) of 1937. Its scope and provisions are specifically aimed at rural communities, their juridic status, and their welfare, and it is described as "a decisive step in the social and agrarian reform of our country" (Cisneros Cisneros 1949). Its details will be discussed in Chapter XII (B, 1, a).

Attempts at safeguarding agricultural labor and at improving its position are also made in other directions. The Labor Code of 1938 contains special provisions regarding agricultural labor, including share croppers.[40] It defines, for the first time, agricultural employer and agricultural laborer and states the rights and duties of each. It charges the former with the obligation of providing pasturage, water and wood, and hunting and fishing rights for the agricultural employee; requires him to furnish adequate housing; and exacts, in certain specified cases, the establishment of elementary schools for the workers' children. The employer is enjoined from retaining fines beyond a 10 per cent maximum from workers' wages or from making deductions for advances. Tools and materials for work have to be provided by the employer (huasipungeros often have to furnish their own tools and animals for hacienda work). The Code also seeks to abolish the truck system[41] and mixed wages for cash wages, fixes minimum wage rates for the various occupations and regions, including agricultural labor, and otherwise seeks to regulate the manner of payment and remuneration.

Whether, of course, the provisions regarding agricultural labor are observed is highly doubtful. The Labor Code is far more stringent in the case of other categories of labor and provides more adequate machinery for the enforcement of provisions for industrial, service, and white-collar workers. Moreover, its definitions and interpretations of what constitutes a labor contract leave "usage" and "custom" sufficient scope to perpetuate many of the conditions which are described for hacienda workers (Serrano Moscoso 1946:74, 75, 76). However, the provisions for agricultural labor must have had some effect in various regions and under various circumstances and probably have contributed to some extent to a mitigation of the worst conditions, particularly where lines of communication have been opened up.

Finally, the Social Security Reform Law of 1942[42] provides for eventual extension and obligatory application of its provisions to those groups so far excluded from the compulsory insurance system: agricultural and domestic workers, self-employed craftsmen, houseworkers, and farmers. One among a number of investigations made preliminarily to ascertain the conditions of such rural independent and semidependent farming groups (Buitrón 1947b, 1949a) raised doubts with regard to the feasibility of their incorporation into the social security system in view of the role which the family still plays in providing for an individual's life contingencies (Buitrón 1947a).

In presenting this legislative framework, no endeavor is made to assess its efficacy. Only its existence has been recorded to show wherein consist the attempts to protect the rural population resources and to promote new stable units on the land, to restrict latifundist tendencies and to loosen the ties of the haciendas and to create ties of another character-- small landownership. Whether these legislative attempts will result in an increased labor supply for agriculture and in increased agricultural production remains a question.

NOTES

1. In view of the prominent place which latifundism occupies in the following, it must be made very clear here that the term refers primarily to a form of land tenure, specifically large-scale concentration of land in one hand, and includes a specific tenancy system. Latifundism does not necessarily entail large-scale production (per unit of land). In this respect it is distinguished from the form of land utilization of the modern plantation system--a form more characteristic of the coastal area of Ecuador.
    The terms minifundia, minifundium, and minifundism are modeled on Spanish usage and refer to small-scale property usually worked only by the owner and his family; they are equally applicable to single-crop, multicrop, or truck farming, or to horticulture.

2. Carrera Andrade 1946; Cisneros Cisneros 1948:150 ff. and passim; Franklin 1943:78-80, 250, 259-60; Parsons 1945:186, 188-89; Maes 1941; Saenz 1933a:50,54, 102; and sources cited throughout this chapter.

3. I made an attempt to establish positive correlations between the prevalence of latifundism, the density of the rural population, and the incidence of ruralism. The findings suggested in the text are part of the results. On the whole, the attempt remained inconclusive because of insufficiently defined concepts ("urban," "rural," "Indian") and insufficient information on "actual" as compared to gross densities, a matter which hinges on the concept of living space in mountainous territory. Nevertheless, and with more adequate statistical data on cantons (in contrast to the large units, the provinces), significant positive correlations of this kind can probably be established. Preliminary computations pointing in that direction, on the level of the provinces, have been made on the basis of the following materials: Cisneros Cisneros 1948:102-5, 115; 1949; Dir. Gen. Est. Censos, Census 1950 (1952):Tables 2 and 5; OIAA 1945; Rodríguez Sandoval 1949:7-8 (who used the estimates of Paz y Miño 1942 and Samaniego 1943).

4. For the distribution of land among state and other public bodies and private haciendas in the three zones of Ecuador, see Benites 1950:

285-95; Carrera Andrade 1946; Cisneros Cisneros 1948:150-51; Franklin 1943:76.

5. Inventoried in Cisneros Cisneros 1948. See also García 1939:120-23; James 1950; Monsalve Pozo 1942.

6. Some of the principal materials are: Buitrón 1947a and 1948a; Buitrón and Buitrón 1947; Cárdenas 1954; CEPAL 1954:74, 76-78; Cisneros Cisneros 1948:79-89; Ecuadorian Commission n.d.:27, 74-76; Franklin 1943: 79-80; International Labour Organisation 1949:55-58, 94, 95-96; Jaramillo Alvarado 1936, 1943, 1946; Maes 1941; Moomaw 1946:164 ff.; Murra 1947: 818 ff.; Parsons 1945:8-9, 188-89; Poblete Troncoso 1946:205; Saenz 1933a: 102-28 and passim; Soule, Efron and Ness 1945:91-92.

7. IEAG 10 and 11 (1953) deal in some detail with the tenancy, especially the huasipungero system, as found in two haciendas in Chimborazo province. The field investigations were made in 1952 and 1953, and the study is the only one known of this scope as regards specificity and detail.

A good summary of the general features of concertaje, including its legal aspects, is found in Rubio Orbe 1949. Cisneros Cisneros (1948:87) considers the yanapa and the huasipungo systems as distinct modalities of the old concertaje.

8. "...the immense majority of the Indians of the Sierra," according to Rodriguez Sandoval (1949:3, also 4).

9. Although the exercise of this latter function had become rare, Saenz (1933a) gives a few examples of its survival into the early thirties and cites instances of compulsory education in the dotrina, with sessions held once a week at a Chimborazo hacienda for its huasipungeros, who had to pay for this instruction by extra work assignments. IEAG 10 and 11 (1953:86-87, 96, 141-42) mention these practices, especially as regards children, but no extra work assignments. Cf. Cevallos 1873: 133-34. On the colonial encomienda and modern latifundism, see Benites 1950, passim.

10. Buitrón and Buitrón 1947; Buitrón 1948a, 1949c, 1951b.

11. Bol. Ind. I, No. 2 (1941):25; Ecuadorian Commission n.d.;7; Murra 1947:818; Parsons 1945:8-9; Saenz 1933a:117, 187, passim.

12. Acosta Solis 1945:13-15, with reference to Tungurahua.

13. Maes 1941; see also Jaramillo Alvarado 1946. However, it should be pointed out that medium and small-scale landownership was characteristic of the province for a considerably longer time, according to Cevallos' specific observations on this matter (1873:297).

14. Maes 1941; Jaramillo Alvarado 1943; see also IEAG 10 and 11 (1953: 35-36) on the "free Indians" of Chimborazo Province. A few chapters of Gil Gilbert's novel (1942) turn on this motive and motif.

15. The literature here used provides a number of specific instances of such land purchases. It also makes quite frequent reference to the matter as a general phenomenon. Specific cases are mentioned for Imbabura Province, especially the cantons of Otavalo and Cotacachi, by Buitrón and Buitrón (1945), Buitrón (1947), Cisneros Cisneros (1948:186), Parsons (1945:8), and Saenz (1933a:117). For the provinces of Carchi and Cotopaxi: Cisneros Cisneros 1948:209-10; Cisneros Falconi 1951a,

1951b; Plaza Jan. 1950; Jaramillo Alvarado 1946; Tello 1949; Zambrano 1951. For Pichincha and Bolívar, Cisneros Cisneros 1948:192, 196, 197, 263, 340. For Chimborazo: Dale 1946:135; J. Davis 1946:40. For Azuay, Monsalve Pozo 1942. For Loja: Jaramillo Alvarado 1946; Saenz 1933a: 123-24. General references to such events are to be found in Jaramillo Alvarado 1943; Moomaw 1946:173; Murra 1947:819; Soule, Efron and Ness 1945:238; Unión Panamericana, Noticias, No. 16 (April, 1944):4.

A number of instances are detailed for the years 1936-37 in Bol. Min. Prev. Soc., Año I, 1937, Nos. 2-3:17-18; No. 5:1-2; Nos. 6-7, passim, and pp. 61-62, 63, and table following p. 112. Whether it was Indians in particular who benefited from allotments from expropriated haciendas is a question. Garcés (1941:26) speaks of a "microscopic proportion" of Indians and Mestizo-Indians who obtained land in this manner. See also newspaper editorials reprinted in Previsión Social (No. 8, 1941), discussing charges that the distribution of vacant state lands was being made to the wrong people, such as employees, businessmen, and other nonfarmers.

16. Cisneros Cisneros (1948:126 ff.) reproduces the complete registrations for 1939, 1941, and 1943. Data for 1945 in El Trimestre Estadístico, Año I, Nos. 3-4, 1945:77.

17. Recently the tendency toward the breakup and parcelization of latifundia was briefly considered within the context of the question of new, incipient class formations in Ecuador, by García Ortiz (1951:21) and Paredes (1951:46), the former considering it a sporadic phenomenon, the latter ascribing it greater importance.

18. Monsalve Pozo 1942. Cisneros Cisneros (1948) mentions a number of communities in which communally owned lands finally did come under individual ownership.

19. Land prices have greatly increased since at least 1940. Unit prices for various types of land, particularly in the highlands, are given in J. Davis 1946:40; Ecuadorian Commission n.d.:6; Moomaw 1946:174-75; Parsons 1945:186.

20. Ecuadorian Commission n.d.:7. Cf. Cisneros Cisneros (1948:131), summarizing the situation in a few terse sentences.

21. John Collier, Jr. See Parsons 1945:8; Garcés 1941:25, 26.

22. This is by no means a new problem, as is very clearly indicated by Hassaurek (1868:303) in his discussion on highland hacienda economy of the sixties. See also Borja-Cordero 1924:81.

23. Ecuadorian Commission n.d.:7; El Comercio, Quito, Oct. 8, 1950.

24. Cf. E. Romero (1947:115), who holds that the reason for Ecuador's "underconsumption" (underproduction) of foodstuffs lies in the absorption of the rural population into industrialized agriculture, i.e., plantation agriculture producing for export. Cf. one of the main motifs in Gil Gilbert's novel (1942).

25. Pan American Associates 1945:280; Zevallos Menendez 1946:5-6. During the war, "thousands of Ecuadorean laborers were employed in the cinchona industry," according to Rainey (1946). During that period, too, some 22,000 persons were engaged in gold-washing in the Litoral and Oriente (Ojeda 1946).

26. IRS IV, 52, 1947; Ecuadorian Commission n.d.:7, 76. In more recent

years, rice has become one of the most important crops both for domestic consumption and for export.

27. Bruzzone 1946; Cisneros Cisneros 1948:87-88; Ecuadorian Commission n.d.:21; Franklin 1943:269; Garcés 1941:30-31; Moomaw 1946:167-68. See also IRS V, 11 (Feb., 1948) on the general labor supply situation before, during, and after World War II.

28. See nn. 26 and 27 above; also Pan American Union 1944:22; Romero 1947:138-39; J. Davis 1946:48; Saenz 1933a:178.

29. These statements are based on the following: Saenz 1933a:180; J. Davis 1946:40, 45-46; Leonard 1947:71. See also Buitrón and Buitrón 1947: 71 and passim; Beals 1952.

30. Dir. Nac. Est. Censos, Census 1950 (1952: Tables 1, 2, and 4), from which the following results are computed.

31. Such immigration is minimal. A very small farming immigration in Carchi and Esmeraldas hails from neighboring Colombia to the north; Loja, in the south, is conceivably recipient of an infinitesimal trickle of Peruvians. European and other "young" immigration hardly exists such as to count in this particular question.

32. Beals 1952, for Nayón; Cisneros Cisneros 1948:218, 225, for Cotopaxi Province; 246, 248, 262, for Chimborazo; 266, 270, for Bolívar.

33. The 1950 census was held during the last days of November, the month during which internal migration is at a minimum (see introductory statement, Dir. Nac. Est. Censos, Census 1950 (1952:9). It may be noted that one of the rice-harvesting seasons in the Litoral occurs between October and December, one planting season between December and January (James 1950). These are two operations presumably drawing seasonal labor. In December, too, a second cacao harvest occurs.

34. This matter is well discussed by Saenz (1933a:119-28, 139-40, 191); see also Romero 1947:56-59; Rycroft 1946:281-82; Franklin 1943:10-13. See also Moomaw 1946:173, 174.
    A pertinent and incisive critique of the agrarian-cum-Indian problem formulation and agitation is presented by Moreno (1940:262 ff.).

35. See the agrarian policy proposed and detailed by the Ecuadorian Commission(n.d.:28, 29-30).

36. See, for instance, Maes 1942; Parsons 1945:8; Romero 1947:48. See Cárdenas (1954), Table 6 on p. 321, which details land use by size-classes of property.

37. The underutilization of hacienda lands may be due to lack of labor, capital, or markets. No information on hacienda economy and its problems was found, except in the most general terms here indicated. CEPAL (1954) deals only with export- and tropical-products agriculture.

38. The latest project contemplated Italian immigrant settlement in the western lowlands, for which see Plaza 1950.

39. Such legislation is extensively summarized in Serrano Moscoso 1946: 111-15. See also Maes 1941:10; Saenz 1933a:121 ff.; Soule, Efron and Ness 1945:238; and the recent compilation of specifically Indian legislation by Rubio Orbe (1954).

40. On the Labor Code (and social welfare legislation generally, including the social security system of 1942), see Ecuadorian Commission n.d.: 77-79; Maes 1941; Owen 1941; Poblete Troncoso 1942:161-62; Serrano Moscoso 1946:74-110; Soule, Efron and Ness 1945:208, 219-20; IRS V, 11 (1948) and V, 101 (1948).

41. According to Garcés (1941:33-34), the truck system (wage-payment in kind) has disappeared in urban centers but continues to exist in various forms in rural areas and among agricultural workers. Inferentially, the injunctions against truck shop, remunerations in kind, and regulation of advances are being used by employers as a handle for refusing "supplies" to their workers; see Buitrón and Buitrón 1947:78.

42. On the social security system, see De Quiros 1945:22 ff., 36, 41, 80; Galarza 1943; Lopez Arteta 1944; Mulliken and Roberts 1946:162; Meneses Pallares 1942.

IV / THE CONTROLLING CONDITIONS: A SUMMARY

The foregoing has dealt with three main sets of conditions which have to be taken into account in considering Ecuadorean economic development in general, industrialization--on whatever scale--in particular. These conditions are conceived as eminently "controlling" conditions and are extraneous to the population under discussion, i.e., they are factors which are least under the control or volition of prospective industrial workers. What amounts to the latters' "viewpoints" and aspirations, be they imputed, derived from observable behavior, or "real" (that is, self-expressed), constitutes in large part the subject matter of Part II.

The first set of conditions, subsumed under the heading of "geography and economy," needs little further discussion. On the whole, there is little to encourage immediate, all-out and all-over industrialization. On the score of Ecuador's raw material resources, as known so far, and the present stand of its extractive industries, such industrialization would appear at least premature. A greater general deterrent to industrialization consists in the deficient communication and transportation system. The general orientation in matters of economic development is clearly and primarily toward agriculture. Although Ecuador has a sizable and fairly diversified secondary or manufacturing industry, it is in fact, in outlook, and by tradition a predominantly agricultural country which continues to seek the solution of its various economic and social problems within and by means of agriculture. Previous developments and plans and policies during the last few decades do not point toward solid and sustained industrialization efforts comparable to those of some other Latin American countries. So far as can be seen, Ecuador at present is neither anti-industrial nor even strictly preindustrial; it may be characterized as a-industrially oriented. Nevertheless, industry during the last few years has increased its volume of production at a rate "apparently greater" than Ecuador's population increase.[1]

The second set of conditions relates to the potential quantity of man-power, and the third to its immediate availability for industrialization under present conditions.

The scanty data do not permit the drawing up of a human resources budget, much less a rural manpower budget. However, it appears that if there are any real surpluses available for industry, they are infinitely small. This is due not to absolute numbers but to the relative fixity of budget items, as it were, and the difficulty of reallocating potential surpluses to other than present purposes. As has been pointed out, the rural agricultural population, from which such surpluses might be expected, is in part stabilized (even though on a level which signifies underemployment), in part in process of stabilization, so much so that deficits are even engendered.

The latifundia-minifundia problem is at the hub of the question of the derivation of industrial labor. Without raising any claims to prescience, some comments regarding possible developments in the foreseeable future in the interplay of latifundia and minifundia are in order.

To the extent that geographical and cultural isolation breaks down and that, simultaneously, legislation concerning agricultural labor, minimum wages, etc., becomes effective, the latifundia will have to exchange their debt-bound labor for free wage labor. From all indications this is what is already occurring in some regions and localities. If this labor--the largest part, so far, of agricultural labor--follows the traditionally and generally prevailing patterns, it will seek to establish itself on land of its own, either by migration to vacant lands or by gradual acquisition of latifundist lands. In either case, latifundism as a labor-retaining reservoir stands to be considerably weakened. But as long as such labor is capable of being drawn off into small landed property, no full-time labor for industry is likely to be produced by the mere weakening of latifundist barriers to mobility.

As for the development of minifundism, no palpable obstacle is seen at the present time. It is sporadically supported officially, but the development itself is not likely to proceed at a rapid pace (the development of minifundia due to fragmentation is not here considered). At any rate, there is no indication of systematic withholding or of systematic unburdening of land on the part of the large haciendas. The amount of cultivable or otherwise productive land, whether privately or publicly owned, is itself a question of debate. But this question is, after all, far more a matter of the position of agricultural technology than of absolute limitations, and will remain so for at least some time to come; in this respect, it is analogous to the scarcity of agricultural labor, which, on analysis, is not so much absolute as relative to, first, the demands made on agricultural production under the formula of higher levels and standards of living and, second, the technical equipment of agricultural labor and the present system and conditions of large-scale agricultural exploitation in the highlands.

Whichever way we look at the problem, the fact remains that agricultural labor is scarce, and industry will have to compete with agriculture for whatever employable labor there is and will be. (This consideration is apart from intra-agricultural inter-regional competition, if any, but which seems to be indicated in the higher wages paid to lowland plantation workers.)

Other developments might offset the necessity for this competition: first, concentration of agriculture, particularly of latifundist agriculture, on livestock breeding which, under prevailing techniques and with existing and expandable pasture lands, would require lesser numbers of agricultural workers; and abandonment of an agricultural protective policy in favor of considerable food imports; or, second, rationalization, modernization, and mechanization of farming methods for large and medium-sized farms.

Some attempts have been made in both directions, but they have so far been confined mostly to the lowlands or western Andean foothills and to large-scale enterprise. In most cases of small-property farming, the latter alternative is unlikely to materialize in the near future, and, in any case, whether in large, medium, or small-scale farming, with private, communal, or co-operative landholding, developing a modern agricultural system of production would require investments which none of these farm-size classes is likely to be able to afford. For quick results, such developments would, furthermore, require educational and training campaigns of unprecedented dimensions. Over-all relaxation of the existing agriculture-protecting policy is very unlikely.

Hence a potentially competitive situation for an incipient manufacturing industry as against agriculture will have to be taken for granted.

Within this limitation and from the point of view of quantitative availability of labor, these conditions seem to apply for any industrialization program: industries will preferably draw on highland populations, as these are large and dense; they will furthermore have to draw upon the rural and agricultural populations in areas where small property and minifundia prevail, where landlessness is somewhat pronounced, and where ease of access to industry and hacienda is approximately equal, if for no other reason than to make labor price competition felt.

It should be noted, however, that the construction of the very means by which isolation is broken down (highways, roads, railroads) again withdraws appreciable numbers both from agriculture, as at present, and from industry, potentially, particularly since this latter occupation can be engaged in seasonally. In other words, competition for labor would be, or is, three-cornered as between agriculture, crucial government public works, and industry. Competition from public works is keen (if this is what it can be called, in view of a certain amount of compulsory public works contribution), and at times government has offered such inducements as land to roadworkers.[2]

It is for all these reasons that industrialization would have to proceed on regional and even local bases. Even within regions it would have to be of an interstitial character rather than general and comprehensive. Apart from the other factors, such as raw material resources, this conclusion is arrived at mainly on the basis of the quantities of potentially available industrial manpower, which, under one viewpoint, constitutes a "mina de potencial humano" (CEPAL 1954:13).

This accommodation to the controlling conditions is held to be a realistic possibility; hence the main subject of the analyses to follow is the quality or qualities of prospective industrial labor drawn from the rural highland populations.

NOTES

1. As cautiously observed by CEPAL (1954:112). The observation is based upon a small sample of industries. It may be added that there are no reliable data on the rate of increase of the Ecuadorean population.

2. Thus, in the middle thirties, government appears to have offered such inducements to highland Indians to work at roadbuilding in tropical areas, areas which Indians are notoriously reluctant to enter. Indians were offered three sucres a day for roadwork and, in addition, 15 to 20 acres of land for 100 days of roadwork (Von Hagen 1940:281).

PART II

QUALITATIVE ASPECTS OF HIGHLAND INDIAN LABOR

"Failure to realize that the peasantry of the
Andean countries constitutes a definite and
very special portion of their population, and
failure to understand the ancient social institutions whereby the peasantry is governed,
explain why so many British and American
business ventures dependent upon peasants
for labor have met with incomplete success
or even with disaster. The trouble has been
that their directors have proceeded on the
assumption that they were dealing with an
ordinary proletariat."

--Means 1925:429-30

INTRODUCTORY

Modern industry ordinarily finds it desirable or actually stipulates that its workers have certain qualities. Among them are relatively patent and single traits, such as specified manual skills, work experience, and training and formal education of a certain kind; health and generally good physical condition; and habits of work that guarantee a minimum of interruptions and disturbances in the process of production. Such habits are relevant to industrial discipline in the more technical sense, and hence the question of work habits and customary work patterns as well as the manner in which prospective industrial workers spend their nonwork time will be of interest to industry at the outset. The chapters immediately following will consider these matters in some detail.

Subsequently there will be considered qualities of a more social nature and hence of more complex character which are important to industry in its associative aspects or as a social system. These "social qualities," too, relate to industrial discipline in that they indicate the manner in which discrete human elements interact as individuals and as natural and functional groups. Because of the importance of industrial discipline in this sense, industry will have to consider the composition of a working force in terms of its internal homogeneity and compatibility and in terms of its probable relation to outsiders; existing possibilities of communication and existing channels of contact within and beyond its constituent groups will also need to be appraised.

An industrial enterprise such as a manufacturing plant, whatever else it may be, is an association of many people combining their efforts and energies and activities toward the purpose of production. It is in the nature of industrially organized production that an industrial plant has a definite social order of its own. The detail arrangements of such an order need not be identical throughout all countries and at all times. It is conceivable, for instance, that they partake of features common to the general social order of the country within which an industry is located, and that the whole cast of a manufacturing industry reflects a "national character" and repeats, in miniature, a larger social order. However, certain features by which the association of human beings in industry are ordered are, and must be, independent of the features of its larger, as well as of the smaller, social orders--although the possible extent of such independence cannot yet be foreseen.

These "neutral" and indispensable requirements of organized industrial association, expected or exacted from industrial workers, can loosely be stated from the point of view of managerial personnel as qualities which make for uninterrupted production and frictionless work discipline: ability to subordinate, to take orders, to co-operate in co-ordinated teams and in functionally, hierarchically, or otherwise structured groups, to communicate and to receive communications and orders, and, to varying degrees, to assume leadership. A measure of homogeneity and uniformity of the human "raw material" in cultural and social respects (such as language, habits, customs, aspirations, etc.), while not indispensable, may aid the task of initial industrial organization and facilitate the development of such industrial "virtues" as have just been mentioned.

The main problems to which Chapters X to XIII will be devoted concern the dispositions or "qualities" of Indian workers which are "social" in that they account for the specific manner in which discrete human elements interact so as to make a specific society possible. These social qualities, expressed in the manifest social relations as they exist in Ecuador, will be considered in their bearing on industry as an association. Our consideration starts from the recognition that an industry (and, for that matter, any other deliberately organized form of association) cannot ignore the kind of society within which it is to take root, the component individual elements of which are to be inducted into industrial life and within which it is to live and to thrive.

Apart from the technical, somewhat narrow sense in which the question of "discipline" is considered, especially in Chapters VIII and IX, it arises again in the following chapters but in different contexts. The subject of inquiry in the section on social relations is those qualities which make for what may be called "discipline-in-society," or associative discipline. It thus turns, on the one hand, on the kind of relations that obtain between Indians and non-Indians (since that distinction is made in actuality) and, on the other hand, on the kind of relations prevailing among Indians. This inquiry is made in order to assess the chances that Indians, as they are, would fit into an industrial organization, with its objective, matter-of-fact, demands for smooth functional subordination or superordination, and for co-ordination and co-operation with and among like elements. (The requirements concerning reciprocal managerial functions will also, though more briefly and indirectly, be indicated.)

The justification for such an inquiry rests on the possibility that an industry might have to start with a social tabula rasa: it might have to hew all channels of communication itself, or it might have to create forms of social relations virtually ex nihilo, as might be the case in closed caste societies. Hence it is a purpose of the chapters here under preview to point to some of the existing forms of social relations, including "established routines of relationships" and established channels and modes of communication, and to assess them either as obstacles to industrial social arrangements or as relations that are capable of application or utilization in the industrial social situation. To make it brief, the most hard-boiled, most rational-minded manager will probably agree that "it doesn't pay" to go out of one's way to hurt the susceptibilities of the managed.

An inquiry into the various social relationships and their correlative behavior in Ecuador means, first of all, an examination, in somewhat formal terms, of the social structure of Ecuador in general; next, an examination of the various ways in which members of its component strata and groups apprehend and act out their positions vis à vis members of other strata and groups (Chapter X). As a result of such an examination we ought to be able to state whether or not, and to what degree, there exist groupings and relationships that would help or hinder industrial association and the industrial formative process.

Another set of questions that should find answers concerns institutions or organizations which permit inference of the existence of a behavior that insures the frictionless association which modern factory production demands. It might even be possible to indicate the existence, either within general Ecuadorean society or within Indian society, of institutions or organizations that might be suitable models for certain detail arrangements within the industrially organized association. These questions are approached in terms of objective homogeneity and subjective solidarity, with the further specific question in mind as to what, if anything, might act as a divisive factor (such as status privileges or other recognized

grounds for differentiation) in the homogeneity of outlook, attitude, behavior
and action that is supposedly desirable in industrial organization. Preindustrial social cleavages may insinuate themselves into the industrial
situation and there perpetuate themselves "unfunctionally" (Chapters XI
and XII).

Our inquiry into the properly social qualities of prospective industrial Indian workers takes also into consideration two points of a "historical" rather than "functional" nature. In the first place, manufacturing
industry must, in principle, be considered an intrusive element so far as
the existing society and culture of Ecuador are concerned. Second, the
realistic assumption must be made that higher managerial and other technical personnel in industry will consist of non-Indians, that is, of a human
element extraneous and perhaps radically alien so far as the Indians are
concerned. For both reasons, it is important to know the ideas that are
held regarding Indians (no matter whether they are "true" or "false") and
the ideas held by Indians about people and things, familiar and strange.
Preconceived notions, prejudices, and superstitions are as much part of
the reality with which we deal as are programs, hopes, beliefs, policies,
and aspirations.

A few opinions on Indians as workers have been culled and are here
offered, such as they are, as leitmotifs to the succeeding inquiry and
analysis of the qualities of Indian labor; they are reproduced, without
comment, to draw attention to the irritation which the Indian seems peren-
nially to evoke in his taskmaster.

The observers of the 1860's and 1870's find that the Indian "does
nothing voluntarily, not even when paid for his labor, but is pressed into
service of the government for a certain time, at the expiration of which
he is discharged and another forced into his place." And "soured by long
ill treatment, he will hardly do anything unless he is compelled. And he
will do nothing well unless he is treated as a slave" (Hassaurek 1868:195,
also p. 134 and passim; Orton 1875:112).

A generation later (Rivet 1903:79):

> Futile, incapable of attaching himself to consistent work, to
> bring forth sustained effort, the Indian is a flighty servant, ir-
> regular, and disappears as soon as he has amassed a little money
> and even without pretext. ... Capable of accomplishing a task and
> accomplishing it well, provided it be always identical, he cannot do
> anything demanding some initiative...less lazy than indolent, the
> Indian sees in his work the means to ensure his precarious existence
> and none...by which to improve his lot.

According to the experience of a paymaster for a road section gang,
"the Indians work very well and actually do more than some white men.
However, they stop for all festivals and usually work only five days a week"
(J. Davis 1946:47-48).

Yet a gang of twenty such workers, called up to clear a mountain
road of a landslide, impresses the traveler with its slowness, lack of
effort, and inefficient movements. The relevant passage is worth quoting
in full (Flornoy 1945:33):

> Ces Indiens-là /near Baños/ sont bien des fils d'opprimés. Ils
> ignorent l'effort des bâtisseurs de route, le noble geste des bras
> haut levés, la sonorité des grands coups de pic sur le roc. Je

voudrais leur montrer comment on attaque la terre. Ils me regardent humblement: attaquer la terre! Eux, ils la déplacent, avec crainte. Ni les Inca, ni les Espagnols, ni les colons fouetteurs ne les menacent plus, et pourtant ils mènent toujours leur besogne à petits coups de pelle résignés. Les jurons me viennent a la bouche... /In the course of the road-clearing work, another rockslide falls and injures one man badly./ On me regarde: este-ce que le patron a compris?

Is it possible to relate such inefficient and unwilling behavior to distinctly Indian qualities and traits?

A. Skills

In considering various isolable qualities of prospective industrial Indian workers, the question of skills is raised first of all because this would ordinarily be the first question raised by an industrial employer. To be sure, in comparison with other questions, this one may appear somewhat trifling if not entirely question-begging, for incipient industry in a nonindustrial country would not expect to find a labor force that was highly skilled (in the industrial sense). However, the peoples of many nonindustrial countries and many so-called primitive peoples possess highly developed native crafts, hand-manufacturing processes, and a great variety and a high degree of manual skills, ingenious tools, mechanical and technical devices, and technological knowledge. It seems important, therefore, to furnish some information at the outset as to what may be expected of Ecuadorean Indians. What skills, i.e., manual skills as such and technical and technological knowledge, can be presumed? Information on this point would permit of an estimate of the chances for the transfer of native manual skills and practical knowledge to those required in industry, of the speed and success of any necessary retraining, and of the amount and kind of needed basic training.

As has been shown previously (Chapter II), the vast majority of Indians are engaged in agriculture in one form or another, to which activity sidelines may be added which, though still largely supplementary to farming, have developed into important craft industries in some areas. Among these are all sorts of textile industries, and these take first place in Indian craft manufacture. It is said that there are "more than 20,000 weavers" in the highlands, "producing for their own use or the market." Other crafts or skilled trades engaged in are leatherwork, felt hat-making, adobe, tile- and brickmaking, ceramics, masonry- and stonecutting, quarrying, bricklaying, construction of subterranean conduits (socavones), carpentry, and other minor trades.[1]

Work along most of these lines is typically pre-empted by Cholos or Mestizos or the small-town urban element; in some regions, nevertheless, Indians begin to appear in such skilled occupations, as independent artisans. Carpentry and other allied woodworking trades in particular are poorly represented among Indians, whereas all types of construction work in adobe, brick, and stone, and the preparation of these materials, seem to be somewhat Indian specialties.[2] On the other hand, there is hardly a craft exercised to any extent by Indians in which Cholos do not also participate. With the exception, perhaps, of spinning and weaving, there are no crafts and trades that are considered typically and exclusively Indian.

Hence materials handled by Indians more especially are those used in a large variety of textile articles, such as cotton and wool, cabuya fiber (for sacks, bags, ropes, cordage, coarse thread, and sandal soles), toquilla straw (from the fibers of the leaf-stem of the lowland toquilla palm used for "Panama" hats) and other fibers and straws such as bamboos, reeds, grasses (mats, baskets, fans, and other basketry articles), and horsehair (hair sieves).

Operations in the preparation of these materials and the manufacture of these products include laundering and other fiber-preparing steps, carding, spinning, weaving, dyeing (with natural plant and mineral and synthetic dyes), embroidering (as on shirts and blouses, rugs and carpets), knotting, twisting, plaiting, braiding, and felting.

Tools and mechanical devices are few and primitive. In particular, iron tools are conspicuously rare, and those in use among various craftsmen and artisans among the rural population were found to be few and poor in quality. Weaving looms are generally home-constructed.[3]

Mechanical devices involving the wheel are rare or completely absent in some localities. Thus in the Valley of Otavalo, wagons are not used at all, all transportation being by human back or donkey.[4] It was in relatively recent times that the spinning wheel was introduced in that region (the only use of the wheel among the Indians there, as far as could be ascertained), and it has not superseded the old form of spinning by hand-rotated spindle.[5] The plow used in Otavalo is a wheelless affair and is advanced only to the extent that it is ox-drawn and may have a metal shoe or plowshare.[6] Weavers in that region use a Spanish-type upright loom with pedals, introduced there around the turn of this century, but the native horizontal or belt (backstrap) looms are still used widely for the making of sashes and other fabrics of narrow width.[7] The stock of tools as customarily used by Otavalo Indian farmers consists of spades, hoes, sickles, machetes, and wooden digging sticks, but not all these implements are possessed by any one individual. Axes, adzes, and small knives are rare.

To give an example of the stock of skills of Indians, those typical for Otavalo men and women may be summarized. An adult male Indian will be able to farm and care for livestock, to spin by wheel, to dye, and to weave; he may be able also to build a wattle house himself, but this is not a general rule, and to engage in the locally specialized trading. Women, apart from household work and farm chores, know how to sew and embroider, how to spin and twist yarn by means of the spindle--or some other phase of textile production--use a sewing machine where they can afford one (in which case a second wheeled item is added to their technological inventory), and make pottery--without the use of the potter's wheel--where the craft is hereditary through the female line.[8]

Thus there exists a certain degree of division of labor, or specialization in skills and manufacturing operations, along sex lines. Men rather than women weave, especially where the pedal loom exists as is the case in Otavalo, while women will help in, or be in charge of, all other subsidiary textile operations. Men spin on the wheel, women by means of the native spindles; in regions other than Otavalo, however, these are seen also in the hands of men. Pottery is a women's craft in parts of Otavalo and hereditary only in some families. Elsewhere, as in the ceramics-producing cantons of Cotopaxi Province, men seem to specialize in that production and its marketing. Both sexes work equally in agriculture, though plowing and other heavy work such as clearing a field fall to the men; nevertheless, women will do the plowing if they have no male help. In Quito, women work in bricklaying tasks alongside their men. Long-range, wholesale transportation is in the hands of men, but otherwise it is the women who carry the burdens to and from the markets.

While, generally, specialization proper tends to run along ethnic or ecologic-regional lines (highlands, lowlands), subregional and local specialization may also be discerned. Within these settings, there may then be further ethnic subspecialization.

The matter of regional or local specialization is of some importance if skills are considered in terms of high manipulatory ability. Such ability would be found, for instance, among the weavers of cloth, as in the Otavalo region; of rugs, as in the Riobamba area; of straw hats, as in the provinces of Cañar and Azuay, also in Loja Province, and in some communities north of Quito.[9]

So far, the question of skills has been discussed largely with reference to independent Indians, whether farmer-craftsmen or laborers. On the whole, economically better situated farming Indians and marginal Indians or Cholos seem to engage in a greater variety of handicrafts and skilled occupations beyond the traditional manufacture of textile articles. And, although on the whole skills appear meager and few, such Indian or Cholo rural populations offer a lively contrast to what may be expected from hacienda-bound huasipungeros, as shown by recent sample studies made in various parts of Pichincha Province. The proportion of those of the general working population of villages and hamlets who exercise some skilled craft or trade other than farming, service, commerce, and transport is very much higher than that of the huasipungeros, namely, 44 per cent of the former (including a small proportion, 6 per cent, of factory workers), as over against 2 per cent of the latter. Skilled occupations among specifically Indian populations also appear to be fewer. In the case under survey, only 23 per cent of the total Indian working population ply some skilled trade or craft.[10]

It is hardly necessary to point out that, generally speaking, the stock of skills, of technical and technological knowledge of the average farming Indian, is limited. It may be, however, that some assumptions regarding the existence of some rule-of-thumb knowledge of chemical processes may be made. This would apply to fermentation processes (as in homemade customary beverages or cheese), to tanning, and to such processes as are involved in the making of dyes, felt, bricks, tiles, glazed ceramic ware, charcoal.

Some specific, albeit minor, difficulties that might be encountered in training for, or in retraining of, skills may be mentioned. Thus the relative paucity of iron tools and particularly the virtual absence of contrivances involving the wheel even in transportation, or of any other of the mechanical principles customarily employed in industry, do not augur favorably for ease in introducing Indians in general to machine production or to the handling of tools other than the customary and primitive ones. In order to emphasize this point, an example from Peru and Bolivia may be drawn upon. Though found to be very satisfactory workers in other respects and contrasting favorably with Cholos in disposition and diligence, a complaint is frequently voiced regarding those Peruvian and Bolivian Indians trained to the use of machinery and technical processes in modernized haciendas and mines, namely, that they forget such training and "have to be trained again and again how to master the intricacies of machinery" (J. Davis 1946:37, 87, 88; Moomaw 1946:170). Applying such experience to Ecuadorean Indians--and there is no reason to think that it is not applicable--industrial training programs would have to take this propensity into account and, above all, to trace its causes. Among others, there might figure precisely the lack of pre-existing knowledge and concepts regarding mechanical and other technological principles inhibiting the process termed by educational psychology "transfer." The alternative, consisting in piecemeal, rote learning of a few operations, might account for this "forgetting" of such training.

Furthermore, if manual skills are at least in part a function of established motor habits, some difficulties might be encountered even on that level. There are indications that many rotary motions--such as in coiling pottery--are systematically made in antisunwise (or clockwise) fashion.[11] These are ritual observances, and, though they may not actually figure as such in consciousness, they are manifested in habits, which habits would, of course, have to be put to the test in actual situations. Trivial as the matter may appear, it is possible that such habits are sufficiently well established to make the regearing of machinery preferable to a lengthy dishabituation process. Similarly, there are hints on preferred or habitual body positions. Thus it is said that in the Riobamba region the "Indian prefers the crouching position. On even a little-elevated seat he feels ill at ease, and even if he could have the use of a chair he prefers the 'Turkish' sitting manner."[12]

In view of the scarcity of concrete and specific information on these matters, any prognosis as to the applicability of the skills which Indians do have to the requirements of industrial manufacture can be made only with the utmost caution. However, it seems safe to say that knowledge of modern tools and mechanical devices and of their underlying principles-- an essential element in real skill--cannot be presupposed. Nor is it likely that the induction of Indians into skill-demanding industries will be facilitated by simple transfer of existing skills and manipulatory abilities to the machine methods of production characteristic of modern industry.[13]

B. Education

The discussion of the education that Indians have is here limited to its more formal aspects. It thus centers largely on the questions of primary schooling and on facilities for vocational training beyond primary schooling, so far as they are relevant to industrial desiderata. It is true that industry in its incipient stages might not be greatly concerned over the question whether its unskilled labor is literate or not. The sole requirement may be ability to count. However, education does assume some importance in selecting semiskilled and skilled labor as well as supervisory personnel, and in these respects the question is of technical importance. Furthermore, the degree of mere literacy prevailing within a given industrial extablishment influences the character of its internal communication, and, while literacy alone does not obviate all verbal communication and instruction, it is a short cut.

The state of education, a matter of great concern in Ecuador, has found somewhat more description, especially of the critical and proposal-making kind, than that of manual skills and technical knowledge possessed by rural highland and Indian groups.[14] There is no doubt that during the last two or three decades educational facilities have been increased and improved and that government and educators spend considerable effort in shaping modern educational policies, oriented to practical training, and in seeking to implement them. The fact remains, nevertheless, that schools in rural areas are insufficient in number and deficient in quality as measured against modern requirements and that schools as a general rule have not yet reached the Indians.

Literacy in Ecuador is low, and among rural groups, especially among Indians, conspicuously so. The 1950 Census registers as illiterate 43 per cent of the total population aged ten years and above.[15] The rate is considerably higher than this national average in a number of provinces and cantons, particularly in the highlands, where it reaches incidences of 65 per cent to almost 80 per cent in a number of those cantons which are considered to have predominantly Indian populations, but also in the more remote areas of the other two zones.

Various precensus estimates and other data on the incidence of illiteracy among various ecological, occupational, income, and ethnic groups[16] give percentage figures for rural and especially Indian groups of 70 to 90 and over, even though about one-third of the Indians are said to have attended school at one time or another. An exceptional case appears to be that of Nayón, an Indian or Indo-Mestizo village in the province of Pichincha, whose literacy rate is suspected to be far above the national average and probably above that of the city of Quito (Beals 1952).

Where schools exist, enrollment in and attendance of elementary schools, under the compulsory schooling system, is low relative to the number of school-age children (6 to 14 years). But, a comparison of data for the early thirties and forties reveals a marked tendency toward improvement (provided the figures can be taken at their face value). In 1933 Saenz estimated that only 33 per cent of all school-age children of Ecuador were attending school;[17] data for 1944 allege that 60 per cent were actually enrolled, with daily attendance only slightly lower. Among the reasons indicated for this still not satisfactory enrollment and attendance were lack of facilities in the rural areas and unwillingness of parents to send their children to school (Ebaugh 1947:15).

Where schools exist in the rural communities and small villages, attendance by Indian children is low, by Indian girls very slight indeed. Even among Indians of the more advanced regions, as in northern Pichincha Province and in the Otavalo region, Indian attendance is minimal. Thus in a girls' school in the town of Otavalo, only one Indian girl was enrolled among 70 students; in the boys' school there were 15 Indian boys, all in the lowest two grades, in a total enrollment of 180 students.[18] In nearby Peguche, a relatively well-off parcialidad of Indians, a new one-room school existed, but in the early forties was reported to be little used by Indians.[19]

If Indian attendance at primary schools is low, that at secondary and other special schools is even more so. Statistical data breaking down enrollment into "races" (White, Mestizo, Indian, Negro), even though such a breakdown is deceptive,[20] give an indication of this. At six rural normal schools (teacher training schools for rural elementary schools) with a total student body of 343, barely 7 per cent were classified as Indian. In the fifteen professional schools (vocational training schools) with a total student body of 1,720, not even one per cent was registered as Indian. In the three newly established "complementary schools" (agriculture and trades) with over 300 students, 4 per cent were classified as Indian. There is no breakdown for all the elementary schools, secondary schools, universities, and four other institutions of higher learning.[21] The data are for the middle forties: taken together they point to Indian attendance at any kind of school as an exceptional matter rather than a rule.

On the other hand, the number of educational institutions has doubled since the middle thirties, according to the statistics here used. An effort is also being made to adapt the rural schools to the requirements and characteristics of the population which is to use them and to modernize the educational curriculum with stress on instruction in practical matters, with training in agriculture to receive foremost attention in rural primary schools as well as in normal schools and in special agricultural training establishments.[22] Educational policy is moving away from the classical system of the three R's and rote learning and toward relating schooling to the daily life of the rural dweller, particularly the Indian (Dale 1946:118; Jaramillo Alvarado 1943, No. 13).

Of the various types of schools that exist within the educational system, the so-called praedial schools (escuelas prediales in the Sierra, de recinte in the Litoral) deserve special mention because of their relation to large-scale enterprise. These elementary schools have to be maintained by large farming and industrial establishments--haciendas, plantations, mines--the latter in regions where there are no public schools; these may offer facilities also for adult education. Some two hundred and forty such schools were said to exist in 1942 (Cisneros Cisneros 1948:134; Ebaugh 1947:21). In the case of the haciendas, the requirement to maintain praedial schools seems largely a dead letter, and what schools of this type exist were found to be poorly equipped and poorly attended by Indian children.

The attitude of adult Indians toward schools, even where these do exist in or near their communities, is reported to be generally one of indifference if not of outright resistance to sending their children to school, especially the girls. For one thing, pasturing is essentially a children's job, and children at an early age are counted upon to do farm and household chores. Their attendance at school therefore greatly affects the household.[23] Also, despite many proposals along this line there are no special Indian schools, and unless the children know Spanish, the official language and the language of instruction, they are handicapped at the outset. In the Otavalo schools previously referred to, there are no Quechua-speaking teachers.[24] Further reasons that have been suggested for Indian resistance to schools are that Indian children are kept in a subservient position when they do attend schools, are held to do the menial tasks there, made the butt of jokes over their costume, or, as literates, are in due time inducted into the army (J. Davis 1946:79; Rodríguez Sandoval 1949:118-19; Rycroft 1946:289).

Resistance toward schooling on the part of the Indian population seems to be weakening, at least in regions where isolation is less pronounced, where schools have existed for some time, and where the people are economically better situated. Of one such community in the canton of Cayambe it was reported in the early forties that 80 per cent of the younger children had been in the two recently established schools (Parsons 1945:184-85). Contact with legal and administrative matters (and perhaps, as one author suggests, with co-operative organizations) also seems to weaken resistance. Saenz reports of Otavalo Indians that they begin to show a desire for their children to learn to read and write so that they may be able to serve as tinterillos (go-betweens for Indians--pettifoggers--in their relations with civil and ecclesiastic authorities).[25] It is in that region, too, that Indians are said to voice a wish for some training in business matters, such as arithmetic and bookkeeping, as they find they need it in their transactions as producers and traders of textiles.[26] The modern type of rural school, combining elementary schooling with instruction in farming, when efficiently organized, seems also successful in drawing and keeping Indian pupils and in engaging parental support.[27]

Education, or rather perhaps the spread of the idea of education (always of the modest scope indicated here), received in 1944 an impetus from a campaign to stamp out illiteracy in Ecuador started systematically by the Ecuadorean Newspapermen's Union (Unión Nacional de Periodistas--U.N.P.) in co-operation with and under sponsorship of

official and other organizations. It is said that within one year the direct
efforts toward adult instruction in reading and writing (by the Laubach
method) turned out about 8,500 people able to read and write, thousands
of others were under instruction, and some 50,000 or 60,000 new "citizens"
(i.e., literates) were claimed to have been made or to be in sight by 1946.[28]
Whatever the concrete results of this venture, and while it is probable
that so far they are confined largely to urban and more accessible areas
with foci in Quito and Guayaquil, it is likely that they help in breaking down
resistance to schools and the Indians' own doubts as to their ability to
learn the art of reading and writing.

In considering the total educational situation, little can be expected
from Indians in general and at the present time. For industrial unskilled
labor, literacy might not be necessary beyond an ability to count, which
stipulation can be met: the Indian language has a full set of numerals, and
counting does not seem to pose a problem.[29] The general state of illiteracy
will present problems, however, in the matter of communication, in that
all instruction, all accounting for wages, etc., will have to be oral.[30] The
fact also might limit the number of otherwise qualified workmen for tasks
requiring reading, writing, and the calculation in numbers. It is therefore
likely that despite increase in the number of literates in the general population and despite increased attention to the country's educational system
and its expansion and improvement, industry will have to shoulder part of
the burden, whether or not it be of the kind that would have to assume it
anyway under the law requiring provision of educational facilities (Serrano
Moscoso 1946:77).

The special factors which are likely to render schooling attractive
or unattractive to Indians have been noted. Indians seem to avail themselves of educational facilities if such are provided, are near at hand, cater
to their interests, and are a demonstrable and concrete answer to needs
they themselves feel.

NOTES

1. On Ecuadorean handicrafts in general, including articles for the tourist and export trade, see: Foreign Commerce Weekly, XXXV No. 4 (April
25, 1949):14-15; Hanson and Platt 1945:26 ff.; IRS V, 74 (Oct., 1948); WTiC
VI, 14, 8 (May, 1948). On Indian or Indo-Mestizo crafts and trades (including in part eastern and western lowland tribes): Cisneros Cisneros 1948:
150 ff. and passim; J. Davis 1946:61-66; Garcés 1946b; IEAG 1953, No. 3:
168-76 and passim; Rodríguez Sandoval 1949:50-60, 62-69, 112-13 (one of
the best sources, with some good descriptions of a number of processes
employed in Indian manufacture, on skills and some organizational aspects
of trades exercised by Indians); Salinas 1954; Zambrano 1951; Bol. Ind.
VI, No. 1 (March, 1946):30 ff. On rug-weaving specifically: Franklin 1943:
111; Long and De Gangotena y Jijón 1946: Spinden 1948. Others consulted
on the subject: Buitrón 1947a, 1951a; Buitrón and Buitrón 1945 and 1947;
Collier and Buitrón 1949:160-64 and illustrations, passim; International
Labour Organisation 1949:80-86; Parsons 1945:9-10, 14-15, 20-27, 30-31,
170 ff., 183-84; Santiana 1949 and 1952b; Saenz 1933a:46, 50-68, passim.

2. Something like an almost complete break seems to have occurred
since the sixteenth, seventeenth, and eighteenth centuries, when artisans
were largely recruited from the Indians and trained by monastic personnel. The flourishing colonial architectural, masonry, plasterwork, stone-
and woodcarving, and silver, gold, and painted works of that period stem

mainly from such Indian and Mestizo craftsmen and artisans, many of them real artists (see, e.g., Benites 1950:130-39). An echo of such stone-carving skills may be found in the case of the new basilica of Cuenca, in construction these past seventy years or more.

Work in wood, however, especially in carpentry and cabinet-making, seems to have decayed entirely among the Indians of today, with the exception of a few localities such as Queros (canton Ambato, province Tungurahua), where it is limited to the carving of utility ware.

3. An attempt is under way in Otavalo, famed Indian hand-weaving center, to substitute modern hand looms for the old-type kind to help increase production; also to standardize native dyes, and to produce closer weaves and uniform patterns and colors, so as to increase exports and to make this domestic cloth more acceptable in the domestic market. See Buitrón 1951d; The New York Times, November 20, 1952; Rubio Orbe 1953, who suggests industries that would be suitable for the region.

4. These observations do not apply, of course, to motorized transportation through the valley. Buses, and also the railroad, are used by Indians for their trading trips to Quito, Ibarra, and elsewhere. Orton states (1875:79) that at the time of his visit in 1867 "there were not six carts in Quito" and that the first carriage was introduced there in 1859.

5. Winding devices for spooling and warping on the rotary principle, used among the most professional Indian weavers, would seem to be the exception; see illustrations in Collier and Buitrón 1949:68, 168, 169, 173-75.

6. Parsons 1945: 177 and passim. On the plow, see HSAI 2 (1947), plate 161, top, and Collier and Buitrón 1949:53, 56.

7. Parsons 1945:25 ff. and illustrations, plates XI-XV; Collier and Buitrón 1949:71, 73; IEAG 1953, No. 3:128, 169.

8. Parsons 1945:53-54. Farming techniques, procedures, and tools are described at some length by Rodríguez Sandoval 1949:45-50; IEAG 1953, No. 3:32-44, 57-64 (for Ilumán, Otavalo canton); IEAG 1953, Nos. 10 and 11:42-45, 107-11, 113-19, 123-24 (Chimborazo haciendas). See also Rubio Orbe (1953) on farming implements and technical "know-how" or lack thereof in farming in the Otavalo region; and Acosta Solis (1945:13-15, in Tungurahua.

9. For example, see J. Davis (1946:62-63), on the speed and accuracy with which members (in this case, women) of a home rug-factory operate their loom. The writer had an opportunity of watching such a father-and-son team in Guano, near Riobamba, engaged in knotting a rug. Cevallos (1873:316-17) extols the sons of Guano as the most industrious of the republic: "the whole population appears to be one workshop" dedicated to textile (wool and cabuya) and also chemical industries.

On the manufacture of toquilla ("Panama") straw hats and the organization of this important cottage industry, see Du Frane 1945; Ferdon 1950: 10, 13, 27, 29 (largely with reference to the coastal fiber-producing and "Panama" hat-making centers of Jipijapa and Montecristi); Hanson and Platt 1945:15, 67-68; WTiC, VI, 14, 8 (May, 1948).

The following deal with the industry centered on Cuenca: Basile Ms. (probably the most comprehensive and detailed study of the subject); Bennett 1946:7, 13-14; CEPAL 1954: 126-29; Cevallos 1873:62, 327; International Labour Organisation 1949:84-86 (summarizing a study published originally in Boletin del Instituto Nacional de Previsión, Quito, March, 1946); Linke 1954:134-37; Monsalve Pozo 1946. During World War II the industry in that region was said to have implicated a population of at least 200,000 and directly employed up to 85,000. The re-appearance on the world market of products made in other countries, and other factors, plunged the Ecuadorean industry into a crisis, about halved the number of persons occupied in it, and poses now a real problem for the affected provinces.

For data on the straw-hat cottage industry north of Quito, which more recently has come into prominence, see Buitrón and Buitrón 1947: 62-63 and Table VII.

For the location of important cottage industries and specialized crafts, see particularly Cisneros Cisneros 1948:150 ff.; and Rodríguez Sandoval 1949:50 ff.; also Villavicencio 1858, passim.

10. Buitrón and Buitrón 1947, Tables VII and VIII (compiled). Cf. IEAG 1953, Nos. 10 and 11:124, passim: among the ninety-odd huasipungero families of two Chimborazo haciendas, no skills other than farming and livestock care are represented.

11. Parsons 1945:25; also in children's plays and games, dances, processions (pp. 52, 80, 100, 102, 105, 115). However, Parsons explicitly notes (p. 27) an exception in the case of the spinning wheel operated by men.

12. Rivet 1903; cf. J. Davis (1946:62) on the operation of the Spanish-type foot loom by Indians "from a standing or partly sitting position," and Parsons (1945, plates XIV and XV), illustrating Otavalo Indians' half-leaning or sitting position while working on such looms. Chairs, stools, benches, as well as other furniture customary in the Western world, are rare in Indian houses or are not used; see, e.g., Rodríguez Sandoval 1949: 71, 110.

13. The mayor of Otavalo is quoted as saying that "the Indians employed in the local cotton mill were among its best operatives" (J. Davis 1946: 87), and elsewhere under comparable conditions, as in the Huancayo area of central Peru, Indians are said to learn modern factory weaving methods easily and "have proved to be excellent specialised workers" (International Labour Organisation 1949:82, n.4). Whether such Indian master-weaver operators (if such they are) are representative of the bulk of Indians remains a matter of doubt. In the Huancayo region such weavers would be likely to be spoken of as "Cholos" (Indo-Mestizos). Judgments of this sort very much depend upon the situation and how it is viewed; thus Linke (1954:132) says that the majority of factory workers in the textile industries nowadays are Mestizos, whereas in the phrasing of CEPAL (1954:66), they are "urban Indians."

The literature on Ecuadorean Indians, taken together, conveys a suggestion that the diversity of skills is greater among women than among men (see Saenz 1933a:190), but this possibility has not been explored here.

Neither has consideration been given here to the eastern and western lowland Indians who are spoken of as "savages" or "uncivilized," for their numbers are small and they live in isolated, dispersed groups. However, on the score of manual skills alone, both as regards variety and workmanship, they seem to be far superior to the highland Indians. See, for example, Barrett 1925; and Stirling (1938:78-95), which contains a description of the delicate operations required in making a blowgun, for which also compare Fejos (1943:47-50), for a Peruvian Amazonian Indian group.

14. Comprehensive discussions on that subject will be found in Saenz 1933a:128, 143 ff., 153, 192 (for the early thirties; he also provides statistical data on Indian voting in elections, which is minimal since literacy is a requirement for the franchise). On the state of, and recent developments in, education, and on educational institutions and programs, including

vocational training facilities, see Cisneros Cisneros 1948:136-44, 334; Ebaugh 1947; International Labour Office 1951:215-22; Linke 1954:84-89; Moomaw 1946:200-2, 207, 209; Romero 1945; Rycroft 1946:281-95.

15. Dir. Gen. Est. Censos, Census 1950 (1952:Table 9). The census considers as illiterate those who do not know how to read and write, or only read, or only write.

16. Benites 1950:262, citing 1942 official estimates; CIAA 1944:79; Maes 1941; Rycroft 1946:288-89; Suárez 1934:9, 19, 35, 40, 83; 1942.

17. Saenz 1933a:143. Of a sample of 60,000 school-age children of the fifteen provinces (highlands and lowlands), 58 per cent were found to be illiterate, 25 per cent semiliterate (Garcés 1941:41-42). These figures agree closely with those cited for the entire enrolled school population of 1938 with, respectively, 43 and 28 per cent of the total (Romero 1947: 60-61). Corresponding data for 1942: 60.15 and 19.38 per cent (Dir. Nac. Est. 1944; also IRS V, 11 /Feb., 1948/, giving the same figure for general literacy). While, according to the 1939 official estimate, the Indian population constituted 57 per cent of the total population, only 26 per cent of the children attending schools in 1942 were Indian (Rubio Orbe 1949).

18. Parsons 1945:13. According to Collier and Buitrón (1949:165-82), most of the Indian traders of Otavalo are able to read and write, and Otavalo schools are now "crowded with Indian children." As of the 1950 Census, Otavalo canton is among those with a conspicuously high illiteracy rate: over 74 per cent. In September, 1950, a twelve- or thirteen-year-old resident of Otavalo town told me that there were many Indians in elementary school, but only one Indian boy--complete with braid and in Indian costume--was attending secondary school (colegio) in that town.

19. Parsons 1945:53. A feature story by Lilo Linke in El Comercio (Quito) of April 6, 1954, indicates that this situation has changed since Mrs. Parsons made her observations; still, Indian children attend school only during a fraction of the school week.

20. This breakdown is deceptive of actual Indian enrollment since in everyday life ethnic identification is made on the basis of dress, language, and other nonbiological criteria. Hence it is possible that the large Mestizo group contains a few "Indians," i.e., students who have mastered Spanish and may have abandoned their Indian dress and other Indian traits for the duration of their study or permanently.

21. Romero 1945. Data are for the year 1944-45. Similar observations are made regarding students at the Agricultural Normal School at Ambate and at the technical training school in Quito where heaviest student enrollment was in mechanics but where only a few Indian students were found and those were enrolled in the weaving and tailoring courses (Moomaw 1946:200, 208).

22. See previous notes, especially 14; also Plaza Jan. 1950 (with emphasis on agricultural training, on the seven rural normal schools, and two new schools for "practical agriculture"); Poblete Troncoso 1942:242.

23. Buitrón 1949c; Buitrón and Buitrón 1945; IEAG 1953, No. 3:229-30; Parsons 1945:184-85; Rubio Orbe 1946; Saenz 1933a:145; Streich and Streich 1947; Suárez 1942. Also Linke 1954:58.

24. Ebaugh 1947:60-61; but see Parsons 1945:13, n.25. However, Quechua is part of the curriculum of one school training teachers for highland rural elementary schools. Lilo Linke, writing in El Comercio (Quito) of April 6, 1954, tells of Colombian nuns who learned Quechua in order to teach school in Peguche; the Indians, however, consider the schools to be for Spanish and do not like to see Quechua employed, although few of the children know a word of Spanish on starting to school.

25. Paredes 1951:40-41; Saenz 1933a:145. On tinterillos, see Chapter X, C.

26. Personal information, John Collier, Jr.; and Collier and Buitrón 1949: 194; Rodríguez Sandoval 1949:118-19.

27. Rodríguez Sandoval 1949:118-19 and Ebaugh 1947:19-20, on such a school in Nayón, the small community already mentioned.

28. Albernez 1945; CIAA 1944:79; García Ortiz 1951 (who has a guarded statement on the possible role of this campaign in the ongoing formation of a "middle class"); The Inter-American IV, No. 7 (July 1947):7; UNESCO 1947:29-32; International Labour Organisation 1949:39-40; Vallejo 1946.

29. See Parsons 1945:154-55; Rubio Orbe 1946, on the abilities in arithmetic shown by Indian school-children.

30. The fact that all rendering of accounts as regards wages, advances, shares, etc., with Indians on haciendas are of necessity verbal and have to be accepted by them on the say-so of the hacienda administration is no doubt one of the factors contributing to Indian indebtedness to haciendas and other enterprises. See IEAG 1953, Nos. 10 and 11:48-49 and passim on account-keeping and "settlements" between hacienda administration and "indios propios."
        How "literacy," in the sense of ability to "draw" one's signature, contributes to Indian indebtedness is shown in IEAG 1953, No. 4:23-24.

A. The Problem of Health in Ecuador

Health and nutrition seem to take a place in the minds of those dealing with Ecuadorean problems next to, and often closely related with, the
agrarian and agricultural complex. Moreover, the question of the population's state of health is treated not only as a technical problem, but
emphatically as a basic social problem in Ecuador.

It has been suggested (Carlson 1943:291-305) that Ecuador became
increasingly "health-conscious" following the health and sanitation work,
especially as regards the yellow fever menace, which the Rockefeller
Foundation initiated in Guayaquil and neighboring areas around 1920. Since
that time a number of municipalities have installed sewage systems and
other health controls with respect to which the country as a whole is very
deficient.[1] In recent years and in connection with the reorganized social
security system, governmental and semigovernmental bodies have instituted educational and other programs, measures, facilities, and activities
designed to safeguard public health.[2] In addition, this development has
been intimately connected with the young pharmaceutical industry,[3] on the
one hand, and has been in part supported by the good-neighborly interests
of organizations--notably Scisp (Servicio Cooperativo Interamericano de
Salud Publica)--and foundations outside Ecuador, on the other.

Alertness toward the problem of health in Ecuador has no doubt been
stimulated also by the truly harrowing picture which the studies of the late
Dr. Pablo Arturo Suárez revealed. His chief study[4] is one of the very few
out of Latin America which, until quite recently and despite its limitations,[5]
could lay claim to being a comprehensive survey and assessment of the
total situation, based on field research. Hence it is understandable that
writers other than Ecuadoreans, in treating of health in Latin America in
general, have drawn on these data as indications of the general state of
health beyond Ecuador, i.e., as typical of Latin American health conditions.[6]
Within Ecuador itself, health conditions vary from region to region. Thus
regions like Otavalo and Loja are given relatively cleaner bills of health
by expert as well as by lay observers.

B. Existing Facilities

Over against the increasing awareness of the state of health of the
Ecuadorean population stands the realization of the insufficiency of all
existing health facilities. Medical services and hospitals are, by modern
standards and in relation to the felt and acknowledged magnitude of the
problem, sufficient only for a fraction of the population.[7] As is natural,
it is the larger urban population that is provided with the greater number
of medical and hospital services, and it is only in very recent years that
smaller towns or cantonal capitals also have been, or are to be, provided
with public health centers.[8] In the middle forties there were a little over
150 doctors to care for that five-sixths of the total population of Ecuador
that did not live in the five largest cities of the country, whereas these
latter were serviced by about 500 doctors. This information is not too

much at variance with Suárez's earlier estimate according to which 95 per cent of the landless rural Indians receive no (modern) medical attention of any kind.[9]

Despite the campaigns waged against specific endemic and epidemic and other contagious and infectious diseases,[10] it is safe to say that it will take many years to draw the rural population into a comprehensive medical service system. Medical training programs have been initiated, and hospital and other public health facilities, in part of a health-educational nature, are being established, although at a slow rate. Hence, despite all the lively interest in the population's health, the present status of existing and projected facilities leaves no room for complacency.

C. The General State of Health

The general level of health of the Ecuadorean population as a whole can perhaps be best appreciated through what is known of the kind and extent of epidemic and endemic diseases, on the one hand, and through such data as are available regarding causes of death, on the other. For both sets of indices the distribution will be noted.

The data on endemic and epidemic diseases[11] are presented at some length, not only because the prevalence of such diseases provides a yard-stick for the country's general state of health, but also because many of them very frequently are followed by complications and extended states of debility. For this reason their prevalence assumes importance beyond their mere incidence. Their debilitating effects among survivors have a tendency to be lingering and cumulative.

Among epidemic diseases, some of which are endemic particularly in the highlands, are named typhus, typhoid fever, and paratyphoid; small-pox; and plague. During an eighteen-month period following January, 1945, 1,999 cases of typhus were officially registered for all of Ecuador, 93 per cent of which occurred in the highland provinces; 54 cases of smallpox, 68 per cent in the highlands; and 46 cases of plague, all of which occurred in the southern highlands where obdurate foci still remain in Loja Province. In 1942-43 and again in 1950-51 there were serious outbursts of bubonic plague, both in Chimborazo and Loja. During 1942-43, there were in addition epidemic outbursts of typhus in the northern provinces, of bacil-lary and amebic dysentery, diptheria, and smallpox, the latter recurring with severity in Loja in 1948. Rabies, long endemic in the country, flared up in the north, and in subsequent years spread to the center and also to the lowlands.

Various "cause of death" compilations[12] provide a more comprehen-sive picture of the kind and incidence of diseases. Thus for the country as a whole, the principal causes of death in 1945 were officially given to be, in order of magnitude, whooping cough (infants and children), bronchitis, "colic," diarrhea and enteritis, malaria, tuberculosis, pneumonia, grippe, bronchopneumonia, dysentery, cancer, nephritis, and typhoid fever. Malaria and tuberculosis were said to be the greatest killers in 1940, the former particularly in the Litoral but also in the lower inter-Andine valleys, the latter specific to the highlands and highland cities such as Quito. Between 55 and 60 per cent of all deaths are due to infectious and parasitic diseases and to diseases of the respiratory and digestive appara-tus, up to 30 per cent alone being accounted for by the two first-named types, to judge from data provided for the years 1942 and 1946; the differ-ences between these two years are very slight.

Data summarizing the leading causes of death in Pichincha Province and Quito City for hospitalized and unhospitalized adults and children from 1920 on show a steady recurrence of bronchopneumonia and respiratory diseases, diseases of the digestive system, and infectious and parasitic diseases. The most common admissions to Quito hospitals in the thirties were for tuberculosis.

Registration figures of causes of death in the canton of Otavalo in 1944 not only show the diseases causing the major number of deaths but also indicate that their victims are in the vast majority of cases children under one, two, and ten years of age. Killer number one for all three ethnic groups (Indians, Whites, Mestizos) is whooping cough, accounting for over 28 per cent of all registered deaths. Over 36 per cent of all deaths were due to a miscellany of intestinal diseases (defined as colic, dysentery, intestinal infection, intestinal occlusion). Bronchitis and pneumonia accounted for 18 per cent of the deaths, the remainder being listed under "congenital debility," senility, and other vaguely defined states of malfunctioning.[13]

As for the state of health among the living population, especially of the highland and rural dwellers, discussion is focused here primarily upon the more prevalent diseases, particularly in terms of their effects upon the efficient functioning of the human organism in its daily life and in the optimum performance of work. Most conspicuous in the literature on the subject of public health[14] are such debilitating ailments as goiter, anemia, avitaminoses, and a variety of intestinal, respiratory, and skin troubles due to parasitic and other infections. Sample studies by Suárez in Pichincha Province in the early thirties established that 85 per cent of the rural population were infected with amebic and helminthic parasites; more than a third of the people so infected were adults. Other and later surveys of school children indicate quite generally that 80 per cent are infected with one or more intestinal parasites, 50 per cent suffer from inadequate nutrition resulting in disposition to tuberculosis, 50 per cent have skin diseases, all have poor teeth, and 40 per cent of those living in tropical regions have malaria and hookworm.

The incidence of debilitating and degenerative diseases ("incurable" in the terms of Suárez) is high, particularly goiter, cretinism, paralysis, skeletal deformations, etc. Sample studies in a number of communities in the nothern and central highlands resulted in findings of goiter affecting up to 70 per cent and more of the population sampled. In summing up his findings, Suárez arrives at the conclusion that one-half of the total rural population of Ecuador are sick at any one time and that, of these, 25 per cent are incurably ill[15]--a much-quoted conclusion.

Taken together, these various statistical data and surveys indicate that states of physical debility and incapacity are widespread among the rural highland population. As for highland Indians specifically, some supplementary information is available.

The pathology of the Indians is said to differ considerably from that of the other population groups.[16] Diseases for which the highland Indians show a marked disposition are whooping cough, ordinary and modified smallpox,[17] measles, typhus,[18] typhoid fever and paratyphoid, grippe, pneumonia, tuberculosis,[19] bubonic plague, cholera, puerperal fever, malaria,[20] pian, carate (mal de pinto), and a variety of other parasitic skin diseases, intestinal amebiasis, helminthic diseases (among which particularly hookworm), toxic gastroenteritis, intestinal occlusion (at least in part related to helminths), goiter, conjunctivitis, and other eye troubles--to name the principal afflictions. In brief, the population specified as Indian is subject to more or less chronic disabilities, due to parasitoses, deficiencies, and disorders, however caused, of the digestive and respiratory systems, and to the sequels of a host of contagious and infectious diseases.[21]

D. Health and Disease among Indians

The foregoing data may be compared with what highland Indians themselves subjectively, as it were, experience. An attempt at an inquiry along such lines is made here for two reasons: first, because such information supplements objective data derived on the basis of modern natural sciences, modern medicine, and, last but not least, modern health standards, by data indicative of subjective feeling tones;[22] second, such information provides hints as to more propitious manners of attack on diseases in given localities where traditional attitudes are most likely to be quite uncongenial to the theories as well as to the practices of modern diagnostic, therapeutic, and preventive medicine; in other words, a knowledge of Indian assumptions and beliefs regarding health and disease would facilitate directing the approach to, and attack on, diseases among them in such wise that it might constitute an answer to their concepts and to actually felt needs.[23]

What Indians express in terms of their own experiences and conceptions, and what is known of their practices regarding health, diseases, and curing, is for the most part imbedded in magical or supernatural beliefs.[24] But the question as to what kind of "dis-eases" Indians themselves complain of elicits symptoms which, while certainly not sufficient for proper medical diagnosis, are nevertheless telling of interferences by bodily disabilities in the ordinary business of living.

Mrs. Parsons (1945:65, 167, 196-98) obtained from Indians in Imbabura and northern Pichincha descriptions of symptoms of maladies which are customarily brought for treatment to the curandero or curandera ("curer," "sorcerer," or witchdoctor of either sex). Symptoms of common malaises are: pains in head, neck, and back; no appetite, lassitude; loss of animation; no pleasure in play or work; constant nausea; unquenchable thirst, drying up. Such ailments are supposed to be due to fright or shock induced by a supernatural agent and are recognized under the general terms of espanto or susto ("fright," "shock").[25] Other ailments, caused by what is called mal aire or mal viento ("bad," "evil air" or "wind") may be anything such as "fever" or ataque (any fit or illness involving nerves, pains in the lung, rheumatism, toothache), but a description of specific symptoms lists swelling lips; pains in arms, shoulders, cheeks; swelling and pains in various parts of the body such as legs, chest, stomach, or genital organs. Symptoms of various other maladies, believed to be caused by the rainbow, are tumors and abscesses; blisters on face, hands, and feet; or itchiness and welts on the body.[26] Finally, lesions of the skin of the feet (due to parasites), cough, and symptoms indicating rheumatism are spontaneously complained of by Indians.[27]

For their ailments, Indians have recourse to home therapeutic methods and to self-administration of homemade remedies and native herb and mineral drugs as well as of some modern drugs and medicines so far as these are available in markets or retail stores (such as boric acid, milk of magnesia, aspirin, cough mixtures, etc.).[28] The use of such modern medicines seems to be entirely eclectic, while that of native medicines is systematic to the extent that traditionally handed-down knowledge and lore is systematic. The same applies to the traditionally known therapeutic methods used in home-curing or in the hands of

professionals (fregadores). They are based on a mixture of folk empiricism and magic; the important point is that their efficacy is believed
in.

Professional curers are also resorted to.[29] With them, the dividing line between curing based on empirical knowledge, divining, and witchcraft is vague. They may limit themselves to the exercise of one of these
activities, such as herbalists (yerbatero) might do, or combine any two
or all three; hence they are variously known as curanderos, curadores;
brujos or hechizeros; adivinos or ojiveños (respectively, "curers";
"witches," "sorcerers" or "magicians"; "diviners," i.e., "diagnosticians,"
in the case of disease). Whatever their special skills, they seem to be
handed down from father to son (Rivet 1903:64), or they are acquired among
lowland Indians to whom would-be professionals repair for extended training sojourns.[30]

It is perhaps because of the lack of distinctiveness among specific
curing, divining, and magical functions that a certain ambivalence attaches
to the position of the curandero. Indian curanderos may, because of their
skills and successes, enjoy great fame and prestige far beyond their home
localities, and are consulted not only by Indians but also by Mestizos
and Whites (at least in the Otavalo region).[31] On the other hand, there
seems to be a tendency (this again applies to observations made in Otavalo)
for curers not only to be regarded with skepticism among some Indians
but also to be feared as practitioners of sorcery or black magic.[32]

At any rate, the existence of an Indian "medical personnel" and the
use of its services by Indians is quite general. To judge from extended
descriptions of curandero medicines and practices (Parsons 1945:69-77;
Collier and Buitrón 1949:147-48; Disselhoff 1940), it may be doubted that
they are of objectively therapeutic value. But the techniques which they
employ must, in the concrete situation, carry some conviction: after having
diagnosed a disease as caused by gusanos ("worms") and having applied
the proper treatment, the curandero eventually produces a vermiform object about two inches long from out of the patient's mouth and shows it to
the patient in evidence of a successfully effected cure.[33]

Use by Indians of modern medicine and medical services, where
they are available, seems on the whole to be highly selective. But resistance to all forms of modern medicine appears to be the more general
rule and has often been observed and frequently commented upon. This
resistance may be quite understandable in view of their own established
health facilities and personnel, primitive and inadequate as they may be,
in view of the conviction which the cures of curanderos carry, be it for
the techniques employed (the "hocus-pocus") or for actual successes in
alleviating specific ailments, and in view, finally, of the "magic," good
or evil, which must seem to them to underlie a great deal of modern medical techniques. A few observations on this resistance may be cited, some
of them being of a general, others of a specific, kind.[34]

Hacienda Indians (huasipungeros) "do not take medicines and drugs,
and 'rather have themselves killed than being forced to take a laxative.'
When they are beset by sickness they go to the curandero for help who
cures them with brews and spells."[35] The Indian, says Rivet, does not
take care of himself (in the modern medical sense) or, if so, only very
badly. "Ignorant of medicine, he treats himself with remedies of a dubious
empiricism; if he has fever, he bathes in icy water," or else consults
wandering ojiveños (sorcerer-diviners), who exploit him (Rivet 1903). In
discussing the spread and control of malaria in the inter-Andine, one
authority observes: "There is one evident difficulty /in combatting

malaria⎤ . The Indian does not like to take the medicine of the White. He prefers to consult the curandero and thus remains an important carrier of the gamete, infecting all the Anopheles that bite him" (Hanson 1941; Franklin 1943:258).

As for hospitals, the attitude encountered in Otavalo among Indians is quite negative, ostensibly because there are "too many sick people" in the available hospitals[36] and the hospitals are too far away. Physical examination by doctors is likely to encounter strong resistance, at least initially, as may be inferred from the experience of one who attempted to secure anthropometric measurements from Indian children in Otavalo canton. His work was made difficult because of "the prejudice that exists among the Indians by which they hold body measurements to be a prelude to sickness and disease, for which reason parents and relatives of the children refused outright to give permission to make measurements."[37] "Superstitions" of this and similar kind may make attention in terms of modern medical practice difficult even where it is most manifestly called for. Parsons (1945:215) reports a tale whose content suggests that specific beliefs are likely to result in dissimulation of sickness and concealment of injuries in order to avoid medical examination and treatment--the sinister rites of sinister outsiders (see Chapter XIII, below).

E. Health and Medical Problems for Industry

From the foregoing a few conclusions can be drawn. There is no doubt that on the score of its state of health the labor potential is appreciably reduced because of permanent or temporary physical unfitness or disabilities. We recall that the estimates of the proportion of so-called incurables among the total rural population amount to 12 to 13 per cent and that it is estimated also that for every man of that population who is physically fit another one is sick,[38] i.e., not fit to work at maximum efficiency.

Such proportions of sick to well individuals are high enough. Even if health standards for industry as they prevail today in advanced countries were to be relaxed, this problem would still be appreciable. Moreover, the problem of maintaining workers in physically fit condition remains.

In addition, though the realistic assumption could be made that it would be the physically fit anyway who would seek industrial employment, the numerical reduction in fit workers would make itself felt when it came to systematic recruiting of larger numbers of workers as industry expanded within and beyond a given area or region. Recourse to less healthy labor forces might then be necessary, and this, in turn, would necessitate physical rehabilitation on a major scale (humanitarian considerations quite apart).

Since health facilities in Ecuador are limited and are likely to remain limited in comparison to standard medical needs, industry itself might have to take a share in health-rehabilitating programs in order to increase the number of those physically fit to work. Depending on its size and the region where it locates, it might even have to assume all the burden of health maintenance of its labor force.

These are tasks which industry does not ordinarily have to assume in older industrial countries. To underline the contrast between industrialized and industrializing countries still further, it is, on the one hand, the very standards of efficiency which today's industrialism has reached that dictates the higher health requirements and health expectations. On the other hand, in Ecuador it is the relative paucity of the population that is available for industrialization that makes economizing with its human resources imperative and which consists of repairing what is in bad condition and in preserving what is in good condition. The role of industrialization under such conditions is, therefore, a unique one and of unique importance.

In practice, the tasks outlined above are of course nothing new to industrial enterprise in Latin American countries. Larger mines in Ecuador (as they do elsewhere) have provided these facilities either voluntarily or in observance of concession contracts with the government which stipulated the provision of hospitals and other medical services. At any rate, such tasks are in the nature of major-cost items.

What is more--and here the second conclusion is drawn--the efforts made in the pursuit of public and industrial health tasks are likely to meet with major difficulties as far as the bulk of Indian and, inferentially, the general rural population is concerned. The value of modern health services, of medical attention, and of public health programs is by no means known to them nor can it be assumed to have been convincingly demonstrated to them in any one individual case. To be sure, there is disease and sickness and full awareness of them. But the Indians have also their own means and personnel to counter these problems to their own satisfaction. The situation is, in short, one in which the modern physician finds himself in outright competition not only with tradition (which is not the case in regard to education or the position of the teacher) but also, very concretely, with the curandero. And since the modern physician ordinarily is not able to give immediate demonstration of his success, his position is weak, initially, vis a vis the curandero. The divergence between modern medical and native traditional conceptions of disease does nothing to equalize the relative positions of modern and native medicine. In some cases where modern medical services are near at hand and where they are cheaper (e.g., free medical service) than that of the generally expensive curanderos, advantage may be taken, at least temporarily, of such facilities, and it is here that some of the opening wedges may be made.

Impediments to effective health rehabilitation and maintenance arise largely from the facts that, first, Indians lack knowledge of, and experience with, modern medicine, and that, second, Indian beliefs, having religion or magic as matrix, will render difficult the application of certain medical techniques at the outset (examinations, taking samples for laboratory tests, etc.). Consequently, there may be outright fear operating against modern health programs involving, as they do, alien procedures and alien settings. It is not within the scope of this study to offer suggestions on how modern health concepts, techniques, and practices can be accommodated to those of the native Ecuadorean population. From her own experience among Otavalo Indians and with her highly intelligent and curious informant, Mrs. Parsons concluded that "an outpatient clinic without knowledge of Indian home life and without the service of the district nurse will remain somewhat ineffectual in Indian Ecuador" (1945:169). The problem, we take it, is not solely one of health education among Indians.

If the total picture of the situation thus gained seems unfavorable and the tasks already tremendous,[39] there remains the question of whether there are other factors which mitigate or which aggravate the difficulties. The answer is in the affirmative in both respects. In the following, therefore, consideration is given to a number of other factors that are related to the problem of health. The constitution and physique of Indians will be

discussed, as well as their nutrition, diet and dietary habits, and the
question of the consumption of alcohol and other items that are considered noxious to health and to sustained efficiency. Some of the matters
presented in the following chapters are of interest to industry quite independently of questions of health and hygiene.

NOTES

1. That cities and towns, not to mention rural localities, are highly
deficient in modern sewage, potable water, and other sanitation installations can be amply inferred from a number of descriptions and statements of needs. See Ferdon 1950:16 ff. (on coastal Ecuador only);
Franklin 1943, passim; Garcés 1946; Inter-American Development Commission n.d.:149-51 (statement of the Ecuadorean Delegate); IRS V, 101
(Dec., 1948); Streich and Streich 1947.

2. Andrade Marín 1942; Buitrón 1949a; see also annual reports by the
Ministers of Social Security and Labor: Tello 1949; Alcívar Zevallos 1951.

3. Richard T. Turner on the pharmaceutical industry, in Hughlett 1946:
311-14; Tello 1949.

4. 1934; see also 1942. Others of Suárez's published studies were not
available except in paraphrases in other sources. A more recent, very
useful, and ample survey of a different character and with special
reference to the Indian population is that by León (1946).

5. Suárez's pioneering studies are based on samples (mainly Quito,
for the urban population, and a number of communities in the northern
and central provinces, for the rural population). His 1934 publication
contains no indication of the size and number of these samples, nor of
the criteria, other than that of low-income level, under which they were
selected. There is no information on the diagnostic and other methods
used. It is therefore a question whether and how far his findings apply
to all of highland Ecuador. It also should be pointed out--and this does
not apply to Suárez alone--that the standards by which health and disease
are assessed are those of modern biology and medicine and are also derived from the standards of life set by the most advanced sectors of
Western society. Hence such findings generally fail to indicate (a)
subjectively felt states of health or disease or disabilities, and (b) the
precise bearing of objective findings on actual performance or efficiency
under specified conditions, requirements, or expectations.

6. See, e.g., García 1939 (Colombian); Maes 1941 (North American);
Poblete Troncoso 1942 (Chilean):87-90, 133; Soule, Efron and Ness 1945:
26, 36, 42, 50-51, who, however, have used other more recent studies as
well.

7. Soule, Efron and Ness 1945:350-51 and charts on pp. 53, 56; Clothier
1946:251-67; see also Mrs. Parson's observations on the subject (1945:
64, n. 134); Streich and Streich 1947.

8. Clothier 1946, on medical training programs; and "La Sanidad en
Ecuador," Bol. Of. San. Panam. 26, No. 4 (April, 1947):305-13, review-
ing the period 1942-47 and the activities and establishments of institutions in the field of public health during that period. In his 1948-49
report, Dr. Tello mentions about 29 hospitals throughout the country, old

and new, remodeled or enlarged, under construction or projected, as also health centers, first-aid stations, public dispensaries, etc. On the subject of rural medical centers, see Buitrón 1951b.

9. Clothier 1946:254, 270; Maes 1941; Soule, Efron and Ness 1945:54; Suárez 1934:83.

10. Among these campaigns are: yellow fever (of long standing, on which see García 1950 for the year 1948); malaria, tuberculosis, venereal diseases, plague, rabies, pian (Tello 1949; Alcívar Zevallos 1951).

11. The following were used for the distribution of such diseases, statistical data (incidence and mortality), and compilations therefrom: Bol. Of. San. Panam. 21 (1942):208, 740; 23 (1944):92, 93, 95; 26 (1947):84, 305-13, 364; El Trimestre Estadístico, Año I, Nos. 3-4 (1945):68; II, No. 5 (1946): 43; III, Nos. 6-7 (1946-47):44. Also, Alcívar Zevallos 1951; Garcés 1946; Gonzalez H. 1941; Izquieta Pérez 1944; León 1946; Saenz Vera 1941 and 1949; Tello 1949. See El Comercio, Quito, Oct. 11, 1950, on a serious outbreak of typhus in Tungurahua.
    According to general admission, all vital registrations are deficient, particularly in the countryside and in remote areas; hence, actual disease incidences and mortalities are bound to be considerably higher than those given in official statistics.

12. From sources as in n. 11; also Andrade Marín 1942; Bol. Of. San. Panam. 21 (1942):132-38; Buitrón and Buitrón 1945; Dir. Nac. Est. 1944; IEAG 1953, No. 3:184-91; Samaniego 1942; El Trimestre Estadístico, Año III, Nos. 6-7 (1946-47):39-43.

13. It is interesting to compare such new data on highland diseases with information such as that given by Orton (1875:91-94) for Quito and the highlands more generally: then, "consumption" was unknown in Quito; "intermittent fevers" and dysentery uncommon; "inflammation of the lungs" rare; typhoid fever and "catarrhal affections," however, were ordinary; digestive disorders frequent, etc. Similarly Hassaurek (1868:116-19); see also Enock 1914:192-205. The literature here used provides other hints on the history of diseases in Ecuador, such as on malaria, rabies, smallpox, tuberculosis, and typhus, which assailed the early Spanish conquerors and was known to them as "Tabardillo" and under other terms, and which even has a Quechua name, occelasta (Benites 1950:58; León 1946). See also below, nn. 17-20.

14. León 1946 (his data contradict, though only in minor part, those of Suárez); Samaniego 1942; Santiana 1952a:120-28, 135 ff.; Suárez 1934: 48-53; Soule, Efron and Ness 1945:50-52; Garcés 1941:36; Bol. Ind. II, No. 2 (1942):12 (on a study by Dr. Julio E. Tobar); Bol. Of. San. Panam. 26 (Sept., 1947):800-1; IRS V 101 (Dec., 1948).

15. Suárez 1934:53-56, 83. Similarly, the Ecuadorian Commission (n.d.: 75) express themselves briefly but in quite gloomy terms on the health conditions of "many city dwellers and almost the entire rural population." Cf. the results of a sample analysis made by the Oficina de Estadística Regional (1949) of the first 1,000 health cards (fichas de salud)--hence a random sample--for the city of Guayaquil, according to which 72.4 per cent were "sick," of which 55.3 per cent were affected by parasitoses, about 18 per cent by venereal diseases, and the remainder suffered from anemia, tuberculosis, and heart diseases.
    There are two sets of observations for two Pichincha Province communities, one of which indicates a sickness incidence of 24 per cent at the time of observation, the majority suffering from gastrointestinal

infections, parasitoses, skin infections, eye troubles (Buitrón 1949c), the other listing the following diseases being represented among a group of 26 patients: tuberculosis, intestinal parasites, venereal diseases, goiter, ringworm, malnutrition, alcoholism, anemia, eye diseases (Streich and Streich 1947).

16. León 1946. See also Clothier 1946:268; Rodríguez Sandoval 1949:77.

17. Parsons (1945:64) mentions periodic epidemic outbursts of smallpox in the Otavalo region and comments on pockmarked Indians who survived the disease. It seems that during the last few decades some immunity has been built up against its fatality, for Rivet (1903:63) held that the Indian population would be three times what it is if it were not for that disease. León (1946) states that smallpox had ravaged the population ever since colonial days until about twenty years ago but that its appearance now is sporadic, while other forms of the disease are frequent without causing major damages.

18. Typhus, typhoid, and paratyphoid, as far as Indians are concerned, are said to be of a benign type. Though frequent among Indians, the incidence of typhus during epidemic outbursts tends to be lower among Indians than among Whites and Mestizos and, in particular, the death rates from these diseases tend to be considerably lower among Indians.

19. León remarks that until the beginning of the twentieth century, tuberculosis affected only Whites, Mestizos, and Negroes, and only exceptionally the Indians. Since then, almost all Indian settlements have been attacked as well. Cf. n. 13, above.

20. Malaria is said to affect 200,000 annually throughout the country (Garcés 1946) and is most prevalent in the Litoral and Oriente. Although probably prevalent since precolonial times (the question of malaria in the New World is under dispute), it is found to reach its fatal stages especially quickly among Indians, according to Rivet (1903), himself originally trained as a physician. The problem of manpower shortages and that of the reluctance of Indian workers to go into low-altitude zones is intimately related to the malaria problem, especially since its fairly recent spread into some of the inter-Andine valleys below 2,500 meters. In most recent years, inter-American and national antimalaria campaigns operating with DDT have registered good progress in combatting and eradicating the carriers (Alcívar Zevallos 1951; Tello 1949). In this regard spectacular changes may occur within the next few years. On the subject of malaria in Ecuador, see also Andrade Marín 1941; Franklin 1943:257-58, 269; Hanson 1941; León 1946; Leonard 1947; Parsons 1945: 62; Rivedeneira 1942; Soule, Efron and Ness 1945:43; Wandemberg and Rivedeneira 1941.

21. Among contagious and infectious diseases to which Indians appear to be relatively little susceptible in comparison with other groups are named scarlet fever, german measles (rubeola), and infantile paralysis; the statement regarding the latter rests on the study of an outbreak in the province of Pichincha involving 64 cases of which 70 per cent were Whites, 21 per cent Mestizos, the rest Indians and Negroes.

22. On this point, see Hoffer 1947. This article exemplifies a method by which to determine the need for medical attention of a rural population by listing symptoms collected in interviews and comparing these with a subsequent survey of proper physical examination data.

23. The following are particularly relevant for this discussion: the very useful recent study by Erasmus (1952) on "folk" (not necessarily "Indian") versus modern medicine in Ecuador; Foster 1951 and 1952 on aspects of public health programs in Latin America generally; Parsons 1945, with a wealth of data on Otavalo, as also IEAG 1953, No. 3:108-16, 230-47.

24. Apart from the literature cited throughout this section, the following offer useful background material: Ackerknecht (1949) and Gill (1940), covering health, curing and preventive practices, underlying approaches and concepts, materia medica, ethnobotany, ethnopharmacy, and ethnomedicine largely of non-Andean and/or pre-Columbian Indians; nevertheless, these have enough relation to modern Ecuadorean highland Indians (and "folk") to make these references pertinent.

25. Children are particularly susceptible to espanto, but cats and dogs are also subject to it. (This, together with the described symptoms, suggests ankylostomiasis.) The concept of the disease called espanto or susto is widespread in Latin America. See Erasmus 1952. Gillin (1947: 130-33) studied the cases of seven individuals in a north-coastal Peruvian community and tentatively suggests that these cases bespeak some emotional crisis, on the basis of an "underlying history of malnutrition, malaria, tuberculosis or all three," and with symptoms of anemia, irritability, low fever, etc., and general debility. See also Gillin 1948a.

26. Belief in these and other diseases is by no means limited to the Indians but is shared to a considerable extent by Mestizos and Whites of all classes.

27. Personal information, John Collier, Jr.; see also IEAG 1953, No. 3: 230-32 for a longer list of ailments and their Quechua terms.

28. Collier and Buitrón 1949:15; Clothier 1946:238; Parsons 1945:30, 62-63, 64. Native herbs and other medicines consist largely in cathartics, sudorifics, calmatives, poultices, and other such "simples." Rodríguez Sandoval 1949:121-22; Erasmus 1952; León 1946. IEAG 1953, No. 3:233-43 has long but unsystematic lists of such herbs and their application.

29. On this subject, see Collier and Buitrón 1949:145-49 (with illustrations); Disselhoff 1940; Garcés 1941:36; Parsons 1945:62-77, 167-69, 195-99 and passim; Rodríguez Sandoval 1949:85; Santiana 1949; IEAG 1953, No. 3:232, 244-47, 262-63.

30. Parsons (1945:139) has two folk tales containing this motif. Collier and Buitrón (1949:145) and Disselhoff (1940) report this as a fact. Such schooling is obtained among the Jivaro of the eastern lowlands, and the Colorado of the western lowlands. The bewitched patient of Ilumán will even go to Santa Domingo de los Colorados as a last resort for a cure (IEAG 1953, No. 3:232). Clothier (1946:240) speaks of "two schools" for witch doctors reported to exist in Otavalo and Cuenca--the only reference of this sort. In Cotacachi canton, which adjoins Otavalo, there is a parcialidad, Calera, which is much visited because of its famous brujos and curanderos, according to Cisneros Cisneros (1948:182).

31. Parsons 1945:73. While in Otavalo (October, 1950) I was told of a witchcraft "case" that had occurred there in the previous month and had involved a white man who had consulted a brujo on behalf of his wife. The nature of the professional advice had resulted, it appears, in a public disturbance. El Comercio of Quito (October 11, 1950) carried the tale of the capturing of a brujo on complaint of a number of patients, his victims, whom he had been defrauding of several thousands of sucres.

32. Parsons 1945:64, 68-73, 169. She remarks that apparently little black magic is practiced in Otavalo by individuals or even by professional sorcerers or curers in their capacity as sorcerers. But magic as such is feared, be it for its own sake or because of the known stand of the church in this matter.

33. Disselhoff 1940; Parsons 1945:72. The concept of worms as disease agents or infestations gains in interest in view of the prevalence of hookworm and other helminths. This matter is mentioned here merely for the possible "analogical handle" (to coin an expression) which this concept offers to those engaged in introducing modern medical practices and notions among Indians; elsewhere the object may be a lizard.

34. Buitrón 1951a, and rejoinder by Santiana 1952b; Erasmus 1952; León 1946; Rodríguez Sandoval 1949:120-22.

35. Saenz 1933a:95, quoting P. F. Cevallos, 1887 (1873:130). Cf. Hassaurek (1868:303), who, speaking of the cheapness of keeping hacienda peons, says that they have their own curanderos and do not require medical attention at all. "Very few Indians would submit to scientific medical treatment. They have no confidence in white physicians." In a similar vein, León 1946.

36. Parsons 1945:167. Her informant, a particularly alert Indian woman, had consulted the three local white doctors, refused to take their prescriptions, and finally sought aid from the curandero; see also pp. 63-64.

37. León 1947. Resistance to performance of autopsies (as prescribed by law in case of death without medical attention) probably also belongs in this class (Bol. Of. San. Panam. 26 /1947/ :305-13).
     The Indians' notorious "camera-shyness" probably also belongs in this category. See Buitrón and Buitrón 1947:15. Mr. John Collier, Jr., told me of an Otavalo Indian who, after finally consenting to being photographed, deeply resented the picture showing him in three-quarter length, without his legs.

38. The rate among employed working people in the United States is one out of every twenty off the job due to sickness at any one time, as of 1949.

39. In comparison to the school problem (which is, after all, of relatively lesser interest to incipient industry) these problems are formidable. The specific tasks with regard to the furnishing of schools and educational facilities are comparatively easy since (1) no complex of concepts, institutions, and personnel compete with the school as such; (2) schools have practical importance to the Indians which they can recognize and for which they even ask under favorable circumstances; and (3) schools, unlike medicine, are a means of orientation toward, and a vehicle into, the modern world surrounding or permeating the Indian world--a matter of which they take positive or negative cognizance, as the case may be.

A. Constitution and Physique[1]

If, on the one side of the ledger, we find a disease-ridden and weakened population, it may be pointed out that, according to some ob- servers, the health and nutrition of Ecuadorean Indians are on the whole better than those of other countries with large Indian populations (Garcés 1945; León 1952; Ricketts 1952; Saenz 1933a:49, 188, 189). Although it is certain that a large proportion of the rural population of Ecuador does not qualify for industrial work on the grounds of physical fitness or is not as fit as would be desired and ordinarily expected, some qualifications re- garding the total Indian picture appear necessary. The impression left by the various portrayals of the health of the rural Indian groups is con- siderably mitigated by the many assertions of the excellence of the Indian constitution.

Thus the traveling observer of the sixties comments more than once (Hassaurek 1868:27-28, 72, 282, 303, 313-14) on the stamina, the endurance, the frugality, and the "iron constitution" of the Indians and marvels at their almost indestructible health once they are beyond infancy, although he finds, as other have since, strong regional variations with regard both to physical appearance as well as health.

The author whose findings otherwise lead to the greatest pessimism says nevertheless, with regard to the Indian specifically, that "he is capable of undergoing great and prolonged physical efforts without fatigue and without discouragement. He travels long distances without growing exhausted and that with heavy loads on his back. Being a frugal eater, though his food may be insufficient, he is resistant to prolonged fasts when circumstances so demand without becoming weak. He sleeps on the hard and damp ground without ill effects to his body" (Suárez 1942; cf. León 1952; Rivet 1903:63; Santiana 1949:259).

This is the tenor in which the constitution or the stamina of Ecua- dorean Indians in general is assessed. Assertions such as these are even more emphatically made about the Indian populations of regions such as Otavalo and Loja. These Indians are singled out as the most robust and healthy, or at least the most healthy looking.[2] It is in Otavalo that the Indians are compared favorably with both Whites and Mestizos on the score of longevity and incidence of infant mortality, despite the relative though probably slight advantage of medical and sanitary facilities enjoyed by these more urban groups. It may well be, as the investigators suggest in discussing their statistics (Buitrón and Buitrón 1945), that as open- country dwellers these Otavalo Indians are less exposed to contagious diseases than are urban or close-settlement dwellers and that their diet is more "nutritious." In other areas, as in northern sections of the prov- ince of Pinchincha, Indians are compared favorably with their Mestizo and even White neighbors also on the score of cleanliness and health (Streich and Streich 1947; Buitrón 1949c).

From these general and fragmentary sketches it appears, first, that survivors of early youth have a hardy constitution and hence might not offer quite as unfavorable material as clinical findings would indicate and, second, that the chances that healthy labor, fit for industrial work, would be found in rural, specifically in open-settlement, populations appear to be relatively better than in urban populations or in small-town or village, close-settlement populations. It should nevertheless be pointed out that precisely such a rural, dispersed-dwelling population would be particularly vulnerable to new contagious and infectious diseases because of its lesser immunity toward them.

Ordinarily, industry makes no, or no precise, specifications in regard to the biological-organic properties of its human material, such as height, weight, muscular strength, etc. Questions incident to such properties of human physique might arise, however, as purely techno-logical ones, as, for instance, in the case of imported machinery and tools or in connection with specific operations blueprinted among and for populations of different biological properties, to which an Indian popula-tion is expected to adapt. Such questions are clearly analogous to the ones regarding motor habits, preferences with respect to position,[3] etc., which have been mentioned previously (Ch. V, A).

Thus, to take one case in which standardization of equipment would have to be taken into account, consideration would have to be given to the fact that the average height of Indians[4] is less than that of North Americans. More important, perhaps, is the distribution of musculature in Indians. Arms are weak and little-muscled relative to legs. The lower limbs, and neck and back, are the loci of maximal physical strength, and it is these muscle parts on which reliance is habitually placed (Hassaurek 1868:89; Orton 1875:111; Rivet 1903:59). Indian laborers are quoted as being able to carry as much as 250 pounds on their backs,[5] and that for considerable distances. This suggests that specific machine and other operations requiring any amount of physical exertion might be more easily performed if designed to call these, rather than other, muscle parts into play (pedals vs. handles; traction vs. lifting, etc.). Clearly, if it is a question of eliminating such operational difficulties, these observations mean fitting the machine to the man rather than the man to the machine.[6]

B. Diet and Dietary Habits

Among a host of more or less well-defined factors which are blamed for the unsatisfactory living conditions or, specifically, for the unsatis-factory health of so large a part of the rural highland population, two are most frequently mentioned. One is lack of a quantitatively and qualitatively adequate nutrition; the other is alcohol. It is held that these, singly or in combination, sap the energy and resistance of the Indians and are causative of or mainly contributory to the low-health level of this type of population.

Estimates on food consumption in terms of calories indicate that some undernutrition prevails among the rural population. According to one set of data, average caloric intake for the lowest rural income groups is 1,690 and for all rural low-income groups 2,000.[7] Indians specifically, according to another set,[8] obtain between 1,496 and 2,308 calories from their food, and independent farmers no more than 2,275.

In terms of modern standards regarding the composition of diet, that of the rural highland population or of the Indians does seem deficient. Typical Indian diet has been more often described than almost any other aspect of Indian life.[9] Staple items, roughly in order of importance in the daily fare, are maize, barley, potatoes, quinoa, other native cereals and tubers, wheat, a number of bean varieties, various gourds and squashes, some vegetables such as cabbage, onions, and wild herbs, and always aji (a pepper). Meat is universally rare, mostly a dish for festive occasions, and ordinarily one of the few items that is bought with the exception of cuy (guinea-pig), which is kept in all Indian homes. Other food items that are bought are salt, sugar (unrefined, in the form of brown cakes, panela), and fats. Milk is hardly ever drunk fresh even where it is available, although many dairy articles, including fluid milk, are handled and actually produced by Indians; milk may be used occasionally in cooking or made into cheese for the market and also for home consumption. The same applies to eggs[10] and chickens. In short, the typical diet of Indians is high in carbohydrates, low in fats, albumins, proteins, and some minerals, with certain vitamins virtually absent. Its composition varies little from region to region and depends on local crops and products. But these qualitative and quantitative variations are also a matter of economic situation and of level and kind of income, although perhaps not as much as some students seem to believe; among Indians, at least, it is doubtful whether the economic element enters decisively into the composition and quantity of their food.

At any rate, León, in discussing nutritional deficiencies among Indians, points out that they are free, generally, of kidney and liver troubles and uremic diseases (in contrast to Whites of the Sierra); that there is no beri-beri or pellagra; and that such deficiency diseases as scorbut, rachitic conditions, and bone deformations are rare--in this, contradicting Suárez's findings. He also considers dental caries rare among Indians, another statement that is open to challenge.[11]

The line between undernutrition and malnutrition is in any case difficult to draw for any specific population under specific conditions (e.g., climate and altitude, kind of work, etc.) and where nutritional and feeding habits have been established over generations. Thus to what extent the one or the other or both inhibit full efficiency or productivity in work cannot be predicted in any precise manner from dietary or nutritional quantity-analyses alone. It would be yet more difficult to decide whether undernutrition or malnutrition, as established by modern nutritional and somewhat abstract standards, is actually felt by Indians themselves.[12] Established dietary habits and behavior suggest other aspects that are pertinent to the question as to what industry may expect of Indian workers and their expectations of the employer.

Hassaurek and Cevallos make some observations on dietary behavior or feeding patterns that may well point to chronic undernutrition. Thus Hassaurek discourses on the fabulous quantities that the ordinarily "frugal" Indians can devour when opportunity offers and when eating at someone else's expense.[13] The rule for Indians is two meals a day, with snacks in between, again depending on economic as well as other circumstances.[14] Hence the behavior just commented upon might constitute some evidence of subjectively felt undernutrition.

On the other hand, it has to be taken into account that enormous meals are invariably associated with some festival or other social function, including certain work arrangements, as shown by any of the numerous descriptions of Indian fiestas and other social gatherings, be they for a work party or for a celebration, properly speaking. Hence the feeding behavior just alluded to does not constitute conclusive evidence of actual food needs in the organic-functional sense, i.e., responses to chronic undernutrition. But it is, at any rate, evidence for expectations that Indian workers might have in regard to the quantity and type of food to be provided by the employer.

With this suggestion in mind, reference may be made to a comment reported of a North American mining official in Ecuador regarding his Indian and Cholo workers, whom he frequently found to "improve in physical condition noticeably for the first two weeks after they came to work at the mine."[15] Whether these improvements were due to any of the advantages mentioned in that context, namely, the observation of the eight-hour day, wages and their manner of payment, or the "balanced meals" obtained at the mine, is not made clear. But considering the points made above, the last-mentioned factor might have been the decisive one in producing such beneficial effects.

The immediate conclusion to be drawn for industry employing Indians and operating within a largely Indian milieu is that the provision of food will fall to a large extent upon industry, not only because of the general economic and agricultural situation that has been discussed in Part I, but also as part of the provisions for physical rehabilitation and health maintenance that are likely to be necessary for the attainment and safeguarding of the Indian workers' full efficiency. Also, Indians might expect the provision of the customary foods on the part of the employer anyway, and in quantities larger than those available to them as independent workers.

C. "Addictions"

1. Narcotics and Stimulants

A great deal has been written on the habit of Andean Indians to chew coca, a habit which, particularly today, is viewed with alarm and to which much of the unsatisfactory state of health of the Indians is attributed. Their general condition and low level of living is also often ascribed to the "vice" of coca and their "addiction" to chewing this leaf.[16]

In view of the concern with which the habit is viewed within and without the Andean countries, it is important to state the case for Ecuador. There are general statements which include Ecuador among the countries (the others being Bolivia, Colombia, Peru, and parts of the Andean areas of Argentina and Chile) in which coca-chewing is more or less widely practiced.[17] Actually, a perusal of the literature dealing with today's Ecuadorean highland Indian yields only two instances of that kind, both clearly marginal and localized: one in the north, Maldonado (Carchi Province), that is, in an area adjoining regions of Colombia where coca is in fact cultivated and chewed;[18] the other in eastern Azuay Province, which is, at that, apparently not certain.[19]

Neither of these two instances is sufficiently well supported, much less described, to constitute together clear-cut cases of coca consumption in highland Ecuador. They suggest, however, the necessity for further investigation. Meanwhile it may be taken as fairly certain that, whatever the damages coca is said to engender in constant users, Ecuadorean highland Indians are generally not now subject to them,[20] and it is to this circumstance that some writers attribute the superior health and well-being of Ecuadorean Indians as compared with other Andean Indians.

Other narcotics with active principles and stimulants seem to be known in the highlands, most of them derived from Oriente Indian culture, but find no more than limited use. Ayahuasca leaves (banisteria caapi) are found for sale in the Otavalo market, but their purpose could not be ascertained by Parsons. Datura leaves are handled by curanderos or are used to sweep the house of the dead, i.e., in clearly ritual acts, and various daturas (sanguinea, arborea, and stramonium) as well as other plants having somniferous and aphrodisiac properties or producing hallucinations are used in the adulteration of chicha ("maize beer"). Cigarettes are smoked but not, apparently, habitually or in great quantities; rather they seem to be associated with festive and ritual occasions.[21] In brief, no "addictions" are reported for Ecuadorean highland Indians.

2. Alcohol

The "alcoholism" of the Indians is another factor which is held to affect in various ways their physical and mental well-being. The undoubtedly high consumption of alcoholic beverages by Indians (as well as by other groups) is deplored on a number of grounds: it diverts corn and sugar to the production of alcohol--in part by illicit distillation--thus aggravating food scarcities; it diverts money from needed food to alcohol. To the consumption of alcohol is ascribed the general cultural and economic retardation of the Indians, and thus it is condemned also on moral grounds. Finally, the cumulative injurious action of alcohol on the organism is emphasized.

There is no doubt that the consumption of alcoholic beverages is high among low-income urban and rural groups of Ecuador, and high particularly among the Indians regardless of level of income. That much can be inferred from the many comments of observers, most of whom note the role of alcohol in Indian life.[22] Observers and commentators are at variance, however, as to whether consumption of alcohol has increased or decreased in recent times. Parsons observes that "among Imbabura Indians there is more drunkenness from chicha than from rum" but thinks that "consumption /of liquor/ and intoxication among Indians have certainly increased" in recent periods, while Garcés believes there is less drinking in Otavalo on holidays than formerly.[23] Whatever the trends in the consumption of alcohol may be, its level is high. On the basis of a rather careful calculation, Suárez found that annual per capita consumption of cheap liquor (mostly chicha and guarape, fermented cane juice) among low-income manual workers in Quito, most of whom are Indians, was over 120 liters (Suárez 1934:11-13). There are various sets of contradictory figures on annual per capita consumption[24] of aguardiente (distilled cane liquor, "rum") and of other alcoholic beverages, including chicha, beer, guarape, and other native drinks such as chahuarmishque (fermented maguey or cabuya juice).

It has to be pointed out that the Indians' "addiction" to chicha, guarape, and aguardiente is an extremely complex affair of which only one aspect is being considered at present, namely, the problem which it might constitute from the point of view of sheer physical efficiency. However, not only is the evidence for a direct correlation between alcohol and physical efficiency of the Indians scant, but the suggestions or opinions on this point are frequently in conflict with each other. Thus the consumption of alcohol and malnutrition are causally related,[25] the implication being that better wages and with them ampler and better food would decrease the consumption of alcohol and both lead to the improvement of Indian health. On the other hand, cognizance is taken of Indian belief that chicha is food;[26] and it has even been pointed out that chicha does constitute a not inconsiderable source of vitamins of which ordinary Indian diet is deficient, for which reason the prohibition (of 1944) against the manufacture and sale of chicha, particularly of chicha de jora (made of sprouted maize), is regretted.[27]

The lack of factual data by which a direct relation between the consumption of these beverages by Indians and their general health, nutrition, and efficiency, could be established leads to further seeming contradictions. Thus Suárez, in his discussion of the general constitutions of the Indian and the injurious effect which the frequent consumption of guarape has on Indian health, nevertheless concedes that the Indian "sustains the toxic action of the liquor which he consumes with frequency and does not thereby become incapacitated for performing his customary work on the day following a night of heavy intoxication."[28] The noxious character of Indian drinking is disputed also by pointing to the contrary evidence of the Indians' well-tilled fields (Rodríguez Sandoval 1945).

Elsewhere Suárez cites official figures for the morbidity of the population in general due to "social" factors, which constitute 13 per cent of the general morbidity. In this group is included chronic alcoholism (Suárez 1934:54; also León 1946). But it is somewhat doubtful whether this would include Indians or the rural population at large, since, as Mrs. Parsons notes quite reasonably, "diseases from chronic alcoholism are diseases of old age and would not be apparent in Peguche /Otavalo Canton⌐, even if properly diagnosed, since old men are scarce" (Parsons 1945:124, n. 83). Furthermore, the Indian, while disposed to the "diseases" of alcoholism and "chichism," offers a little-propitious target to cirrhosis of the liver and delirium tremens.[29]

In considering the general against the more specific statements on the matter, and in the absence of further material sufficiently conclusive to judge the degree of physical injury upon the alcohol-consuming population, it is probably safe to say that even frequent and heavy intoxication does not directly impair the general health nor in itself impede the working efficiency of Indians.

On the other hand, as has been noted before, the "addiction" to drinking has drawn and still draws a great deal of more or less understanding criticism. Two examples will suffice. Says Hassaurek: "...to eat to excess and to get intoxicated are their chief wants and their only tastes." And Suárez: "Drink is the passion and the one and only dream of the Indian, however situated" (Hassaurek 1868:187; Suárez 1942). Still, he and others have linked drinking with fiestas or other occasions of which copious quantities of liquor are the ingredient; nevertheless, the critics of Indian drinking call for the control of the manufacture and sale of chicha and aguardiente as well as for measures toward the bridling of fiestas themselves on the ground that both are injurious to the health and the general economic situation of the Indians. Various attempts have been made along these lines but it does not seem that they have met with any noticeable success. Apart from the tendency to attack symptoms rather than to deal with the basis of the high alcohol consumption, the issue itself is further beclouded by the position of the government, which has a monopoly on the manufacture and sale of aguardiente and which derives revenues from alcohol taxes and licenses.[30]

However, there are other aspects of the Indians' alleged alcoholism which, on analysis, are far more important to industry and to industrial conduct than its bearing on health and efficiency as such. These have to do, on the one hand, with the meaning of, and the attitude toward, drinking among Indians and, on the other hand, with certain aspects of industrial discipline. These implications of the "alcohol problem" will be considered in the following chapter and in their proper meaning contexts.

NOTES

1. "Constitution" and "physique" are here employed in their ordinary connotations: "constitution" as meaning "bodily predisposition or idiosyncrasy as regards health and strength"--the organism's ability to take punishment and to withstand efforts, fatigue, exposure to heat and cold, diseases and sequels. "Physique" refers to "bodily structure and development"--body size, weight, appearance, proportions, distribution of musculature, etc.

2. Franklin 1943:174; Garcés 1946a:11, 14; Saenz 1933a:29. Other modes of regional variations in this respect are noted by Franklin (p. 215), who finds that the urban Cholos of Cuenca (Azuay Province) have a better physique and enjoy better health than the Andean people in general.

3. The problem of skills and physique as practical questions relating to established motor habits, posture, and even dress, as indicated here, has apparently received little attention in anthropology. It is touched upon by Kroeber (1948:348-50) as a "culture process" or factor making for the persistence of culture, and by Gillin (1948b:256 ff.). Herskovits (1952a:153-54) rightly considers motor habits and the retention of work habits a fruitful field of study. A most interesting statement of the matter is that of Haudricourt (1948, esp. pp. 58-60); see also Mauss (1936) and Bailey (1942).

4. Physical characteristics, including posture, of highland and some eastern lowland Indians are described by Santiana (1947). For anthropometric and descriptive data on some Indian groups of Imbabura Province, see Gillin 1936 and 1941. For a general description of Riobamba Indians, see Rivet 1903. Some anthropometric data relating to growth indices are given for Otavalo children of both sexes, aged 2 to 17, in comparison to Quito school children; included are data on over-all height, weight, arm length, chest and other measurements (León 1947).

5. Clothier 1946:221. For an illustration of one type of Indian pack-carrying, and on average performance, see Rainey 1946:353.

6. A case involving Peruvian Indians may serve to illustrate this point--a practical problem relating to the adaptation of physique and motor habits to technology. The incidents, related by Osgood Hardy (1919), occurred during some construction work employing Indians. The author tried to apply some North American labor methods in lieu of the old and antiquated methods of the Indians. "I purchased two modern wheelbarrows, only to have them lie idle for the first three weeks, until I succeeded in partially educating several Indians to their use." (Indians carry their bricks and other building materials on their backs.) "I decided that a longhandled shovel would save their backs--but in ten minutes after they had received them they had thrown them aside and were doubled up with their shorthandled, acute-angled, hoe-like spades." Clothing may also become part of that problem. "I made four ladders on an American pattern, but the Indians never ceased to complain because the treads hurt their bare feet."

In his semifictional account of his work as radio-engineer in Peru, Storm (1948:131 ff.) tells the tale of a strike of switchboard operators. The switchboards had been manufactured in England and installed at a level that would have been adequate for English operators. To the shorter Limeñas they were a constant source of excruciating shoulder- and backaches.

The author had an opportunity to watch similar discrepancies in the case of American-made cottonseed oil presses, operated by Peruvian workers by means of improvised stepladders and straining.

It is evident that the entire problem here posed belongs in the sphere of interest of applied physical anthropology, whose studies have been of such importance in the design of uniforms and equipment and in the layout of submarines, airplanes, etc., for the British and American armed forces. On this field of "human engineering" see Clark 1946; Daniels and Hertzberg 1952; Darcus and Weddell 1947; Hertzberg 1948; Hertzberg and Daniels 1952; King 1948; Morant 1947 and 1948; Newman 1953; Randall 1948; White 1952.

7. Suárez 1934, passim, and 1942. On comparing his data for low-income rural and urban groups, the rural groups seem to have a slight edge on the urban. Also, the Buitróns (1947:42-46) note a slight tendency toward a more substantial or plentiful diet among huasipungeros in Pichincha Province as compared to the free peons of the villages and hamlets, who may or may not have land on which to grow their own food. It is interesting to note that in this instance, and in regard to nutrition, the very lowest rural income group is somewhat better off than the higher ones. While the samples furnished by the Buitróns are too few to furnish a basis for general conclusions, they nevertheless suggest a nexus between money incomes and the state of the food markets in Ecuador. Whatever the food market situation is, huasipungeros do not earn enough cash to buy foods except in minute quantities (salt, sugar, fats).

8. Ecuadorian Commission n.d.:75-76, crediting these data to Suárez. Cf. Linke 1954:81 ff.

9. Buitrón 1947a; Buitrón and Buitrón 1945 and 1947:39-53; Clothier 1946:231; Gillin 1941; Hanson and Platt 1945:28; Hassaurek 1868:28; IEAG 1953, No. 3:68-93; No. 4:34-40; Nos. 10 and 11:60-64, 127-33; León 1946; Maes 1941; Parsons 1945:17, 18, 22-23; Rodríguez Sandoval 1949:27-28; Romero 1947:116-18; Santiana 1949; Saenz 1933a:46 ff., 92-95, 188; Soule, Efron and Ness 1945:26; Suárez 1934:34, 38-39, 42 and 1942. Almost all these sources also comment on the insufficiency of Indian diet.

10. Clothier 1946:230 (who points out that nonconsumption of milk by Indians protects them, on the other hand, from contamination from these sources); Parsons 1945:167, on the refusal of her informant to drink milk and eat eggs when these were prescribed to her by the doctor, on the ground that they were upsetting her digestion.

11. León 1946; Santiana (1949:259 and 1952a:120-28), on the basis of his own and others' observations (he being a trained dentist), disputes the "popular belief" regarding the good dentition of Indians. Gillin's own very detailed examination of 134 adult male Imbabura Indians shows a very high incidence of caries and loss of teeth (1936, 1941). Toothlessness is glaring, even to the most casual observer, particularly among the Indians attending the weekly fair at Riobamba.

12. The literature nowhere offers a single instance of outright complaints, voiced by Indians themselves, about their food situation; Rodríguez Sandoval (1949:76 and passim) reproduces a few Indian comments on the sensation of hunger and satiation.

13. Hassaurek 1868:27, also p. 130 and passim; Saenz 1933a:92-95, citing Cevallos' work (1873:130), whose descriptions, he says, are generally true for conditions observed some seventy years later.

Cf. Saenz 1933b:40 (page reference is to the English translation, 1944), where he reports similar observations concerning Peruvian Indians. He concludes that poverty is not the only reason for the Indians' insufficient diet; rather it is his habitual parsimony or frugality.

The relative abundance of information on what Indians eat invites comparison with the virtual absence of information as to when and how they feed.

14. Parsons 1945:22-23, where she also discusses eating etiquette and ceremonial. Three meals a day are indicated by Buitrón and Buitrón 1947:45, 47; Rodríguez Sandoval 1949:76 has three meals as a rule, with refreshments in between; also IEAG 1953, Nos. 10 and 11.

15. Franklin 1943:69. See also Mathews (1947:161, n. 21), according to whom "exceedingly interesting results were reported from a voluntary health program" of that mining company. Also Troncoso (1946), on the hospital and feeding arrangements at that mine.

16. Popular accounts on coca and the physiological (laboratory) effects of coca-chewing: Gutiérrez-Noriega and Von Hagen 1950; Hodge 1947.

17. Bejarano 1945; Espinosa Bravo 1949 (with a map showing the distribution of coca-chewing which apparently includes Ecuador); United Nations Bulletin III, No. 17 (Oct. 21, 1947):525, reporting on a speech by Juvenal Monge of Peru, according to which he included Ecuador (but omitted Bolivia) among the coca-chewing countries.

18. Rivet 1926, reporting on funeral customs in Maldonado where he observed a coca-leaf pouch among the items being put into a man's grave. León (1952) identifies this parish (together with regions adjoining the Curaray River in the Oriente Province of Napo-Pastaza) as an area where the plant is cultivated on a minute scale and from where Ecuadorean pharmacies derive very small quantities.

On the areas in adjoining Colombia where coca is cultivated and chewed (though outlawed in recent years), see Hernandez de Alba 1947: 919, 928, 934. On linguistic grounds, the (Ecuadorean) Maldonado population seems to be related to southern Colombian Indians rather than to the mass of Quechua-speaking Ecuadorean Indians (see Ferdon 1947 and map).

19. Garcés 1941 and 1945 (in which he sets the record straight in answer to Bejarano /1945/); León 1946 and 1952, where he rightly points to the possibility of coca, when taken in the form of an infusion, having been confused with another plant, having narcotic or stimulating properties, such as is widely used among eastern lowland Indians.

20. Coca plantations did exist in various regions of Ecuador in colonial times, and coca leaves constituted part of the remuneration of mitayos employed in gold-washing and mining enterprises. See Perez 1943; Murra 1947:810; and especially León's brilliant article (1952) on the history and decline of cocaism in Ecuador, in which he relates its disappearance in rather early colonial times to the effectiveness of anticoca legislation, on the one hand, and to the minor importance, in comparison with the other Andean areas, of mining in Ecuador, the mines being the coca-consuming centers.

21. Parsons 1945:63, n. 126; 72; 121, n. 59; 198; 202. On the use of datura among curanderos, see Disselhoff (1940) and Cooper (1949b), the latter noting that it had been introduced into Sierral practice by curanderos who learned their art among the Jivaros; León 1946.

22. Buitrón 1948b, where he lists "alcoholism" among the six main problems of the Indians. Cisneros Cisneros 1948:150 ff.

23. Parsons 1945:122, 171, 178; León 1946, according to whom consumption of aguardiente has increased among Indians since the decree of 1944 prohibiting the making and selling of chicha. Garces 1945.

24. Cisneros Cisneros 1948:98-100; Ecuadorian Commission n.d.:18-19; Garcés 1941:43; also Rodríguez Sandoval 1949:108 on the number of aguardiente outlets; and IEAG 1953, Nos. 10 and 11:148-49, according to which there are 800 alcohol-dispensing establishments in two parishes of Chimborazo Province.

25. Garcés 1941, 1945, and 1946a:13; Saenz 1933a:82, 92-95; Soule, Efron and Ness 1945:26-27.

26. Garcés 1941:43 ("it is monstrous to find that the Indian still believes that chicha is food"); also his other works.
     Cf. León 1946; Santiana 1949:244, 246, 254-55. Both animadvert against Indian drinking, but Santiana points out that chicha, when made by the Indians in their own homes, is healthy and pleasant, clean and nutritive. According to both authors it is the White and Mestizo chicheros (tavernkeepers making and selling chicha) who adulterate the drink by adding toxic ingredients such as huantuc or guanto (datura sanguinea) and others (see above, n. 21, and text); it is this "souped-up" chicha which is held to do the real damage among its Indian purchasers. See also IEAG 1953, Nos. 10 and 11:81, on such practices among Indians.

27. Buitrón and Buitrón 1947:53. According to Saenz, the alcohol content of chicha does not exceed 6 to 8 per cent (1933a:48); according to Clothier (1946:228), it varies between 5 and 20 per cent. For a chemical analysis of guarape, see Suárez 1942.

28. Suárez 1942; cf. Hassaurek 1868:28, who asserts that "the vice of drunkenness does not affect /the Indian's/ iron constitution."

29. León 1946. These data are reproduced for what they are worth; their evaluation must be left to the specialists in biology, medicine, psychiatry, etc.

30. Apart from the sources already cited in this chapter, see also Ecuadorian Commission n.d.:18; J. Davis 1946:72-73; Linke 1954:157; Rubio Orbe 1949.

A. The Problem and a Background

The previous chapters have been devoted to a consideration of the skills, education, and health of prospective Indian workers as relatively isolable and obvious qualities which as such are of the most immediate interest to an incipient industry and which, by themselves, are held to be most amenable to testing and comparison in terms of given standards. The real and putative circumstances and conditions influencing these three qualities of the human "raw material" have also been taken into consideration and weighed in order to arrive at a first conclusion regarding the Indians' fitness or capacity for industrial work and its present-day requirements.

The following two chapters are to continue and conclude this survey of "single" qualities by examining an apparently integrated group of habits or routines which are pertinent to the question of industrial discipline. Modern industry holds certain expectations regarding a number of seemingly distinct qualities: it refers to them as "punctuality," "regularity" of appearance at work, "reliability" of attendance, "steadiness," "sobriety," "perseverance" on the job and assigned tasks, observation of working schedules, etc. It is apparent that, when reduced to a common denominator, all these discretely enumerated qualities have to do with time. The scheme into which the following considerations are cast has to do with the problem of time in social life, with the nature of "discipline," and with allied categories, namely, "work" and "leisure" as distinct cultural conceptions.

"Discipline," in the more technical sense, is here understood as "the fitting of individual actions in such a way that the character of each and its relations to the rest can be accurately controlled in the interest of the end to which the whole is devoted. The importance of discipline lies in being able to count on the individual doing the right thing at the right time and place. [1] (There are other aspects of industrial discipline, but these are dealt with in Chapter XII.)

Discipline, in this sense, has to do with time. Time, indeed, is here the key concept. From an economic point of view, time is a budgeted commodity; timekeeping, on the other hand, in terms of its social function, provides a "useful point of reference" by which to co-ordinate "diverse groups and functions which lack any other common frame of activity." [2]

It will be seen that the present scheme of inquiry and analysis (in contrast to the question to which these two chapters are addressed) owes much to points raised by Henri Bergson (1944, esp. pp. 360-74), especially with regard to the "natural articulation" of time as over against scientific time. We substitute for science (which "admits of no essential moment, no culminating point, no apogee") the requirements of modern industrial organization of production. This substitution is perhaps not too unjustifiable since "scientific time and space are, in a sense, closer to...the average individual" of modern life, who "apparently...has become so habituated to the scientific time conception, which has infiltrated into the common sense point of view, that he finds it difficult to remove himself to a level which is psychologically more primitive." The modern (urban-industrial) individual thus tends to describe (and feel) time in Newtonian terms rather than in more "empirical" terms (Benjamin 1937:279; Johnson 1947, esp. pp. 15-31, and passim).

Outside modern physical science itself and its philosophy there are other hints as to the real and palpable differences in the apprehension and articulation of time, and of timed or timeable phenomena, situations, and events: these come from a comparison of "Standard Average European" and non-European languages and language structures and forms (Whorf 1941; Hoijer 1953), although there is a question whether and how far linguistic patterns and conceptions of time inferred therefrom influence actual behavior-in-time, or vice versa.

At any rate, for present purposes it is being assumed that individual, "inner," private time is not only the strictly individual affair which it is (in terms of psychology) but may have groupwise, generally common features and thus a like general structure for peoples of like social and, particularly, cultural situation. In other words, we have shifted durée, individually empirical, "experienced time" from the individual psychological to the sociological level; and we have concretized it.

Other observations have contributed to the present approach to time. Thus the phenomenon of the divergences in the use of time between modern urban and rural populations is, of course, known in a general manner. Rural sociologists sometimes comment on these differences, though only in very general terms and without drawing particular conclusions therefrom.[3] West characterizes well the distinctive characteristics of rural work as contrasted with most urban work: "...great variety in rural tasks," "the individual control of speed with which these tasks are performed," freedom from noise, tedium, and enforced, unsocial co-operation with other workers, and "the immediate, personally understood and simple relationship between work and livelihood" (1945:100).

Also the quite general tendency of deploring the budgetwise use and consumption of time in modern civilization according to the clock, the speed and artificial "rhythm" of modern urban and industrial life as over against the "natural" rhythms and leisurely flow of life ascribed to rural and peasant groups, is called to mind. Such perhaps romantic, nostalgic comparisons and expressions of petulance and resentment toward modern time regimes bespeak quite well an actual difference in "felt" or personally experienced time on the level of groups.

In this context it is not without interest to note that problems of "acculturation" are occasionally singled out for treatment in terms of time-behavior. "For example, an important item, among many such problems may be found to be Puerto Rican work rhythms and tempos at variance with those which New York employment imposes."[4]

Of further illumination for our posing of the problem are Richards' observations regarding "the rhythm of work" among the Bemba of Northern Rhodesia, by which she means the difference (from our point of view) in the kinds and amounts of tasks performed daily, the apparently "erratic" change in working hours, the sheer bodily rhythms--in short, everything which distinguishes Bemba handling or "conceptions" of time, of periods, of work habits and work rhythms from those of industrially implicated man.[5]

"Time-budgets" are beginning to figure in recent ethnographic literature, particularly in studies on the economy of non-Western or non-Westernized peoples. These studies tend to emphasize the time spent on activities that are geared to main and supplementary ways of making a living within a given economy and within a given culture. There are few detailed observations along these lines. And as these tend to be related to given propositions of the science of economics, they tend to omit from their tabulations those activities that cannot somehow be identified as "productive." Else they are designed to give the lie to the "myth" of the lazy, undisciplined primitive man and his desultory working habits.[6]

It may be added that for the present question it is not significant whether differential time regimes are functions of specific cultures or directly or indirectly causally related to specific occupations (thus perhaps being "determined" by climate, the latitudes, the seasons, geography, etc.--as they well may be); our primary interest here is to show that differential time regimes exist and that their coexistence may have practical significance.

For if the modern industrial organization of work is viewed as a system of timing, a survey of the use of time such as is here proposed may serve as an analytical and diagnostic device by which to appraise traditional time uses in their potential bearing on industrial requirements.

Time, accordingly, is the broad frame of reference within which to examine the use to which Ecuadorean Indians put their time habitually and customarily; the manner in which it is divided up into "work" and "nonwork" activities or the Indians' distribution of events in time; and the systems and patterns in which work itself is carried out so as to gauge the nature of the work process itself in time.

The terms "work" and "nonwork" have just been employed and must be explained. For purposes of this discussion, "work" is not understood to be only that activity by which something is produced or effected according to intention, plan, or purpose. The definition here also, and very emphatically, includes the attitude, set, or approach toward the specific task of producing or effecting and the spirit and behavior in which this goal-directed activity is carried out. In other words, work is intentionally sober and unadorned activity related to the execution of a task or project.

Whether or not the product of such activity or the activity itself has a market value, and whether the task requires effort, sacrifices, or expenditures of any sort, or whether these are subjectively felt, is for the present purpose not of primary importance. Neither reward nor punishment enters into the present definition of work. It is meant to be applicable to the activity called "work" in modern industrial society as well as to the activities in a society such as the one under discussion.

The considerations leading to this unorthodox formulation of the concept of work as an operational concept are well illustrated in a generalization regarding the native populations of the Pacific Islands: "...in such cultures it is hard to draw a clear line, as Westerners do, between work and recreation. Much of the fishing, gardening, clearing, and other pursuits counted by Westerners as work is done in friendly cooperative groups under pleasurable conditions which approach recreation, while preparations for a feast, practicing a dance or clearing a sports ground for a meet may have all the vigor, discipline, and competitive spirit of hard work" (Handbook...1948:185).

As will be noted at the proper place, the distinction between "work" (however defined) and "recreation" (as above) or, better, "leisure" would be out of place in regard to certain activities of a nonindustrial society, such as that of Ecuadorean Indians. In order to avoid the use of a concept which is bound to be misleading here, the admittedly clumsy terminology of "work" and "nonwork" has been chosen.[7]

"Leisure" is a phenomenon (and a "problem"[8]) that is specific to modern society, on the one hand, and of special strata of aristocratically oriented societies, on the other. This is one reason why the concept is inapplicable to Ecuadorean Indians, as will be shown, and why a neutral term had to be selected which would not conjure up our own notions.

By way of a not too far-fetched illustration, reference may be made here to the problems encountered by the Spanish in the sixteenth and seventeenth centuries in their attempts to exact from the Indians of Peru (then including most of present-day Ecuador) and Bolivia a required amount of work and to educate them to "systematic habits of work." Some aspects of the matter, pertinent to our discussions, are pointed out thus (Kubler 1947: 392-94):

> The Spaniards do not seem to have comprehended that, for the Indian, no work was worth doing which was not infused by ceremonial symbolism...; work was punctuated by ritual and festive occasion; work itself was ceremonially performed /In precolonial times7 . In Christian life, work and worship were separate concepts. The day of rest evoked no response from the Indian whose understanding of leisure was in terms of ceremonial exercise. Under Christian direction, the tributary was expected to do unadorned work for six days, divorced from all forms of ritual behavior. His daily devotions were a separate category, and labor, far from being a form of piety, was degraded into physical toil, without spiritual compensations.

Although the treatment of the problem may be somewhat novel, the problems to be discussed are, of course, old and well-known ones. Their presentation will be perhaps rather unorthodox, but they are cast into this form in an attempt to furnish a somewhat more distinct background to the problem arising from industrial requirements that consist in training "human beings to renounce their desultory habits of work and identify themselves with the unvarying regularity of the complex automaton," the modern orthodox mechanized factory, and to make the independent craftsman, for example, "renounce his old prerogative of stopping when he pleases, because he would thereby throw the whole establishment into disorder."[9]

What, then, are the large and small elements in Indian comportment that could "throw the whole establishment into disorder"?

B. The "Problem of Alcoholism" Reconsidered:
   Alcohol, Fiestas, and Industrial Discipline

The preceding chapter ended with a reference to the problem which the Indians' "vice of drinking" constitutes apart from, and beyond, its bearing on health and physical efficiency. This reference is taken as a convenient starting point from which to embark upon an examination of those aspects of the Indians' "passion for drink" that have far more immediately important implications for industrialism and industrial discipline than its real and alleged effects on health and constitution for which precise data are lacking anyway. Here, then, attention is given first to the traditional and customary place of drinking in the Indians' way of life and thereby to an attempt to seek for its proper contextual referent. As it turns out, a discussion of this matter provides also a vehicle by which to introduce essential aspects of Indian life and Indian ways of doing things--aspects which are of direct relevance to the question of industrializing this population.

In calculating the per capita annual consumption of alcoholic beverages among low-income manual workers of Quito, Suárez points to an important aspect of the problem of "alcoholism"; he estimates that about one-third of the working days are spent annually in the consumption of, and intoxication with, chicha and guarape. The importance of alcohol as a time-dissipating and work-interrupting factor is further underlined when he turns to Indians specifically, of whom he says that "the days spent in fiestas and intoxication are no less than 30 per cent of all working days" (Suárez 1934:11-13; 1942).

If constancy in work, reliability of attendance, care, etc., are what is expected of Indian workers, it is likely that such expectations will be frustrated in many instances. Suárez has clearly related the consumption of alcohol (the main target of his critical analysis) to fiestas and holidays-- the occasions for drinking. The implication is that any lack in the desired constancy in work is not directly due to addiction to drinking as such but to the relative importance of fiestas and other social events as over wage work. Hence it is to this side of the problem to which we address ourselves.

That the importance of fiestas is not confined to Indian life but is a general characteristic is borne out by a report of a Quito newspaper, according to which, "Ecuadoreans work two-thirds of the year and have holidays the rest of the time.... /From January/ up to October, 1945, Ecuador has had 206 working days and 98 holidays, counting Sundays, Saturday afternoons, and civic and religious holidays."[10]

While a multitude of holidays is observed by the whole of the Ecuadorean population, as may be expected in a Catholic country, the tendency toward extending religious holidays beyond their calendar dates seems to be especially marked among Indians. Fiestas of one sort or another are frequent and may each last a number of days. They are given in celebration of the locally important saints as well as in observance of the Catholic calendar of general holidays. Else they are held to mark and celebrate a personal event, a baptism, a funeral, and, particularly, a wedding. Depending on the occasion, fiestas may include a mass or other forms of church attendance, processions and pilgrimages, dances and music, and always a great deal of eating and drinking. They may last days and nights; wedding celebrations lasting eight days are quite common. "Every holiday," says Rivet in speaking of the Indians of the Riobamba region, "particularly the more important ones, such as Holy Week, Easter, Corpus Christi, Christmas, All Saints Day, and the local holiday of La Merced, is followed by an orgy of eight days."[11] These long and protracted affairs tend to implicate the whole community or the whole extended family (the two may be coextensive) and draw at least the presence, if not the active participation, of everybody in the community and its environs.

But fiestas are not the only occasion for drinking; the role of drinking in Indian life and activities, whether work or nonwork, is much more pervasive. Any kind of gathering is an occasion for more or less drinking. Such occasions are the fairs and weekly markets, the Sunday mass which is followed by visits to the tavern, and collective work parties (mingas)--including housebuilding and harvest celebrations.

Since important areas of Indian life and activities are pointed up by the consumption of alcohol (and thereby brought to special notice as quasi-recreational or quasi-leisure activities), it might be well to compare explicitly two sets of evaluations of the role of alcohol in Indian life.

Some observers have taken pains to probe directly into the Indians' attitudes toward, and their motives for, drinking. The results show first, that no moral stigma attaches to drinking as such and that in Indian eyes it is not a "vice" or "addiction." Second, as already noted, Indians ascribe particularly to chicha important therapeutical properties and hold it essential in the restoration and maintenance of physical and mental well-being; the beverage, therefore, figures frequently in the "snacks" and "refreshments" taken during work. Finally, and most importantly, the observation of definite rules regarding eating as well as drinking in company points away from pathological addictions. Drinking, from the Indians' point of view, is a social--not to say "sacramental"--affair: "only dogs drink alone." It is eminently a matter of good form and sociability and thus co-extensive with good relations with and among relatives, neighbors, friends, or anyone else. The drinking type of conviviality expresses regard for others and enhances one's own prestige.

This does not mean that Indians themselves do not criticize drinking. Some Indians of the Otavalo region have been sounded out as to their views in that matter. In these instances heavy drinking was condemned on purely economic grounds, i.e., as a money-wasting and time-consuming activity. However, no such criticism was offered in regard to drinking at fiestas and other celebrations. Here as elsewhere, on the contrary, the ability to drink with one's friends is considered a direct and positive reflection on a man's economic and social abilities.[12]

The main purpose of this presentation has been to locate the Indians' "alcoholism" with regard to its social and cultural context and with regard to the consequences it might have for industrial production (other than those connected with the question of the workers' personal health). Some inferences for industrial production can be summarily stated.

It has been shown that drink-punctuated activities are by no means haphazard, whimsical affairs but are, in large part, occasioned by definite events which, to Indians at least, are important. So far as these occur with a certain regularity over the year, they can be foreseen and, quite literally, taken into account. There is a marked tendency for church holidays and fiestas, as well as for some of the personal life events, to be celebrated during the off-seasons, i.e., at times when farming activities are slack. Needless to say, the traditional calendar of events does not necessarily reconcile with industrial activities which are not bound to the yearly cycle of seasons.

Apart from these relatively solid and highly visible occasions, there are others which make probable a high degree of less foreseeable tardiness, absenteeism, and other industrial work-disruptive behavior. Late arrival at work or failure to appear at all may well be due to a worker's inability to refuse a proffered drink on pain of violating for good cherished or valuable relations.[13] The probability of such "undisciplined" behavior is heightened if and when the very forms or, better, formalities that accompany drinking are considered.[14] The drinking pattern as it exists--which constitutes, as has been seen, a whole complex of motives and behavior-- and as viewed and understood in its institutional and social context is likely to interfere in small but numerous ways with the industrial work process by individual discontinuities and interruptions, and thus to contribute to instabilities in the industrial work pattern.

C. Time Regimens and Work Schedules

In the foregoing, consideration has been given to the outstanding activities and behavior of Indians in their use of time that is not, or not wholly, devoted to work. These considerations are now carried a little further in turning to the specific questions which concern the Indians' use of total time. Particular reference will be made to their nonwork time, that is to say, that parcel out of total disposable time that is not given over to activities constituting work exclusively (in the sense already defined) but which is nevertheless consumed in structured activities or devoted to pursuits which represent a complex of meaningful intentional actions. How, then, is time distributed as between work and nonwork, and what kind of work-continuities can be discerned? And what, if anything, has time not devoted to work to do with work habits and attitudes toward work? What propensity toward continuity of work can be discerned?

In the introduction to this chapter the well-known differences in principle between the use of time in industrial and agricultural life have been touched upon in a very general manner. Rather than elaborating on these, we shall indicate here what can be gleaned from scattered information relating to the use of total available time by Ecuadorean Indians specifically. There are, of course, no time budgets. Furthermore, such information as exists concerns almost exclusively the Indians of Otavalo who are, after all, a somewhat special group and, so far as is known to date, not in all respects typical of Ecuadorean Indians at large. They are, perhaps, typical of potentialities.

As is natural enough, it is the seasons which punctuate alternations between work and nonwork, and between different tasks, for a farming population such as the Otavalo Indians.[15] There appears to be a tendency to engage in craft work in greater concentration during the periods between the peaks of cultivation, sowing and planting, and harvest. At least one observer has related the development of craft industries working for the markets to the fact that holders of a sufficient amount of good bottom lands yielding one crop, enough to provision the household with food and requiring but one farming cycle, have thus sufficient time to devote to the manufacture of textiles and other articles.[16] At any rate, work in this area is not uniform nor does it consist of identical tasks throughout the year.

Alternations between work and nonwork are, as has already been stated, at least in part seasonal, in part they follow the official church calendar, and in part they are spontaneous according to the more or less formal occasions celebrated by feasting gatherings and emphasizing the festive rather than the properly work activities of life. These are the holidays and fiestas and the other celebrations of personal life events already mentioned.

The weekly routine is described as follows for the Otavalo farmer-craftsmen:

> Fiestas aside, the passing of time...in the valley is punctuated by the Sunday Mass in the parochial church and by the Saturday market in Otavalo or the nearer town market...The week's work

in weaving, hatmaking, or pottery making is regulated so as to finish products for the market. The Friday bath...is also preparatory. [17]

Apart from fiestas, celebrations of personal life events, mass, and market, there are few discernible occasions of such importance as to distract from working time. The fact that there are but the fewest hints on that matter would itself point to the virtual absence of structured or deliberately planned activities by which to "pass the time"--nonworking time, that is. However, the festive occasions themselves require some time for preparation. Thus Indians who act as musicians at fiestas practice their music long in advance (Parsons 1945:116). There is a single account on the preparations for a fiesta, according to which a series of ceremonial as well as functional meetings are held over a period of some nine months before the fiesta of San Luis in the Mojanda area (Otavalo canton). This is an individually sponsored fiesta, and the preparatory meetings involve the sponsor and a large "staff" of functionaries and helpmates. These meetings are themselves little celebrations during which arrangements are fixed, roles assigned, formal invitations made, and "refreshments" served. The main affair, the fiesta of San Luis, is followed by another feast given for the main helpers (Santiana 1949: 261 ff.).

More telling than the absence of any systematic observations on how nonworking time is spent is the fact, stated explicitly by Mrs. Parsons, that there are no games for adults[18] that are played spontaneously. Exceptions are weddings, when games are played on the days preceding and following the main event, i.e., as part of a fiesta, and wakes, when some kind of imitation and forfeit games are played.[19] The comment of the "school-bred young Indian" reporting on these games as played at wakes by Indians in Cayambe canton (Pichincha Province) is illuminating: "Because they have no appropriate times to play games, the Indians choose to play them at a wake, where it is not suitable to play any of these games."[20]

The assertion that "Indians have no appropriate times to play" is certainly a valuable hint in several respects, all of which have bearing on the expectations that may be held concerning specific work qualities of Indian workers; these consist of habits of, and attitudes toward, industriousness and bespeak a positive attitude toward work.

First, the above statement is in line with an observation, made particularly of Indians such as those of Otavalo, i.e., largely self-employed, independent farmer-craftsmen: the continuous application to tasks of one sort or another, the filling in of every moment with some kind of work, is frequently cited as characteristic of Indians. Within his own round of activities, the Indian is said to be never idle. In other words, in being self-employed he does employ himself constantly. The industriousness of Indians under such conditions is a matter of agreement among observers. It is held to be typical of Indian women to be occupied with spinning while walking along the road, while selling in the market, and while gossiping with each other, and men are similarly seen engaged in some braiding or cording work, or even spinning, as they walk.[21] The significance of the observed and asserted industriousness of the Indians lies in the contrast to the trait which is alleged to be characteristic of Whites and Mestizos in so far as these consciously or traditionally share the Spanish-colonial "aristocratic" contempt for manual work and assume the attitude of the classical type of the hidalgo toward making a living by personal physical efforts.[22] Among Indians, there is nothing to point to a horror laboris, a consistent tendency to avoid working.

Such observations have subjective corollaries in the attitude of Indians regarding industriousness. The comment cited above itself indicates that Indians bestow a positive value on it. Otavalo folk tales contain the motif of industriousness finding its material reward, laziness its punishment. In Peguche (Otavalo canton), hunting is disparaged as the pursuit of the lazy. Men and women having the reputation of being industrious are looked for as desirable mates; and Indian pedagogy stresses industriousness above all.[23]

Finally, the comment on the Indians' lack of time for playing reflects on the use Indians make of the total time at their disposal. Time is used, above all, for work; next, for fiestas and other social events which are in part obligatory though festive, or even create economic values (e.g., housebuilding) without, however, having the character of work (as previously defined). Between work-time, properly speaking, and the massive time-consuming festive occasions there is no residual and recurring time that is taken care of by what we would call "leisure activities."

Indeed, it would be highly misleading to define Indian activities that are not, or do not have the aspect of, work as "leisure" activities. In the first place, no instance has been encountered which would indicate that a concept of leisure, comparable to our own, exists among Ecuadorean Indians, must less that a "problem" is constituted by any available "leisure" time, that is, of having to fill a regularly recurring span of time that is set apart from working time (excluding the time spent in recreative or, better, restorative activities such as eating and sleeping) with activities specially reserved for it. In the second place, no value is bestowed on leisure as such,[24] a trait which again distinguishes Indians from their non-Indian conationals.[25]

These were the reasons for which it has been found inappropriate to discuss the use of time by Indians in terms of work and leisure. There is no leisure; and there is no leisure problem within the setting of their own life and their own conditions. No pattern exists to meet that problem, should it arise and as it is bound to arise in the modern industrial situation. Therefore, that problem is likely to be acute[26] and will be the more acute the more remote an industry is from Indian population centers, the farther it removes the individual Indian worker from his usual social milieu, and the more it is thus apt to throw him upon his own resources -- a situation for which he is entirely unprepared since, as has been seen, he has no such resources of his own.

On the other hand, except for the more or less solid occasions giving rise to fiestas and their preparation, there is nothing in nonwork time activities that would tend to impinge greatly upon industrial work. In other words, there are, quite literally, no real distractions apart from fiestas (and, perhaps, litigations)[27] and the specific forms of conviviality by which good social relations are cultivated among Indians. These, as has by now been amply shown, are important.

This inquiry into the distribution of total time has constituted a rudimentary attempt to draw attention to the problem arising from any necessary rescheduling of traditionally timed systems of activities in adaptation to industrial production methods. The adjustment of people both as organisms and as manipulators of time to radically different time regimens and regulations having their own arrangements of activity sequences is clearly a practical problem which needs at least pointing out (Richards 1939:392-98; Herskovits 1948:271-72 and 1952b). For it is quite possible that all sorts of difficulties which industry might encounter with Indian workers (manifesting themselves, for example, in onsets of fatigue, unpunctuality, absenteeism, etc) could be referred to divergences in time habituations or in time schedules rather than to any single condition or quality of Indian workers or, again, to their "culture," "society," or "existence."

There remains the question of task continuities. It must have become evident that the lack of sameness of tasks and activities throughout the year does present a contrast to the industrial time regimen. This matter will be further considered in detail in the following chapter within the general question as to what habits and patterns and "sets" characterize the work of Indians.

NOTES

1. Parsons 1937:507, paraphrasing Max Weber's concept of "discipline."

2. Mumford 1934:27. In reference to the succeeding, see also his suggestive remarks on the history of the clock as the key-machine of the modern industrial age, and his formulations of its consequences for the ethos, habitus, mentality, or pattern of average urban and industrial Western culture (pp. 12-18, 196-99, 269-73, 345).

3. See Sorokin, Zimmerman and Galpin (1930-32, III:360), where attention is drawn to this matter and a very sketchy set of data offered comparing timed activities of Russian industrial workers with those of Russian peasants.

4. From a report on Puerto Rican Communities in New York, research study on community organization conducted by the College of the City of New York, Prof. John Collier, Director, in News Letter of the Institute of Ethnic Affairs, Inc., Washington, D.C. (Vol. III, No. 2 /March 1948/:6; my emphasis).

5. Richards 1939:392-98; see also the context in which Herskovits (1948: 271-72) discusses that matter.

6. Bücher 1909:408; also Thurnwald 1932:213-14. For examples of work-time budgets in anthropological literature, see Firth 1946:93-97; Foster 1942:35-38; Herskovits 1940:71-79; 1948:268-72; Tax 1953:85 ff.; Wagley 1941:25-26.

7. On this point and for much of the following discussion, cf. Curle 1949; Firth 1948.

8. From the growing body of literature and (apparently inconclusive) materials on leisure in modern society, see, e.g., Greenberg 1953; Denney and Riesman in Staley 1952:245-81, and particularly the roundtable discussion, "Leisure and Human Values in Industrial Civilization," pp. 50-91 with the illuminating remarks of its Hindu participant; also pp. 205-7.

9. Mumford 1934:173 and 174, quoting Andrew Ure, "The Philosophy of Manufacture...," London, 1835.

10. Reported in The Inter-American IV, No. 12 (Dec., 1945):29. (At that rate, and over the same nine months' period, the number of days that would obtain for the United States would be about 65.)

Rodríguez Sandoval (1949:92) allows for ten holidays and other celebrations, and figures "rest days" to amount to totals of 78 to 130-40 annually; weekends with many city workers extend from Saturday noon to Tuesday morning. In the country, feasts and family celebrations alone may amount to 20 a year.

There is perhaps some slight exaggeration in the allegation that the number of national and church holidays reduces the school days in Quito to 79 a year (Bemelmans 1941:51); there are about 180 days in the official school year.

The school calendar for a nine-month session of the Social Service School lists 10 official holidays (national and church) and 14 days of recess and vacation (Ministerio de Prevision Social y Trabajo 1951).

For a list of 33 holidays and fiestas of national and local importance, see Hanson and Platt 1945:28-29. For a calendar of fiestas in Otavalo communities (probably not complete), see Parsons 1945:95-112; ten prescriptive holidays are listed, and others are of local importance.

11. Rivet 1903:75. (Supposing that this is an exact list, and the Sundays are added to it, a total of 102 days are holidays or nominally nonworking days in the Riobamba region.) See also Buitrón 1948b; Hassaurek 1868: 265-67; and Santiana 1949, on the feasts of San Juan, San Pedro, and San Luis which last for five and eight solid days; IEAG 1953, No. 3: 102-4, on the fiesta of San Juan in the villages of Imbabura Province.

12. For these data and instances, see, particularly, Parsons 1945, passim; Rodríguez Sandoval 1945 and 1949:82, 83, 94-95. Also Buitrón 1948b; Buitrón and Buitrón 1945 and 1947; Clothier 1946:229; Cooper 1949b, esp. p. 545; J. Davis 1946; Garcés 1945; Cisneros Cisneros 1948: 98-100; IEAG 1953, No. 3:99-108 and Nos. 10 and 11:78-79, 82-83, on the subject of largely Indian alcohol consumption; León 1946.

13. For a number of concrete instances, see Rodríguez Sandoval 1945 and 1949, passim; Parsons 1945:123, 152-53; Hassaurek 1868:266; IEAG 1953, Nos. 10 and 11:82-83.

14. For an extensive discussion on Indian eating and drinking ritual (etiquette), see Parsons 1945:121-24; also Rodríguez Sandoval 1949:13, 17, 105, on formal banquets.

15. Parsons 1945:18-19 gives an abbreviated schedule of farming tasks: the months in which specific crops are sown or planted and harvested. A more detailed list is found in Collier and Buitrón 1949:49 ff. See also Buitrón 1947a. Buitrón and Buitrón (1945) show that Indians generally celebrate the traditional ceremony of wedding after the harvest.

16. Buitrón 1947a. He indicates, however, that other factors also enter into the development of household industries, such as nearness to markets. He noted, and correlated, the lack of sufficient land with absence of household industries producing for the market. Land-poor farmers have to supplement the food they grow themselves with food given them in remuneration for help they render at harvests or for other tasks performed elsewhere. Those who have sufficient land, but lands situated in the bottoms or on the slopes and upper altitudes, are faced with two farming cycles and have, consequently, no time for occupations such as weaving.

It should be added, however, that sufficiency of land is not the only condition for the development of a cottage industry. As the case of the toquilla straw-hat industry in Azuay and Cañar seems to show, it was utter insufficiency of land that led to its initial development and to the later rapid expansion during World War II (Basile Ms.).

17. Parsons 1945:111. Markets are held on different days in different towns. Also Santiana 1949:244-45. Cf. IEAG 1953, No. 3:166-67, 168, 171, 172, on weekly and annual schedules among almost full-time household textile producers.

18. Parsons 1940 and 1945:38; children play games, and the concept of games and playing is otherwise known, as can be inferred from folk-tale motifs. But Parsons observed no Otavalo Indian groups playing the national ball game, pelota or guante (pp. 53, 102). However, see below, n. 20.

19. Parsons 1945:194-95, 200-2. Ethnologically speaking, the games played at wakes have a ritual, ceremonial background, but in the cited instances this meaning of playing games or gambling at wakes ("forfeits") seems to have been forgotten. Today's games are said by the Indians to be "Spanish," i.e., intrusive to the native aboriginal culture or a fashion descended from an upper class.
    On the subject, and for data on Andean "recreative culture" and illuminating comments on the apparent poverty of games, see Cooper 1949a, esp. pp. 505, 512-14, 516-19, 522-23.

20. Parsons 1945:202. "Except in certain ceremonies, the Mojanda /Indians/ never play," says Santiana (1949:153), without saying what these ceremonies are. See Buitrón 1951a, taking issue with this statement, and Santiana 1952b, answering that now pelota is being played by some youngsters; also Rodríguez Sandoval 1949:122. Very "advanced" Indian groups, such as Indians from Otavalo who have become residents of the city of Ibarra, are said to maintain football teams of their own (Rubio Orbe 1953).

21. Garcés 1941:37; Saenz 1933a:55-56, 64; also Rivet 1903:72; Stübel 1897:311. And personal observations. The trait is nevertheless more pronounced in women--a familiar enough phenomenon. See also Collier and Buitrón 1949:62 ff.

22. Compare the statements on "Indians as workers" in the introduction to Part II.

23. See Parsons 1945:129, 32, 54 and n. 51, 155; in Cayambe, however, hunting is not disparaged (p. 189). For a possible reason for this difference in the evaluation of this activity, see Hassaurek (1868:294), according to whom "friends of the chase will find an abundance of deer" and other game animals in that region, and "the sport is very popular among the natives." Whether "natives" here means the local gentry, the Indians or, as is most likely, Indian drivers is not made clear. In any case, there are concrete precedences for the popularity of hunting and the lack of stigma attached to it in that region.
    Rodríguez Sandoval (1949:87-91) has many examples of Indian opinion on industriousness, on work well performed and their esteem therefor, and their contempt for the lazy and inept.

24. A close examination of Indian beliefs regarding life after death would probably be extremely rewarding in this respect, as it would be in many others. No such examination has apparently been made even by careful observers and investigators, perhaps because such beliefs do not stand out conspicuously from the matrix of Catholicism and also because of the secretiveness and lack of articulateness of Indians in matters touching cult, ritual, and belief connected with the supernatural.
    However, from some observations made by Parsons, it appears that the ideas of reward and punishment stand in the foreground of beliefs and ideas on afterlife, while those of rest, release from toil, are hardly elaborated. Heaven, the reward for good conduct on earth, is a

"place of pleasure" and, perhaps, without work; it is by no means apparent that it therefore is one of idleness or leisure. Hell is first and foremost a place of punishment and torture; there is no suggestion that it is a place of eternal toil. As a place of punishment it appears to be a more favored theme for church paintings than any other religious theme. See Parsons 1945:87-89, also p. 173 (Table), pp. 179-80, and plate XXII; Parsons 1940; Murra 1947:821; Bemelmans 1941:87-89; also Rivet 1903: 73-75, on the model which the hacienda situation and the harsh tyrannical taskmaster furnishes for Indian conceptions on the deity and the afterworld.

25. Of the Ecuadorean "Mestizo Middle Class" it is said that "leisure" (ocio), not being employed, turns into boredom (Paredes 1951:49). Cf. Tumin (1945), who compares the "non-material culture pattern" of Ladinos (Whites) and Indians of a Guatemalan highland community, two-thirds of whose population is Indian or so designated. While, according to him, work for the Ladinos is an evil to be avoided and manual work in particular is despised, leisure is a value, and boredom a serious problem, Indians do not even have a formal conception of leisure time; for them there is no problem as to how to fill up the hours, a man's virtue is proportionate to his reputation as a hard worker at hard manual tasks, etc.
    Another variant on the theme is presented by Reichel-Dolmatoff (1953), on a Mestizo community with a strong Indian background in the Sierra Nevada de Santa Marta, northern Colombia.

26. The Ecuadorean Constitution prescribes the eight-hour day as the standard limit, and the Labor Code strictly regulates the maximum of hours that may be worked per day or per week for various categories of workers, including limits on overtime, nightwork, etc.

27. The question of law-suits by and among Indians has not been considered here as a "pastime." It will be considered in different contexts (Chapters XII and XIV).

IX / THE USE OF TIME:
WORK HABITS AND WORK PATTERNS

The discussion of Indian work habits and patterns is divided according to the two methods or systems that can actually be distinguished, one that is individually performed, the other that is performed collectively or co-operatively.

A. Individual Work

In the case of individual work the larger part of the generally very scanty information again derives from observations made of Otavalo and similarly situated Indians. The daily round of chores and routine tasks of a basically farming population such as this one, generally living and working some distance from populated centers, is limited, humdrum, and sufficiently unspectacular to explain the scarcity of detailed information.

Such as these observations are, they refer to the alternations between given tasks, or the pattern of changing from one kind of work to another. Household and farming chores do, of course, impose to some extent their own regularly changing pattern of activities within the working day, as every housewife knows.[1] In the case of household industries such as weaving, work has been characterized as a constant alternation between and changing among heterogeneous tasks. Thus, though a man may be busily working from sunup to sunset, it is not sustained work at one task but a going from one to another and still another and back to the first, such as from weaving to hauling water to cleaning wool and back to weaving (Buitrón 1947a)--a working pattern which is no doubt relaxing but which certainly is not that of orthodox industrial production. There is, as we are informed (Buitrón 1947a; Parsons 1945: 51, 60, 61, 156, passim), remarkably little specialization of labor in connection with tasks within the household and in farming work (cf. Chapter V, A), men and women performing a great many identical tasks and women helping men in almost everything. Weaving in Otavalo is practically the sole work performed exclusively by men and this only if done on the pedal loom. Where crafts prevail, men tend to do the skilled work, while women and children give proportionately more attention to farming and the care of livestock (Moomaw 1946:188). Children, depending on their ages, help in any task. From all this it can be inferred that the men's alternating work pattern just described is not imposed only by the inherent requirements of household and farm, since women and children could, in principle, look after these.

However, there is a rudimentary division of labor along the lines of modern industrially organized work. Some Indian weavers have enlarged their household "manufacturing establishments" to such an extent that they employ others (peones), who are paid by the piece; these weaver-peons are explicitly stated to observe a nonalternating pattern of work in that they apply themselves all day to a single task only (carding, spinning, weaving, dyeing, etc.).[2]

An observation kindly communicated by Mr. John Collier, Jr., throws some interesting light on the kind of discipline maintained within such an enlarged household enterprise (described to be working on orders, not "speculatively" for the market): there, the head of the family and master of the enterprise would not permit one of his sons to take out even a few minutes to satisfy the curiosity of his visitor regarding the preparation of some dye mixtures. The context of the incident made it clear that no resentment of an outside intruder or secretiveness was involved but that it was merely a matter of loss of time and the maintenance of shop and/or family discipline that were at stake.

It is in such larger household enterprises as alpargate- ("sandal"-) making or the weaving of straw hats or rugs that the various operations are broken down and divided up among the members of the family or household, including the children (Buitrón and Buitrón 1947:61; J. Davis 1946: 63-64).

One other feature of work patterns deserves mention, because it too reflects upon the treatment of work and the working process as a non-continuous one. That is the manner in which work is assigned, as in haciendas, or engaged for and undertaken by free peons or independent artisans. This feature constitutes a "task" system or a "task-within-time" system. Thus, in haciendas, the huasipungeros are assigned to various farm operations every morning, each assignment consisting of a definite task (tarea)[3] such as plowing or weeding a field of so many furrows of specified length. Similarly, they are held to take turns performing special services, for instance, serving a term of so many months as cowherd or house servant.

Free laborers (peones) hire themselves out "by the job" (per obra) as well as, though more rarely, by the day. Independent artisans such as masons and bricklayers, stonecutters, woodcutters, etc., who work from place to place, undertake work by the job and do a fixed amount of work for a fixed sum of money, sometimes within a stipulated period of time.[4] Similarly, the peons employed by the few larger weaving enterprises (or incipient factories, from the organizational point of view) in the Otavalo area are paid by the piece woven or the amount of wool spun, regardless of the time they spend on a given task (Buitrón 1947a).

Working time, then, is used for continuous, but disjointed, activity, each activity tending to be a whole task without being necessarily related to the next in actuality or in concept. The alternation of tasks in time might, under given circumstances, be related to, or accentuated by, back-and-forth movements occurring in space.

With the exception of carriers and traders, who often and regularly journey long distances, Ecuadorean Indians on the whole are not travelsome.[5] What traveling there is normally occurs within the area surrounding a population center, be it ever so small, provided it has a church or chapel, a cemetery, a market, inns, some administrative officials, etc., and some opportunities for casual little jobs. Within such an area, Indians may move freely to and fro, but such mobility is deceptive because of its short range and because of its circuitlike character. Ecuadorean Indians' attachment to their homes is much emphasized by observers: they do not venture forth on long-distance traveling (as Guatemalan Indians, and to some extent also Peruvian and Bolivian Indians, do so conspicuously). What is of interest here is that a basic lack of venturesome mobility leads to a high degree of spurious mobility, which is mentioned here because it may affect directly the work pattern and accentuate the disjointed character of working. Thus Rivet, in proof of the attachment of Indians to their homes, miserable as these may be, says: "Cases of Indians are cited who work far away from home and who, after a hard day's work, make a long trip at night to visit it and return the following day to accomplish the daily task."[6] The majority of the free peons of a sector of Pichincha Province, which is said to be purely Indian, work in and around the city of Quito; some of them stay at the place of work from Monday to Friday and go home over weekends. But others commute back and forth daily (by foot), making a daily trip of 20 kilometers (12.5 miles).[7]

B. Collective Work

In contrast to the meagerness of information regarding individual work patterns, descriptions of collective or co-operative work institutions and patterns are both more frequent and more extensive. Passing reference has been made already to one feature of these traditional work arrangements, namely, their festive character. Being clearly extraordinary affairs, these mingas (also called ayni, convite, cambia mano, and by other terms) are conspicuous and have invited the attention of casual and expert observers alike far more than those everyday, continuous, and hence unspectacular activities which would throw light on individual work habits.[8]

A distinction should be made between mingas as arranged by Indians themselves and those which are ordered by local Indian or non-Indian civil or ecclesiastic authorities or by the large landowner.

In the first type, the minga is strictly an in-group affair, "a reunion of friends, neighbors, relatives for the execution of work for one of the members of the group." For a harvest, for other farming tasks too extensive to be executed by an individual farmer and his household, or for the building of a house or the transport of construction materials, an Indian raises a contingent of necessary hands by inviting his relatives and friends to help him in the particular undertaking on the basis of formal and informal reciprocity. While such work parties function essentially on a co-operative and reciprocal basis, the organizer of a minga furnishes food and drink, and the mingueros themselves may contribute housebuilding materials. They may also receive gleanings of the grain harvest or gifts of corn harvested. What with the serving of food and drink and the conclusion of the enterprise by dancing and general feasting, such a minga has all the earmarks of a fiesta rather than of work. All "have a magnificent time and it is more a fiesta than work."[9]

The second type of minga is held at the instance of bodies or persons generally not members of the in-group. Local public authorities call mingas for cleaning or repair of public squares and streets, for road work, for the building of a trail or sections of highways, for the digging of irrigation ditches, or for other works of a public nature. Functionally, at least, such mingas take the place of taxes. Minga service is obligatory, and summons for such work service have to be honored on pain of having some personal or household good confiscated to be redeemed by work or a money payment. Nevertheless, work performed on that basis may also partake of the festive character of Indian-arranged mingas, depending on the nature of the task to be accomplished and on the generosity of the local authorities, or of the single official arranging for a minga, in furnishing the drinks. Tools and also food are provided by the mingueros themselves.

Church mingas for the repair of church or chapel, etc., tend to be on a smaller scale and are informally arranged at the instance of the local padre through Indian chapel officials. Mingas for the benefit of a

hacienda are nominally voluntary, and participants are formally invited
rather than called up for service as in the public works mingas. Whether
these mingas are undertaken by the Indians willingly or unwillingly, they
too tend to be accompanied by liberal rations of chicha or aguardiente.
"Chicha," as Rivet puts it, "is the promised recompense for the worker."[10]

While there is no indication that these collective and convivial work
parties engender anything comparable to the machinelike rhythm of work
which is said to be characteristic of collectively organized and executed
tasks among other nonindustrial or preindustrial or primitive peoples,
the alacrity and speed with which work in minga is executed[11] have been
commented upon, quite apart from the good will and spirit prevailing under
the best of circumstances. Since this type of collective work has been
given attention here in so far as it may be relevant toward estimating
work habits or patterns which might be brought into industrially organized
work, the matter is summarily discussed.

There is no doubt that Indians can be organized into collective work,
but hardly on the ground that minga furnishes the appropriate model. This
conclusion needs some emphasis in view of the hope sometimes expressed
in the literature dealing with the "Indian problem" which takes the existence
of mingas as the traditional and natural expression of Indian co-operative-
ness and hence as capable of being utilized for modern institutions and
activities. The evaluation of minga vis-à-vis industrial requirements is
arrived at by considering three aspects not pointed out or made explicit
in the literature that has been used here.

Negative evidence for the nonapplicability of minga in industry is
derived from the fact that not a single instance has been cited of its use
in craft work or, for that matter, in any kinds of work except those specified above (agriculture, construction, public works).[12]

Mingas, with the possible exception of those that are held for public
works or only with a hacienda's own conciertos, are seasonal affairs.
Where farming tasks are involved the point is self-evident, but it applies
equally to housebuilding mingas, which are usually held during the agriculturally slack periods. This is one reason why mingas must be considered extraordinary events rather than matter-of-course and everyday
work arrangements.

It has also been shown repeatedly that food and drink may constitute, among other things, the reward for efforts made on behalf of someone else. Workers bidden in groups for a special piece of work are, as
has been seen, regaled by the bidder. Hence there is a chance that, in
the event of an occasion requiring special or extra efforts, Indian workers
will expect like treatment, be it by way of extra compensation, be it by
way of "refreshment." Industry on occasion may, therefore, have to
furnish the accustomed drinks--not necessarily as incentive but simply
in answer to ordinary Indian expectations.[13]

Provisions of this sort are unusual, to say the least, in modern
industry. The tendency is rather in the opposite direction, for reasons
of "discipline" if for no others. Yet it needs pointing out that a totally
"dry" industrial situation may not always answer native customs and
expectations.[14]

In sum, institution and work pattern of minga provide no precedent
for the standard industrial work pattern. Minga does not meet that requirement of industry according to which work ought to be performed
soberly, regularly, and continuously. Minga does indicate, however, that

common undertakings and work co-operation are not alien to Indians. It is on this ground--and the sporadic and apparently shrinking existence of common landholdings--that Indianists sometimes tend to hold certain hopes for the future shape of Indian economy. For Ecuadorean Indians, however, such hopes do not seem well-founded as far as industrial production is concerned. This type of collective undertaking lacks the substantiality of objective, functional work--in other words, of sustained activities geared exclusively to production.

C. The Problem of Adapting Native Time Regimens and Work Habits to Manufacturing Industry

The most general conclusion that can be drawn from the matters presented in these two chapters is that work as a whole for the individual tends toward diversification in time and in kind. Apart from the seasonal, there are special kinds of diversification that are related to household-farming-craft and service combinations. Whatever these combinations are, the exercise of any particular occupation other than that of daily tasks tends to be reserved for agricultural off-seasons or to be wedged between daily agricultural chores. Furthermore, work other than daily routine tends to be intermittent due to the punctuation of time by nonwork occasions. These occasions are numerous but relatively few in kind. Such as they are, they require massive, rather than evenly distributed, consumption of time. Moreover, from the Indian point of view and from the point of view of his social relations, they are unavoidable and imperative, a matter that has already been hinted at, but which will find more extended discussion at another point (Chapter XIV). In all, work is not only diversified in kind, but also exhibits discontinuities in time.

Both these features of work appear to be accentuated if daily work processes and individual work patterns, as in cottage industry, are considered. Daily work processes are discontinuous, and daily tasks are diverse and heterogeneous. The latter, moreover, are not related among themselves but related by virtue of the setting within which they are performed. Similarly, assignments to work and hiring out for work tend to be piecemeal, consisting of isolated tasks. The discontinuousness of the work "process" may be further emphasized due to special conditions such as distance between home and working place and the ensuing traveling back and forth, whatever the reason may be therefor (attachment to home, lack of facilities for lodging at the working place, etc.).

The manner in which Indians use their time, their habits and patterns of work, in no way predisposes them to the industrial production regimen and to the sustained routines by which uniform tasks are executed over relatively long stretches of time daily and every day; nor to a system of production that is based on budgetwise allocation of time to intentionally productive and intentionally nonproductive ("recreation and leisure") categories; nor to one wherein, finally, time is of the essence not only for technical (i.e., budgetary and calculative) reasons, but also for reasons of social organization (i.e., considering the social function of timekeeping).

In all these respects, the work and time-scheduling methods of Indians are not applicable to industry if the industrial system is viewed as a system of timing. There is a divergence between their habits of using time and those required by, or characteristic of, modern industry. The periodicities and rhythms of industrial life are not "naturally" those of Indian life. What is to be expected on the average and initially from prospective Indian industrial workers is a tendency toward a disjointed kind of work pattern that will express itself in daily performance as well as in delays and tardiness, irregular attendance and absences of varying durations, and a high degree of labor-turnover.[15]

An exception to this prognosis is perhaps presented by those who have already been habituated to or schooled in sustained work at uniform tasks and continuous daily work processes through large family-household industries and through the familiar and recognized authority. Such workers, however, will not be numerous, and they will presumably have fewer incentives than any other types of workers to enter modern industry. The same observation would seem to be applicable to Indians who are engaged in trading occupations, although they are the ones who have "acquired a notion of the value of time" that would in part answer that of industry.

The customary "task system" poses some special problems. First, supervision of those habituated to that system will tend to assume special importance and is likely to require a far more detailed organization in the assignment of tasks than is normally expected in industry (the necessity for oral instruction due to general illiteracy is here recalled).

Second, the "task system" has some implications with regard to hiring or job contracting and remuneration. Inasmuch as work consists, in the ordinary Indian situation, of a series of distinct jobs or tasks, time remuneration, as customary in industry and as preferred in most labor legislation, is not apt to strike a familiar chord among Indian workers. For instance, it is reported that Indian and Cholo workers, newly inducted into mining work, frequently fail to realize that large (for them) balances of wages are being kept for them by the paying office; instead, they ask the boss for little "advances," just as they used to ask the hacienda patrón for little advances against future crops and work obligations.[16] Thus there may be anticipated a pronounced disparity in understanding of work and remunerations as between these and modern industrial workers. For Indians the work unit, the finished product, is a completed task, and it is the completed task or product that is paid for. In other words, the conceptual and contextual precedent for remuneration is piecework remuneration, not remuneration for any slice of time spent working. It is hard to see how the confrontation in the industrial situation with a continuously incomplete task will make sense to the Indian, must less that a reward is bestowed for it. After all, Indians deal, no matter what the task, with visible wholes, not parts, of a product, even where operations themselves are divided among various individuals. The whole is, quite literally, not lost sight of, even in large household industries, where there is division of operations but not real specialization.

It should be clearly understood that piecework remuneration in industry is not advocated here as an incentive for Indians to work harder, or to avoid idling or cheating on the job; as such, piecework is of doubtful value since incentives have to come from somewhere else. Besides, Indians are industrious and work-habituated, thus "disciplined" to that extent. The justification for piecework remuneration rests here on existing work habits and work patterns and on this form's being understandable to Indians. In fact, this is a practice they may expect from an industrial employer, much as they might expect, analogously, the furnishing of food and drink as part of their regular remuneration or in support of any special efforts.

NOTES

1. See Parsons (1945:185) and Santiana (1949:243-44) for the only--and at that, very sketchy--descriptions of a "typical day," which include that kind of tasks. Also Collier and Buitrón 1949:63-64.

2. Buitrón 1947a. For a fuller description, including time scheduling, of household textile industries in Ilumán, see IEAG 1953, No. 3:164 ff.

3. The unit of work performed in Chimborazo haciendas is a raya, one man-day's work, women's and children's work being counted as one-half raya, and as such is entered in the daily work books and other accounts of the hacienda and kept track of by the huasipungeros. See IEAG (1953, Nos. 10 and 11:19, 35, 47-49, and passim), for these and other details connected with work-assignments on haciendas.

4. Buitrón and Buitrón 1947:61-62, 66-67, 71; Buitrón 1949c, Table 2. A wedding fee, to be paid by the groom, may include (besides a cash payment) a tarea of fifty stones for the church (IEAG 1953, Nos. 10 and 11:60). See also Saenz 1933a:108-10, on hacienda work regimes; Serrano Moscoso 1946, summarizing labor legislation and labor contract provisions; and Moomaw 1946:166-67.

5. Buitrón and Buitrón 1945:10; Garcés 1941:23, 24; Parsons 1945:10 (also for the points following in the text).

6. Rivet 1903; similarly, Moomaw 1946:172. See also such behavior of a huasipungero, assigned by his master to woodcutting far away from his homestead, as described in Icaza's novel (1934).

7. Buitrón and Buitrón 1947:72. That "time values" change among certain groups is explicitly declared by Rubio Orbe (1953), in reference to Otavalo Indian vendors of textiles who travel long distances using autobus, railroad, and even airplanes.

8. On mingas, see Buitrón 1947a; Cisneros Cisneros 1948:187; IEAG 1953, No. 3:48-50; IEAG 1953, No. 11:135 (who also mention a new form, minga de Oyari, which is an abbreviated minga held from daybreak to breakfast-time among huasipungeros and Indian farmers who, after concluding the job, return to their regular daily tasks); Collier and Buitrón 1949:116-23; Garcés 1941:31; Murra 1947:820; International Labour Organisation 1949:94-96; Parsons 1945, passim; Rodríguez Sandoval 1949:95-96; Saenz 1933a:95-99, 111, 129-30, 190; Santiana 1949; Zambrano 1951:190.

9. Buitrón 1947a, commenting on such a housebuilding party.

10. Rivet 1903. The types of mingas held on behalf of persons or bodies who do not reciprocate in like manner by contributing personal help on another occasion have often been cited as survival forms of forced labor or tribute labor (mita), which was current in precolonial and colonial times and during republican times. These mingas have, on this ground and on others, been assailed as abusive of the Indians. It is difficult to draw the line between the voluntary and the forced aspect of minga in these cases, and there is no doubt that such systems lend themselves to impersonal and personal abuses, even though features may be incorporated that bespeak the meaning of voluntariness and reciprocity that is of the essence of minga. Thus there may be present the hacendado's bounty of chicha at a potato-harvesting minga, but the

overseer's whip may figure just as prominently (see Franklin's eye-witness account of what is to all intents and purposes a minga /1943: 80-81/). For a publicly arranged minga for the building of a trail, see Ferdon 1945. Daily newspapers sometimes carry announcements of local administrative officials for a minga to be held, say for the build-ing of a section of highway or railroad, to which the populations of the respective localities are bidden.

11. Indians' working "rhythm" is slower than that of members of the other ethnic groups; and they are "less agile" than Whites and Mestizos, "lacking in nervous energy, and rarely execute forceful movements" (León 1952; cf. Florney 1945:33 with his description of Indian pace of work and his own irritation, cited in the introduction to Part II). One of the reasons given for Indian boys not taking part in playing football at school is that "they are very heavy-footed /pesados/ and are no good" (no sirven) (IEAG 1953, No. 3:228).
It is certain that Indians normally will not "snap to work" nor exhibit the kind of pep to which we are used, say, in an American soda jerker. The problem, if it is one, permits of several explanations and may be a matter of incentive and interest, of health, or simply one of habituation, analogous to the question of physical makeup and motor habits already discussed.

12. Cf. Zambrano (1951:190), considering all craft work: "...this work is carried out individually or by families and has nothing of the communal."

13. This should be distinguished from the fact that rations of food and drink are often part of the actual compensation for regularly and in-dividually employed workers, such as hacienda peons. The above point should also be distinguished from the discussion regarding the necessity for industry to furnish its workers with food, from the point of view of health and physical efficiency.

14. A reminder of the grog-drinking British Navy and the dry American Navy seems not too impertinent here; also of the tea and coffee "addic-tions" and the work-breaks of, respectively, British and American workers.

15. Developments made during the second World War regarding arrange-ments of industrial work within the plant seem very pertinent to this particular point. These developments are reported to have occurred in the arrangement of work processes in mass production and consist of changes in the assembly layout in concept from the orthodox layout in space (or time). See Drucker 1946; also Digby 1949; cf. Staley 1952: 32 ff. on alternatives of organizing work processes in a factory.
It is to be wished that industrial and educational psychologists of the Gestalt school would interest themselves in this particular problem, as well as in the whole question discussed in these two chapters and in those problems which relate to skills and technical education discussed in the previous chapters. One such approach that has come to notice regarding training in specific skills is that presented by King 1947-48.

16. Franklin 1943:81-82. Cf. IEAG 1953, Nos. 10 and 11. This point and those raised further in the text may be compared with a suggestion that "it is conceivable that the pattern of working men's habits and social attitudes might be changed by altering the wage time span, that is, by paying wages at monthly or quarterly intervals instead of at weekly in-tervals" (Cohen 1949: esp. pp. 155, 156).

X / THE PLACE OF THE INDIANS WITHIN
THE GENERAL SOCIAL STRUCTURE OF ECUADOR

A. Ecuadorean Society - General Considerations

To apprehend the structure of Ecuadorean society various criteria could profitably be used. Simple differentiation of its population into groups could, for instance, be indicated by reference to habitat. That such differentiation exists has been shown in discussing Ecuador's geography and its population distribution. Different modes of life do prevail among the coastal, ethnically mixed population, the montuvios, and the highlanders, or serranos, who are identifiable and, in fact, largely identified as Indians. But no question of, for example, relative social power would be involved in this sociozonal classification.[1]

Another possible classificatory scheme would express social differentiation in terms of the population's urban-rural composition. The distinction can be safely, but only impressionistically, stated to be of great importance. However, there is a dearth of agreement and of empirical data as to what constitutes urban and rural, both for demographic purposes and for purposes of social analysis, in particular, of social stratification.

For instance, García Ortiz (1946:170-71) conceives of the "urban" (lo urbano) as a human conglomeration limited to a perimeter within which houses are built, streets laid out in symmetrical order and grouped about a plaza, the whole designed on a rectangular grid-plan; the rural settlement, on the other hand, the habitat of the campesino ("rural dweller"), is characterized by a planless dispersion of dwellings. One difficulty in this scheme, however, is that the urban dweller or the dweller on the urban periphery does not necessarily lead a life that is associated with an urban setting (a matter evidently taken into account by the census category of "suburban"). The proportion of ecological urbanites who are farmers in smaller towns and laid-out villages is generally high. Yet, the bipolar urban-rural differentiation of the total society cannot be ignored, for the simple reason that the attitudes and evaluations of urban and rural express a hierarchical order of social values, entirely comparable to the attitudes particularly of Latin Europe (France, Italy, etc.) and areas contiguous to it. The Ecuadorean campesino, the chagra ("country dweller," "peasant"), is a specimen of humanity that ranks beneath the cuidadano (which means, significantly, both "urbanite" and "citizen"); the campesino is a country bumpkin, a yokel, but in a far more accentuated sense than his Anglo-American congener, the backwoods farmer. The attitude (cf. Caplow 1952:258, 260) is very likely correlated with the centralistic political organization and the opposition of the capital or metropolis to the "provinces," and with the general stream of life in which the modern and the traditional are so antithetical.

The social structure of Ecuador could be seen in terms of two dimensions or two principles. One indicates society as composed of groups distinguished on historical-cultural grounds, albeit in biological terms, as Whites, Mestizos, and Indians (and/or Negroes, as the case may be). This principle does not by itself necessarily imply stratification. It merely points to the coexistence of groups within each of which social stratification proper might autonomously be possible.

The second principle indicates a general, all-pervasive stratification involving "ranking" in the sense of evaluated statuses. In the case of Ecuador it is the kind that can best be spoken of as constituting an estate society.[2]

Throughout this and the following chapter we shall be concerned with social relations in these two terms, namely, with estate (stratificatory) relations, on the one hand, and those arising from the coexistence of ethnic groups or plural or parallel cultures, on the other. The present somewhat formalistic description of Ecuadorean social structure is offered in part in order to facilitate a better understanding of matters subsequently to be dealt with and in part, and mainly, to indicate the social setting within which industrialization might occur.

Over-all Ecuadorean society is here likened to a society structured along estate lines. It is at least the author's view, derived from a consideration of all available indications, that the criteria by which to designate this society as a caste or class society are not present to the same extent as those by which to diagnose an estate-ordered society. In the interest of brevity the case shall not be argued at length here. An estate society, at any rate, is what one might expect in view of the historical precedents and the historical development of Latin American countries, in so far as they continue, to so marked a degree as does Ecuador, the tradition of the social order of the Spanish and Catholic world of the late fifteenth, sixteenth, and seventeenth centuries.[3] That this tradition is, in an appreciable measure, continued is best attested by those writings which inveigh against it.

Within such an order--a society still organized on the estate principle--the uppermost estate group is composed of those who continue that tradition: a nominally Spanish-derived criollo element, which leads a mode of life that is, or tends to be, leisurely; whose model is still the tradition and ethos of the hidalgo ("knight"); which may still enjoy the possession of landed estate or else languish in genteel penury; which is active in matters political, military, literary, intellectual, etc.-- the stratum that today is ordinarily spoken of as blancos ("Whites"). The status accorded to it, or arrogated by it, is extended, of course, to those who now engage in modern occupations (such as business, industry, the professions), are educated, live in the city, wear modern-style clothes, and partake to a greater or lesser extent (and sometimes no more than vicariously) of modern metropolitan life.[4] Their status or rank, however, is by no means bound only to the fact that they are lily-white or that they are wealthy. Neither the one nor the other attribute is decisive by itself.

The low-status group within such an order is traditionally constituted by the Indians, that is, historically speaking, the vanquished and conquered tribute-paying and service-rendering mass of the natives, now an illiterate and, at least in the terms of the superordinated status group, an uneducated group, politically inactive and nonparticipating, low manual laborers and grubbers in the soil par excellence.

Such is the historically derived bipolar structure. As will be seen presently, much of the relationship and behavior manifested between "Whites" and "Indians" can be referred directly to this type of structure.

But there exists an intermediate stratum or group which shades out into both extremes, the "Mestizos" or "Cholos." This group or stratum owes its origin to the racial, as well as to the cultural, mixture of the Spanish with the aboriginal people. Today, the Mestizos represent a somewhat more urban element (thus they may be urbanized Indians)[5] and, occupationally, the class of manual workers as well as that of craftsmen, artisans, and shopkeepers of the cities, towns, and villages.[6] So far as three strata are distinguished in highland Ecuador, the Mestizos tend to hold an intermediate status position. Yet there are important and significant exceptions--exceptions which are not related solely to the indefinite and fluid terminology and conceptions by which distinctions are expressed for these three groups or strata. Although such a third stratum or group is terminologically distinguished, and although certain criteria of a relatively superficial nature provide the bases for such distinctions, the "typical life chances" within the social as well as within the economic order are in fact very largely identical for Indians and Mestizos. This identity may further extend to the "style of life" or the "mode of living" of both these groups, particularly in the rural areas.

The existence and recognition of this interstitial or middle group bespeaks an atypical aspect of what is otherwise here considered to be an eminently estate-stratified society, an aspect which is of the utmost importance: this society is not rigidly departmentalized. Whatever barriers exist to social mobility are not inherent in the system (except, perhaps, in the matter of access to the top social stratum of the "old families," and even that has been breached in the course of history) but somewhat extraneous to it. These obstacles consist in geographical isolation, lack of communication and educational facilities, etc., rather than in factors immanent in the social setup. The attributes and symbols, at least, of a superior status are accessible to members of the lower status group, certainly in theory, and appreciably so in actuality.

Furthermore, relatively little significance is attached to the racial or genetic makeup of any given individual, even though he or his group may be spoken of in terms denoting "race" in the biological sense.[7] What we have, then, is an "open"-estate society,[8] which means that there are no tendencies toward the kind of major and minor coagulations which pose the well-known problems of such industrial or industrializing countries as, for instance, the United States, the Union of South Africa, or India.

Considering this dynamic aspect of Ecuadorean social structure, it is of course difficult to distinguish its estate-orientation from class-orientation. It is true that to all appearances there is a restructuring along (economic) class lines taking place, particularly within the urban areas. Furthermore, the relations of the various groups to each other in Ecuador, as in other Latin American countries in general, have very largely been treated polemically and in terms of "class" in the generic as well as in the more strictly economic sense. But neither is the process leading toward a class society all-pervasive nor are the class interpretations exhaustive of this "social reality." A few observations to this point follow.

First, stratification in terms of economic, i.e., propertied, and also occupational, classes runs through all three ethnic groups. Indians as well as non-Indians may, for instance, be propertied, though the property scales may differ; equally, employers and employees are found in all groups, although employer status among Indians is rare. Second, the moving of Indians into the category of Mestizo or White cannot be predicated upon the sole fact that an Indian is economically

well off. There are examples of Indians acquiring the attributes of
Mestizohood, such as costume, because they cannot afford the clothing
associated with the status of Indian. Thus it is possible for Mestizos
to become the lowest status group, as has occurred in Otavalo. There
are Indians who, because of wealth and education, qualify for, and in
fact acquire, a White status directly.[9] In brief, improvement in the
economic position does not, by itself, lead to classwise ascendancy.[10]
On the contrary, there are tendencies for Indian groups to develop even
greater differentiation as over against the other two strata or groups
on the basis of Indian economic improvement. These tendencies can
be inferred from the hypothesis held by Murra ("...In the case of Otavalo,
/acculturation conditions/ indicate that contact with a cash economy has
strengthened, rather than weakened, Indian life")[11] on what appears to
be quite substantial grounds and apparently also, though more implicitly,
by Buitron, both guided by observations of Otavalo Indians. And while
such a hypothesis might apply to only a minority of the Ecuadorean
Indian element, it indicates possible processes and developments which
would be incomprehensible under a class interpretation of Ecuadorean
society.

In sum, and seen from an over-all perspective, Ecuadorean society
in general is such as to provide scope for change in personal status, however understood. There is scope for drifting or stepping into another
"station" as opportunity arises. Within the limits of opportunities and
conditions other than social, choice is possible regarding one's "style
of life."

This statement on the character of Ecuadorean society serves to
forestall any misapprehensions regarding a rigid inflexible structure
into which industrialism would have to accommodate itself as best it
could. The very difficulties that arise for the social scientist who attempts to capture Ecuadorean "social reality" into neatly packaged
categories[12] should testify to the fluidity of the Ecuadorean social structure, although, by and large, it is not a class structure.

In the balance of this chapter we propose to show how reports on
the character of the Indians and how their specific behavior vis-à-vis
non-Indians bear out both their estate position and their cultural differentiation.

In descrying manifest behavior as a function of an estatal order and
in terms of manifest forms of subordination and superordination, a first
hint will be provided as to the behavior that may be expected to assert
itself at least initially in an industrial situation. As has already been
indicated, we shall, incidentally, dwell on the ideas held by members of
one group or stratum about those of another, since such ideas might, by
themselves, predetermine relations within industry.

We shall be concerned also with a detailed analysis of intergroup
or interstratum contacts, particularly so with reference to the occasions
giving rise to such contacts and to the manner in which they are made.
The bearing of such analysis on the question of recruitment of industrial
labor and on the problem of continuing transgroup or transstratum communication within and beyond the industrial association will be apparent.

B. Indian-White Relations

Three sets of evidence are offered by way of indicating the relations
that obtain between Indians (including Indianized Mestizos or Cholos or
"Indo-Mestizos") and Whites.

The first of these consists of a sample of the impressions which Indians have made and are making on non-Indian travelers and casual observers. It is from these impressions that a sort of "image" of the Indian is derived.[13]

The second set consists in Indian behavior vis-à-vis the non-Indian observed and described in greater detail.

The third set, not sharply distinguished from the foregoing, consists of the criteria which are employed by Indians to differentiate themselves from non-Indians by personal characteristics and personal attributes, behavior, and verbalizations.

Hassaurek has dealt at length with the "Indian character," and there is much in his observations and comments that reflects convincingly the social relations obtaining between Indians and Whites. Here is how he sketches the Indian:

> He salutes you submissively as you meet him, but the white man hardly deigns to answer his salutation....The Indian is like an outlaw, at the mercy of everybody, and everybody's slave. But his stupefied and beastly nature never revolts. He is the personification of abjectness, beastliness, and servility.

> They /i.e., the 'common people' of the interior as a whole/ seem to have learned submissiveness and humility from the Indians, who are perfectly helpless and rightless. Everybody kicks them, everybody insults them, but they never resent. Indian farm laborers, after having been whipped at the command of their masters, address them, hat in hand, and as polite and pliable as if nothing had happened....He is always humble, always submissive in words, but generally very backward in actions.

> It is neither in him, nor in the circumstances in which he lives, to be anything else /but a beast of burden and a drudge/ . He is destitute of all ambition, of all energy, of all industry, of all spirit of enterprise. He is accustomed to being a slave....Like children, the Indians live for the moment only....Their improvidence knows no bounds....All the virtues by which good men excel, are unknown among them. They are completely imbruted; completely stupefied. They have forgotten the ancient glorious traditions of their race....The most that can be said in their favor is that they are not savages; they are humble and submissive, docile and obedient, abject and timid; and...they scarcely ever commit acts of violence....And yet these poor creatures are, after all, the most useful members of Ecuadorean society.

> The Indian does more work than all the other races together.... He is harmless and inoffensive, good-natured, and easily manageable. But his position in the social scale is in inverse proportion to his usefulness. He is far below the North American Negro. The work Indian is a term of contempt, even among Indians themselves....Filthy, servile, superstitious, drunken, indolent, as they are, they claim our sympathy and commiseration. [14]

Rivet, in discussing the Indians in the region around Riobamba (Chimborazo), for the most part debt-bound serfs, sums them up in similar terms some forty years later: guarded, slavish glances, excessive politeness, servility, fearful and sly, thievish (though honest among their fellow-Indians) and lying.[15] And like others since, Rivet elsewhere compares the eastern lowland Indians, the "savages," favorably with the tamed highland Indians.

The Jivaro does not have the submissive, humble, cringing appearance, I might almost say servile, of the civilized Indian; much to the contrary, everything in him reveals the free man, passionately loving liberty, incapable of putting up with the slightest subjection. [16]

Saenz, too, finds the Ecuadorean Indian amiable and submissive in his daily work and, in contrast to the Mexican Indians, humbly saluting his superiors on the road. Toward the white man he shows a natural reticence and, though supposed to hate the White "with a concentrated hatred," manifestations of hate are rare (Saenz 1933a:165-66).

The descriptions of Indians and of individual encounters with Indians, scattered throughout Franklin's book, convey the same impressions: the Indians and Indianized Cholos "cringe and grin in obeisance"; in refusing a service to a gringo ("foreigner") they are nevertheless "very humble, very polite"; the hand extended to catch the other's to kiss is covered with the poncho. [17]

One observation is worth quoting in full (Franklin 1943:260):

The feudalism of Cayambe is palpable. The attitude of each individual defines at a glance his place in the crystallized, rigid class system. The Indian of Cayambe, while he is more given to self-assertion than the indios anejos (hacienda serfs) of Tungurahua, Leon, and Chimborazo, is a churl. It is in his gait and his address.

These examples may suffice to convey a picture of the most general type of interestate behavior and comportment. Social distance between "high" and "low" strata and their members takes the extreme form of utter subservience so far as Indians in general are concerned. Hence the traits just characterized express the "normatively patterned relationship" in such interstratum situations.

That this behavior and comportment is the general norm is underlined when the exceptions which exist (and which are duly noted as exceptions by observers are considered.

First, here is an example of change of behavior that can be related directly to a change in the social environment. Franklin compares urban workers with rural Indians in these words (1943:107, also 108):

The railroad and factory workers are an anachronism in Quito. Happy, grimy industrial workers, they have a devil-may-care grace about them, a literate, sophisticated sense of humor, and a metropolitan habit of conversation. They do not cringe. Their words are not punctuated by the apologetic "sinurr" /senor, "sir"/. They are like industrial workers everywhere.

More important, perhaps, are the observations of the same author regarding the differences in the behavior of Indian and Cholo mineworkers toward their boss--the context indicating that these miners were but recently recruited from among that servile rural workers' stratum for work at a North American-owned and -managed mine. The author finds himself "particularly impressed with the fact that the sudden appearance of their boss did not cause them to cringe and grin in obeisance as they had been accustomed to on the land from which they had come....They did not stand by, watching, the foolish smile of praise on their faces, as they would have done in the presence of an overseer, or the lord of the hacienda, before their contact with the Mine."[18]

The bearing and comportment, or the "estate behavior," of other identifiable groups in the highland region also provide a marked contrast-- always on the basis of impressions--to the people elsewhere considered Indian. According to Franklin's observations of the Cholos of the Cuenca region (Azuay Province), "class divisions are stricter and more carefully observed...than anywhere else." There, the pride of the Cholos is as great as that of the landed families of ostensibly pure Spanish stock. The Cholos of Cuenca "are erect men, who look you in the eye...whose physical manner has nothing of the subservience of the typical Andean Cholo, but who, on the contrary, conveys a certain pride of race and of class which excludes the foreigner and the ciudadano." These Cuenca Cholos clearly differentiate themselves from both Blancos and Indians by having their own markets "run by and for cholos, /and/ who manage to impart to the 'decent' visitor /an allusion to the gente decente, "proper" or gentlefolk, the white upper stratum/ and to the Indian a sense of in- trusion into a world not his." These Cuenca Cholos further differentiate themselves by a distinct and typical dress, by language mannerisms, their Spanish containing not only the usual Quechuanisms but also the vowel pronunciations peculiar to the Quechua language.[19]

Among Ecuadorean highland Indians at large, there are parallel cases of exceptional groups to whom the estatal behavior described in the previous pages does not apply or is at least considerably mitigated. Among them are the famous Otavalo Indians, whose bearing and behavior strike almost all observers because they deviate so markedly from the "submissiveness" of the bulk of highland Indians. Although the con- trasting behavior of many of the Otavalo Indians is often interpreted in terms of "progress" or "transculturation" and is directly or indirectly referred to a comparatively recent spread of the cottage weaving indus- try, there are various hints to suggest that the behavior itself is not a recent development.[20] At any rate, Indians such as those of Otavalo, or of Saraguro in the south (Loja Province), offer a contrast to those of Chimborazo and elsewhere, who "adopt before the white man the attitude of beaten dogs," in that those of Loja and Otavalo are "sure of them- selves, meet the whites openly, without diffidence and hate, without sub- mission and shyness."[21] Nevertheless, even though such as the Saraguro Indians are independent farmers owning their own lands and "are the most progressive of any group with whom we came into contact," they are still observed as they approach and wait "timidly" their turn in a store run by a non-Indian who orders them around, while their children are made to perform the menial tasks at school and to keep apart from non-Indian children.

The fact that there is more information about Otavalo than about any other single group of Ecuadorean highland Indians affords an oppor- tunity to study Indian-White relations in greater detail there and to note the subtleties that characterize them and the behavior by which they are expressed. The estate-focused relation between Indians and Whites in that region is perhaps best brought out in the words in which Mrs. Parsons has characterized it (evidently not as unwittingly as has been the case with many other characterizations usefully employed in this chapter):

...the attitude of the Indians is not at all subservient; rather it is a matter of keeping in their place as a guaranty of inde- pendence. It is more indifferent and impersonal toward Whites

than, shall I say, the American Negro attitude; and the nearest
comparable relationship I know of is, curiously enough, that
between masters and European-born servants in large households
of the northeastern Atlantic seaboard /1945:10/.

A number of examples, especially culled from Parsons' text, show
how distinctions between Indians and Whites (or Cholos considered as
Whites) are actualized, detected, and verbalized by Indians themselves.[22]
They are expressive alike of status distance and cultural differentiation
and thus may, or may not, have been born of oppression. At any rate,
no Indian is seen at night in the streets of Otavalo town. Indians rarely
cross the town's plaza or sit on its benches.[23] They usually keep to one
side of the church. And ordinarily Indians "...always give a White person
the right of way." Indians and Whites have separate cemeteries (Franklin
1943:261). Indians use none of the flour mills, nor the Cholo hand mills,
to grind their corn, but use the old metate and grinding stone, which,
however, are manufactured by Cholos.[24] No Indians are seen participating in handball games, while, on the other hand, no Whites (except Parsons
and her Quito Chola companion) were attending a particular celebration
of Indians--a matter over which the observer exclaims: "In pastime or
pleasure, how much apart they remain, Cholo and Indio!" There are
differences in the manner in which, for instance, Holy Week is celebrated,
the Whites simply attending church services and feasting and dancing at
home, the Indians with elaborate rituals and public celebrations lasting
over several days.[25] Palm Sunday mass is attended by most Indians at
a different hour from the Whites.

Filth and disorder are often held to be a general characteristic of
Ecuadorean Indians. But in the Otavalo region filthy and littered rooms
and a dirty house are marks of the Cholos; the Chola, also, takes orders
from her husband as no Indian woman would.[26] And the beggers observed
by Parsons are Cholos, begging from Indian households.[27]

That the Indians are fully aware of the difference between themselves and the Whites and that differentiation toward Whites on their
part is conscious if not deliberately cultivated is strongly suggested by
incidental intelligence from Parsons and other sources. It is "because
we are Indians" that Otavalo men wear their hair long in contrast to
Whites (on the other hand, they recognize that Riobamba Indians wear
theirs short "because it is their custom").[28] And there is much to suggest that Otavalo Indian differentiation as over against Whites is com-
mingled with contempt. Thus Mrs. Parsons finds that Whites are not
considered desirable spouses because they are lazy and do not know how
to farm. (In Tungurahua Indian circles, too, a man who wears "White"
dress, shoes, and plays pelota, is considered lazy and not eligible as a
husband /Rodríguez Sandoval 1949:99/). Jealousy is a non-Indian trait
in the eyes of Indians: "Only cholos fight over women."[29]

Specific forms of individual and groupwise avoidance also bespeak
the social distance obtaining in Indian-White relations. This distance
is manifested, on the behavioral level, in the remarkably noticeable
"freezing up" of Indians in their encounters with non-Indians, specifically with "Whites."

While dealing with this phenomenon (conceived of as a function of
Ecuadorean social structure and as indicative of the gulf between Indians
and non-Indians), we shall evoke the all-important problem of "communication" within and beyond the industrial association.

Change in behavior, marked particularly by Indian personal (in addition to geographical) inaccessibility and uncommunicativeness toward Whites, has been commented upon frequently and stated in various ways. Thus even in Otavalo,

> in his relations with the whites, the Indian changes completely. He is no longer full of merry spirit, of jest, of good will, strength, life, but becomes a humble individual, silent, without will /of his own/ , apathetic, lifeless....Even though there are a few whites who try sincerely and disinterestedly to help him and consider him as equal, the Indian remains distrustful /Buitròn 1947a/ .

In Otavalo, the uncommunicative Indian offers a sharp contrast to the urban Cholo, and indifference or scorn toward the tourist, i.e., the white man, is marked. The Otavalo Indian does not allow this tourist "to forget that you are not talking with him, but making him talk to you" (Franklin 1943:263). The questions of the inquisitive white stranger are on occasion answered with silence, and the queried Indian manages to sidle away. The Indians' predilection for using bypaths and rough trails rather than highways is explained as a safeguard toward retaining their independence, to keep sheltered from prying eyes, to avoid strangers; and there are concrete examples of Indian behavior in warding off the curiosity of their white neighbors.[30]

Still more marked is the distance-behavior of Indians of Saraguro (Loja Province), of whom Franklin says (1943:174):

> I found it very hard to engage any of them in conversation, either in Spanish or Quechua, since they seemed to have a definite will not to understand what was said by an outsider. This was strikingly different from the giggle of the Otavalo, who thinks a foreigner funny, but tries to make sense out of what he is saying, in spite of all. The Saraguro, on the other hand, is likely to say "si, patron," or "ari, patron" /"yes, master"/, to any question, however phrased.

As the matter is expressed for the Ecuadorean Indian in general, "he does not appear to expect anything from the White, but only wants to be left in peace" (Saenz 1933a:166). The attitudes of Indians who "reject modern culture" are summed up as being either of "cold indifference" or of "depreciation and arrogance" or of "humility that borders on servility," toward Whites, and epithets are employed by Indians with reference to Whites that denote "intruder," "carried hither by the wind," "irreligious enemy" (auca), "base one" (Rodríguez Sandoval 1949:121).

There is no intention here of stretching too far the matter of the uncommunicativeness of the Indians vis-à-vis the non-Indian or the outsider by relating it to their estate position exclusively. Many reasons combine to make access to the Indians, in the literal as well as in the figurative sense, difficult. That difficulty is the _fact_ in which we are now primarily interested.

Among the _reasons_ which may account for the unsatisfactory results in questioning Indians on, for instance, the value of their land, production costs, profits, etc., are undoubtedly, as is pointed out by J. Davis (1946 : 67), the very manner of questioning and the questions themselves; their content and terms cannot but be unintelligible to the Indian. Else he may have reason to fear their purpose--hence misleading, wrong, or no answers.

Again, historical as well as daily experiences with Whites may play a decisive part in creating and reinforcing distrust and a measure of xenophobia. Isolation as such, due to broken territory or distance to population and market centers, and other obstacles to regular contact with the outside world have to be taken into account in searching for causes and reasons for the Indians' uncommunicativeness. Linguistic barriers must, of course, be considered by themselves.

The Buitróns were led to study the matter somewhat more systematically in the course of their inquiry into the living conditions of the rural population of the province of Pichincha. They arrived at the conclusion that the reasons for the marked tendency to avoid Whites, the display of evasiveness, and the general taciturnity found among appreciable segments of that population are to be sought in the relative economic situations of Indians and Cholos. Since their experiences add to the factual material on the subject of Indian uncommunicativeness or Indian-White uncommunicability, it is worthwhile to recount them at some length, together with the arguments and comments that led the Buitróns to their conclusions.[31]

Despite the good will and interest of the investigators, they found that

> there was no lack of individuals in all parts /of the province/ who were extremely distrustful, who were sure, despite all our explanations, that our investigations served no other end but to establish new obligations (impuestos). It took much patience and lengthy and repeated explanations to overcome the distrust which, unfortunately not without reason, some people had.

Some of the campesinos, however, could not be convinced of the investigators' sincerity, in which cases data were secured from more amenable neighbors. But families were also found who grew quite enthusiastic once they understood the object of the investigation and who had no doubt of the investigators' sincere desire to help them, "because up to then nobody had taken the trouble to journey to their homes and converse with them and to learn personally of their needs; they told us fully of their troubles and begged not to be forgotten."

> In El Inca and in general in the zone extending from Nayón to Calderón is where we encountered the greatest resistance to answering our questions and to permitting observation of the homes. Those who have traveled through the region know that it is inhabited by a large Indian population, still wearing its typical dress. The majority of these Indian families own their own land. From this point of view, that is, on the basis of land ownership and relative economic independence, the Indians of that zone very much resemble those of Otavalo. This parallelism and the fact that the Indians of both zones are equally distrustful and shy in the presence of Whites aroused our interest and made us recall the popular and widespread belief that the Indians are distrustful and intractable by nature or that these manifestations are a part of their very spirit, or their idiosyncracies, and that they have no relation to the conditions of their life or any other extraneous factor whatever. Our experience during our contact with the Otavalo Indians and now this one with the Indians of El Inca-Nayón-Calderón has confirmed this popular belief up to a certain point.
> The Indians of Otavalo, excepting of course those of the parcialidades who are considerably advanced in the transculturation process such as those of Peguche, Ilumán, etc., and the Indians of

El Inca-Nayón-Calderón, hide on the approach of a White in their house or abandon it precipitously. When cut off in their retreat and an attempt is made to engage them in the nicest manner in conversation, their answers are evasive, false, or intentionally stupid. Sometimes they exasperate the most patient investigator....

Due no doubt to the possession of land, the Indians of these regions are in a better economic situation than the many Indians who, not possessing lands of their own, have to work as free peons in the villages and haciendas and as huasipungeros or peones conciertos in the haciendas.

In comparing their experiences in Otavalo and in this zone, the Buitrons were at first inclined to accept the popular theory of the "naturally" distrustful and intractable Indian.

But when we carried on the investigation in /other cantons of the province of Pichincha/ we found that the Indians of these zones are neither mistrustful nor shy; nor did they flee or avoid the Whites when they saw them approaching their houses; nor did they resist being interrogated; nor did they answer with evasive, false or deliberately stupid replies; nor did they resist being photographed and it never occurred that they asked to be paid for the photograph that had been taken of them. We have then two Indian groups exhibiting entirely different behavior. What can be the cause of that difference?

In analyzing the conditions of life of the Indians /of these cantons/ we found that they do not possess land of their own and that almost all work as huasipungeros. They live in houses furnished by the hacienda, cultivate lands furnished to them, with oxen and even tools that are furnished by the hacienda. They are Indians who have lost everything. What distrust can they have under such conditions? What do they stand to lose in answering questions which, let us suppose, are designed to establish new obligations? What can they fear on being photographed when all the misfortune the 'evil eye' can bring has befallen them already? Or else if it did befall them, it would matter little to them!

Hence it is understandable that the mistrust of the Indian does not stem from his nature, from his manner of being, but from the material conditions of his life, from something that he is still in danger of losing.

It must be owned that the Buitróns have argued their case on the basis of their own, factual experience and that, moreover, they have argued it logically and plausibly. Still, one may doubt whether their logic is that of the Indians. The communicativeness of the "dispossessed" does permit of other interpretations. In the case of the landless "free" peons, we recall that some of them go from place to place in search of jobs, even though in a narrow circuit; one wonders whether this degree of mobility has not sufficed to lead to a measure of "transculturation" such as to make them face the camera and Whites generally with greater sophistication than their landed, relatively self-sufficient and immobile fellow-Indians. And in the case of the huasipungeros, the "dispossessed" par excellence, it is equally plausible to argue that they have been taught systematically and for generations to "answer civilly."[32] As Franklin puts it for the Saraguro Indians in pursuing the same line of thought, "since the Saraguro has his own house and land, which he owns outright, as does the Otavalo, he cannot be forced into subservience quite so easily as the Indian of León /Cotopazi Province/ and Tungurahua."[33]

However that may be, here we have a set of experiences, arising from a concrete, practical, prosaic task, permitting observation of contrasting attitudes. For our own immediate question, that of approach to Indians and communication with Indians by and in industry, an important hint has been provided; it cannot be taken for granted that any Indian is a hail-fellow-well-met individual, or that discussion with him in terms of equality is the "natural" thing for him, or that any topic will be understandable or of interest to him. If it is not his "being," it is, at any rate, his "existence" that calls for delicacy in approach and for an understanding of customary social relations for successful communication. Our hypothetical industrial personnel manager will have to observe the "etiquette" of Indians as well as that of Indian-White relations, at least initially; otherwise, the Indian industrial novice is likely to become confused, frightened, or, worst, resentful.

But the case regarding the nature of Indian-White relations is not yet concluded. They are further illuminated by other kinds of behavior indicative of "distance." Such behavior may be verbal, as in derogatory expressions (both in terms of reference and terms of address) applied to members of the other group or acted out in various ways; again, it may range from conscious abstention of "imitating" or taking on things and symbols of the superordinated group to open hostility.

There is no disputing the fact that over the centuries a goodly number of things Spanish, European, and White have become part and parcel of Indian life. Nor is there any doubt that many individual Indians today are moving out of their orbit into other strata or groups. Regardless how they may be designated (change, acculturation, transculturation, assimilation, education, urbanization, mestizaje, etc.), these are processes that have been and are continuously operative and by virtue of which Indian life is subject to constant changes--losses and accretions implying acceptance, at highly differential rates and degrees, of modern or originally non-Indian items and patterns. These processes are extremely important, but they are also very difficult to analyze, both as historical and as ongoing phenomena, and, indeed, are not by themselves of concern here. Rather it is the momentary or systemic countertendencies that are to be recorded here as indices of "distance" in Indian-White relations.

There are instances of outright refusal to accept or imitate things considered by Indians to belong to the world of the Whites; many of these are seemingly of no other but utilitarian significance, but they are nevertheless rejected, at least on the verbal level, because they belong to the world of Whites. (That they may happen to be incompatible with existing patterns is, needless to say, a totally different matter.) Among the "symbols" singled out for nonimitation or rejection, then, are shoes, modern city dress, tile roof and wooden floor, saddle and stirrup (for mounts), schooling (e.g., to be teachers for Indians) and literacy (which also happens to subject a person to army service), army service itself (as "useless," a lazy man's pursuit), and the selling or mortgaging of land to Whites.[34] The maintenance of distance from the Whites through such rejections is often referred to an Indian "inferiority complex." As phrased by Indians, however, it is fear of criticism by the group and of adverse gossip (murmuración) that leads them into such negative decisions and evaluations. Either interpretation points to groupwise attitudes as to what is "becoming" to a given status. These are not attitudes bespeaking a class setup.

On the other hand, there are many hints to the effect that deliberate "imitation" of Whites and things White is of the derogatory, ridiculing, or even covertly hostile kind. The clues are taken, in the first place, from some discriptions of Indian dances and from such games as do exist.

For the various dances as also for processions at fiestas there is a good deal of traditional masking and dressing up in roles. Among the impersonations of historical figures, including the conquistadores and other dramatis personae, contemporary White "types," such as hacienda overseers, soldiers, etc., also figure prominently.[35] Similarly, the games which are played at wakes in Cayambe, reputedly "Spanish games" (in contradistinction, as phrased by the Indians, to "Inca games"), contain roles such as that of the teniente politico, priest, sacristan, etc., that is, of Whites in the roles of offices not ordinarily held by Indians. One game consists of the enactment of piano playing, the various participants acting out the roles of "keys" and emitting the appropriate notes on being struck by the piano player. This example is cited merely because it parallels another, in which the ridiculous is emphasized, contained in a semifictional account in which an Indian's attempt to make White life appear ludicrous is clearly conveyed (Parsons 1945: 202; Bemelmans 1944:263-65).

In fact, the impersonations in Indian dances and games are not only straight dramatizations of a traditional theme in ritual form or commemorations of historical events; they also seem to contain elements of malice directed specifically against non-Indians. Imitative mimicking of Whites and white personages can be inferred from descriptions of Indian dances and of Indian masks caricaturing the Spanish; from the laughter which the performance of a clown-dancer imitating others dressed as Blancos draws from the onlooking crowd; and finally, and most suggestively, from the threat, overheard by Hassaurek, of an Indian toward a person who had offended him, that he, the Indian, would mimic the offender at the dance of San Juan. At an Indian dance festival held at Quito, Whites are ridiculed in one of the dances called Los Abagos ("The Underdogs"?), representing the Whites in costumes of rags and tatters, denoting badness, the Indians as angels.[36]

That mimicking elements in dances, dramatic performances, and games suggest a covert hostility toward Whites and contain traces of animosity, albeit masked in conventional forms, is the more plausible as overt manifestations of hostility seem comparatively rare. Special occasions, however, such as fiestas, give rise to behavior by which resentment of and animosity toward Whites, non-Indians, or other outsiders may be displayed. Thus, when drinking, Indians tend to become boastful and self-assertive, though they are reputed even then never to attack Whites.[37] Nevertheless, instances are recounted when the Indians' normal politeness toward Whites disappears during fiestas. On San Juan's Day, White Otavalo townsfolk are apprehensive of the Indians because at this time "their usually submissive neighbors tend to be self-assertive and overbearing. For one thing, the dancers dress like Blancos and carry whips. They are heavily policed by the town authority."[38] While these precautions are only partially prompted by Indian "overbearing" behavior during fiestas, they nevertheless seem to indicate a traditional fear on the part of Whites of Indian revolts and uprisings--a fear which persists from colonial days and which has the character of a "convention" much as other traits ascribed to Indians are matters of conventional beliefs.

Yet fears of open Indian hostility appear not entirely groundless. Local uprisings, revolts, and skirmishes[39] involving Indians have occurred intermittently since Spanish days. Especially did the latter part

of the eighteenth century see a series of "rebellions," on a lesser and far
more localized scale than the famous movement of Tupac Amaru in Peru
(1780) but starting a decade earlier. It is of interest to note that these
early centers of unrest--Otavalo (Imbabura), Patate (Tungurahua), Guano,
Guamote, Columbe (Chimborazo)--not only enjoy a comparatively better
economic situation (crafts and/or owner-farmers) and viability, and are
in part the most "Indian" groups, with relatively intact cazique organization and communal land purchases and holdings, but also seem to have
continued in major or minor measure a tradition of obstreperousness (as
seen from the White point of view). The best-known in this last respect
are the Indians of Salasaca,[40] who may have been implicated in the 1770
uprisings of the Indians of Patate (which parish was also the scene of a
bloody uprising of hacienda workers in 1923). The Salasaca Indians themselves (whose territory today adjoins that of Patate) enjoy something of
a reputation for intractability: they obstructed the building of a highway
through their territory some years ago, more recently (1945) forced a
visiting Mexican anthropologist to flee, and of late figured in the news as
having committed marauding attacks on relief columns working toward
the disaster-stricken areas following the 1949 earthquake of Ambato. In
general, it seems that it is Indian groups in the north and central highland provinces (Pichincha, Imbabura, Chimborazo, Tungurahua, and,
apparently since more recent times, Cotopaxi) among whom a sense of
provocation--to put it in the most neutral terms--is alive.

It would be rash, however, to consider all these Indian revolts and
uprisings as directed primarily against Whites qua Whites. The character of the recorded outbursts makes it clear that they were directed
against specific abuses and the White perpetrators of them, that they
were born of vexation or misunderstandings as to issues and purposes.
Bloody incidents occurred in the course of litigations--one of which,
at least, is reported to have lasted some eighty years--between haciendas and Indian communities over boundaries or other rights to land
and water resources. The activities of health inspectors combatting
rabies by killing dogs throughout the countryside (Linke 1946), or of census takers,[41] have provoked serious incidents. Still other local uprisings are evidently in the nature of "strikes" and part of an incipient
labor movement spreading among agricultural workers.[42] It is entirely
a matter of conjecture--but these cases of turbulence may be the only
ones among Indians that are not quite so spontaneous, nor quite as
ephemeral and undirected, as other episodes. So far, at any rate, there
is little to indicate the existence of a state of permanent, active, and
overt hostility, much less open warfare, between Indians and Whites
as social strata or otherwise. Nevertheless, there are a few communities, whose number is not known, which have been isolated for such a
long time that they have kept a certain independence and are little influenced by Whites. Visits by non-Indian outsiders are risky, so much
so that even the priest on his visits on holy days has to be escorted in
and out (Murra 1947:819).

The main results of this survey of modes of behavior prevailing
between Indians and non-Indians have largely substantiated our initial
suggestion that Ecuadorean society is an estate-oriented society. Distance markes the relation between Indians and non-Indians. And the
behavior of the former toward the latter ranges all the way from "keeping their place" to "keeping apart."

Here, then, the main points will be summarized of which the promoters of industrialization have to be aware in entering this situation.

Indians as a whole impress the outsider by behavior denoting social distance from, specifically subordination to, the non-Indian. Attitudes and behavior of a subservient and compliant nature are pronounced among the mass of hacienda-bound workers and also among "free" peons.

Apparent--and important--exceptions to or deviations from this typical behavior have been noted, most significantly (on the face of it) in the case of recent recruits in mines (which, nota bene, were under non-Ecuadorean management). At first glance, this case suggests that the usual interestate behavior disappears with relative ease with a change from one social milieu to another, particularly where the latter is, so to speak, extraterritorial.[43] But that behavior here is plastic and adaptable simply indicates again the lack of rigidity of the Ecuadorean social structure. Nevertheless, this one case does not properly constitute a sufficient basis for generalization. It cannot indicate, for instance, whether behavior changes will occur in the case of massive recruitment and systematically stimulated inductions of Indians into industrial situations and into manufacturing industries. In addition, it is not possible to tell whether the startling abandonment of outright servile behavior is more than skin-deep and only "for the duration" of mining or industrial employment.

A variation of behavior bespeaking social distance occurs in the case of relatively cohesive Indian communities which, perhaps on the basis of economic near-self-sufficiency, perhaps for historical reasons, have preserved a measure of cultural independence and integrity and a degree of nonofficial autonomy. In the case of such Indians, attitudes and behavior of standoffishness, constraint, and uncommunicativeness are combined with tendencies toward invidious comparison and self-assertion as over against non-Indians.

Distance-behavior thus appears to be compounded of latent or manifest but, in any case, perpetuated subordination and of voluntary differentiation--a differentiation, incidentally, that extends to other interethnic (inter-Indian) relations (see Chapter XI). We may venture to say that, among such Indian groups, Indian-White relations have unilateral aspects: from the point of view of most "Whites" relations may be conceived as essentially up-and-down relations, while from the point of view of these Indians the same relations tend to assume the more "tolerant" meanings of relations toward outsiders or strangers.

At any rate, the hard core of the problem consists in the fact that there are relations of distance, marked by secretiveness toward, avoidance of, and uncommunicativeness toward "Whites." Whether social distance is maintained on the basis of differentiation in status or on that of differentiation in "culture," access to Indians is difficult. Uncommunicativeness and avoidance; the lack of a "common universe of discourse"; and an ever-present fear of strangers or outsiders and mistrust of their motives--these are the palpable obstacles to free and direct social intercourse between Indians and non-Indians. Degrees in these types of distance-behavior and attitudes have been noted and their significance discussed; whether these traits are inversely related to the economic positions of Indians is not altogether proved and remains a matter of doubt.

Another fact has been established, namely, that the total highland Ecuadorean social situation is pregnant with divisive tendencies arising from status privileges and obligations, on the one hand, from cultural differentiations, on the other. Yet, and this matter cannot be sufficiently emphasized, this situation does not consist of a segregation of "races"

or "castes," brought about and maintained essentially unilaterally by
one of them, but of separation, primarily of estates and secondarily of
ethnic groups (by virtue of their cultures), bilaterally observed. It is
this separation that might insinuate itself into the industrial situation.

Inasmuch as interestate attitudes and behavior are likely to persist at least for a while within the industrial situation or during the
process of industrialization, it may be that those Indians who enter
industry from the concierto and similar dependent situations will turn
out to be preferable from the point of view of industrial discipline.
Habituated as these hacienda Indians are to subordination, a greater
degree of compliance and obedience[44] may well be expected from them
than from those Indians who have been their own masters, either as
free peons or as independent, self-employed farmers and craftsmen.
However, it may also be anticipated that such discipline-habituated
Indian workers will require constant, close and minute, and, above all,
personal supervision. For we have clearly seen that their capacity for
subordination, prima facie so favorable for the industrial situation,
is not a "functional" one from the point of view of the industrial association. The "established routines of relationship" between the would-be
managers ("Whites," strangers, outsiders) and the would-be managed
(Indians) are the sharp opposite from "task-conditioned" relations.

It is also obvious that the industrializer, be it in the person of
the manager, the recruiting agent, or other industrial functionary in the
position of having to contact and deal with Indians, faces distinct problems,
and the question of getting in touch and communicating with Indians outside or within the industrial situation is apt to become a matter of prime
concern. Direct and unmediated approach by persons and for purposes
unfamiliar to Indians, as for instance in labor-recruiting campaigns,
is not likely to meet with success. Finally, "conventional" and other
ideas and beliefs held by "Whites" about Indians (and presumably trans-
mitted to the newcomer to Ecuadorean society) may be considered barriers in their own right to Indian-White rapprochement for industrial
purposes.

C. Indian-White Contacts

In view of the palpable obstacles which beset social intercourse
between Indians and non-Indians, it is necessary to inquire into the
specific, recurrent, and face-to-face contacts that Indians and non-Indians
do have, after all, and which are incidental to the ordinary business of
life. This inquiry serves not only to illuminate further the kind of relations that prevail between Indians and non-Indians but also examines,
first, the relation of the Indians to the institutional life of Ecuador in
general and second, the channels of approach to the Indians. Since, as
has been amply shown, the direct approach to Indians tends to present
difficulties, can it be mediated and, if so, by whom?

For over four hundred years, the relations between Indians and
non-Indians as groups have been in the nature of a continuous and relatively close political and economic symbiotic connection or, more precisely, of a functional interdependence. Yet the governing institutions
of a political and legal, religious, and economic order are not institutions
of the Indians; they are creations of the Whites, and they are perpetuated
chiefly by the Whites. The main point is that Indian co-ordination with
these institutions is indirect; it is realized through the institutions' own
formal representatives and functionaries. It is eminently in this manner
that quasi-individual Indian-White contacts occur.

In what capacities are non-Indians commonly known to Indians, and what are the roles the former play in the understanding of the latter? Summarily, the answer is: the priest, the teniente político and the police, mayordomos (stewards of haciendas) and landlords, and lawyers (Buitrón 1947c; J. Davis 1946:82; Franklin 1943:263).

The relation of the priest to his Indian parishioners is variously described. Saenz arrives at the conclusion that the low or parish clergy of Ecuador, in contrast to that of other countries such as Peru, Guatemala, or Mexico, has had and still maintains close contact with the Indians; this clergy is not absenteeist as in some of the other countries, and the parish clergy is very largely recruited from the Indian element--two circumstances which Saenz thinks explain "the benevolent attitude of the clerical class /of Ecuador/ toward the Indian."[45]

In general, however, contact with the priest seems to be neither close nor frequent.

The majority of Indians are beyond the spiritual ministrations of the Church. Except for the occasional festivals and market days and for the population concentrated in some of the comunidades, they rarely have contact with the Church; the free Indian habitat is usually too remote and inaccessible for the clergy to visit. The large haciendas provide a chapel on the estate where at long intervals mass is held for the owner's family and his peons. [46]

And, "relations /of the Otavalo Indians/ with the priest do not extend, except in connection with baptism, to even the most casual relations with the congregation" (Parsons 1945:10).

Relations with functionaries of the church or with types of religious functionaries other than the secular priest are, however, by no means quite as distant nor contact with them so infrequent. Mrs. Parsons' observations seem to indicate that the function of the regular parish priest are eminently sacerdotal, while pastoral activities tend to be in the hands of other religious functionaries.

Contacts with the priest among the Otavalo Indians are limited, barring the passive attendance at church services or the celebration of a baptism or a church wedding. Other occasions for contact occur incidentally to the rendering of personal services by Indians, and such occasions are specific. Thus there is a traditional obligation for the newly married bride to serve a term of eight days in the curacy, but in Otavalo that service is commuted or commutable into a cash payment. There is also the payment of tithes and first fruits to the church; again, in Otavalo the rights to these have been sold by the church to merchants who collect the produce. Finally, there are also faenas ("work stints") in lieu of payment for a baptism or wedding.[47]

More direct and frequent contacts seem to prevail where a monastic order exists whose members often substitute functionally for a curacy in the supervision of its charges. Parsons describes the Franciscan padres as visiting Indian homes and as otherwise instituting certain religious services connected with the Third Order of San Francisco, besides running schools.[48]

Relations with another category of religious functionaries authorized or perhaps only tolerated by the church are much more intimate, and it is possible that Saenz's "low clergy" should be identified with one such functionary, the maestro rezador, as portrayed by Parsons. From her account it appears that this personage is a layman with permanent tenure of office who functions as a more effective intermediary between Indians and church than the priest. Judged by surname, mother tongue, and dress, this praying master is himself an Indian but literate and qualified to execute some religious rituals and to officiate at certain occasions. Apparently under the authority of a higher ecclesiastic, he visits Indian homes up and down the country for more or less extended stays and, in return for his prayers and benedictions, receives lodging and food in them. He partakes of the life of the household as a welcome guest without, however, being shown particular deference; altogether, his relations with his Indian hosts seem to be on an easy and informal footing. Elsewhere, and more generally, these functions are restricted to praying, and are exercised professionally, by poor Cholos in connection with funerals and mourning and commemorative rites.[49]

In the realm of governmental institutions, contact and relations with the teniente político, or with the functionaries of political authority in general, are almost as attenuated as in the case of the priest. The teniente político is in charge of the parish (now understood as a secular administrative unit, and the smallest such unit in Ecuador), which may be "urban" or "rural." Only exceptionally is an Indian, so recognized, appointed to that office.[50] Others of the local political administrative apparatus are a secretary, judges, and the police. Except for the lower ranks of the police, this apparatus does not ordinarily include Indians as such. It functions largely in an urban setting, however small (parish town or village), and is thus comparatively remote from the Indians. Occasions for contact with the local authority are few and simple and consist in the payment of fines (as for disorderly conduct during fiestas), in registering births, deaths, and marriages where such registration is enforced, in furnishing minga labor or faenas for street cleaning, repairs, etc., and in attending law-court matters. Contacts, moreover, tend to be indirect and are often accomplished through the Indians' own alcaldes (headmen) and other more or less informal intermediaries. The scant literature on that subject, for the most part critical toward this setup, reveals little else beyond negative criticism. But there is at least one suggestion that the teniente político may act as a real and effective leader in specific tasks.[51]

Indian-hacendado relations are characterized as "feudal" in the literature, which dwells on the stifling, oppressive, and exploitative features of the hacienda and is silent on any others. Here, too, contacts are few and indirect, as they are effected largely through the mayordomo or administrador (overseer, "steward"; "manager") in his dealings with hacienda peons or, in the case of free Indians, through the mayordomo on the one side and the Indian headman on the other, as occurs, for instance, in negotiating a calling-up or invitation to a minga on behalf of the hacienda. It may be reasonably assumed that the frequency and directness of contacts between mayordomo and Indians vary inversely with the size of the hacienda and the number of its Indian workers. On the very large haciendas such contacts are probably also mediated, and the straw bosses or Indian headmen, as lieutenants of the mayordomo, assume proportionately greater importance. On festive occasions there may be face-to-face meetings between Indians and hacienda owners,[52] as well as in the annual giving of the camari--an obligatory contribution of eggs, chicken, guinea pigs, etc., by hacienda Indians to their landlord, overseer, and foreman, and a reciprocal present to the Indians in the form of liquor.[53]

While the representatives of these institutions--church, government, and landed employer, landlord, or neighbor--"have reality for the Indians," contacts are limited to the most essential functions which bring them about at all. Such as these contacts are, they are marked by the kind of behavior which even on the conspicuous level does not seem to be associated only with that of "mutual economic convenience," as Mrs. Parsons characterizes Indian-White relations in Otavalo (1945:10; cf. Santiana 1949:241). In those rare cases in which this status behavior does not predominate, it is undoubtedly due to the individual and strictly personal qualities of both, or more likely one of, the partners in a contact situation. Such cases are atypical, but instances exist.[54]

The fact itself that contacts as a rule are indirect or mediated deserves some further consideration. The intermediaries mentioned so far, through whom contacts between Indians and non-Indians are effected, act formally, i.e., in their capacities as representatives of formal and official institutions and bodies and personages. Their functions are formal functions; their authority is essentially delegated authority; their intermediacy is an institutional one. The maestro rezador, the Indian alcalde[55] and even the hacienda mayordomo and the Indian mayoral ("foreman"), bridge, ex officio, the gaps, respectively, between the Indian parishioner and the church, the Indian "citizen" (better, perhaps, "subject") and the government, and the Indian worker and the landowner.

There are, however, intermediaries on a relatively informal level who do not depend directly on official institutions and bodies but who nevertheless facilitate a direct linkage between individual Indians and non-Indian individuals or organizations.

The lawyers have already been mentioned. Involvement of Indians in lawsuits, litigations, or conflicts with the law makes necessary frequent recourse to the lawyers. But these "live and practice their profession in the cities, far away from the Indians" (Buitrón 1947c). However, it appears that some lawyers acquire increasing firsthand contact with Indians.[56]

It is largely such legal involvements that have given rise to a class of intermediaries who are called tinterillos[57] but whose function of intermediacy extends to other problems as well. Tinterillos (or quilcas, quishcas as they are termed in Quechua) are, to paraphrase Saenz, smart people who have set themselves up as helpers of the Indians. "They are the intermediaries between /the Indians/ and the civil and ecclesiastic authorities for all minor questions. The Indian takes no step without them for the arrangement of whatever real or supposed problem. If he wants a baptism, a mass, the reading of responses for the dead, or a wedding, he goes first of all to the tinterillo or quilca whom he entrusts personally with the arrangement of the matter with the priest." The function of the tinterillo becomes more important in cases where the Indian has some real difficulties with the authorities, with his neighbors, or with Whites. Often these tinterillos are small shopkeepers or tavern keepers who thus not only have the Indians as their customers but also as their clients.[58] That literacy qualifies an Indian or Cholo for the "office" becomes apparent from Saenz's reference to the Indians of Otavalo, who gradually manifest a greater desire for the schooling of their sons so that they may serve as tinterillos--a proof, according to Saenz, of the Indians' felt need for "some people having their confidence who are capable of dealing with the authorities and with the mestizos in general for the settling of their problems."

For actions involving objects of some value (such as real estate), "the Indian has to present the proper claim of his rights, and it is then that the lawyer (abogado) and not the tinterillo starts functioning."

But before either tinterillo or lawyer is approached, the ñaupador (counselor /?/ in the community)[59] is consulted. The ñaupadores "furnish the information as to whether the matter in hand belongs in the jurisdiction of the tinterillo or of the lawyer."

In Otavalo, the roles of intermediaries (tinterillo, abogado, ñaupador) appear to be assumed to a wide extent by the compadres (the godfathers to the children of individual Indians; in other words, an Indian's "gossips") and on a strictly individual basis.[60] It is asserted even of these relatively "emancipated" Indians that they almost never "approach the civil and religious authorities personally to solve their problems." The Indian always does this by way of a White as intermediary. For this he chooses Whites who suit him as godparents for his children. Hence, "the baptismal godfathers of Indians are always Whites." These aid the Indian in cases of difficulties with the law, arrange for him the christening with the priest, and serve him in similar matters.

The importance of the compadre for the Indians of the Otavalo region is well brought out by Parsons' observations. Although, according to her, "godparents may be Indian or White," "in some families white persons of some distinction are preferred," as "White compadres are an asset for anyone who has business in Otavalo /town/ or Quito." This was the case in the family of Parsons' informant: there an Otavalo town official, a leading merchant, and a Quito physician were the compadres. They were chosen for practical reasons which are illustrated by one instance in which that family was able to afford to disregard a summons to minga work and to have the ensuing fine revoked thanks to its compadre connection with the municipal officer in charge of public works.

The key men or intermediaries in the relations between Indians and non-Indians and the kind and mechanisms of contact between these groups have now been determined. The most powerful, respected, or feared entities (priest, government official, landlord) are physically relatively remote from the Indians although virtually ever-present in their lives in some form. They are in positions of command over, but rarely in direct contact with, the Indians. For effective communication and dealing with Indians they require intermediaries (lay clerics, police, mayordomos, etc.) whose roles, however, are rather in the nature of agency than of intermediacy. True intermediaries, that is, persons whose authority rests less in the office than in the business and problems of Indians, are few. One type of these particular key-men roles has its background not only in the remoteness between Indians and non-Indians but also in the complicated legal system, the Indians' illiteracy and ignorance of the law, and in the frequent involvements in civil lawsuits. These concern mainly land but also questions of habeas corpus and also the fines and threats "by which the tenientes politicos, through their accomplices and agents, the alcaldes, eternally badger the Indian (Franklin 1943:78, 79; Saenz 1933a:134).

The compadres, as in Otavalo, seem best to fulfil the function of being intermediaries between Indians and non-Indians in that they have the least involvement with specific bodies or institutions (they may, of course, be so involved, but this is incidental to the compadreship). They are sought out by the Indians not so much because of pressing specific needs (such as to have to come to terms with the law in a given case) as for the attainment of advantages generally to be wrested from a world that is alien and superimposed upon their own.

It is interesting to note a parallelism for this intermediacy pattern which occurs in quite a different area of Indian life, at least among the

Indians of Otavalo. There, the conception of the saints is that they are "the 'advocates, abogados, of the dead,' and one had better stand in with them"; to which Mrs. Parsons remarks specifically that this is "a point of view I have never heard advanced in other Indian circles"[61] (i.e., among Indians of the North American Southwest and of Mexico).

One important exception to the indirectness of contacts between Indians and non-Indians exists in the market. There, dealings are direct as between members of the two groups. Whether they give rise to any but ephemeral and impersonal relations cannot be said, but it is conceivable that non-Indian wholesale buyers of Indian products, such as textiles, have lasting and direct and possibly personal relations with individual Indians, perhaps via the compadreship, thus reinforcing established business relations.

In the market itself, dealings are nevertheless not quite unhampered by the differential distribution of relative power among estate or ethnic groups or, briefly, between Indians and Whites. Thus a non-Indian shopper may appeal to the policeman to force the Indian seller to lower her price.[62] Also, "for the right to sell their wares on the market square, in a certain town in Ecuador, extra taxes are placed on the Indian which the white merchant does not have to pay," consisting of a tax for the right to enter the market town, another for the right to sell wares, and a third on the wares that remain unsold at the end of the day.[63] But there is no segregation by ethnic groups within the market; there is grouping according to specialization and products (Parsons 1945:30-32).

In summarizing the main results of this survey of Indian-White contacts, it appears that the occasions for contacts between any one Indian and any one White tend to be limited to matters that lend themselves to being easily isolated, strictly business matters, as it were, whether these be with the church and its representatives, government and its officials, or landowner and employer and his agents.[64] Apart from these business-like and mediated contacts, others are apparently so few or appear so trivial as not to find mention in the literature. At any rate, there is no direct dealing, as a general rule, between Indians and non-Indians, and certainly none as between social equals. The intermediaries who have been discussed, both formal and informal, are therefore really key men: They are the keys that make Indians and non-Indians interfunction when called upon to do so. Even so it is doubtful whether what we have called informal intermediaries (tinterillo, White compadre, occasionally abogado) exist to any great extent among the mass of Ecuadorean Indians, in particular the mass of hacienda peons. These types of intermediaries seem to exist largely among independent Indians.[65] There, perhaps (and this question is open to further specific inquiry), some form of clientships or retainerships have become elaborated around compadres, i.e., prominent Whites, tinterillos, and managers of chicherías and possibly other small establishments.[66] If this were found to be the case, the approach to Indians as groups might turn out to be thereby appreciably facilitated. Otherwise individual Indians would have to be sought out via their individual intermediaries.

The foregoing examination of the kind of contacts that usually occur between Indians and non-Indians again demonstrates relations between them to be distance-relations. The fact that the occasions giving rise to contact are few and the contacts themselves tend to require mediation not only is probably a function of the total social structure as previously described but also can be independently related to the remoteness (in every sense) of the country's dominant institutions from Indian life. These institutions have their own representatives and functionaries ("formal" intermediaries). Yet intermediaries whom we have termed "informal" (because not institutionally delegated), and who act on behalf of the Indians, are required in order to render contacts effective and enduring. In other words, if institutions, or organizations and individuals acting in their interest, wish to reach into the Indian sphere, they require the assistance of a lower-echelon intermediary, preferably one "retained" by Indians. The converse necessity for Indians to come to terms with non-Indians and their institutions yields this lower-level intermediacy to some extent.

The applicability of the results of the foregoing analysis to an industrializing situation involving Indians is obvious. As the behavior associated with Indian-White relations may be expected to persist in a novel situation such as the industrial one, the intermediacy pattern as it exists between Indians and non-Indians may likewise be expected to carry over into incipient industry. Moreover, such a new industry in any given region or locality, and reaching beyond the urban environment for its labor, might well take advantage of the intermediacy pattern: rather than employing a direct, individual, and unselective approach lacking "proper introduction," by which it risks prejudicing "friendly relations," it might endeavor to establish contacts and relations by seeking out those personages who enjoy a measure of Indian confidence. These potential contact or key men have been pointed out.

In addition, industry will very likely have to create its own, quasi-institutional, special functionaries, such as labor recruiters,[67] foremen, etc.; these would, however, have to be specially schooled in the delicate tasks of contacting, and maintaining contacts with, Indian workers and would-be workers.

While this chapter has emphasized the Indians as a social stratum (one "estate" among others), we shall consider them in the following more specifically as a distinct ethnic group, starting with the question, "Who are the Indians?" and, "Who is an Indian?" In examining them as such, those elements of their social organization and of their culture will be pointed out which are pertinent to the problem of industrialization with Indian participation.

NOTES

1. The political, better perhaps the party-political, life of the country is said to move back and forth between the liberal, progressive element represented by the Costa and the conservative element represented by the Sierra. The polarity of Guayaquil and Quito is traditional (since Independence) and almost proverbial. It does not, of course, extend to matters political alone, but also to the status, in terms of their economic roles, of the coast, which produces exportable surplus (plantation agriculture) and the Sierra, which works mainly for the domestic market (hacienda agriculture). Cf. Benites 1950:235 ff.

2. The scheme followed here is in the main that of Max Weber, as translated by Gerth and Mills (1946:186-93) and Parsons and Henderson (1947:347, n. 2 and pp. 424-29); also McIver 1937:166 ff.
    To the best of our knowledge, no attempt has so far been made to apply an analysis of modern societies of the type of Ecuador in terms of estate, while analyses in terms of "class" abound, particularly among Latin American writers. It is an open question whether class analyses are really exhaustive of the social "realities" of many of the Latin American

countries, especially those of the Andean and Middle American regions. There have also been attempts, mostly by North American social scientists, to identify the relations between, say, Indians and non-Indians ("Whites") in terms of "caste." These attempts have not, in the writer's view, been wholly successful. But there is no doubt that, within given communities, relations may well appear to be eminently caste-ordered.

In principle, an estate order ought to be distinguished from estate relations, the latter being our real topic. However, this distinction is not always carried through here.

3. As García Ortiz (1951) points out, the Spaniards of the conquest were leaving a society from which feudalism was making a slow and reluctant exit, only to encounter a society in the New World (Incaic Peru) that was entering on a definite, formative phase of feudalism. Similarly Benites 1950:87, with reference to the subsequent formation of the encomiendas (fiefs) in newly conquered Hispano-America. It should be added, however, that feudalistic features are only a part of an estate order.

4. Benites (1950:158 and passim) provides very illuminating sketches of the hidalgo ("petty knight," military noble), his origins, ideals, and position in colonial society, as well as of the changes in systems and nomenclatures of Ecuadorean social stratification from early colonial to modern days. The stratum under discussion is small and in itself stratified, and is considered to be composed today largely of members of a new "middle class" (Paredes 1951; García Ortiz 1951), a proposition which is open to doubt unless considered exclusively within urban settings. On this point, see also Beals 1953; and Jaramillo Alvarado (1943:57, in No. 12), on the absence of a cultured powerful middle class. Franklin (1943: passim) has a number of vignettes on society (gente decente), shading into "upper middle" and "middle middle class" in cities such as Quito, Cuenca, Loja. For characterizations of nineteenth century Ecuadorean society, see Hassaurek (1868:121 and Orton (1875:68 ff.)

5. The processes of adjustment of rural highlanders or Indians to, and permutations resulting from, life in the cities have not yet found any investigators. See J. Davis (1946:45-47, 83) for a few points on the subject: Beals (1951 and 1952) suggests the possibility that Indians may become "urbanized," i.e., modernized, without becoming permanent residents in large cities and without first having become rural Mestizos, i.e., having passed through a phase of acculturation of two hundred and three hundred years ago.

6. Beals (1953) calls this indefinite stratum a "Middle Group" and considers it (as does Tschopik 1952) as such in that it tends to be oriented to a European rather than an Indian way of life, or one in which Spanish rather than aboriginal patterns predominate. The designation is coined to prevent this group from being identified with a nascent "middle class" (as attempted by García Ortiz 1951) or to avoid a treatment of Mestizos in terms of "class" (as does Paredes 1951).

7. The term raza does not necessarily correspond to "race" in its modern, biological meaning; neither does the term casta cover any of the standard sociological meanings of "caste."

8. Beals (1953:336) suggests that among the Latin American countries with large Indo-Mestizo components, Ecuador is probably the least rigidly structured as concerns social mobility.

9. Buitrón and Buitrón (1947:54 ff.) have drawn emphatic attention to this matter; also Buitrón 1947a.

10. This is, however, the position of Saenz (1933a) and that of the majority of writers dealing with Indians and the process leading to Mestizohood
(mestizaje). This process of "acculturation" or "transculturation" is held
to be the result of economic improvement and can be furthered by such
improvement.

11. From an abstract description of a project by John V. Murra, "Community Study of Otavalo, a Quechua Indian Community," in NRC 1946:
44; also Murra 1947:820.

12. Cf. Mishkin 1947:414, in considering the parallel case of Peru.

13. Cf. the parallel conspectus of opinions on the Indians as workers in
the introduction to Part II.

14. Hassaurek 1868:90, 133-34, 186-88. In almost identical phrases, also
Orton (1875:111-12), who finds that the Indian has "shrewdness and penetration, but lacks independence and force." Otherwise the Indian is
characterized as "submissive," "servile," "timid," "superstitious,"
"indolent," "abject, but not without wit." Cf. Stübel (1897:317), who speaks
of the Indians' fateful "Milde und Duldsamkeit." as well as of their
"Verschlagenheit." ("Humility," "mildness"; "patience"; "cunning."

15. Rivet 1903:78-79. Cf. J. Davis 1946:106, speaking of hacienca Indians
of this region and of others: "The hacienda Indian is docile, languid,
slovenly, ambitionless and filthy in his personal habits. He will not
look you in the face as he talks to you."

16. Cited by Stirling (1938:3), from Paul Rivet's "Les Indiens Jibaros,
Etude Géographique, Historique et Ethnographique," L'Anthropologie
18 and 19 (1907, 1908). The above quotation is Stirling's translation.
    Similar comparisons between lowland and highland Indians are
made by Bemelmans 1941:124; Cisneros Cisneros 1948:92-93, 98; Flornoy 1945:67-68; Gill 1940: passim.

17. Franklin 1943:70, 83, 77-78. The last example may be considered
a bit of a joke. The immediate understanding of this hand-kissing act
by those not familiar with Indian etiquette would naturally be one by which
to impute servility to Indians, and one specific to Indian-White status
behavior. However, as Parsons points out, hand-kissing is derived from
both Inca and Catholic custom, and Indians kiss the hand of anyone they
wish to honor, be he Indian or non-Indian. While handshaking is not customary among Indians, in shaking hands an Indian will sometimes cover
his hand with the poncho. See Parson 1945:61, 114, 156; also Buitrón
1951c; Rodríguez Sandoval 1949, passim. On the poncho-wrapped hand,
see Gill 1940:15, 245.

18. Franklin 1943:70. Franklin's observations may be compared with
the surprised comments by a member of a team of journalists visiting
that mine over a little episode consisting in a worker's offering
cigarettes to the "gentlemen" of the press! (Troncoso 1946.)

19. Franklin 1943:215-17; similarly Von Hagen 1949;64 ff. Except for
data on the straw-hat cottage industry centered in this area, other information on this group is woefully lacking. It must be added that
Franklin's and Von Hagen's picture of Cholo well-being in that area
is considerably overdrawn in light of other reports on the plight of the
straw-hat weavers. However, this is certainly one of the rural Mestizo
groups of the Andean area in general "which are as unique and identifiable as are the Indian cultures" remarked upon by Beals (1953:329,
336) and Tschopik (1952).

20. For instance, Hassaurek (1868:276-77) remarks on the reputation Otavalo Indians enjoy in Quito. See also Ceballos 1873:240.

21. Saenz 1933a:166; cf. Hewett 1939:117; Franklin 1943:173-74, 261 ff.

22. The following examples are from Parsons 1945:10, 102, 79, 22, 102, 96, 9-10, 167, 10 (n. 9), 97, 158, 167, 28, 54, 59 (in that order).

23. Indians prefer to walk in the middle of the street in Otavalo town, rather than on the sidewalks, according to Franklin (1943:262).

24. According to my own observations in the Fall of 1950, I found Indians (as judged by dress) using one of the flour mills.
    Mr. John Collier, Jr., tells me that the whole-wheat bread sold in the market of Otavalo is eaten only by Indians.

25. On celebrations and games, see Chapter VII, C. In Otovalo, at school, "a few Indian boys play handball with the Cholo boys" (Parsons 1945:53).
    Up to about fifty years ago church holidays were celebrated in public with the joint (voluntary or compulsory) participation of all strata-- Whites, Cholos, and Indians. See Rivet (1906) for a description of the Good Friday procession in Tulcan in 1902, and reasons for the change since then.

26. One of these examples from Parsons' observations illustrates perfectly the reasons for the indefiniteness of criteria by which to tell Indians and Cholos and even Whites apart. In one of these dirty households Spanish was spoken (White or Cholo trait), but the men wore their hair braided Indian-fashion and the women spun with the native spindle and wore the Indian skirt.

27. The number of beggers and vagrants in rural sections is apparently high (see Suarez 1934:38). There is strong evidence that this "occupation" is generally recruited from Mestizos or Cholos, for Indians are "insured" against public mendicancy through their families. See Rodríguez Sandoval 1949:31-32, 90-91.

28. Parsons 1945:28. Cf. Rivet (1903:58), who explicitly notes the short hair of Riobamba Indians.
    One observer twists the long hair of Otavalo and Loja male Indians into "aggressiveness." According to him (Dale 1946:104-5), these Indians are the most aggressive types in Ecuador, for although they had contact with Whites and other Indians who wear their hair short, "they will persist in their old custom of wearing their hair long. Apparently they have attached new meaning and values out of proportion to the inherent significance of long hair, and look down upon Indians who do not observe this custom."

29. Parsons 1945:54, 59. Statistical data relating to the age of Indian, White, and Mestizo women at marriage tend to indicate that the criteria according to which mates are selected do indeed differ between Indian and non-Indians. See Buitrón and Buitrón 1945, tables and explicit comments on that matter; also Parsons' observation (1945:57); also Rivet (1903), who notes that the age of the bride does not play a role with the Indians as it does with the Whites.

30. Parsons 1945:10-12, 107. On the subject of the Indians' avoidance and distrust of Whites and of the outside world, see also Collier and Buitrón 1949:91; Santiana 1949:239, 243, 245.

31. Buitrón and Buitrón 1947:13-16. The study of Otavalo (Buitrón 1947a) to which reference is made was another pilot study, similar in scope, though less exhaustive and detailed. There, population and other data were secured with the help of the local Indian alcaldes and a member of the Otavalo police who, "himself an Indian, had served on the force for many years and knew almost all the Indians by name."

32. See Benites (1950: 111, 211), for references to enforced politeness in the eighteenth and nineteenth centuries.

33. Franklin (1943:173), where he points out that "Ecuadorians consider the Saraguros refractory workers," while "a nearby American-owned mine holds the opposite point of view." Some cases of obstreperous behavior of Saraguro road workers are there discussed.

34. Andrade Marín (1946), citing instances described in a work by Lic. Segundo Maiguashca, "Rehabilitación del Indio a la Cultura" which discusses the case of an Indian group near Quito whose economic circumstances are better than average and which has schools and other innovations. Other examples in Rodríguez Sandoval 1949:35, 118-21; and IEAG 1953, No. 3:229-30.

35. For extensive descriptions of dances in Otavalo canton, see Parsons 1945:105, 109, 110; Hassaurek 1868:265-83; Collier and Buitrón 1949:104-5; Cisneros Cisneros 1948:186-87, 199.

36. Instances from Orton 1875:110-11; Parsons 1945:105,107; Hassaurek 1868:273; R.V.L. (Rafael Vallejo Larrea) in Previsión Social, No. 10 (Jan.-April, 1942):49-53; (on the "Los Abagos" dance and music, see also Caluccio 1953:17). See also Hewett (1939:117, 118-19) on this aspect of Indian dance comedies "from Peru to Mexico"; and Rivet (1903:79) giving vent to his impression of Ecuadorean Indians in terms that seem very apropos to this discussion: "Moqueur, malicieux, donné d'un réel talent d'imitation, il ne sait que mimer les actes auxquels il assiste et qui le frappent, sans y ajouter rien de personnel." For Peruvian Indians, cf. Valcárcel 1945:181; and Gillin's remarks in Tax and others 1952:260.

37. Buitrón and Buitrón 1945; Hassaurek 1868:271, 298; Parsons 1945: 123 ff.; Saenz 1933a:96-97; Rubio Orbe 1949; Rodríguez Sandoval 1945; Santiana 1949:252.

38. Parsons 1945:108-9, see also pp. 102-3. Elsewhere (p. 111) the reason given for the presence of the police is the bloody quarrels among Indians which are common on such occasions.

39. For references on these points, including "cases," see Benites 1950:152-53, 250; Cisneros Cisneros 1948:209-10; and Tello 1949; Cuestiones Indigenas, 1946, unpaged appendix of illustrations with captions, on the Puruhá of Cotopaxi; Rubio Orbe 1946:66; Saenz 1933a: 118, 119, 127; Rodríguez Sandoval 1949:39, 41.

40. The Salasaca "record"; Buitrón and Buitrón 1946; Cisneros Cisneros 1948:238; Dale 1946:104; Rodríguez Sandoval 1949:86, 87; The New York Times, August 10, 1949; see also sources in n. 39.

41. On precensus experiments and experiences during the taking of the 1950 census in Imbabura and Chimborazo, see Garcés 1950; Buitrón 1951e; Dir. Gen. Est. Censos, Census 1950 (1952:9-10); Linke 1954:10.

42. The labor movement in general had its real start in Ecuador in the early twenties following the first systematic, organized, and bloodily quelled workers' strike in Guayaquil. On the labor movement among agricultural workers, including Indians, especially as concerns one Indian woman leader, see: Bol. Ind. IV, No. 3 (1944):199; Jaramillo Alvarado 1946; Lear 1944; also Saenz 1933a: 118; Mulliken and Roberts 1946:159.

43. This argument is not to be construed as argument in favor of foreign ownership and management of industrial enterprises in Ecuador. From the few available accounts, the mine in question seems to have offered unusually good working conditions. But it must also be pointed out that working and other conditions, particularly in the case of foreign-owned mines, are minutely prescribed by the Ecuadorean labor code and by special contracts of concession. Compliance with stipulations regarding such conditions is zealously and rigorously watched over by Ecuadorean authorities, the press, etc.

44. The understanding of discipline, here in the narrow sense of automatic compliance, follows that of Max Weber and his distinction between discipline as "habituation" and as "rational" discipline. See Parsons and Henderson (1947:152) and Gerth and Mills (1946:253 ff. and pp. 261-62).

45. Saenz 1933a:160 ff., where he documents the concern shown by individual ecclesiastics and the higher clergy as a group with the Indian problem. In a manner, Saenz's contention is confirmed by Benites' discussions of the conflict between the lower (criollo or mestizo, i.e., Indian-derived) clergy and the higher (Peninsular, i.e., Spanish-immigrant) clergy throughout the colonial period, and of the role of the village priest during the wars of independence in siding with the forces of emancipation (1950:155, 175 and passim).
On the other hand, Saenz's reference to the recruitment of the parish clergy from among the Indians is obscure. He may have had in mind the colonial "formative" period; or else he might have been thinking of the kind of lay religious functionaries of local chapels or churches, or ambulant prayer masters, both of whom are discussed.

46. J. Davis 1946:72; similar observations are made by Father Rodríguez Sandoval (1949:124-25).

47. Parsons 1945:56, 81, 209; see also Buitrón 1951c. According to Saenz (1933a:92), personal service by the bride in the cura's home for a term of one month is rendered in the region of Riobamba. This once standard custom is still alive in the province of Chimboraza, according to IEAG 1953, Nos. 10 and 11:21, 59.

48. Parsons 1945:149, 160, 164-65 (the main source on this subject, on which otherwise there is practically no information); see also Rubio Orbe 1953; and Bemelmans 1941:86 ff.

49. Parsons 1945, plate XXI and pp. 55, 84-85, 76, 153-54, 161, 164 on one such maestro rezador. See also Buitrón 1951a and 1951c; IEAG 1953, No. 3:269-70; Rivet 1906; and Rodríguez Sandoval 1949:102-3 on these rezadores, also termed rechazidores and cantadores.

50. For a thumbnail sketch of the role and official and unofficial functions of the teniente, see Franklin 1943:137. On this subject and the following in our text, see Saenz 1933a:130 ff.; Parsons 1945:5; Santiana 1949:239.

51. Ferdon (1945), describing a trail-building minga under the direction and personal leadership of the local teniente.

52. Parsons 1945:12-13, 209; also plates **XXXVIII-XL**, showing Otavalo Indians making an offering of chicken to the hacendado; as pictures they are more revealing of the relations between the "two parties" in that region than any of the meager reports: the hacendado and his people up above on the balcony, the Indians down below in the court-yard, the latters' leader, withal, on horseback. Icaza's classic novel (1934) offers a grim portrayal of relations and the manner of contacts between hacienda Indians, on the one hand, and hacendado, mayordomo, priest, etc., on the other.

53. IEAG 1953, Nos. 10 and 11:84-86, 136. These recent (and only) accounts of hacienda Indians and hacienda organization bear out the above statements. Contacts with the patrón are very limited indeed.

54. Parsons 1945:149-50, 151, 163, with brief sketches of her chief informant, an Indian woman who "furnishes an illustration of the oppor-tunities for acculturation through unusual personality." In this indi-vidual case, relations between Indians and non-Indians, and contacts, are both easier and closer than is the case in general.

55. Indian headmen or officers of an Indian community. Theoretically, they are elected representatives of their Indian bailiwick; in practice they are appointed, as a rule, by the teniente. In neither case, however, are they given official status or recognition by the national government. See below, Chapter XI.

56. Franklin (1943:76-79) tells of a Quito lawyer who specializes in cases involving Indians and the legal interests of Indian communities, and who deals with his Indian clients directly and in their language.

57. The term tinterillo (as also the corresponding Quechua term) is one of depreciation: shyster lawyer, pettifogger, parasite solicitor, scrivener. Saenz is the main source for this discussion (1933a:134-35, 145, 192); see also Buitrón 1948b; and Rodríguez Sandoval 1949:29-30, 85.

58. In a different context, but suggestively, Parsons draws attention to the importance of chicherias or estancos (taverns, public drinking yards owned and run by non-Indians) as Indian meeting places, successors to the great house of the native chief of early times, where today "we see... ancient Indian practices going on, ceremonials of dance and song and ritual feasting" (1945:181-82).

59. This personage is encountered only three or four times in the literature here surveyed. Saenz and Rodríguez Sandoval mention him briefly, as discussed in the text. Other mentions, to be discussed else-where, refer by this term to an Indian religious, ceremonial role. Both roles seem to imply the concept of "Elder."

60. On the compadres in their capacity of intermediaries, see particular-ly Buitrón 1947a; and Parsons 1945:44-45, 151, 163. The compadres, whether they are Whites or Indians, occupy a position of power and respect among the family with whom they are associated in this capacity. It is significant, however, that the formalities and ceremonies by which a person is invited to become one's "gossip" differ according to whether the prospective compadre is Indian or White. In the latter case, the whole ceremony appears to be abbreviated and, above all, lacks extended drinking together (Parsons 1945:42-46, 54, 99, 211; see also Buitrón 1951c on these ceremonies involving Indians and Whites). See also Collier and Buitrón 1949:20, 143-44; IEAG 1953, No. 3:204-6, 217-19.

61. Parsons 1945:81-82. Cf. Mishkin (1947:465), where he discusses a superficially similar conception of the role of the souls of the dead among southern Peruvian Indians. Some scholars specializing in Middle American ethnology might not consider the conceptions of the Otavalo Indians regarding the saints as singular. But the point here is that such conceptions may reflect a specific social milieu.

62. Collier and Buitrón 1949:19; on forced street-sweeping labor for which Indians are singled out after the market, p. 20.

63. Dale 1946:103. The information is given for what it is worth. Discrimination is certainly involved here, but whether it is directed against Indians as such, or against out-of-town traders and nonresidents, or whether it constitutes a price-regulating discrimination or a sale-enforcing measure, is not clear.

64. See also J. Davis (1946:82) remarking on the nature of contacts of Indians of the Andean countries generally with the "outer world."

65. Negotiations between a group of Indians and a hacendado for the purchase of the latters' lands were carried out by a "white" inter-mediary (Buitrón and Buitrón 1945). Hacienda owners or stewards also figure as intermediaries for Indians who retain them as attorneys in cases of conflict with the law. The honoraria exacted are such that the Indian client ends up as a serf (IEAG 1953, Nos. 10 and 11:53-54).

66. Canteen-keepers and shopkeepers are frequently accused of em-ploying semicoercive or fraudulent methods in delivering Andean Indians over to labor recruiters or of abetting and aiding in such labor-recruiting methods.

67. In agriculture, hacienda mayordomos or specially commissioned individuals act as labor recruiters. Garcés (1941:34-35) indicates that such labor recruiting is relatively new and has come to the fore due to the "labor crisis in agriculture," self-recruitment of agricultural labor being no longer sufficient for hacienda requirements.

In previous chapters "Indians" have been discussed summarily in demographic terms and in terms of socioeconomic position. Also, certain selected qualities, such as skill, education, and behavior connected with the use of time, have been discussed at some length as qualities typical of "Indians" though not necessarily specific of Indians. A loose equation of Indians with the rural highland population or a peasantry in general has been explicitly or implicitly admitted throughout. In the chapter just preceding, however, Indians were treated in a more specific sense in that they were identified as Indians by virtue of their position within the larger Ecuadorean society, i.e., largely in terms of particular behavior patterns that obtain between members of different social strata, one of which was equated with "Indian." But no comprehensive, explicit, and exclusive declaration of the "essence" of Indians has been advanced as yet.

Now, therefore, they will have to be introduced without reference to their relations to other, non-Indian elements, namely, as a distinct ethnic element. As will be noted, their recognition and definition is an unusually complicated matter; some reasons for this complexity--really a perplexity--will have to be indicated. Furthermore, the question will be raised whether Ecuadorean Indians are all alike or whether, and in what respects, they differ among themselves.

These questions have direct bearing on the problem of industrialization. If, for instance, Indians were found to be a homogeneous or uniform population, certain qualities or features might be inferred to hold good for all who are, or are regarded as, Indians, hence render the "qualities" of "raw" human resources calculable for a prospective industrial enterprise. Moreover, such objective uniformity of a population may, or may not, be indicative of a subjective we-feeling or group coherence in which industry would be interested; for on such coherence may hinge some of those social qualities which are prerequisites for industrial organization, namely, capacity for teamwork, for "discipline-in-association" or associative discipline, for a measure of self-organization, and/or for the assumption of leadership functions.

In dealing with these questions there is no intention of describing Indian culture in all its ramifications and manifestations; instead, we shall again confine ourselves mainly to social relations as they prevail among Indians and to those features of Indian life and society that are pertinent for assessing Indians' suitability for industrially organized work.

To begin with, the question, "Who are the Indians?" cannot be answered with anything like neat precision. Among the Ecuadorean population the broad racial substratum is Indian. It presents itself as a continuum analogous to, but by no means coincident with, the continuum in social stratification as discussed in the foregoing chapter. White-Indian admixture exists in varying proportions, though, on the whole, White admixture among the population considered Indian is probably less than Indian admixture among the populations considered Mestizo or White.

The distinction actually made between Indians and non-Indians builds up upon the historical fact (and the awareness of this historical fact) that the present population was preceded by an aboriginal Indian one, the point of reference here being the point of first contact between Indians and Spanish. Today's Ecuadorean Indians, however, should by no means be equated with that aboriginal population. Rather we are faced with the existence of a biologically somewhat, and of a culturally considerably, hybridized population. It is true that in it many genuinely aboriginal single culture elements or "traits" survive; some of these, though probably not many, can be so identified with certainty. But, even on close scrutiny, composites of such elements or "complexes," such as housing, agricultural techniques, organization of work, family organization, etc., are already difficult, if not impossible, to sort out according to provenience into pre-Columbian (pre-Inca and Inca) and post-Columbian (European, specifically Spanish) elements. At any rate, aboriginal Indian and Spanish cultural elements are fused at the level of a peasantry which represents today's Indian culture. Hence it should be understood that, in enumerating any "traits" as "Indian," we are not concerned with the question whether these traits are diagnostic of aboriginal culture or not, or whether some of them are shared with those otherwise recognized as Cholos or Mestizos, or even Whites. For the sake of operation, we shall mean by "Indians" a population, usually so considered by whomsoever, preponderantly rural and peasant in character, a hybrid human stock among which the aboriginal strain may predominate, and representing a syncretic culture, compounded of aboriginal and intrusive elements, having the flavor of the antiquated, conservative, and outmoded and, if one wishes, the quaint. The people representing this culture have, in the course of time, elaborated some, modified others, of its features, be it by way of spontaneous and perhaps automatic changes occurring in response to changing conditions, be it in response to directly operative extraneous factors, or to explicit measures imported from without.

Such modern end-products of comparatively recent contact and change "in Latin American countries in which the Indian racial ingredient remains heavy" are aptly characterized by Kroeber in these words (1948:431):

> Mostly they are devout Catholics, but with considerable pagan absorptions. Their dress is not the old native one; but it often is distinctive of locality or class, like peasant costume. The rest of their life is a similar mosaic of indigenous and Spanish elements in complex and unpredictable combinations. There are millions of such "Indians" in these countries, with a culture that is not pre-Columbian, not Spanish or colonial, not modern Occidental, but some of each, plus local developments evolved from the mixture during four hundred years. There has been an enormous amount of acculturing going on in these centuries. But the product is better characterizable as a hybridization than as an acculturation, if that word is allowed to retain its usual implication of assimilation into something superior or larger. These millions of "Indians" are not "assimilated," either nationally or culturally.

The fact that the Indians of today's Ecuador are presumably neither "pure" racially nor undiluted or pristine culturally does not mean that there are no palpable Indians or that the existence of Indians as Indians is illusory. They are distinct and distinguished from Ecuadorean non-Indians not only as a stratum but also as an ethnic group, i.e., respectively, not only on grounds of social evaluation but also on grounds of historical and cultural differentiation.

This twofold aspect of Indian existence in the social space has been alluded to before; it consists in vertical sub- and superordination by "ranked" social strata and in horizontal co-ordination by ethnic groups and is a feature that is perhaps unique to the Andean social world; at any rate, it seems to obtrude itself nowhere else as forcibly: Indians are socially distinguished over more than one perspective, i.e., duomodally.

These distinctions are relative. Throughout, the fluid character of the social structure of modern Ecuador will have to be kept in mind, with its indeterminate stratum that is in the making or in a continuously repeated remaking. In the summary picture of the ethnic situation that follows, we shall again encounter an interstitial or buffer (perhaps also transitory) group in the Mestizos or Cholos. This statement is but a corollary of what has just been indicated regarding the mixture of elements in varying, though unknown, proportions as being today's Indian culture. Hence what are essentially dynamic processes will perforce have to be stated in static terms for the sake of presentation and analysis. This caution is also necessary lest permanence be imputed to Indian culture. Though to all appearances retarded, when compared to our modernly derived expectations, it has received accretions, sustained losses, undergone elaborations and modifications in the course of a development of several centuries. To understand it now as frozen into its present status quo would not only deprive our chief question of all sense but would also be a fundamental error regarding this culture.

We shall first consider in some detail why Indians are Indians, by what tokens they are so defined, and what constitutes "diagnostic features" for their culture and for individual Indians and for Indian groups. In the course of this consideration we shall point out some specific difficulties besetting attempts at defining Indians, thus substantiating several points already made. We shall next discuss the features by which Ecuadorean Indians are judged to be homogeneous; and taking the real or alleged homogeneity as a clue we shall raise the question (in Chapter XII) whether there exists a generalized specifically Indian "solidarity" and attempt to descry the limits of inter-Indian compatibility and of co-operative action, at the same time noting divisive tendencies as well.

In pursuit and elaboration of these problems we shall devote a cursory examination (in Chapter XII) to Indian group life, projecting it against the question whether organizational or other phases of Indian life as it exists now can be built into the industrial system. We shall raise the specific question whether existing social relations among Indians lend themselves to being perpetuated within the industrial situation or whether they absolutely contravene industrial requirements as defined earlier. Thus, is there a value in attempting to keep them viable, or is their dissolution imperative for the sake of industrial organization? And must existing relations therefore be broken off short, or can they be advantageously integrated into the industrial work situation? Thus we shall inquire into Indian organizations with regard to their foci of interest, scope, functioning and vitality, and in that context pay particular attention to leadership and authority and to the grounds on which they are possible among Indians. In pointing out the organizational functionaries, the "key men" in Indian society, we shall attempt to furnish a list of potential "spokesmen," "contact men," or leaders paralleling that of the "intermediaries" discussed in connection with the question of Indian-White contact.

A. Criteria of Ethnic Distinctiveness

In those Latin American countries in which the proportion of the indigenous population is high relative to the European-derived population, a great deal of though has been spent over the question as to how to define an Indian and what criteria to use to arrive at a comprehensive and valid definition. The attempts at finding such a generally applicable and empirically justifiable set of criteria have not, so far, been successful anywhere, and there is reason to doubt that an all-purpose definition of today's Indian will ever be successfully and satisfactorily established. Taxonomical classifications are notoriously unrewarding where the material to be classified constitutes a continuum, and this is precisely the situation with which we are confronted.[1]

Apart from the logicoscientific, the empirical reasons for the bedevilment of the questions as to "Who is who?" and "Why?" in Indian Latin America, including Ecuador, are complex and shall not be dealt with here at length; they are largely of a historical-intellectual nature and have to do with changes in social valuations as well as, latterly, in scientific interest itself.[2] The main point is, to repeat, that, looked upon as a whole, the Ecuadorean population consists of a continuum of groups whose biological and cultural characteristics blend into each other. This is the fact with which we are most concerned at the moment. If, in the following, some criteria are laid down as conspicuous marks of differentiation between the Indians, Mestizos or Cholos, and Whites, it should be remembered that thereby only approximate definitions of the various ethnic groups are offered and that the validity of the criteria or traits differs from region to region, from situation to situation, and even from era to era; that their applicability varies with the purpose in hand; and, finally, that they vary also with the observer of, or participant in, a given situation.

A few words shall be said first on the general ethnic picture of Ecuador with particular reference to that interstitial fluid ethnic group, the Cholos or Mestizos, because it is on that group, so recognized, that class and ethnic (cultural) changes articulate. Their social evaluation differs somewhat from that in other Latin American countries where that term is employed, such as Peru. And, as we have seen, their social position differs from region to region within Ecuador. In the following we give a few examples as to how they are defined. In this manner, not only is an idea conveyed of the fluidity of ethnic categories as it obtains in Ecuador, but an approximation as to "who the Indians are" is gained, so to speak, by a method of exclusion.

Thus Parsons:[3]

> It would be difficult to classify /the population of Ecuador/ by race, except roughly, as is common practice, as White, mestizo or half-breed, Indian and Negro....Between race and culture there is considerable confusion in Ecuador as elsewhere. A mestizo or Cholo is thought of both as a half-breed and as a person of low economic status and cultural inferiority derived from Indian contacts.

> /Cholo/ was a term of contempt /in early Spanish days/, as it is more or less today in Ecuador; one would not use the term in speaking to a mestizo.

In contrast to the Cholos in Peru where, according to Saenz (1933b: 123-24; 1933a:174-76), the term has a broader and somewhat endearing meaning, the Cholos of Ecuador, where the term has a derogatory connotation, "form a restricted class; they are really Indianized rural Mestizos and, at best, the urban lower elements."

The Cholo is a Mestizo, product of the crossing of the Indian with another Mestizo. The term has a social connotation that is subtle, but quite recognizable....The Cholo hardly escapes the condition of the Indian, lives as a rule in the territories of the Indians, is the Mestizo of the rural parishes and villages and also the common low people of the cities. His rustic costume, distinct from that of the Indian, is characteristic, but preserves neverthe-less obvious /Indian/ survivals....The resemblance in occupations and in bearing (postura) has not yet been lost entirely...

The ethnic picture of highland Ecuador is thus described by Ferdon (1947:161-62):

Most of these natives are now distributed over the plateau as hacienda workers....Others have drifted into villages or towns where they have acquired the white man's dress and certain of his customs. Many of these are locally referred to as cholos, or mestizos, and although blood mixture with the white man is in-ferred, it is not necessarily fact, customs and dress being the main criteria. However, a few small groups have withstood the onslaught of the Spaniard and have maintained a semblance of cultural continuity /Otavalo, Salasaca, Zaraguro, and others/. There may be other such units tucked away in the mountain valleys or high paramos of the Andes...

Here, then, are some characterizations of the Cholos. Taken to-gether, they are consistent with the manner in which the term has been used up to now. The Cholos or Mestizos accordingly constitute an ele-ment that is not too remote from the Indians, except that it is marked by a tendency toward urbanization. And Cholos are implicitly included in the definition of Garcés according to which an Indian is "everyone who, belonging to the autochthonous stock (raza), lives in such a manner as to participate in the tendencies and usages common to it"[4] and who aptly differentiates between "mestizo-indio" and "mestizo-blanco" (Garcés 1941: 14).

B. Criteria of Ethnic Identification

Apart from such general and abstract, though comprehensive, definitions indicating ethnic distinctiveness, what are the conspicuous and socially used marks by which the ethnic groups and their members are discerned in everyday life?

The most outstanding and generally the safest single criterion by which the two or three ethnic groups and their members are in practice identified is dress or costume. The costumes worn by individuals are in general sufficiently typical for Indians as also, though not always, for Cholos or Mestizos to serve as differentiating marks as over against the dress worn by Whites, i.e., standard modern European attire.[5]

Dress, according to the explicit statement of the Buitróns (1945), is the sole classificatory criterion for purposes of local registration of Indian, Mestizo, and White births, marriages, and deaths in Otavalo.

Yet costume by itself is neither an exact nor absolute classificatory criterion.[6] It is, however, the most ostensive mark of a person's status, ethnic as well as social, and in a way the least arbitrary token of its wearer's identity.

The importance of dress as indicator of ethnic identity is shown by some examples furnished by the Buitróns. In one case, they refer to two brothers, one of whom dresses as Cholo or Mestizo, the other as White: the brothers were accordingly enumerated in official registrations as Mestizo and White, respectively. On the other hand, in certain regions of Pichincha Province, as also in Otavalo, the maintenance of Indian traditional costume is in part related to ability to afford it: "Mestizo" dress, consisting in cheap, modern-style clothing, is not as expensive as Indian-style costume; hence poorer Indians revert increasingly to the cheaper factory-made attire and on that score tend to be considered Mestizos (Buitrón and Buitrón 1945; 1947:54, 56, 58). It is at this point that dress starts to serve as an economic class mark. And it is over dress and the spending of money thereon that a first differentiation sets in between "lower-class Mestizos," who spend money on "showy clothes," and Indians.[7]

Language can serve as a nonarbitrary criterion of identification and classification for almost all purposes. It is in terms of mother tongue that Ecuadorean Indians could be objectively defined, and are socially defined. The question of language anyway merits some discussion in view of the problem of interpersonal communication presented by it.

Quechua is the language spoken by Indians, or by persons considered Indian, in highland Ecuador.[8] But language does not figure as a population-statistical item in any surveys or estimates of population, and there are no figures to show the extent to which Indians, or for that matter non-Indians, are bilingual. According to most observers, ability to understand or speak Spanish is generally limited to relatively few (otherwise) Indians, although there are probably few communities in which someone does not speak or understand Spanish or has a working vocabulary of it. Indian ability to use the language varies according to region and to distance from towns, with occupations that entail the making and marketing of craft products, also with age and with the extent to which Indians have access to, and avail themselves of, schools.

As it is, the Quechua spoken, for instance, in Imbabura Province, is reported to contain 15 to 20 per cent of Spanish or hybrid terms and phrases, much as Ecuadorean Spanish of the common people and particularly of those considered Mestizos contains Quechua terms, constructions, and pronunciations. Dialect differences within Quechua seem sufficiently marked to make mutual understanding among Indians from different localities oftentimes difficult.

Names, i.e., surnames or patronymics, do not seem to be used as readily to identify their bearers as Indians or non-Indians as is general appearance, dress, or language. But Parsons provides a valuable hint as to the roles which surnames, together with other indices, play in marking a person as Indian or non-Indian. Speaking of a small place in the canton of Cayambe, she reports that Indians may adopt Spanish surnames "when they prefer to be considered Cholos" and live close to town, and "when a person has acquired sufficient money to think he can and should pass for a Cholo, and occasionally some of the poor relatives change names at the same time."[9] This is one of the few clear instances so far encountered in which surnames figure as one of the vehicles by which to enter, socially, into another estate or group, and it is cited here because it justifies the inference that surnames do count in social identification. In fact, surnames are used in establishing the "race" (raza) of the deceased in local registers, as in Ilumán, or the registrant is asked whether the deceased was an Indian (natural).[10]

Racial features are possibly used in the compilation of some official statistics, the classifications being White, Mestizo, Indian, Negro, and sometimes also Yellow (Chinese, Japanese). In neither of the two examples which have come to attention[11] are there indications or instructions regarding the exact differentiating features according to which the breakdowns are to be made. Presumably, the compilers are guided by skin color and/or other physical features; none of these, however, can be considered as constituting absolute or safe guides by themselves.

To the criteria of dress, language, surnames and perhaps, physical features may be added, as group features, residence and occupation. These have been previously discussed and may be summarized here with special reference to Indian group identification.

Indian settlements typically do not form closed villagelike centers. They are generally open settlements, in that dwellings are characteristically dispersed throughout their parcialidades (but may sometimes form small, more compact caserios), are sometimes separated from each other by fairly long distances, and are marked off from each other by ditches, gullies, ravines, and other natural features. Closed and planned settlements, on whatever scale, are inhabited by a White, or more often, by what is (therefore) considered a Mestizo population, the latter fanning out into, or blending with, the Indians of the surrounding countryside. Hence, more often than not, Indians will be found to live in scattered, open settlements (parcialidades) rather than in closed, "nucleated" or compact villages or towns, although there are exceptions (Nayón).[12] It is in this sense that it is said that Indians are typically rural, open-settlement dwellers (campesinos).

As has been noted earlier, Indians are eminently peasant farmers and agricultural workers even if also or additionally engaged in some special handicraft manufacture. Some Indians have transportation and ambulant trading as their full-time occupation. Hand-manufacture of various articles as full-time occupations and skilled trades such as bricklaying,[13] carpentry, etc., are considered more typical of Mestizos, as a rule, than of Indians. There are some occupations, largely service occupations, which are said to be filled preponderantly by Indians: carriers, muleteers, domestic servants, barracks-stable boys, the street-sweepers in the larger cities and, of course, road workers in general.[14]

Other features are not so much classifying as they are typical qualities which, in the eyes of the observer, heighten the chance of a man's being an Indian when found in association with dress and language, the latter being the most exclusive and relatively least equivocal feature of Indian distinctiveness which may simply be corroborated by any of the others here named. Generally speaking, identification of an Indian is almost always a matter of context, setting, and a multiplicity of features corroborating each other. To say that Indians share a common way of life or a common culture (costumbres, "customs") is something of a tautology, though it is sufficient for a very general appraisal of the matter. It is insufficient when it comes to analyzing tangibles and isolated traits. Many so-called Cholos or Mestizos (so defined by virtue of only one trait or by virtue of such "highly visible" features as dress and/or language and/or residence) share the Indian way of life in many respects, and behavior and attitudes do not differ from those of Indians. This applies not only to the frequently shared levels in matters educational and economic, the general level of living, but also to beliefs and practices in everyday life.

On the level of polemics (to which no disparaging meaning is attached here), "Indian" is frequently equated with "rural proletariat,"[15] in the clear recognition that the lines between the rural Cholo and the Indian are too fluid and too little discriminating to permit of distinction for practical purposes, such as welfare action. Excepted from this equation are groups such as those of Otavalo and Saraguro and other Indian groups which have maintained a more clear-cut cultural continuity[16] in the midst of Indian-Spanish hybrid peasant culture and can probably be defined ethnologically without logical and empirical qualms.

On such an ethnological basis, i.e., on the basis of historical-ethnographic comparison, Mrs. Parsons lists a number of traits [17] (besides traits of "material culture" and institutional complexes) which refer to behavior, attitudes, and concepts and which are typically Indian, such as "not undressing to sleep,...great emphasis in general upon the social importance of eating and drinking in company, including the religious importance of offering food to the dead and to the gods or their representatives...the contemporary attitude of irresponsibility for conduct during drunkenness...--all these are characteristic Indian ways and attitudes," including "attitudes toward property." "The distribution of fields and houses is pre-Conquest /i.e., therefore, Indian/, together with the lack of any proclivity for concentrated town life....This accounts for the Indians' attachment to their lands in the face of tremendous pressure to dispossess them. It may account also in part for their submission to the /colonial/ encomienda system and to the present-day hacienda system, where, like cats, as one hacendado put it, they cling to the place they are used to." "Prescriptive, standardized, and comparatively unchanging styles are characteristically Indian."[18]

Two other methods of ethnic identification may be mentioned, both of which require definite and well-circumscribed contexts. One is descent or family affiliation, so far as these are known in small, ethnically mixed communities. In such a setting, "it is known who an individual is, who are or were his parents and grandparents; hence it is natural that /the members of the community/ consider him an Indian or non-Indian without giving weight or importance as to how he dresses, what language he speaks, etc. However, it is necessary to state clearly that, when this genealogical knowledge is lacking, the classification is a cultural rather than a biological one."[19]

The other method is one of explicit or implied self-identification on the part of the Indians. Individuals refer to themselves as "natorales" (naturales, "natives") in contradistinction to blancos (the term, however, is also used by Indians to refer to individuals whom they consider ill-bred, gauche, ignorant of good manners).[20] However, such spontaneous self-identifications are probably operative only in specific situations, namely, under some stress and irritation, on the one hand, and in the presence of an observer known to be sympathetic, on the other.

C. Homogeneity and Heterogeneity of Ecuadorean Highland Indians

This brief survey regarding the criteria by which Indians are defined in Ecuador has indicated certain features that are, or are believed to be, common to them. These features, in tending to be exclusive, imply a relative Indian homogeneity. Whether Indians, so defined and looked upon without reference to a non-Indian world, constitute a homogeneous assemblage is, of course, largely a matter of perspective and context. Some observers are more impressed by the differences they discern among the

population that is considered Indian than by similarities, and stress
differentials that are due to economic situation, geographical location,
variations in the degree of acculturation to Ecuadorean national or modern culture including linguistic acculturation, and basic historic (i.e.,
pre-Hispanic and even pre-Inca) and quasi-tribal differentiations which
are still operative.[21]

Saenz, on the other hand, asserts that the character of the Ecuadorean Indian population is one of basic homogeneity. He contrasts
Ecuador with other Latin American countries with large Indian populations, such as Guatemala and Mexico, and on comparison finds that Ecuadorean Indians constitute a remarkably homogeneous population. It is
his impression that the similarities in features making for this "homogeneity," namely, language, "culture," intensive farming, cottage industries, regional trade in markets, food habits, political and religious
institutions and practices as they obtain throughout, are greater than,
and outweigh, the dissimilarities or variations in details in all these
spheres. He admits, nevertheless, that differences within the Ecuadorean Indian population merit further study--differences which are due
in minor part, however, to differences in economic situation (1933a:
30-31, 99, 186 ff.)

Taken together, the data contained in the literature here surveyed
and used bear out Saenz's impression fairly closely. However, from the
scant information on income and consumption levels it does not appear
as though the economic, as a differentiating element, is decisive. Thus
Buitrón finds that the better-income Indian groups of Otavalo, i.e., those
participating more actively in a cash economy by the sale of handmade
goods, purchase food additional to that which they themselves produce;
have clothes of better quality and more of them; build houses with tiled
roofs rather than with thatched roofs; use some market-bought European-
style kitchen utensils. But there are no differences in the style of
clothes, or in the basic ground plan of the houses, or in the system of
farmwork, or in the tools and methods used in farming, and none in the
scale of preferences for which money is spent or would be spent. Moreover, elsewhere he asserts that "many of the campesinos who have land
of their own" and who engage in craft industry or commerce "continue
to live in the same poor and dirty houses and feed themselves in the
same manner as those who do not have land, or industries or commerce,
and who live in homes and on land furnished by the hacienda in exchange
for their work"; this indicates "that the economic factor is not the only
one which keeps the campesino in the situation in which he is found."[22]

Similarly, little difference was found in dress and in the amounts
of food consumed by income groups in the sample studies made by Suárez
in the central highland provinces, while some differences were found in
the degree of literacy, cleanliness, the amount of furniture, etc. Differences in income were not, it appears to that investigator, expressed in
the quantities and qualities of food (Suárez 1936:39-40; 1941).

Considering these various observations, we may suggest by way of
a first, tentative conclusion that differences in economic level do not
tend to operate in such a way as to produce palpable differences in Indian
style of life or culture, and that established preferences and tastes are
relatively impervious to alterations in economic status. In other words,
it appears that any such differences are superficial and do not impinge,
at least not immediately and automatically, upon Indian tastes or preferences so as to alter basic patterns of living.

Other inter-Indian group differences are attributable to specialization by parcialidades or parishes in certain craft manufactures or other

distinct occupational pursuits, some of which may make a community notable. Cases in point are the Indians of Pelileo (Tungurahua Province), who are said to be famous as packers and carriers, or the masons of Latacunga (Rainey 1946; Rodríguez Sandoval 1949:64). The lists of parcialidades in Pichincha Province show occupational specialties engaged in by the majority of inhabitants in addition to farming: carriers and traders, day laborers and artisans, firewood collectors, and weavers of various articles and in various materials, also subspecialized according to specific textile product.[23]

Other differences are noticeable only on closer observation of groups on wider comparative bases. Among these are differences in physical makeup or physical type, perhaps even in temperament,[24] differences which are not wholly without interest for industrialism, as has been pointed out before.

There are variations in such cultural details as express themselves in regional and local peculiarities in costume items. Thus the shape or color of hats, base color of poncho, etc., and the manner in which the hair is worn vary and identify their wearers as natives of specific villages or localities.

Differences in other details of "material culture" are also slight. Again the fact that differences do not rest entirely on economic factors is forcibly brought home by comparing descriptions of houses, house furnishings, and inventories of such widely separated regions as Riobamba and Otavalo. The Indians of the former region are economically badly situated as compared with those of the latter. Yet the differences in these items are minimal, even down to details.[25]

The literary material on Ecuadorean Indians, such as it is, and seen as a whole, conveys a strong impression of a substantial similarity, not to say uniformity, of Ecuadorean Indians. The similarity is great on linguistic grounds, despite dialectal differences, in respect to technological and material culture as expressed in kinds and styles of articles made and used, and appreciably in the manner and style of life. These seem indeed to override the differences that arise from dissimilarities in natural environment and resources and location relative to larger centers, and even those that might arise from differences in economic situation. Hence it is on that basis that it is fair to say that the Indian population of highland Ecuador as a whole is of a rather uniform and homogeneous character.

Still, these conclusions must be considered provisional, first, because of the paucity of sufficiently detailed studies of various Indians as groups and as individuals, and even as economic groups; second, because of the almost complete absence of any descriptive ethnographic and analytical studies of those groups for which variations in cultural details and physical features have been noted. These are the groups which "have maintained a semblance of cultural continuity,"[26] and of these only the Otavalo Indians have been studied to any extent. There is, third, the difficulty inherent in the dynamics of the social situation in Ecuador on which we have frequently commented. With the indeterminate position and the fluid conception of Mestizo and Cholo in mind, it is very likely that any one individual, or even groups relatively close to urban centers, is considered as non-Indian or passes as such if he fails to conform to any of the patterns described in the various chapters of this Part. On that score, the question of homogeneity cannot be considered except in static and therefore somewhat artificial terms.

NOTES

1. In multigroup societies of other parts of the world these difficulties are not encountered either because a single criterion is socially deemed sufficient (race, religion, language, or even the much vaguer criterion of "nationality") or because the constituent groups are, for whatever reason, both self-conscious and articulate enough to identify themselves in terms that they acknowledge as valid or are forced to acknowledge themselves.

The question of definition in reference to Indian Latin America has been discussed by many students from various angles and in various contexts. The following may be mentioned: De la Fuente 1952 (including following discussion); Gamio 1945; Gillin 1947:151-60 and 1949; Mishkin 1947:411-14; Salz 1944; Tschopik, Jr. 1947b:11-15; 1948; 1952. The problem is also considered from time to time in various articles and comments published in América Indígena.

2. These reasons may be stated summarily:

(a) Concepts and criteria used by "objective" or scientifically interested observers of the social scene to designate "Indians," "Mestizos," "Criollos," etc., have changed (and indeed are now in process of reconsideration as indicated in n. 1 above), whereas, within the same social scene, the current popular terms and their conceptual content which are used in actual social intercourse have not changed, or they have not changed at a rate to keep pace with the scientific terminological and conceptual armature; instances are casta and raza, terms which do not necessarily mean caste and race in any conventional scientific sense, and indeed rarely do.

(b) The Indian element as such has undergone re-evaluation at various times, and policies with regard to it have shifted back and forth. Such a shift occurred, for instance, during the first decades following the Spanish conquest and the beginning of the colonial administration in Peru. A re-evaluation of the Indian element is discernible at the present time with direction toward favoring it, at least in some countries. This matter has been touched upon in the text on several occasions: here, reference is had to the pro-Indian, Indigenist or Indianist tendencies among intellectuals, government officials, and other segments of public opinion. These tend toward a broadening of the criteria by which to designate larger parts of the population as Indian.

(c) As a corollary of the foregoing point, the objectives for which comprehensive investigations, such as census enumerations, are made of a population are subject to changes, often within decades. Any one purpose or objective (the pursuit of a demographic, economic, or social welfare policy) makes up and emphasizes, so to speak, its own set of criteria for the definition and identification of whole groups and their individual members. This and the foregoing point is forcibly brought home in the lucid paper by George Kubler, "Colonial and Republican Population Mixture in Peru," read at the 29th International Congress of Americanists in New York on September 6, 1949, part of a larger study (Kubler 1952).

(d) Apart from changes in the social as well as in scientific or generally intellectual attitudes toward, and evaluation of, the Indian and Mestizo element, changes have undoubtedly occurred in the composition of the total population and in the relative size of its constituent groups. The process is related to the open-estate structure as previously discussed; it should also be considered in the context of a possible ethnic differential rate of increase.

3. Parsons 1945:1, and n. 1. In her book, she refers to Mestizos or Cholos as "Whites," since she considers their culture to be derived primarily from Spanish peasant or village culture.

4. Quoted by Saenz (1933a:173) from Garcés' Condición psíquico del Indio en la Provincia de Imbabura. El Indio factor de nuestra nacionalidad, Quito, 1931 (Anales de la Universidad Central 48 and 49).

5. This is one of the few subjects pertaining to Indian and general rural highland life which has found numerous descriptions, for the area at large as well as in regard to regionally typical costume. See Buitrón and Buitrón 1945; 1947:54-56; Cisneros Cisneros 1948:199,220; Collier and Buitrón 1949:64-67 and numerous illustrations; Franklin 1943:261; Gillin 1936; Hanson and Platt 1943:61-62, 67; Hassaurek 1868:27, 124-25; IEAG 1953, Nos. 10 and 11:28-33, 103-4; Rivet 1903:59; Rodríguez Sandoval 1949: 71-72; Saenz 1933a:43-45, 64, 175-76, 188; Suárez 1936:33; Von Hagen 1949: 66-67, 69-70, 81.

6. For instance, church weddings involving Indians tend to feature nowadays white wedding costumes, i.e., conventional, European-style wedding attire, that is specially hired for the occasion, or an infant may be dressed a la white for his baptismal in church. See Parsons 1945:57; and Rodríguez Sandoval 1949:100, 124-26.

7. Compare Paredes 1951 and Buitrón 1949c:66. Rodríguez Sandoval (1949:110-11) has a neat sketch of the often very slow and gradual metamorphosis of the Indian into White--via piece-by-piece change of dress items. On the score of dress, Mestizos also seem to fall into distinct categories; IEAG (1953, Nos. 10 and 11:106) has a reference to cutus, i.e., the Mestizos of Licto (Chimborazo), who wear the cotona, an old Indian-style collarless embroidered shirt (p. 32).

8. Buitrón (1946:51) and Murra (1947:786-820) indicate that about one-half of the Ecuadorean population speak Quechua, presumably their native tongue. Garcés (1941:41) estimates that 85 per cent of the Ecuadorean Indians understand Spanish, but only a small proportion speak it.
    For the question of language in Ecuador in general and with special reference to Quechua and its status in various regions and localities, see Bennett 1946:13; Cisneros Cisneros 1948:93, 94; Flornoy 1945:31; Franklin 1943:217; Gillin 1941; Parsons 1945:3 (n. 12), 150, 159, 163-68, 178-79, 200 and passim; Romero 1947:83-84; Saenz 1933a:30, 74-75, 190; Rodríguez Sandoval 1949:114-17 with a number of sample texts and a very useful discussion.
    No specific data were found regarding the extent to which Quechua is known by those whose mother tongue is Spanish. Hassaurek (1868:305) comments on the ability of all Whites and Cholos of Otavalo to speak Quechua. An obscurely phrased passage indicates that apparently such a situation obtains in present-day Cuenca (Von Hagen 1949:71), and Mr. David Basile informs me that white people in the Cuenca area evidently speak enough Quechua to communicate with their workers or to use it in the market, a situation which I believe also prevails in Otavalo. Elsewhere it is asserted that "practically every European in Ecuador speaks Quechua" (Tannenbaum 1944:177), a statement for which we have neither supporting nor contradicting evidence. It seems surprising that no observer of the Ecuadorean scene, with the exception of old Hassaurek, has proffered an unequivocal statement regarding the general medium of communication between Indians and non-Indians. Rodríguez Sandoval (1949:viii, 5), although he spent his youth in close contact with Indians, applied himself systematically to learning Quechua, both the full and the Quechua-Spanish mixed idiom. IEAG (1953, Nos. 10 and 11:97) tells of a hacendado in eastern Chimborazo who refuses to address his peons in Quechua, hence these are bilingual.

9. Parsons 1945:189-90, where she discusses a list of Indian and Spanish surnames prevailing in that canton. See also pp. 34-36 for the genealogical tables of three Peguche families; ten of the nineteen patronymics can be identified with certainty as Indian, and pp. 164-65, where fifteen surnames are mentioned, ten of which are Spanish. Change or modification of their surnames by Indians as a reclassificatory measure is also noted by Rodríguez Sandoval (1949:122-23). See also Benites (1950:130 ff., 144-45) on name-changing practices during the colonial era.

Indian names are easily spotted, as, for instance, in the civil registry compilations (births, marriages, deaths) carried almost daily by El Comercio (Quito); according to seven samples taken at random from September and November, 1951, issues, Indian surnames constitute an average of about 20 per cent of the totals listed there.

The Buitróns (1947:54) note that the surnames of the Indians of the Inca-Nayón-Calderón section in the northern part of Pichincha Province differ from those of the majority of Indians in that province. This group is surmised to be derived from Inca-transplanted mitayos from the Bolivian Plateau. Patronymics and toponymics provide many clues to the pre-Inca culture history of Ecuador. See references in Murra 1947: 791; and the study by Castro 1948. On toponymics, see summary statement and references in Cisneros Cisneros 1948:93 ff.

10. IEAG 1953, No. 3:184-85.

11. Both in El Trimestre Estadístico, Año I, No. 1 (1945):20 ff.; and No. 2 (1945):21-23. The first of these consists of reproductions of recent schedules to be used by physicians for medical certification of births, stillbirths, deaths, etc., and contains for raza the classificatory items "White," "Indian," "Mestizo," "Yellow," "Negro." The other consists in a set of educational statistics similarly broken down but lacking the category "Yellow."

12. Buitrón and Buitrón 1947:13; Collier and Buitrón 1949, end-papers and illustrations; García Ortiz 1946:170-71 (on lo urbano and el campesino); Parsons 1945:38; Rivet 1903:65; 1926:379; Saenz 1933a:31-34, 187.

13. Of 28 occupations listed by ethnic groups for Pomasqui (a parish north of Quito), those of bricklayers, weavers, and curanderos were filled exclusively by Indians; one-half or more of the persons engaged in sawing sandal-making, quarrying, cooking (females only) were Indian. See Buitrón 1949c.

14. Thus the Quito and Riobamba street-sweepers are "well-known urban classes" (Saenz 1933a:73-74)--classes on which there is virtually no information. The street-sweepers of Quito are, or were, recruited from one community which had a long-term contract with the Quito municipality to furnish rotating squads for this task, each serving one month (J. Davis 1946:46; see also Garcés 1941:39-40).

15. For an instance of a number of statements couched in these terms, see the preface, "Manifiesto Indígenista," to Cuestiones Indígenas del Ecuador 1946.

16. Ferdon (1947) enumerates about a dozen such groups. See also his map.

17. Parsons 1945:170-72. See also the rest of this very suggestive chapter on "Provenience of Traits" of the Indians of Imbabura and particularly of those of the canton of Otavalo. The cultures of pre-Columbian Peru, of eastern Ecuadorean, and other Amazonian lowland tribes (but largely

of the Jibaros), and of the Spanish (or White), furnish the bases for her analyses by which to sort out Indian "traits" and to state cultural "parallels."

18. Some of the above observations offer good examples as to how different interpretations of the same data may come to loggerheads. One may well wonder whether the (historical) "trait" of "unchanging styles," etc., is characteristically Indian or whether it is not generally peasant, i.e., one of the traits by which peasant is defined. Parsons supports her statement with a quotation from the Royal Commentaries of the Yncas, by Garcilasso de la Vega, the sixteenth century chronicler, son of a Spanish conqueror and a Peruvian Inca princess. This authority was, therefore, no peasant himself, but an aristocratic, urban, or rather urbane, observer of his fellow countrymen, no doubt disdainful of the peasant Peruvian.

A neat parallel example of differing interpretations derived from differences in scientific interest or orientation, or in the aims of scientific and other investigations and regarding the search for primary factors in observed social phenomena, is constituted by the case of the often-observed cleanliness of the Otavalo Indians. Parsons (1945:176) sees in Imbabura Indian "cleanliness and sense of order" a Jibaro parallel, suggesting a cultural affinity. Other observers comment on this trait and these Indians' better economic situation in the same breath. Buitrón and Buitrón (1945) account for this trait by reference to the lakes, clear streams, and warm springs of which the entire province is full. See also Buitrón and Buitrón (1947:20 ff.), where climatic and topographic features of Pichincha Province are discussed and where in many cases access to water is very difficult indeed and where, consequently, personal cleanliness is not conspicuous among the Indians. To these interpretations of observable social phenomena rendered in terms of cultural continuity or tradition, economic condition, and natural resources, others could be added phrased in terms of social status (cleanliness as unbecoming to low status) or of a sort of social "camouflage" (dirty, hence poor). Infant punishment is cited as a reason for the avoidance of baths in adult life (IEAG 1953, No. 3:227-28). Evidently, no single interpretation is sufficient to explain the "cleanliness and sense of order" or absence thereof among a given population.

19. Buitrón (1951b) who, for purposes of classifying a given population, followed local concepts according to which Indians are "those who are so considered by the members of the community." Unfortunately, he provides no information as to the identity of the interrogated members who made the classifications.

20. Only Rodríguez Sandoval offers a number of "cases" (1949: pp. ix, 26, 44, 88-89, 91, 120). But see also Parsons 1945:28. The Quechua term runa (literally, "man") is also used as a designation for Indian.

21. See, for instance, Benites 1950:103-4; Cisneros Cisneros 1948:111; also Rubio Orbe 1953; Rodríguez Sandoval 1949, passim; and Santiana 1952:134-36, on the gamut of phases of assimilation and acculturation.

22. Buitrón (1947a), where he points out very clearly, however, that nearness to urban centers may operate in such differentiations as he finds among the Otavalo group, and that this is a factor that parallels, but is distinct from, the level of income per se. See also Buitrón and Buitrón (1947:40-41, 58), where weight is given to this factor as concerns Indian groups in Pichincha Province, also pp. 44 and 46 on the minimal differences in the kinds and amounts of food consumed as between hacienda peons and free peons having land of their own, and pp. 35-36 on the basic similarity between these groups in the matter of style of housing,

while their care and upkeep correlate with the economic situation of their inhabitants. The last quotes are from Buitrón (1948b), again with reference to Otavalo.

23. Buitrón and Buitrón 1945; 1947, Tables VII and VIII, and passim; also Saenz 1933a:59, 64, 67, 68, 71; Parsons 1945:16, 25, 160; McClure 1946; Franklin 1943:111; Longand De Gangotena y Jijón 1946; Spinden 1948. See the extensive listing of local specialties in Rodríguez Sandoval 1949:55 ff.

24. Hassaurek (1868:280, 296) found Cayambe Indians "much more pugnacious and violent than their countrymen in general," when he observed their dances, and "could see at once that they were descendants of tribes entirely different from those of Otabalo" (Otavalo). Villavicencio (1858: 163, 305) is particularly impressed by the Indians of Cotacachi (Imbabura Province). Parsons notes differences in physical type between two communities in the canton of Otavalo (1945:177). Gillin (1936 and 1941) established such differences on an anthropometric basis among communities within the province of Imbabura. Buitrón and Buitrón (1947:54) point out such differences for an Indian enclave within a more generalized Indian and Cholo rural population in Pichincha Province. Similar observations are made on other regions of highland Ecuador: Franklin 1943:172; Hanson and Platt 1945:46; Cisneros Cisneros 1948:132 ff.; Clothier 1946:219. In these more cursory observations, physical and nonphysical features are not clearly separated.

25. Rivet 1903:60; Parsons 1945: chap. iii; Buitrón and Buitrón 1945; Buitrón 1947a; Santiana 1949:240-41; Rodríguez Sandoval 1949:71--all these offer the materials for comparison. Similar ones can be made for dress, tools, food and drink, etc.

26. References to such groups are found in Buitrón and Buitrón 1947:54; Cisneros Cisneros 1948:90-98; Clothier 1946:219; Ferdon 1947; Franklin 1943:174-75; Garcés 1941:27; Hanson and Platt 1945:46; Murra 1947:810; Parsons 1945:172-74; Perez 1943.

   Some of these groups are reputed to be derived from Bolivia and Peru, brought into Ecuador under the Inca policy of forced resettlement colonization (mitimaes). No proper comparative ethnographic studies have been made with a view to ascertaining the historical affinities of these groups with those of the central and southern Andes.

A. Indian Solidarity: Limits and Focus

Indian culture, comparatively speaking, appears to be uniform. Outward features of Indian existence are little differentiated; and so far as these permit inferences as to some covert aspects of this culture, the same applies to individual aspirations, tastes, preferences, or "values." Beyond this homogeneity, no inference can be drawn as to whether Indians all over the Ecuadorean highlands would act in concert or that they <u>feel</u> themselves to be alike, merely because they are Indians.

Yet a general and <u>effective homogeneity</u> or effective coherence among Indians is precisely one <u>of the conditions</u> on which much of the success of industrialization would hinge. Industry is presumably to some degree interested in assembling groups whose members are not strangers to each other and as such would have to be accustomed to each other, for the simple reason that pre-established acquaintance or intergroup familiarity would facilitate communication to and within such groups. Though this principle of assembling working groups is not "functional" from the point of view of industry, it might have a function not only in insuring "discipline-in-association" but in maintaining "morale" on and off the job. In giving this orientation to our question, the assumption is that intergroup compatibility is primarily a function of intergroup we-feelings, or subjective cohesion, of "community of interest, feelings, and action," in short, of solidarity--a sentiment which is not created overnight.

It is this question of the we-consciousness and active we-feeling, if any, among Ecuadorean Indians, to which we address ourselves here. First, is there anything among them that could be called "solidarity" in the above-defined sense? If there is not, the further question would have to be raised as to the levels or the group units where solidarity can be found.

Once this question has been answered, the inquiry will be extended to the organizational aspects of Indian group life, i.e., to the level on which, and the grounds by virtue of which, solidarity exists. Last, the key organizations by which the Indian social fabric might be given extra strength, and the "key men" or the formal and informal leadership of and within the functioning Indian group, will be determined with a view to pointing out those whose pre-existing positions and roles might fit them to assume posts of authority in the industrial working group.

There is little in the literature under survey which would indicate any kind of we-feeling, or of action bespeaking solidarity, among Ecuadorean Indians considered at large. On the contrary, the absence of precisely such feelings of cohesion among Indians in general is abundantly stressed in many different contexts.[1] A consideration of certain recent trends and developments may serve to substantiate this lack of social cohesion on the larger scale among Indians.

In the first place, a literate, articulate interest in Indians qua Indians, a pro-Indian movement, an Indianism <u>on behalf</u> of Indians <u>is</u> not,

needless to say, an Indian movement. On the contrary, and much in contrast to present-day developments elsewhere in the world, Ecuadorean
Indians do not have an intelligentsia of their own, i.e., a modern-educated,
modern-thinking, "progressive" leadership that might, as in other cases,
force or persuade or stimulate by precept a people that such an intelligentsia recognizes as its own, and is reciprocally so recognized, into
some common consciousness and common action and common goals. There
is no Indian group, systematically operating so as to constitute a bridge in
the transition from the traditional or a given status quo to the new, however the latter may be defined. That there is no such Indian intelligentsia
is easily understood in considering, inter alia, the nature of the Ecuadorean
social structure, which permits of a high degree of ethnic and social
mobility and which consequently makes for the absorption of any potential
Indian leadership, intellectual or otherwise, into the non-Indian world.[2]

This is not to say that under a subscriptum, and with an appeal to
cohesion, other than "Indian," associative developments centering on other
common denominators of "Indianhood" might not take place. So far, however, such developments have remained indistinct, ephemeral, and inconclusive.

Thus, since the earlier forties there has existed a Federación
Ecuatoriana de Indios, an affiliate of the Confederación de Trabajadores
del Ecuador (C.T.E., the all-union Ecuadorean labor organization) and
connected with the incipient agrarian labor movement mentioned in
Chapter X. The Ecuadorean Indian Federation held two congresses, one
in 1944 following the organizing C.T.E. congress, the second in 1946 which
was to be attended by representatives of Indian comunidades, "unions,
committees of Indian defense, cooperatives, and tribes."[3]

Since then, little further news on the Federation has come to notice.
At any rate, there is no ground to think that such associations are symptomatic of a pan-Indian "awakening" or even intend Indian action as such;
they probably do bespeak interests and aspirations of workers[4] or of other
extraneous "interests." Whatever the forces that check[5] further and
more vigorous developments, these associations evidently fail in being
sustained by an all-pervasive Indian solidarity.

Where, then, do we find inter-Indian compatibility, cohesion, or
solidarity? The answer to this question will be found ever more definitely the closer the strictly local community is approached.

Whether there is any real solidarity to be found on the level of the
province or the canton (the modern political and administrative units) or
within intermontane basins or valleys is doubtful. Very likely, Indians
know that they "belong" to this or that administrative unit or that they
inhabit a designated natural region. It might conceivably be on these
levels that societal formations of a kind could be found. In fact, the designations often employed in reference to Indian groups of a given canton or
of a territory about a town or of a distinct mountain massif as "the
Otavalo," "the Saraguro," "the Zambiza," or "the Mojanda Indians" tend
to convey the impression of so many distinct tribes or even nations of
highland Indians. Occasionally, a tribal or linguistic designation is used
in reference to a living population of a definite region, such as "the
Puruhá" of Chimborazo Province.[6] These are speech usages that hark
back to the pre-Inca situation, when the highlands were occupied by a
number of tribes, petty kingdoms, "nations" of distinct provenience and
language. Today, however, nothing like such organizational principles
can be detected, hence no in-tribe attitudes inferred. Rivet notes explicitly that "today, notions of clan, of tribe, do not exist any more, or

at least do not exercise any action on Indian social life," Indian aboriginal society having been obliterated through permanent contact with White society (Rivet 1926:376).

However, Indians of distinct parishes and even more so of the small- er unofficial units of the parish, such as the parcialidades,[7] are sufficient- ly we-conscious or in-group-conscious to distinguish themselves on that ground from other comparable units. Common action seems to begin on the parish and on the parcialidad levels. At least this much can be inferred from interparish and interparcialidad hostilities, on the occurrence and persistence of which there are a number of references. Until recent years such hostilities led to open and systematic battles between the different groups, consisting of members of different parcialidades or of peons from different haciendas. These battles were waged particularly at the meeting of the different groups on the occasion of some fiesta.[8] The policing of the dance yards at fiestas (referred to in Chapter X) is a realistic measure to prevent such intergroup quarrels and fighting from ensuing in too much bloodshed.[9] Members of another parish, though it be but a few miles dis- tant from that of the speaker, are referred to as strangers, "other people," "alien people."[10] Lack of co-operation and the existence of much rivalry among the parcialidades of Otavalo canton are explicitly noted,[11] and everywhere a vast number of neighboring Indian communities are involved in protracted litigations, many of them of old standing, over land and use rights of natural resources.[12] Difficulties in inter-Indian communication due to dialect differences have been mentioned before; these differences are cited as the reason for the government's failure to use Quechua in the educational curriculum (Linke 1954:54).

A good measure of the extent of parishwide we-feeling and in-group action is provided by the marriage statistics compiled for the year 1944 for the canton of Otavalo, which indicate the provenience of spouses for Indians, Whites, and Mestizos. In 93 per cent of the Indian cases, both partners came from the same parish. Both the other ethnic groups showed an appreciably higher marriage mobility; that is, a rather larger number of spouses came from other parishes, cantons, or even provinces. The Buitróns, who compiled these data, believe that intraparcialidad marriages, on which no data were available, would show a similar high in-marrying incidence for Indians. And Rodríguez Sandoval declares flatly that people like those of Otavalo and Zalazaca are "strictly endogamous" and that "in general, groom and bride should belong to the parcialidad," whereas Parsons reports that in Peguche (one of the Otavalo parcialidades) "strangers from other Indian settlements are considered eligible spouses or,...even preferable spouses." The few cases of such "strangers" who had married into Peguche show that they came from the same parish, with the exception of one man who, however, still came from the same canton. Thus despite reported Indian opinion on the matter, "the greater number of matches are between neighbors, the outcome of propinquity."[13] There is no particular contradiction between Indian "ideal" marriage selection and "actual" selection if the restrictions of church and custom regarding marriage (endogamy and exogamy) are considered.

In some respects, then, in-group feeling, or what we have termed "solidarity," becomes discernible on the level of the parish. It could be called that unit within which marriage is possible and, where the local community is very small, in fact necessary. At any rate, the parish is customarily what might be called the minimum "endogamic" unit.

However, the most intensive, active, and generally effective we- consciousness or solidarity prevails apparently on the level of the par- cialidad, or a comparable settlement unit under one of the many designations. Some observers, such as Saenz and Buitrón, consider it the functioning unit of group life. On the other hand, Parsons, and also apparently Garcés (1942), are inclined to consider the extended kin group or the larger family to be the basic social unit. The extended kin group, the ayllu, comprises husband's and wife's collaterals, and connotes among Ecuadorean Indians "the consanguineous bilateral group within which marriage is forbidden," an interdiction, sanctioned by custom as well as by the church, which relates to marriage among descendants of common, maternal and paternal, greatgrandparents.[14] A group of ayllus constitutes the llacta, the Ecuadorean Quechua term for parcialidad, and thus designates a group continuously occupying a definite area and having distinctive customs and traditions.[15] Hence the divergence of opinion as to whether the parcialidad (llacta) or the ayllu is the basic social unit is not serious, since there is a tendency for the extended family to coincide with the parcialidad, particularly where the latter is small.

The proper criterion by which to designate the functioning group unit is in both views largely the measure of co-operation which unites such groups in work projects and celebrations, such as housebuilding, agricultural tasks, baptisms, weddings, funerals--the major life events which are matters of common and communal concern, to which relatives, neighbors, and friends contribute and in which they participate jointly.

It is, however, Mrs. Parsons who produces the most substantial evidence in favor of her opinion that it is the ayllu rather than the parcialidad as such that is the co-operating and primarily cofunctioning social group. In the first place, we have her direct and relatively close observations on the composition of permanently and regularly interacting and coacting, and hence co-operative, groups within a parcialidad of the size of Peguche, which, according to her, comprises 122 households.[16]

Accordingly, it is family relations that are close and co-operative; it is the family circle within which visiting and borrowing and lending of tools and other articles occurs, and within which food gifts are exchanged on ceremonial occasions; members of the extended family or the relatives within a community compose the nucleus of the party of helpers building a house for a young couple; at formal assemblages it is by and within the family that contributions of food and drinks or money to purchase drinks are made--always and eminently the family, i.e., relatives connected by blood and/or marriage plus those (provided they are Indian) who stand to an individual in the all-important relation of compadreship. (Compadres, "gossip," are a sort of fictitious kin, or kin by courtesy. Marriage restrictions within the baptismal compadre circle are the same as those obtaining for the proper kin group or ayllu.)[17]

It is obvious that these close face-to-face relations can obtain only within a group of relatively limited numbers. It has been mentioned before that the ayllu, or bilaterally extended family, may be coextensive with the parcialidad or local settlement, or administrative unit if the latter is small enough. Hence a few words on the possible size of both the ayllu and the parcialidad settlement are necessary.

Thanks to Buitrón's survey of 37 parcialidades in the canton of Otavalo, there are some data on the number of houses or households composing these parcialidades which convey an idea at least of the order of magnitudes that are involved.[18] Parsons, on her part, provides some information from which it is possible to gauge the number of members composing the functioning extended family group within a parcialidad of the size of Peguche.

On Buitrón's rough enumeration, the smallest number of houses per parcialidad is 20, the largest 2,500. Sixteen, or 43 per cent, of the 37 parcialidades are credited with a number of households under 100; seventeen, or 46 per cent, had up to and including 400 houses (the majority still below 200); and four parcialidades, or 11 per cent, were credited with 1,000 to, and including, 2,500 houses.

Now, despite the discrepancies in the reported size of Peguche, this parcialidad can be considered to be of representative size within the size range of Otavalo parcialidades (122 to 300 households); it may also be considered as having a population that is somewhat too large for its members to know each other intimately, have constant and direct face-to-face relations, and co-operate with each other consistently and permanently.

How large is the size of the extended family or permanently and constantly co-operating group? Parsons provides two sets of data by which to arrive at an approximate answer. One set consists of three genealogical tables for three families among whom, in turn, many connections by blood and marriage exist (i.e., marriages between third and even second cousins). Together, these tables name a little over 130 individuals who were alive at the time the data were collected (1940 and 1941) and who resided in Peguche. Another set of data enumerates 30 Peguche households the majority of whose members were related by blood and/or marriage in various degrees; these 30 households constituted the first host-group to an ambulant saint's image which made the rounds within that group, then moved on to another such group within Peguche, again a distinct kin and neighborhood group.[19]

Hence, within a parcialidad of the size of Peguche, the functioning group consists of between 120 and 150 individuals who are closely related and who live in as close proximity to each other as a scatter-settlement permits. These are the face-to-face groups whose members have constant or regular contact with each other; within which visiting, borrowing and lending occurs; this is the co-operative, "mutual-help" group.

A parcialidad, a concentration, or other type of settlement, then, may consist of several such groups, as in the case of Peguche. It is the overlapping of such groups that may give a local community the cast of a solidly cohesive group. However, it is important to realize that it is anyone's extended family that is the real center of gravity and the frame of reference encompassing all solidarity behavior, and that the local community, whatever its designation, tends to provide merely the setting for it. It is in this sense that, as Buitrón puts it (1947a), "the parcialidad, like a great and good family, is ever ready to help and support the individual whenever he is in need"; and it is in consideration of this fact, no less than in consideration of the mistrust of Indians toward all outsiders /Whites/, that he arrives at the conclusion that "it is not advisable to attempt incorporation /of the Indians of Otavalo/ into the social security system."

As in any group, no matter how tightly knit, there are occasions for strife and quarrel. However, so little is made in the literature of such negative intragroup relations, and so much is made of the co-operation within the local group, that these indicators of divisive tendencies, if they are such, are offered here merely to complete the picture.

Quarrels and fights occur and are indeed frequent even among close neighbors and kindred, but the occasions which give rise to them are the usual festive occasions when people are in their cups; hence no responsibility is expected for damages inflicted under such circumstances (fines

are levied by the public authorities for drunkenness and drunken mis-
behavior, but this is a matter of a "third party," so to speak), nor are
lasting enmities supposed to be engendered by a drunken fight or by an
exchange of insults.

Fear of witchcraft or black magic may well be indicative of intragroup enmities,[20] but witchcraft being a practice that by its very nature
is secretive, too little is known on that subject to permit conclusions as
to the strength and extent in any group of this potential divisor.

Litigations and lawsuits, particularly over land and inheritance,
seem to be very frequent. Though these are public affairs, we have no
data as to how much such litigations contribute, if at all, to extensive
intragroup and individual enmities and feuds. But there can be little
doubt that factionalism, centering on lawsuits, has to be reckoned with
in any community.[21]

Finally, a good index to group cohesion and particularly to group
solidarity would be furnished by indices of thievery: Who steals from
whom? Rivet, in assessing the "character" of Riobamba Indians, says
that they rarely resist the temptation to steal from non-Indians or outsiders but that they are honest with their fellow-Indians and show their
reciprocal confidence by leaving their homes unlocked. Yet among the
functions of the sorcerer-curer-diviner, described by Rivet in the same
article, is that of locating lost and stolen objects and of indicating the
thief. In Otavalo, a tale about a robbery is told in explanation for the
custom of keeping doors locked, and the curandero is consulted as to lost
and stolen articles and the identity of thieves and robbers.[22]

Outside the local community and kinship groups as solidly cohesive
groups, viable associations or organizations qua Indians are not conspicuous, nor are they in Indian tradition. In recent years, however,
Indians who have gone to the cities to work are said to have formed their
own professional associations or guilds (gremios), complete with statutes,
flags, music bands, such as street-sweepers, porters or carriers, masons,
and the last-named even maintain relations with colleague-groups in
other cities.[23]

Some of the traditional Indian "professions" and crafts tend to be
handed down in the male family line (as in the case of some curanderos,
or, for instance, in adobe-making) or in the female line (as in the case
of pottery-making in Otavalo). But nothing like occupational "castes" is
engendered by these few and, so far, not very well substantiated family
specializations. Nor do we find guilds, such as Indian weavers might have
formed locally and translocally, nor "colleges" of curers or medicine
men. Finally, the rudimentary religious lay organizations or "orders,"
which exist here and there, seem to have no other but local significance.
Dedicated to the service of a saint, they do not constitute a "community"
apart from the local one and hence do not create ties among members
over a larger plane. There are no hints, furthermore, as to the existence
of any type of secret societies.

Thus, once more, the conclusion is that there exist virtually no
solidarity-building group formations transcending the local setting.

Last to be considered in this connection are the possibilities for
both integrative and divisive tendencies resulting from the existence of
social strata among Indians at large and within the local Indian group.
No clear indications were found pointing toward full-fledged stratification

on (economic) class lines among Indians at the present time. The wealthier
and economically more successful individual certainly enjoys more personal prestige within the community than his poorer fellow-Indian because,
above all, he can fulfil certain public functions that are all-important in
Indian life. Furthermore, there are indications that classlike, or, better,
stratificatory distinctions are maintained between "free" Indians and
concierto Indians of the same locality--distinctions which are expressed
in avoidance of intermarriage, as in Imbabura, or in verbal disparagement
in references to less "acculturated" Indians;[24] in such cases it is not
clear how far traditional interlocality attitudes are intermingled with
"class" attitudes arising from differential stages in "acculturation" (ability to speak Spanish, for instance). In Ilumán, an Otavalo parish, "Blancos"
and "acculturated" Indian owner-farmers are said to "understand" each
other better than the latter and the "poor" Indian huasipungeros (IEAG
1953, No. 3:182).

It is, at any rate, only occasionally that the existence of classes or
castes among Indians is being explicitly asserted. There are a few cryp-
tic hints to that effect: "In only one place of these two countries /Peru and
Ecuador/, Saraguro in Ecuador, did we find anything that would correspond to a caste system. Here were three distinct group classifications
each one determining social distinctions and rights." Further, equally
tantalizing references, complementing the preceding statement, to "the
three social strata of local Indian society" in Saraguro, "who will not live
together with elements of other classes," make it clear only that these
"castes" or "classes" are actually composed of Indians and that each of
them has its own mayordomo or manager at fiestas. There is no information on the principles on which this inter-Indian stratification is based.[25]

In any event, there are these references to inter-Indian stratification, but, while its existence cannot be doubted, it is so inconspicuous (at
least to non-Indian observers) and so little substantiated that it would be
rash to infer from it a "class-consciousness" transcending the local setting and to consider it as focal to translocal Indian solidarities.

So far, the question of the focus of inter-Indian solidarity has been
discussed largely with reference to Indians or to Indian groups which are
not subject to the hacienda regime. As for such hacienda peons (conciertos or huasipungeros), there are no data from which to infer any in-
group feeling among them, other than the accounts of battles which used
to occur between different groups of hacienda Indians on fiestas, on which
occasions they converged at one place. Whether these groupwise periodic
conflicts still occur is a question; at any rate, they alone would constitute but tenuous evidence for haciendawise Indian solidarity. Whether,
on the other hand, cohesiveness in the case of hacienda Indians is established on the same principles of locality and family as among "free"
Indians (as is likely), or whether additionally or alternatively it is established on the basis of identification with the master and landlord, is not
known.[26] They certainly are spoken of as "belonging" to this or that
hacienda, and with residence over several generations on a hacienda,
this "belongingness" is no doubt sufficiently internalized to produce
group cohesion around such a focus. But, to repeat, the literature on
hacienda peons is much too vocal on the abuses to which they are subjected to make anything but guesses possible. The paternalistic, protective hacendado commanding his peons' allegiance and creating group
solidarity among them on that basis, if he exists at all, finds no mention.

This survey, in the course of which we have examined a number of
principles by which group solidarity might be possible, has resulted in

the conclusion that it is in fact the local and/or kinship group which is virtually the only group type having effective cohesion or solidarity. As the sphere widens, group ties appear to become progressively tenuous. Kin relations and co-operation remain confined within numerically manageable proportions. For all practical purposes, no other principles of association or group formation, transcending the local boundaries, seem to exist; there is nothing that overcomes the principle of extended family and localism. There is no Indian "community" or "society." There are only distinct local communities, and it is these which, having inner cohesion and operating on the local level, are of importance to industry: from them, the "naturally given" work groups may be drawn, the members of which are used to co-operating with each other, at least know each other, and might for this reason sustain their own discipline.

It now behooves us to examine the local community further, with regard to its organization in political and other self-administrative matters, and to ask what arrangements exist by which local solidarity tends to be reinforced by specific interests. Who, for example, are the leaders in the community, and from what quarters does initiative arise, if any?

B. Indian Group Organization

The fact that it is only the local community which is the focus around which Indian group life is apt to coalesce might easily lead to the impression that such groups are also tightly knit in regard to their organizational forms. Any such impression is, however, considerably mitigated on considering the parcialidad or equivalent community from the point of view of formal political organization or, for that matter, of any organizational tendencies in other directions. On the contrary, the absence of such tendencies is notable; or, if there are any, they are most inconspicuous.

The following survey of local "self-administrative" arrangements will serve to point up the comparative lack of cohesiveness of the local group on formal, systematic ground or on a level where appropriate arrangements for "social control" and for the making of decisions are properly and deliberately "organized," explicit, regularly observed, manifest or open to inspection by the outsider, and subject to rules more or less known as such to everybody. Special attention will be given to the discernment of those personages within the local community who, because of their office, i.e., formally or for other reasons, hold positions of influence and authority among the Indians.[27] As has been stressed several times, such key men are of particular interest to any "action" emanating from outside initiative, including industry; it may be presumed that it is persons having actual command or enjoying authority over others who may supply or, indeed, deny the leverage necessary to move people into industry and who, within the industrial situation, might continue to exercise more effective command functions than strange and superimposed elements.

1. Local Political[28] Organization and Functionaries

So far as Indian local political organization and local administrative apparatus are concerned, they are neither independent of, nor particularly distinct from, those applying for the country at large. Politically, neither parcialidades nor the recently created comunas (see below) nor hacienda peons' groups have a life of their own; administratively, they have no really independent officialdom capable of acting on its own responsibility in no matter how circumscribed a sphere of action. The arrangements by which law, in the formal sense, and order are maintained among the Indian group are merely the extensions or adjuncts of those of the parish, cantonal, or provincial unit in which it is located. Until recent times there were no provisions under the Republic which permitted Indian communities to function with a measure of autonomy in matters political or administrative, formally or in practice, and hence these have generally no corresponding organizations of their own.

(a) Recent Developments: The Comuna[29]

It is in part this state of affairs which the Law of Organization and Regulation of Communal Lands (Ley de Organización y Regimen de las Comunas, briefly, Ley de Comunas) of 1937 aims to change, and this modern development ought to be briefly considered, both for its intrinsic interest and for the light it sheds on the existing situation.

The Ley de Comunas intends to give juridic personality and organizationally explicit form to the politically and administratively amorphous and economically anemic parcialidades, anejos, caseríos, etc. It is applicable to population groups of fifty or more adults who wish to achieve a functional organizational machinery affording them representation before governmental authorities. While thus providing for all rural groups, the law is aimed particularly at the protection of Indian rural communities and, where these own natural resources, from outside encroachments. The comuna, as conceived by the law, is modeled somewhat along the lines of supposedly pre-Columbian communal forms of land tenure and exploitation, incorporates features of Spanish-colonial municipal organization, and also contains elements of modern co-operative associations. These newly and voluntarily created rural administrative, semipolitical, and (where the bases exist) economic units are designed "to play the traditional political and administrative role of the comunidad...where land is communally owned."[30]

The conversion of "unconsolidated" groups such as parcialidades into corporate and relatively self-administrative bodies calls for the creation of an apparatus consisting of a cabildo ("council" or "board") composed of five members--a president, a vice-president, treasurer, secretary, and syndic (sindico, "trustee" or "attorney")--which is to be elected annually by a general assembly of the registered members of the comuna, i.e., men and women aged 18 or over. The cabildo acts as the legal representative of the comuna and administers its economic affairs, its legal matters, and is in charge of functions such as distributing and renting land to individual cultivator-members. However, the formation of a comuna does not necessarily imply that it owns goods, i.e., land and rights to other natural resources, in common; it merely enables population nuclei which are not otherwise "incorporated" (as in a parish) to achieve corporate status, and thus as statutory bodies to acquire or safeguard land, forest, or pasture resources[31] for their own use, or to further other interests and activities of theirs in common, such as craft production. In regard to this last aspect, the form of co-operative as a complement to the comuna is the one most commonly proposed.[32]

Communally owned lands are in principle inalienable.[33] Lands of Indian comunidades and comunas are exempt from rural property taxes.

Communities thus organized under the law are under the supervision or tutelage of the Ministry of Social Welfare (Previsión Social),
which itself may appoint a cabildo where its functions are not exercised
properly and equitably. Otherwise comunas are under the jurisdiction
of their respective parishes, a division of responsibilities that has
drawn criticism.

Claims regarding the number of comunas vary. It has been stated
that between 1938 and 1943 over 1,200 comunas were organized comprising
a total population of over 600,000.[34] Subsequently published figures
indicate barely 900 "legally organized" comunas in all of Ecuador, with
a comuna population of approximately 300,000 (Zambrano 1951). A survey
of the highland Indian communities (concentraciones indo-mestizas) shows
that but 189 (out of a listed potential of 1,472), with an estimated population
of 119,000, appear as comunas, utilizing communal resources, with or
without additional private holdings, for timber and fuel, pasture, irrigation, or for "industrial" raw materials, worked up in craft-fashion (Cisneros Cisneros 1948).

Up to the present, these new creations cannot be considered typical
of Ecuadorean Indian group life, nor do they appear to function well in the
majority of cases. Major shortcomings are due to the confusion of the
cabildo members regarding their rights and duties; failure of the outgoing
cabildo to call the general assembly for the election of a new one; arroga-
tion of powers by the president beyond those assigned him, arbitrary
administration, and lack of internal or external control over his actions.
In brief, the cabildo tends either to abuse its powers or to fail altogether
in exercising its tasks (Cisneros Cisneros 1948:151 ff.; 1949; Zambrano 1951).

Evidently, fifteen or sixteen years are not enough for a formalized
organization to supplant the loose type of "organization" which, at least
since republican days, has characterized Indian group life, which still
characterizes it, and to which attention is turned now.

(b) The General Situation

Such as local political organization is, it has found a number of illus-
trative comments. Thus the "simplicity, the almost total lack of functionaries in the Ecuadorean parcialidad," the absence of any deliberative bodies
and of administrative hierarchies, is particularly striking to Saenz in comparison with the organization in Indian communities and their political life
in Guatemala and in parts of Mexico. From the point of view of his experience with these countries and measured against a policy of assimilation ("integrating the Indian with the life of the nation"), he evaluates the
situation positively: "The Ecuadorean Indian does not suffer from the narrow village localism /i.e., tight local organization/ which is observed in
Guatemala and in the South of Mexico, first, because the village as such
does not exist, since the homesteads of the population lie dispersed about
the parcialidad; second because of the residue of /primitive/ communism"
/meaning the communally owned pasture lands and the communal work
parties of mingas /.[35]

Outside of the recent comuna organization, the Ecuadorean Indians'
only formal provision for self-government is through the national suffrage,
the exercise of which requires literacy and is, even so, subject to the
directives of the parish priest and the other powers that are. Moreover,
"there is no indication of an urge to political organization in Imbabura
today or at earlier periods."[36]

Under these circumstances, who are the persons among Indians who represent such political and administrative matters as are of concern to a parcialidad or to a group of hacienda peons? And what are their roles toward the represented or commanded group and toward the authorities to whom representation is made?

Indian communities, such as the parcialidades of Otavalo, tend to have one or more alcaldes, themselves Indians. (Other terms for holders of offices that are analogous in other types of settlements and in other regions of the highlands are regidores, gobernadores, cabecillas, curacas, and the modern Quechua term, llacta-umas.)[37] Where this is the case, observers speak of a "cazique government" (of the colonial type) as being still intact. "In some regions, the Indian still preserves remnants of his original political organization; the alcaldes are caziques or governors, real chiefs of the Indians; the ñaupadores /"councillors"; see below/ play an important role" (Saenz 1933a:131). This "government," as a systematic, formal and conspicuous institution, does not appear to be as frequent as other general assertions might lead one to believe; in fact, today it seems to be the exception rather than the rule. Cisneros, in his survey of close to 1,500 named communities, mentions the existence of curaca or alcalde forms of government (organización Caciquil y de Curacas, or de Alcaldes; regimen de Curacas y Caciques; regimen Caciquil, etc.) in the case of only 23 Indian communities or clusters of communities, of which 12 alone are in Imbabura Province, the remainder in the central provinces of Cotopazi, Tungurahua, and Chimborazo.[38] In most cases, the secular local authority is vested in the teniente político of the parish. Parish boards (juntas) are provided for under a special law, but do not exist in most cases.[39]

The forms by which alcaldeship is attained vary. In practice, if not formally, the office may be hereditary in some communities. The more general rule seems to be for it to be "elective." Although under recent legislation alcaldes are supposed to be elected by the members of the parcialidad, they are actually appointed by the teniente político or sometimes by the parish priest. Occasionally, the proposal for the appointment of an alcalde comes from the Indians themselves, but there is no information on the formal or actual process by which this is accomplished. As Parsons points out (1945:84), "secular election of Indian officers was never introduced" in Ecuador, a statement which is not to be taken quite literally: provisions for such elections and for a measure of self-government are "on the books."

Nevertheless, in law these Indian headmen or mayors have no official status vis-à-vis the central government. In actual practice, however, an alcalde, a cabecilla, etc., may function as "the official representative of his parcialidad before the authorities of the Republic."

The functions which such headmen perform also tend to be ambiguous. On the one hand, they are described as taking care of the internal affairs of the community, such as organizing mingas for public works, resolving conflicts, even imposing punishments, guarding over morality, performing the traditional native part of marriage ceremonies-- in short, carrying out such administrative, judiciary, executive, and advisory functions as are called for within their bailiwicks.

On the other hand, alcalde functions consist also in the execution of commissions with which the teniente of the parish charges them: to make announcements and to act as sheriffs, to round up Indians for unpaid public works or for work on behalf of a private party,[40] to run shopping and other errands for their administrative superiors. These are for the most part actual, not legal, obligations. Alcaldes receive no pay, but are supposed to serve "patriotically."

The system seems to be similar for hacienda peons in that their Indian headman (cabecilla, "little head," or mayoral) acts primarily as agent or labor recruiter for the hacendado or for his manager; he arranges for hacienda labor, be it for a minga-organized task or for seasonal employment. In general, the mayoral (quipu in Quechua) is a type of foreman and disciplinarian among the hacienda hands, with power of physical punishment and with certain privileges and responsibilities. In some cases he also conducts a weekly morning session during which the peons' children are instructed, by him, in prayer, song, and catechism.[41]

Considering the actual roles and tasks of such officials, it is perhaps not surprising that, as some observers indicate, they are disesteemed by their fellow-Indians. In Otavalo, the alcaldeship is wanted by few. Office holders, because of the actual (not legal or formal) obligations which they have to fulfil, are likely to make enemies for themselves in having to enforce the orders of the teniente and the police; the errands are time-consuming and compel alcaldes to neglect their own work; and they face the accusation of being lazy, a very grievous charge in Indian eyes. Direct expenses also may be incurred by the alcalde in the performance of his task to furnish Indians for public works, in that he has to provide chicha at his own expense.

Furthermore, it appears as though the nature of the formal alcaldeship in its modern garb is by no means understood. According to Collier and Buitrón, the "mayor" of Otavalo appoints every year a committee consisting of president, vice-president, secretary, treasurer, and syndic, which is to sponsor and prepare free elections of community officers. All the members of this committee--very likely either an appointed cabildo of a comuna, or the junta of a parish--are indiscriminately called alcaldes by the Indians, the implication being that they fail to grasp the meaning of, or appreciate, apparatus and arrangement.

Alcaldes or cabecillas in their roles as labor recruiters are also unpopular. There are complaints that "they do not defend the rights of a poor man in trouble with a hacienda or with the municipality; they merely make presents...to the judges and others." If such a one happens to be considered "rich," his unpopularity is doubly compounded, for he is disesteemed for his greed for money and land, for his stinginess, for his unneighborliness, and he is also one who is always "intent on securing peons by foul means."[42]

If authority and prestige on the basis of formal office, such as it is, is small, there are hints that authority on a personal basis or, more precisely, on the basis of personal qualities and achievements, can accrue to an individual. In following these hints of leadership exercised on the "informal" level, we are confronted with a type of political organization and of "functionaries" which is not predictable on as systematic grounds as in the cases described before.

Rivet observed that every Indian village in the Riobamba region has a chief, a "mayoral," who is self-imposed and who has attained to that position not by vote or consent of his fellow-Indians but by virtue of his own cunning or force; an example is given of such a chief, who is "a real king among Riobamba Indians, surrounded with respect, whose advice is listened to, whose orders are obeyed, and who enjoys uncontested power." Similar is the position of the hacienda mayoral in that region, who is found in every hacienda where many Indians work, apropos of which Rivet comments: "...the concern to give themselves a chief is innate in the race. Each time that a group of Indians, small as it may be, accomplishes a piece of work in common, after a few days one of them, the strongest or the most cunning, imposes his authority over his comrades and directs and commands them."[43]

Orton, too, gives some instances of chieftainship of the kind that points to eminently personal qualifications, such as ability to speak Spanish and literacy, rather than to a preservation of institutional elements (1875:179, 181 ff., 185). Literacy among illiterates as a leadership qualification is underlined by the many observations according to which such Indians tend to abuse their skills, position, and authority to the detriment of their fellow-Indians (see, e.g., Franklin 1943:78). The chances are that such literate Indians with command of Spanish are in any event and for these very reasons classed by outsiders as Mestizos or Cholos, and Mestizos are traditionally considered the exploiters of Indians. One is led to think that such persons are sometimes identified as Mestizos or Cholos because of their personal power among otherwise fellow-Indians. Such observations lend a further dimension to the ambiguous position of Indian leaders, official or otherwise.

Nevertheless, these Indian leaders, whether they be termed alcaldes or cabecillas, whether their "office" is "formal" or not, can be very important. Thus during a pilot census held in one of the Otavalo parishes some months previous to the full-dress 1950 official census, it was the alcaldes of legally unofficial and unrecognized status who collected and reassured the Indians who were fleeing all over the hills and thus saved the day for the officials who conducted the experiment (Garcés 1950).

Purchases of hacienda lands in the province of Azuay have been made collectively by Indians through their cabecillas, who collected the money for this purpose from the Indians. The reporter of these cases concluded therefrom that Indians are capable of common organized action once land is involved, despite their meager organizational apparatus (Monsalve Pozo 1942)--action, that is, which does not follow a traditional or formal pattern but which is organized in the face of a novel situation and novel opportunities. Yet it is precisely such a comuna, organized in 1944 by Indian hacienda ex-huasipungeros who had bought hacienda lands, which serves as the type-case (IEAG 1953, No. 4) for the impotence of such a community which lacks traditional organization and leadership, techniques of dealing with the ways of the modern world and the Whites; the lack of this traditional and modern organizational equipment and know-how has left such a comuna in a legally and economically precarious position, virtually without defense against "interested" outsiders, with an enfeebled and practically nonfunctioning cabildo and with internal divisions.

On the whole, modern observers are fairly well agreed on the lack of autonomy of the Indian local community in political and administrative matters and on the lack of an independent and discernible self-administrative apparatus. Alcaldes "generally are only the instruments of the authority and represent no moral leadership among their fellow-Indians" (Saenz 1933a:131). How, in concrete cases, such Indian crypto-authority can nevertheless be effective has already been shown.

In summary, it can be said that the Indians' social coherence or solidarity on the local level generally is not related to a correlative political organization but rests solely upon kinship and neighborhood. Such political organization as does exist is amorphous and on the whole so attenuated as to be incapable of yielding up a consistent, formal leadership.

It hardly needs to be pointed out that the personnel which does man the key posts in local administrative organization is generally not suitable for initiating and facilitating the contacts of industry with Indians. The tendency is for such offices to be unpopular and for their holders to be suspect by Indians and non-Indians, though for different reasons. There may be individual cases of communities and office holders where some genuine confidence is established between Indians and their officials and where some genuine cohesion is created around some such personalized authority. The detection of such a personage, however, cannot be made systematically on the ground of known formal organization.

There is, however, another aspect to Indian leadership deserving of attention. Where effective leading personages exist, properly recognized as alcaldes by their Indians, the office resembles that of the ancient headmen of the ten- and fifty-, perhaps even the one-hundred-, family groups of the Incanate, those petty officers in close contact with their men, actively directing and supervising their work and themselves setting the pace--leaders of the top-sergeant and foreman type. The understanding of this office and role seems to be still alive; today's alcalde is expected by his Indians to set the example, to work as hard as anyone or better, and his very position and authority are predicated on exemplary, active industriousness.[44]

Having established the dearth of effective cohesion on an autonomous secular political level, the question now arises whether there are other "interests" that give rise to formal organization and cohesion and through it to a measure of active solidarity. It is found in examining the religious life of Ecuadorean Indians. What sort of religious organization does prevail, how is it formally organized, where are its key men, and what kind of authority, if any, do they exercise?

2. Religious Organizations and Functionaries

Religion occupies a conspicuous place in Indian life. Its importance is underlined by the fact that data on the overt and more manifest activities connected with this sphere are, comparatively speaking, ample. Ostentatious events such as fiestas centering on a religious theme and pilgrimages related to the cult of a saint's image are, of course, difficult to overlook. Paradoxical as it may sound, the significance of religion for Ecuadorean Indians is equally highlighted by their secretiveness in religious matters, of which Mrs. Parsons has encountered unequivocal examples.[45]

Many observers comment on the religious devotion of Ecuadorean highland Indians and on the high degree to which they are formally Catholicized. In this respect, they are said to offer a contrast to Indians of other Latin American countries, where aboriginal religious forms and concepts have been better preserved and appear, therefore, more conspicuous.[46] In Ecuador, Catholic observances and Catholic beliefs dominate Indian religious practice regardless of the undercurrent of "folk" and pre-Catholic, native beliefs and observances.

This is perhaps another way of indicating that, in matters religious, Ecuadorean Indians are as co-ordinated or integrated, institutionally, with the official Catholic Church, as they are dependent on the official apparatus of the central national state in matters political and administrative. However, within the limits of this dependence on, or integration with, the institutions of the church, there exist clearly discernible though rudimentary organizations revolving on interest in religion and, particularly, on certain forms of religious observances. These organizations are dedicated to the maintenance of local chapels and to the elaboration of Catholic cults (the celebration of a saint's holiday) and appear today to be a matter of distinctively Indian interest. That this is a fairly recent development is suggested by Rivet's observations (1906) from which one can infer that some of these religious, ceremonial observances and their specific forms were by no means exclusively Indian as little as fifty years ago (cf. Chapter X, note 25).

Indian religious organization is local and centers on the chapel of the parcialidad, or the church of the parish, the cult of the local patron saint, and the celebration of his and other major saints' days.[47] According to these two matters of concern, namely, chapel maintenance and service of the saint, two sets of officials can be distinguished, although just barely, for here again Indian secretiveness, lack of specific data, and, probably, also the slightness of elaboration of Indian religious organization itself combine in rendering the discernment of their systematics, if any, difficult.

One set of officials consists of relatively permanent functionaries of the local chapel, who hold office for terms of one, two, or three years: the sindico, who is the keeper of the chapel keys and who is responsible for chapel property, and several alcaldes (alcaldes de capilla, chapel alcaldes, not to be confused with the alcaldes discussed in the foregoing section),[48] who are appointed by the parish priest. They carry a staff or cane, sometimes adorned with silver, as a token of their office. These chapel alcaldes are responsible for assembling work parties (mingas, faenas) for needed repair and similar work on chapel or church or monastery where the latter is in charge of the spiritual life of a parish. They also keep order at fiestas, acting thus as secular officers or sheriffs.

Such a setup is described (Parsons 1945:207-8) in some detail for a community southeast of Quito, Amaguaña, in the Valley of Chillos. There, the priest names two alcaldes and one alguacil (a minor functionary, a kind of sheriff for the priest) from among the peons of the local hacienda. "The duties of the alcaldes are to see to it that the people attend la dotrina /the "Doctrine," catechism/ and Mass, to inform the priest of faults and lapses, to see that people do not fight and injure others when drunk, to take the priest to the sick and dying, and to bury anyone who has no family to bury him, getting the money from the patrones /hacienda owners/ or other moneyed persons. Alcaldes and the aguacil walk in the van of dance processions to keep order and decency. It is not obligatory for the alcalde to provide for feasts /see below/, but he may do so, and for Corpus Christi an alcalde provides a greased pole" hung with foods and other prizes to be retrieved by those who succeed in climbing to the top.

Apart from this instance, little attention has been paid to these chapel officials, perhaps because their functions tend to fuse with those of the second set of religious functionaries, to be discussed presently, or perhaps because the existence of the "alcalde system" in any one settlement depends on whether a priest or monastic order actively stimulates and supports the development of chapel organization on the local level.[49] At any rate, Mrs. Parsons (1945:83, 84), on the basis of her observation in Otavalo, arrives at the conclusion that "in parish church and more particularly in chapel organization lies the nearest approach to self-government to be found in Peguche or elsewhere in Andean Indian Ecuador," even though "under the parochial system Indian officials were and are factors of control by the Church."

The other set of religious functionaries that can, in principle, be distinguished relates to the "mayordomia or prioste system for the cult of the saints." These functionaries are not officials, properly speaking, but are officials only pro tempore, as it were. They are the men who take charge of the locally notable saint (or a holy "day") and who, for the duration of this office, are known under the titles of prioste, mayordomo or, as in Peguche, capitán. They mostly volunteer for this office for a term of one to three years, as is general in Ecuador. Until a few years ago, it is said, it was customary for the priest to designate the prioste or cargador (one who takes on the cargo, the burden), and the custom still prevails in many parts of the country.[50] Such seems to be the case in Amaguaña, mentioned above, a community which apparently is composed of "free" and hacienda Indians. There, the priostes to serve for Corpus Christi and other feasts are appointed by the parish priest. They are chosen from among the landowning Indians, and they serve the hacienda peons as sponsors of the fiesta, while the patrón ("landlord"), on the one hand, and the chapel alcaldes, on the other, contribute certain items to the fiesta.[51] Elsewhere still, the office of the prioste falls to the lot of the Indian (secular) gobernador and (secular) alcaldes (Rodríguez Sandoval 1949:103 ff.).

Whether the office is assumed voluntarily or by appointment by the priest or even by the (secular) alcalde in agreement with the priest, to serve at least one term as prioste is a duty which every man, once married and a householder, is expected to discharge at least once in his lifetime unless he wants to face the serious disesteem of the members of his community.[52] The prioste finances and organizes the celebration of the local saint or of a holiday.[53] He is the leader of the procession of dances that follow the mass, the host who furnishes most of the meals and drinks, the main provider of music bands, fireworks, and other incidentals, the undisputed "king" and chieftain of the celebrants. Other functionaries for these occasions serve under various titles as assistants, cofinanciers or co-organizers, or have specific roles, dramatic and others. These fiestas are, and are meant to be, ostentatious affairs. But little is known with regard to the inner working of these organized saints' celebrations and the manner in which they are arranged.[54]

It is difficult to tell whether, and to what extent, chapel alcaldes and priostes enjoy any authority by virtue of their office or role. In the case of the appointed chapel alcaldes, there is little to indicate that the appointment as such confers prestige and authority upon them. Rather, it seems, they take on the service or are appointed because they already have standing in the community, because they can afford the service with the expense in time and money entailed by it and, perhaps, because they are better able to assemble a work party than others--clearly a matter of the influence they already command in the community. However, all these are surmises, for there is nowhere an explicit statement as to the bases for their appointment, as to their qualifications, and, least of all, as to any influence they might have on their fellow-Indians that would indicate any one person as a likely choice for that office.

So far as the priostes, the nominally or really volunteer sponsors of a fiesta for a saint, are concerned, it seems safe to say that their leadership is a strictly ad hoc matter, namely, for the duration of their sponsorship or of a celebration (about one year). As has been pointed out, such sponsorship is expected of any man, and assumption of this duty is therefore a matter of course, a prerequisite to being considered a full-fledged adult member of the community.

Hence while we do encounter some sort of local organization in the religious sphere, an organization which, despite its vagueness, is certainly more developed than the political-administrative "organization," its functionaries do not, by themselves, seem to constitute rallying points for the community, reinforcing its cohesion. Rather, the presence of such functionaries may constitute indices of the community's vitality and vigor in sustaining a common interest. Nor do chapel alcaldes and priostes seem to derive any special authority from their offices and roles in the religious organization alone.

Yet alcaldes and priostes must not be underrated for our "practical" purposes, which consist in indicating what persons are capable of keeping discipline among Indians on whatever basis and by whatever means or authority however derived. Consideration of Indian religious organization fails to disclose formal, institutional leadership with unmistakable distinctiveness, be it for lack of sufficiently detailed information on the mechanics of chapel and prioste system, be it for weaknesses inherent in them. But considering merely the nature of the more or less temporary prominence attained by individuals as chapel officers or as fiesta-sponsoring priostes, the offices serve to indicate those among Indians who can be presumed to "count" within the Indian community: the discharge of office and tasks requires of these "functionaries" maturity, a measure of wealth (or credit),[55] and a circle of relatives and friends to help in the realization of tasks attendant upon the "office." Its fulfilment, particularly where the office or function is assumed independently of clerical pressure, also indicates the individual's concern to keep in touch with the community and to retain or increase its good will and good opinion toward himself. If these inferred attributes constitute leadership, alcaldes and priostes are apt to command it. And fiestas are, therefore, as good occasions as any to discern socially leading Indians.

3. Other Persons of Authority or Potential Influence

The preceding surveys of Indian organized group life have yielded few personages who by virtue of their special office command general authority or who exercise actual and sustained influence over other individuals in their communities. It cannot but have become all too apparent that, organizationally, communal life on the level of the local group is extremely formless. The truly startling paucity in the nomenclature of offices and roles is but a corollary to this organizational formlessness: terms like alcalde and mayordomo have to cover a variety of (modernly) heterogeneous offices and roles. In some cases, as must have become abundantly clear, it is only by the exercise of specific functions that an officer is recognized as a secular or religious one. This holds if we look at matters in terms of the rubrics into which we classify activities. Clearly, Indians themselves do not divide up their worlds into secular and nonsecular realms, and it is no doubt also for this reason that offices are so little distinguished terminologically.

However considered, the formless local organization corresponds to the virtual nonexistence of authority on formal grounds. Indian communal life is poor in regard to key men. Even a noticeably strong "interest," such as the religious one, has but an attenuated organizational form in which it finds expression. What is more, little or no respect, i.e., influence or authority of a potential nature and on the bilateral or dyadic level (as between counsel and client, doctor and patient, employer and employee, etc.), seems to accrue to holders of office merely because of their office. If it does, it appears to be achieved on a substantially personal basis; as we have pointed out, the office may be but the result of personal and individual achievements and qualities.

In this section we shall, therefore, briefly consider other possibilities which may place an individual in a position of authority, actual or potential, vis-à-vis his fellow Indians.

There are only two or three categories of people who conceivably might constitute sources of influence and authority within their community, be it on formal grounds, be it because of special qualifications. They have been mentioned or discussed before and are only briefly pointed to again in this context.

There are, in the first place, the so-called ñaupadores. Of them nothing is known except through the briefest of references. They are termed "counselors" by Saenz, who indicates that they have some kind of partly secular authority and who asserts that they play an important role in some regions without saying what precisely that role might be. Elsewhere, they figure as a kind of elder attendants or "troubadour-counselors" at Indian weddings,[56] clearly ceremonial roles today whatever else they might have been in times past.

The other category is that of the curanderos or brujos, the witch-curers, whose roles and functions have been discussed (Chapter VI). A perusal of the literature shows nothing by which to conclude that they enjoy any authority, respect, or prestige transcending the strict limits of their "calling." Within these limits, that is, on the basis of his profession which he exercises "on call," the brujo may be an important and respected person in the community, or else he may be viewed with skepticism and fear.[57] Information is both too general and too scant, even for Otavalo, to permit conclusions regarding the possible authority of curers and/or sorcerers in matters beyond their proper professions. There is certainly nothing to indicate that they constitute rallying points to, or leadership in, Indian society, as might have been the case in preconquest times and as is today the case among some eastern lowland Indians where dual leadership, consisting of shaman and war leader, occurs (Parsons 1945:176-77; Stirling 1938:39-40, 121).

Among occupational categories, those of masons or bricklayers (albaniles) seem to enjoy a high degree of prestige among Indians, qua masters of their trade; "they are treated with special consideration and addressed by the significant title 'master'" (maestro).[58]

A further such category is derived from interest in religion. "Prayers are exceedingly important and persons who know them are respected and paid for them, whether priest or layman."[59] Among such laymen could be counted the maestro rezador. And though he may not be shown particular overt deference by his Indian hosts, yet he is esteemed--for his functions, which are specific and circumscribed. Hence his position is, for practical purposes, analogous to that of the curandero, whose authority does not exceed his profession.

If the examination of specific roles or occupations has failed to point out possessors of general authority or actual command over others, it remains to look for other systemic grounds on the basis of which a special form of authority is established, namely, relations of respect, as such, of a "particularistic" character. Such relations are named here in order to indicate the persons who are in position to exercise potentially some authority or influence over others.

One of such relations and for all general purposes an important one is that in which the godchild stands to both his baptismal and his wedding godparents. On formal occasions, such as Holy Week, they are asked for their benedictions, and they are consulted on matters of importance.[60]

Age itself establishes its own respect relations. Respect and courtesy--and a high degree of courtesy at that--are rendered to the older persons within one's immediate and extended family, within the neighborhood, and within the parcialidad. These are addressed with the proper title of respect, taita ("father"), the title given to men of general distinction, such as the maestro rezador or the master who teaches the Doctrine. Disrespect to parents or godparents is considered a grave sin.[61]

Real, material obligations, particularly in conjunction with those imposed by respect relations, also establish situations of authority on the dyadic level. Obligations are incurred by children toward their parents so long as they are economically dependent. Marriages are contracted at a generally early age, and the young couple usually lives with the parents of either bride or groom until they have saved enough to start an independent establishment; until then they "are said in the Spanish phrase to be 'in the power of their father'." Furthermore, a parent drawing up a will might give preference to those of his children who have properly "served" him (Parsons 1945:33, 186), an assertion of parental authority by which children not only are kept "in line" but also might be influenced not to leave the parental homestead during the lifetime of one or both parents.

C. Fitting Existing Relations into an Industrial Situation

In the light of the requirements of industry for smooth interaction of discrete human elements, for intergroup compatibility, teamwork ability, and co-operation--in short, for functional discipline--we may inquire into the prospects of an incipient industry to obtain these social "qualities" and the circumstances and conditions under which they can be secured.

One way by which to circumvent all sorts of initial difficulties would be to select only the young people out of a community as recruits for industry. And, indeed, this has been a general tendency in industrializing situations, the assumption (or rationale) being that young persons, besides having other desirable qualities, are pliable enough to be fitted, in the course of an industrial apprenticeship, to the exact requirements of industry. This is a proposition that has much to recommend it, especially under a long-range point of view. But it is apt to put all kinds of responsibilities--technical, legal, and moral--on industry.[62]

An alternative procedure is given in the utilization of existing associational forms and in the integration of their "natural" (i.e., communal or familial) discipline into the industrial association.

As has been shown, there is no general inter-Indian cohesion throughout Ecuador. Hence inter-Indian compatibility cannot be taken for granted. At best, inter-Indian relations are neutral or indifferent, else there may be rivalry among groups coming from different localities. At worst, hostility and tendencies toward groupwise open warfare may be anticipated.

It is the local community and, within it, the kinship group that offers the greatest possibilities toward insuring compatibility and co-ordination in teamwork, even though it be "functionally diffuse" rather than "functionally specific" relationships on which such an arrangement would be based.

Looked at superficially, the question seems to boil down to an alternative, namely, whether Indians are to be recruited into, and dealt with within, industry as individuals or as collectivities. The assumption might be made that the units in either case have potentialities for use and development and lend themselves to modes of manipulation that are distinct from each other. In our concrete case it would be misleading to pose the question in this manner. Ecuadorean Indians, so far as can be ascertained, are neither markedly "individualistic" nor "collectivistic" in any sociological sense or in the sense in which the terms are employed in ordinary modern loose usages.

True, the relatively independent and somewhat self-sufficient local community has, as has been seen, a solidarity of sorts, hence might be considered as collectivistically oriented. Its cohesion is, nevertheless, attenuated because of its dependence on outside institutions such as in the political and administrative sphere, and because of the incomplete and slight development of sustaining organizations within it and the general lack of accentuation on single, distinct leadership personnel of any kind. The character of settlement itself has also to be considered. Whether the dispersal of the population constituting the local community is slight or not, in any one case, it is nevertheless a fact that habitations tend to be well separated from each other and, because of this lack of contiguity, "individualized," as it were, by spatial isolation.

So far as factual evidence is available, property, except perhaps in isolated cases, is no focus of collective cohesion. For, although some resources, such as forage, pasture and woodland, and water, are, in the best cases, "owned" by a community, the land that matters, i.e., that which is regularly worked, is generally owned individually or at least so possessed. There are no clear cases, for Ecuadorean Indians, of land collectively owned and collectively worked; nor are there instances in which communal resources give rise to any but ad hoc and ephemeral organizations, such as those in defense against encroachments from outside. In the case of water resources, irrigation ditches may be built and maintained collectively, but such cases are not well substantiated and seem to be anyway not common.

In all, the "collectivism" of the Indians, often so hopefully adduced as a basis upon which to engraft modern producers' and consumers' co-operatives (e.g., Rubio Orbe 1953) or as models by which local self-administration (such as the comunas) can be elaborated and secured, is derived from certain mutual-help patterns and from the observation of co-operatively executed tasks and collectively celebrated feasts, both of which may take in the local community to varying extents. However, in view of the results of our examination as to where co-operation actually begins and occurs and also of the specific tasks and enterprises to which such co-operation is limited, it seems that the collectivist character of Ecuadorean Indians is a matter of somewhat mythical imputation rather than a reality for all practical purposes. This applies to relatively intact Indian groups. It would be even more forcefully true in the case of those numerous Indians who find their main livelihood in employment either as casual laborers or as hacienda-bound peons.

This does not mean, however, that Ecuadorean Indians should be considered as highly "individualized." The fact that ties are tenuous so far as the local community is concerned, because there is hardly anything by which to anchor them, is no ground for believing that there are no ties whatsoever. Indian "individualism" is as deceptive a matter as Indian "collectivism." As has been shown, there is a high degree of cohesion on the level of the extended family, which may be coextensive with, or contained within, its physical setting, the local community. To be sure, the extended family or ayllu also appears to be rather vulnerable organizationally because, first, of its tendency, probably correctly observed by Mrs. Parsons, to shrink; this tendency is related, on the one hand, to nonobservance of customary and church marriage rules and, on the other hand, to the fragmentation of land through the prevailing system of inheritance in equal shares. These are, of course, sufficiently familiar processes into which other more remote contingencies enter, such as the rate of population increase, but these are not the subject of consideration here, since all we are concerned with at this moment is to state the potential vulnerability of familial organization in terms of direct "causes."

The second reason why the ayllu is considered relatively weak, organizationally, lies in the lack of additionally sustaining interests and correlative organizations, a lack similar to that recorded and discussed at length for the local community. In brief, the social fabric is loose; it does not receive an extra knit from institutional and organizational elaborations of distinct interests.

Such as it is, however, the ayllu and/or the local community not only provide nuclei from which to draw manpower in small but appreciable numbers[63] but, more importantly for the discussion here, the ayllu contains possibilities for furnishing effective working teams to industry. What is still more important in this context: a team thus composed of kindreds brings with it its own hierarchical arrangements and its own mechanisms for the maintenance of discipline among its members and for their allocation in some co-ordinating fashion. Consequently, there is much to recommend the recruiting of labor and the grouping of workers in the industrial situation on the basis of their kinship relations rather than on the basis of age alone or of other, exclusively technical, qualifying criteria (cf. Herskovits 1952b:99-101).

It is obvious that this suggestion is modeled, in part, along the lines of that old method of statesmanship, modernly familiar as the policy of "indirect rule" as employed in the administration of colonial peoples -- a policy by which many of the details of administrative and law-and-order enforcing functions and responsibilities are left or shifted to pre-existing organizations and their functionaries. In most of these cases, such organizations are much more elaborate and much more formalized, and carriers of authority are much more clearly discernible, than is the case among Ecuadorean Indians--the very fact of their obviousness inviting their utilization. These principles of functional organization can employ the ayllu in so far as it is intact and in so far as it is at all discernible.

In terms of practical application of these principles, this means that the adult male members of the ayllu or extended family can be made to function as a group toward the maintenance of interplant or intershop compatibility, co-operation, and discipline. The burden of this task can be left to an appreciable degree to the authority as it is distributed within its own circle. And even though there are few outward indices showing how and where authority and respect are formally located, there are persons in command of both. They are so recognized and (indirectly) recognizable by virtue of their age, personal qualities, and achievements ("offices"), evaluated in terms of traditional standards and expectations. The employment of such persons for tasks that put them in command of others may go a long way toward obviating the necessity for the imposition of constant and minute supervision of any working group by foremen, bosses and straw bosses, supervisors, inspectors, etc., some of whom, because of the technical requirements of the job, cannot but be outsiders, strangers, "Blancos" so far as the Indian operators are concerned. Hence, supervision coming necessarily and at least initially from these quarters, it is apt to prove itself far less effective than any which a relatively closed and close group itself might exercise by and among its members.[64] As has also been seen, there is a tendency for other, formal functionaries, such as alcaldes, to be suspect and unpopular among their fellow-Indians and, indeed, to be under suspicion from all sides precisely to the degree to which they succeed, because of personal qualities and qualifications, in establishing themselves as real leaders. The distrust that thus tends to accrue to them as tyrants or exploiters of their charges is likely to be absent or at least considerably mitigated where leadership is left to emanate from those who are held in respect and who derive authority within the intimately known and therefore unequivocal kinship group.

In situations of industrialization, no matter on what scale, it does ordinarily happen, though by no means always, that individual workers are hired and facilities rendered for their immediate families to accompany them, especially in cases where labor has to be drawn from afar. Various short-run and long-run considerations prompt such procedure. There is also the well-known tendency for members of the extended family to follow suit and seek industrial employment where some relatives are already employed, in preference to places where there are none.

The matter which has been discussed here has to do neither with such policy considerations nor with small families and the stabilization of a local labor force and the insurance of a larger one in the future, nor with the drift-effect of employment. The present considerations pertain primarily to the requirements for a maximum of congeniality, co-operation, and teamwork within any single industry, plant, or shop, and for a minimum of enforcement of discipline from outside or of education for teamwork specifically. Whatever deliberate action can be taken by industry in this matter might well go toward seeking out kinship groups rather than individuals for recruitment and, particularly, for job placement. Just as the presence of a single family might stabilize labor at a given place, so the kin group might stabilize or sustain the team in actual work. Again, in practical terms, this means that considerably more attention will have to be given to the training of established leaders, hence to the older men, in supervisory tasks, than is customary in mature industry.

The maintenance of the native age-cum-leadership hierarchy for the sake of the Indian team's industrial discipline has, of course, very obvious drawbacks. Among them might be plantwise factionalism among the various groups, particularly in cases where local intergroup and intragroup hostilities have existed before, and its transferral into the industrial situation. The suggested arrangement is also apt to be vitiated in cases where individuals might have become industrial recruits precisely because they chafed under the pressure of local public opinion, traditional parental authority, and other forms of group pressure.

Finally, the question must remain open whether discipline can be maintained in the long run on the basis of the suggested scheme, once technical training, more rapidly assimilated by the younger, entitles these to ascendancy. It should therefore be understood that this scheme can be considered valid only for initial periods of rapid and massive industrialization of Indian labor.

NOTES

1. Ferdon 1947; Garcés 1942. The inability or unwillingness to "associate" is not, however, confined to Indians. Thus Jaramillo Alvarado (1943, No. 12:57) refers to the lack of class consciousness among the Ecuadorean proletariat. Speaking of the "serrano character" in general, Hassaurek (1868:123) comments on "their great distrust of each other, which precludes all spirit of association. Partnerships are not customary; corporations are unheard of. Great enterprises, therefore, are an impossibility." Regarding this lack of a "spirit of association," see also Benites (1950: 159-60) on eighteenth century attempts to exploit mines and other natural resources by means of stock companies and other corporative organizations, and their failures.

2. Literate Indians tend to lose touch with their Indian group (Parsons 1945:13, n. 52); literate and citified, they are disavowed by their community (Rodríguez Sandoval 1949:119), or they lose the Indians' confidence in other ways.

3. Poblete Troncoso 1946:207; various references in Rodríguez Sandoval 1949:87, 118-19; and especially the convocation and agenda for the 1946 congress of the Comité Central Nacional de Defensa Indígena (1946), signed by Dolores Cacuango, secretary; the Functional Deputy for Indians (member of the House of Representatives of the Ecuadorean Diet); and others, with text in Spanish and Quechua; see also Chapter X, n. 42. On some turbulent antecedents to agricultural workers' organizations in the early thirties, see Saenz 1933a:118.

4. Cf. Garcés' statement to the effect that Indians are employed in textile factories since they require less wages and because the Indian "has not yet become an individual in whom revolutionary ideas prosper" (1941:19).

5. During 1953 the Ecuadorean government was reported to have "launched an all-out drive against the syndicalist and communal organizations of the Indians" in the context of riots and killings on haciendas with Indian labor (Hispanic American Report VI, No. 9 /Sept., 1953/), following which the Federación held a meeting of delegates in Quito (personal communication from Lilo Linke, December, 1953).

6. On the antecedents of "the Puruhá," see Costales Samaniego 1950. The Puruhá language is known to have been spoken until the end of the seventeenth century. IEAG (1953, Nos. 10 and 11) deals with Indians of Chimborazo who may be identified as Puruhá (or Puruguay) remnants.

7. A parcialidad or anejo (anexo) is an Indian settlement or residential grouping or "concentration" (concentración indígena or indo-mestiza) which does not have the character of a "planned" town or village. A considerable number of vaguely and inconsistently applied designations exist by which to refer to such rural or semi-urban settlement units, such as: ayllu, barrio, caserío, centro, comunidad, comuna, departamento, diseminación, grupo, hato, partido, poblado, punto, recinto, sección, sitio, tambo. Some are misnomers; some do not refer to Indian settlements specifically; some are used for types of coastal settlements.
Cisneros Cisneros (1948:154-55) attempts to distinguish between the settlement types or nuclei of caserío, parcialidad, and diseminación: thus he considers the first as a more concentrated type of settlement (in contrast with the scatter-settlements), more isolated, and generally an adjunct of, or located within, hacienda lands but also occasionally within the tracts called parcialidad. The parcialidad

seems to be the prevalent type of Indian settlement where Indians own lands, and we shall use it here for most of our discussions in the sense of specifically Indian community.

8. Hassaurek 1868:298-99; Cevallos 1873:135 (dance and battle for the possession of the plaza); Parsons 1945:182; Collier and Buitrón 1949: 101, 104; Santiana (1949:254) tells of the Indians living about the Nudo de Mojanda who wage a battle "by appointment" every year with those of Camuendo, which is followed by a feast of reconciliation and friendship. These cases cogently invite comparison with the "encounters" (institutionalized, formal, but by no means only mock battles) described in detail by Alencastre and Dumézil (1953) for Indian groups of the province of Cañas and elsewhere in the Department of Cuzco, and analogous instances from the Departments of Ayacucho and Junín in Peru.

Whether these brawls or battles are waged in earnest, there is little doubt that they are also highly conventionalized affairs and are, or were, in the nature of "mock battles," or "combat dances." But even if they include such ritualistic elements, they are most apt to illustrate the limits and foci of Indian we-consciousness or solidarity or group cohesion and allegiance.

9. See Flornoy (1945:30), who describes a fiesta scene near Ambato where, in the face of "plumed and masked dancers, dancing and making as though to give battle, the police have to ready their sabres." And Parsons 1945:111, 207 (n. 81), 210 (n. 92).

10. Parsons 1945:7-8 (n. 5), also p. 73.

11. Buitrón and Buitrón 1945; also IEAG 1953, No. 3:275.

12. Cisneros Cisneros (1948:150-294) in his inventory of Indo-Mestizo communities notes a number of such controversies. See also Tello 1949.

13. Buitrón and Buitrón 1945; Rodríguez Sandoval 1949:98; Parsons 1945: 54, 69.

14. Parsons 1945:38-40 (her emphasis). Marriages between second cousins do occur, however, and nonobservance of this marriage restriction seems to be increasing. "As exogamous restrictions are curtailed the ayllu may be expected to shrink... ."
    The Ecuadorean Indian conception, according to which the ayllu designates an exogamous bilateral kinship group, differs from that generally held in the Andean area, particularly in Peru. There, the ayllu means what in Ecuador is designated as parcialidad, and is conceived of as "an association of families united by community, territorial and genealogical links." The Peruvian ayllu, similarly to the Ecuadorean parcialidad, may or may not own land in common. If it has marriage rules, they tend to be endogamic. The modern Peruvian ayllu is, then, the local community, generally a peasant settlement, analogous to the Ecuadorean parcialidad.
    The nature of the classical (pre-Inca and Inca) ayllu has not been determined to the satisfaction of all investigators. Among modern writers on the subject, see Castro Pozo 1947:483-99; Means 1925:428 ff.; 1931:223, 226 ff.; Mishkin 1947:441 ff.; Rowe 1947:253 ff.; Trimborn 1925: 987 ff.; Tschopik, Jr. 1947a:539 ff.

15. Rodríguez Sandoval 1949:9-11, 22, 25, 27-30, on ayllu (including relationship terms) and llacta. Llacta, the term by which Ecuadorean Indians call the parcialidad, is, interestingly enough, the old Quechua term for the one hundred households into which the population was nominally grouped under the Inca decurion system (Parsons 1945:7, n. 5).

The term is also used, modernly, to cover the meaning of "country," "nation" (see Comité Central Nacional de Defensa Indígena 1946).

16. This includes three households of hacienda Indians. Figures on the population of Peguche differ. Buitrón (1947a) credits it with 300 houses, or a population of 1,222. Cisneros Cisneros (1948:180) puts it down with an estimated population of 1,000. These discrepancies are discussed in some detail below, n. 18.

17. Parsons 1945:33, 38, 54, 97, 99, 121, 149, 159, 162, 164-65, 172, 173, 174, 178, for pertinent observations and her conclusions. Also Buitrón and Buitrón 1945. Rodríguez Sandoval (1949:35) notes that land is sold or mortgaged to members of the ayllu and not sold to Indians of other parcialidades or to Whites.

18. Buitrón 1947a. The discrepancies between his, Parsons', and Cisneros' data for Peguche have been noted, n. 16. There is no relation between Buitrón's figures and those provided by Cisneros Cisneros (1948:180-81; 1949) for Otavalo parcialidades or, as Cisneros terms them, concentraciónes. The discrepancies are considerable, and there are no data by which to account for them in any systematic manner.

Buitrón secured his data by relying greatly on the information of the local alcaldes (Indian headmen) and one policeman who knew the populations of their bailiwicks well. He assumes four persons per house or household in order to arrive at his population estimates, an assumed proportion which appears overcautious, both in the light of some of his other studies and in the light of the few data provided by Parsons on figures per household.

Despite these shortcomings, the data are believed to be usable to establish the orders of magnitudes that are of interest here.

19. Parsons 1945:34-37, 164-65. The number of different surnames appearing in the first set is 19, in the second 15, including maiden names of married women.

20. See Parsons' "guess" regarding fear of witchcraft as a result of a specific family feud (1945:169). There is no indication of the cause that gave rise to that feud. In Peguche, "envy is believed to be the prime cause of the kind of enmity that resorts to witchcraft" (p. 68 ff.); again, no information for what people are envied.

Disselhoff (1940), in remarking on the "little fortification" guarding the entrance to one brujo's house, seems to underline the element of black magic in communal relations since, according to him, brujos or curanderos are subject to acts of vengeance for black magic or for failures to effect cures. See also IEAG (1953, No. 3:232, 244) on the employment of "black magic" by one's enemies.

21. Rodríguez Sandoval (1949:24, 37), on lawsuits arising from questions of inheritance. Stübel 1897:295. Buitrón (1947) has a specific case of a Mestizo community, which is factionally divided over one particular event that happened many years ago. The Indians living on the periphery of this community are also divided into factions, but over a lawsuit of their own.

22. Rivet 1903. Cf. Stübel 1897:295, and Orton 1875:110, 112, who infers that Indians steal only from Whites. Similarly, Rodríguez Sandoval 1949: 42-43, 91. Parsons 1945:145, also pp. 69, 73-74.

23. Rodríguez Sandoval 1949:121. Associations according to provenience are by no means confined to Indians in other metropolitan centers, at least as far as observations in Peru show.

24. Rodríguez Sandoval 1949:87, 98-99, 122, which contains a very interesting expression of a Spanish-speaking Indian from one locality as regards Quechua-speaking Indians from another, distinct locality, both of the same canton.

25. Dale 1946:118; J. Davis 1946:71. The appendix of illustrations in Cuestiones Indígenas del Ecuador (1946) has a few notes on the existence of "social classes" among the Indians of Saraguro (province of Loja) going back to ancient times. One of these upper classes is called quinta corona ("Fifth Crown"). Territorial or residential differentiation is also indicated.

26. A verse of a song sung by Indians when drunk begins, "I am the Indian of...," the name of the proprietor being left blank in the text reproduced by IEAG (1953, No. 10:82).

27. Cf. the methodological approach taken by Sewell (1949), who distinguishes between real, i.e., effective, "status" and nominal or formal "official position" of prospective "key persons."
    It should be said at this point that in the Ecuadorean situation it is very difficult to sift community leadership derived from formal institutional organization from that which is due to eminently personal qualifications.

28. The term "political," in so far as it implies action involving decision and/or power, is actually a misnomer, as the material will amply show. It is used for lack of anything better by which to discuss power and decision within the radius of the local community. A field of "custom political organization"--analogous to that of "custom law"--has barely been established in the social sciences.

29. The comuna and the law creating it have found ample and often critical discussion, largely centering on the aims, intentions, meaning, and scope of the law, but in minor part also providing surveys and examinations (though none detailed) of the actual status and functioning of the comunas. See Bol. Ind. I, No. 2 (1941):25; Bol. Min. Prev. Soc., Año I (1937), Nos. 1-2:1-2; No. 5:7-8, 46-48; Nos. 6-7:29-31; Previsión Social, No. 10 (Jan.-April, 1942):146-47; No. 11 (May-Dec., 1942):175-79; Dir. Nac. Est. 1944; Cisneros Cisneros 1948:150 ff.; 1949; Ecuadorian Commission n.d.:28, 76-77; Garcés 1941:18, 26-27; 1946a; García Ortiz 1942; 1946; International Labour Organisation 1949:58-67; Maes 1941; Monsalve Pozo 1942; Rodríguez Sandoval 1949:42; Zambrano 1951.

30. Communally owned lands are technically termed comunidades. By extension, Indian groups and settlements owning such lands are also called comunidades (cf. n. 7). A comuna, in the sense intended by the law, is a nominally incorporated Indian settlement, mostly a settlement of the comunidad type, i.e., with communally owned resources. In the literature, these terms are often employed indiscriminately. Thus IEAG (1953, No. 4:3) distinguishes between two "classes" of comunas: the surviving traditional precolonial type, and the recent, legally organized one.

31. In a very few cases, totora ("reed") stands and clay pits are thus bases for the formation of "industrial" (in contradistinction to the more common agricultural or irrigation) comunas, the cabildos of which rent them for an annual fee to mat- and basket-weavers and pottery-makers, respectively.

32. There is but one clear case on record of an agriculture and livestock co-operative formed of Indian ex-huasipungeros and other hacienda peons who co-operatively purchased a hacienda, aided by the Social Welfare Ministry and bank loans. There are two cases, both in Guano (Tungurahua Province), of cabuya textile producers and rug-makers. Co-operatives have not taken hold in Ecuador, and most of them that have formed quickly fell apart; of a recorded 255 established since 1937, only a few function, which are non-Indian and either definitely urban or consisting of coastal ricegrowers (see, however, latest figures on functioning co-operatives, in Pan American Union 1954:39). Most of the sources listed under n. 29 also deal with co-operativism in the general academic manner. But see also Cisneros Cisneros 1950 and, particularly, Cisneros Falconí 1951a and b.

33. It appears, however, that in a number of cases communally owned cultivable lands were divided and sold as individually owned holdings to members of the community--another trend that contributes to the formation of minifundia.

34. Just 10 per cent of the comunas so claimed own land, and accordingly the average for the highlands works out at less than half an acre per person.

35. Saenz 1933a:131, 132; also pp. 190-91; p. 99.

36. Parsons 1945:5, 176-77. (Mrs. Parsons does not seem to have been familiar with the--then quite recent--comuna law.) On the point under consideration, see also Garcés (1942), who discusses some factors account-ing for this lack of "sociability" on any but the family level; also Murra 1947:815, 820.

37. The main sources used for this discussion on the alcaldes, or native chieftainships, are Buitrón 1947a; Buitrón and Buitrón 1945; Cisneros Cisneros 1948:150 ff.; Collier and Buitrón 1949:94; García Ortiz 1946; Gillin 1936 and 1941; Murra 1947:820; Rivet 1903; Saenz 1933a:40, 89-95, 129 ff.; Rodríguez Sandoval 1941:27-32, 40-41.
　　On precolonial, colonial, and early republican conditions (which furnish instructive comparable data (for modern conditions), see Means 1925; Rowe 1947:253 ff.; Trimborn 1925; Kubler 1947:376 ff.; Hassaurek 1868:307, 310.

38. Cisneros Cisneros 1948:167 ff. His data are, of course, no proof of the statement made in the text above, but only evidence on the compara-tive rarity of the persistence of a native or traditional form of local government. There is no doubt that his "count" is not complete. It should be added that all the data of his inventory thin out markedly as his survey moves away from, and south of, Quito.
　　On the relative rarity of native alcalde organization, see also Murra 1947:820.

39. For the "type-case," see IEAG 1953, No. 3:157.

40. To Hassaurek (1868:307), labor-recruiting appeared to be the chief function of Indian alcaldes.

41. IEAG 1953, Nos. 10 and 11:49-50, 57-58, 96, 141-42; Parsons 1945: 12-13, 189; Rivet 1903.

42. Parsons 1945:189, 187, from accounts written for her by "school-bred young Indians" of a parish in Cayambe canton, where such officers are termed gobernadores.

43. Rivet 1903:65. As to the village mayorales, it seems they have largely disappeared since Rivet made his observations in that region over fifty years ago. As to the hacienda mayorales, it is interesting to note the situation in which they make their appearance and their roles, both of which correspond closely to those of the petty officials of the ten- and fifty-household units under the Inca decurion system. Cf. n. 41.

44. Cf. Means 1925; Trimborn 1925, on the pre-Columbian institution, with Rodríguez Sandoval 1949:89.

45. Parsons 1945:107, 157 (n. 10), 161-62, 164, 169.

46. Saenz 1933a:76; see, however, Parsons 1940 and 1945:5-6, 180, who points out many survivals of aboriginal religion; also Murra 1947:820-21; Rivet 1906; Stübel 1897:306-9.

47. For this and the succeeding text, see particularly Parsons 1945: 81 ff. and 178 ff.; also IEAG 1953, No. 3:219-21; Nos. 10 and 11:79-81, 88.

48. It may be suspected, however, that in practice there are many cases where alcaldes combine secular (i.e., their minimal political-administrative) and religious functions.

49. In the Otavalo region some Indians are members of a lay order, the Third Order of San Francisco (Parsons 1945:149-50). This appears to be a recent development. There is no information as to the functioning of such orders. Elsewhere in the same region, membership in two other religious societies (Daughters of Mary, and Congregation of the Holy Heart of Jesus) appears to be non-Indian (IEAG 1953, No. 3:220).

50. Saenz 1933a:77-79. It is his impression that the general case is that "the community, directed by the parish priest, designates the persons who are to take charge of these festivities." In Ilumán, the priest names the priostes for the fiesta of "La Virgen del Carmen" (IEAG 1953, No. 3: 220-21); in the Cajabamba region, he appoints the priostes to serve for the fiesta of the "Virgen de Balbaneda" and as the "kings" for the fiesta of "Los Reyes" (IEAG 1953, Nos. 10 and 11:79, 88).

51. Parsons 1945:208-11 (this account was written for her by one of her friends, a long-time resident of Ecuador).

52. For this and the following, see Buitrón 1947a; Collier and Buitrón 1949:124-39; Hassaurek 1868:265-79, 283-85, 296-99; Parsons 1945:81, 99-111, 208-13; Rivet 1903:75-76; Saenz 1933a:76-79; Rodríguez Sandoval 1949:103-7; Santiana 1949:259-68.

53. Not all religious fiestas are prioste-sponsored. Among the Indian groups about the Mojanda massif (Otavalo), the fiesta of San Juan and San Pedro, while requiring preparations of two or three months, has no prioste; it has "an essentially popular character." It seems that formerly the white hacienda-owners sponsored this fiesta; they still furnish what we would call a "May pole." The fiesta of San Luis, however, is sponsored, financed, and organized by a prioste (Santiana 1949:259 ff.).

54. See Santiana 1949:261 ff. for the only somewhat detailed description of arrangements preceding a prioste-sponsored fiesta. There are titles for persons in charge of specific tasks before and during the celebration. Cf. Rodríguez Sandoval 1949:103 ff.; Rivet 1906.

55. At least one instance has come to notice, the community of La Magdalena, on the outskirts of Quito, where the prioste is entitled to the honorific term of address "Don" (Castro 1948).

56. Saenz 1933a:131, 135, 92. Rodríguez Sandoval (1949:85) mentions the ñaupador in a derogatory sense, as troublemaker, like the tinterillo (cf. Chapter X, C and n. 59). Parsons (1945:57, 58) refers to the nyopadura, nyupadura, and also speaks of "wedding alcaldes" as does IEAG (1953, No. 3:216).
     One might surmise that this personage is an erstwhile "Elder," one of whose functions was to preside at weddings and celebrate marriages and at such occasions to dispense wise counsel and generally to guard over the community's morals. All these functions or roles still exist, but they are divided among various personages (priest, padrinos or wedding godparents or sponsors, alcaldes, aguaciles, etc.), leaving the ñaupador with shadowy, marginal, and faintly clownlike features.

57. Collier and Buitrón 1949:148; Parsons 1945:64 (n. 133) and 73 (n. 188). Cf. Chapter VI, D, and this chapter, A, n. 20.

58. Rodríguez Sandoval 1949:69; see also pp. 63-64.

59. Parsons 1945:113; see also pp. 42, 97, 158; and Chapter X, C.

60. Parsons 1945:96, 122-23. On the inter-Indian padrinazgo or compadrazgo and its importance both for the "gossip" and the godchild, see Rodríguez Sandoval 1949:26-27, 96-97; and IEAG 1953, No. 3:219. On expected behavior and relations between godparent and godchild, see IEAG 1953, Nos. 10 and 11:66, 135.

61. For courtesy terms, formal behavior between juniors and seniors, and concepts guiding respect behavior, see Parsons 1945:39, 42, 98-99, 120 (n. 52), 122-23, 138-39; and Rodríguez Sandoval 1949:11 ff.

62. Cf. Shih 1944:148-50 on this general point.

63. See above, this chapter, section A, where the number of persons composing an average ayllu was indicated by a rough calculation. On that basis, recruitment of the entire male contingent of an ayllu, from age 12-14 up, might yield "teams" of between 35 and 50 workers who, among themselves, might continue the "natural" solidarity or cohesion of the ayllu.

64. The unfavorableness of the position of non-Indian personnel in charge of, and in constant and direct touch with, Indian workers (see the considerations on Indian-White relations) is mitigated to the extent that such personnel is specially trained to deal with Indians--a training in "social skills" that goes far beyond the ordinary industrial requirements for technical and technological qualifications. The matter has been touched upon before, and there will be occasion to revert to it, as in the next chapter.

Industrialization in Ecuador implicating its highland Indian population is necessarily predicated upon the presence of non-Indian actors. Industrial managerial and technical personnel must be, in the nature of things, strangers to such prospective industrial workers. In turn, Indians are bound to strike such persons as strange beings. Hence, no matter how such a combination and the ensuing situation is viewed, at least an initial hiatus between industrializing personnel (supervisors, foremen, engineers, instructors, etc.) and Indians will have to be taken for granted.

Any industrial establishment, and a manufacturing establishment in particular, is by its very nature an organization of hierarchically ordered authorities. The impact of an inherently "functional" hierarchical order upon a nonhierarchical order is aggravated when its top parts, its "legislative" or "executive" staff, and its bottom parts (in this case, workers) are alien to each other.

In this chapter, which concludes the discussion on social relations, we address ourselves to some aspects of this problem as it concerns particularly non-Indian personnel in direct touch with, and in charge of, Indians, and with emphasis on their position as strangers. Such a position is generally a delicate one; at times, it may be precarious and decisively influence, if not determine, the success (or lack thereof) of industrializing endeavors. The discussion of this problem has special reference to the limits to which "intermediaries" (Chapter VII) can be employed and native leadership (Chapter XII) organizationally used in industry. In this sketchy treatment of the problem of the stranger, the industrializing agent shall be thought of as being essentially "on his own."

Two distinct, but related, questions will be dealt with. One concerns the strange person. In what terms may we expect Indians to define the status of the stranger appearing in their midst and about to establish some sort of modus vivendi with them? The other, reciprocal, question concerns the "strangeness" of Indians in terms of modern man's frame of reference. Thus, what degree of sophistication, if any, may we expect of Indians when confronted with new situations, alien things, strange tasks?

A. The Stranger

In considering the first of these two questions, we recall the two-fold analysis of social relations between Indians and non-Indians as functions of a particular type of social stratification and of ethnic (cultural) differentiation. The nature of these relations has been extrapolated from the kind of behavior that characterizes encounters between Indians and non-Indians, and from it we have concluded upon a range of attitudes, sometimes pronounced, sometimes subtle, but generally negative, which Indians hold vis-a-vis non-Indians. That these negative attitudes, bespeaking social distance and cultural differentiation, present a practical problem to the newcomer, the bringer of things and ideas alien, has been pointed out on various occasions. Yet it would be erroneous to refer all such negative attitudes, all such "distance" behavior, to the prevailing Ecuadorean social structure and only to that. Negative attitudes may include, or perhaps even concentrate on, <u>any</u> stranger, anyone not belonging to the local community. True, there seems to be a tendency for Indians to define in the most obvious terms as <u>blanco</u> (White) the non-Indian, the outsider, the social superior, the city man, indifferently; and if strangers, foreigners, outsiders, persons in command of a situation wear European clothes and otherwise look and behave as non-Indians, they are <u>eo ipso</u> "Whites." One could almost say that for Indians the White is the Stranger <u>par</u> <u>excellence</u>.

But, on closer scrutiny, gradations of "strangers" may be discerned. We turn here to the third, "autonomous" principle underlying social relations[1] to indicate some general tokens by which the stranger is defined in the eyes not only of the Indians but of the folk of Ecuador generally. Is there any kind of common denominator by which Indians <u>and</u> non-Indians together might define themselves as over against still other groups, "third parties," as it were? Excluding consideration of membership in the local group, a stranger may be defined in terms denoting religious affiliation or in terms of his citizenship. We shall here consider both possibilities.

Rivet considers religion to be the only plane on which Whites and Indians, originally the conquerors and conquered, meet, in that the use of church facilities and the services of the priest are common to both.[2] That this joint participation in this sphere is not only formal and passive but has the aspect of a real common meeting ground, or rather a ground by virtue of which to define the nonparticipant as stranger, becomes apparent from a number of hints regarding the use of the term "Christian" (<u>cristiano</u>) and the conception of "Christian."

In the first place, "Christian" as used by the folk of Ecuador,[3] including Indians, means simply "man," "person," "individual," but is mainly synonymous with "human" in contradistinction to beasts and inanimate things.[4] It is also employed to refer to some specific person who is no more than vaguely familiar ("<u>tal cristiano</u>," that fellow).[5]

In the second place, "Christian" is equated with the official language of the country, Spanish, in the mind of the folk of Ecuador, including the Indians. He who speaks "Christian" is not a real stranger, a <u>gringo</u> ("foreigner"), as Franklin makes clear in his account of a number of illuminating episodes (1943:28, 59-60, 75, 195, 200, 201, 203, 248).

To achieve a perfect blending-in with a strange milieu, to be capable of "doing in Rome as the Romans do," is often considered a desirable accomplishment and a substantial aid in gaining access to people outside one's own circle. But, among the episodes related by Franklin, there is one pregnant with quite contrary implications: this author's very ability to speak the language, to conform to the customs of the country, and thus to appear as an Ecuadorean resulted at one time in the refusal of an Indian <u>huasipungero</u> to entrust his young son to him as a guide; for in the eyes of an isolated Indian a foreigner was to be less feared as a potential kidnapper of Indian children than an Ecuadorean, i.e., a native White, a member of the ruling stratum--and it was as such that Franklin was identified. No amount of persuasion could convince this Indian that Franklin <u>was</u> a foreigner, hence not in the habit of abducting Indian children for service.

Evidently, the position of stranger, or rather, specifically, foreigner, may under certain circumstances constitute an asset, rather than an impediment, in dealing with the folk or the Indians of Ecuador.

In the third place, "Christian" means those who are baptized (in the sense of the Catholic Church) and thus excludes the "unbaptized," namely, savages, the wild people, the forest Indians of the Ecuadorean lowlands, on the one hand, and Evangelistas (i.e., Protestant missionaries) and "Masons" (i.e., all unbelievers and heretics), on the other.[6] Non-Indians, one may infer from these meanings of "Christian" among Otavalo Indians, are thus acceptable and accepted by, and form a society with, the Indians in so far as foreigners and/or Ecuadorean Whites are "Christians" in the Catholic sense and behave accordingly.

The potential inclusiveness indicated by this conception does not, however, extend to the nation or country of Ecuador. The citizen status of a stranger does not appear to play a role among the Ecuadorean folk, least of all among the Indians. Franklin, in his encounter with a "Cholo subsistence farmer," is led to wonder whether "he thought of himself as an Ecuadorian or not."[7] Ideas on the political geography and the political life of Ecuador, not to mention those of other countries, among this folk, are the vaguest. Indeed, one of the commonest themes of Indianists centers precisely on the fact that the Indians lack any feeling of belonging to a nation and that they are neither conscious nor active citizens of the country in which they reside. "To integrate the Indian with the national life of the country" is a phrase that recurs interminably in Indianist literature; it indicates exactly the lack of any we-feeling on the national-political plane. Hence, if Indian alcaldes are presumed "to serve patriotically" (i.e., without salary or other recompense), if mingas for public works are supposed to be a "patriotic duty," if their start is marked by the exhibition of the national colors and patriotic speeches,[8] it is very doubtful indeed that such appeals have now much meaning for Indians generally, beyond providing a spectacle. Hence, too, the status of the foreigner, the stranger, is established in any terms but that of his formal citizenship: Indians do not define the foreigner in terms of his nationality. But, as was hinted earlier, it may be that, on occasion, the presence of a foreign White may be evaluated more positively than that of a native White, as one who is not implicated in the "vices" justly or unjustly attributed to Ecuadorean "Whites." In this respect, a foreigner may be in a relatively more advantageous position and obtain "entree" more easily than the Indian's usual neighbor.

B. The Strange

The notions that Indians have about things familiar and strange are part of that basic information which may be of importance to industrial management or supervisory personnel in their dealings with Indians. What reactions may be expected from Indians in the face of innovations such as industrialization implies, or confronted with specific situations or requirements not familiar to them?

Ecuadorean Indians have so often been described as tradition-bound and archconservative that an attempt to controvert the matter can be dispensed with. In fact, we should not expect from them highly enlightened, "rational" attitudes and "progressive" outlooks, whatever these terms may mean. But the question may be raised just in what respects and under what circumstances such traits display themselves which give rise to characterizations of Indians in such pessimistic terms. Do such verdicts disqualify Indians for industrial work? What are the acts which, when demanded of Indians as a matter of course, are apt to jeopardize specific undertakings? A few instances have been collected that seem to confirm Indian "irrationalism" so-called, because of their bearing on the prospective behavior under specific work conditions, and because they highlight "irrational" and, at that, hostile attitudes toward foremen or supervisors, whether or not these are Ecuadoreans or, for that matter, "Christians."

According to accounts relating to Indians of Cayambe (Pichincha Province), foremen, supervisors, or engineers are believed to be in league with the devil or with the spirits (duendes)[9] that are supposed to haunt places where bridges, tunnels, irrigation ditches, or conduits are to be constructed. These seem to be not merely verbally professed Indian beliefs but beliefs that in some measure guide conduct and action. It is asserted that in one instance of constructing a bridge a young peon was required by the engineer and construction boss to throw a number of tools into the river by way of a sacrifice to the local duende, "and during the work on the bridge two young men died," the lives of two young Indians having been part of the bargain with the duende. "Such is the belief about all persons who die in the construction of bridges, caves, ditches--the belief that their souls are delivered to the owner of the work, to the duende, the spirit." "In this kind of work, one takes great care not to hurt one's self, and, if one does, one takes great care to hide the blood, because they say the overseers and the engineers are on the lookout for those who hurt themselves to get the blood and sign the name of the person who is hurt, signing as many names as the number of persons the spirit may have asked for. Once the desired number is secured, they deliver them to the spirit."[10]

It is on the basis of similar "irrational" beliefs that the presence of foreigners may come to be resented. Thus the scientific party of which Rivet was a member, while encamped on a mountain plateau in Carchi Province, found itself actively threatened by the local Indians who ascribed to the foreigners' presence the three months of adverse weather which the angered páramo (high plateau) had therefore sent them.[11]

How "rational" or sophisticated the approach of Indians may be toward the new, specifically toward machines or matters associated with machines, or with novel or "uncanny" work is probably a matter of the first introduction and the skillfulness with which they are exposed toward such novelties. The instances here given serve to show, at least, that "rationality" cannot be taken for granted, particularly where the first impression of a machine conveys no indication whatever of its use or functioning.[12] Here it is of particular interest to note how certain traditional beliefs may act to undermine from the outset the relations between Indian workers and supervisory personnel, or in what terms perhaps already established dislikes of a job or of persons in commanding positions may be exhibited and dressed up in a tale incorporating existing folk motifs. The pretexts (if they happen to be such) of displaying given attitudes are, after all, of no less importance than the attitudes themselves.

Unpropitious reactions toward matters that are "strange" to Indians, though not inevitable, must be expected. A recognition of their conceptions of the outer world, their beliefs, and religious and other practices which give rise to "irrational" behavior would seem indispensable if voluntary co-operation rather than compulsion to work is desired. Not only that: the success of work under circumstances such as those just described, in terms of performance and without otherwise unexplainable refusals to work or nonappearance on certain days[13] or at certain places, or wastes in tools, equipment and materials, would be contingent upon the degree to which foremen or other supervisory personnel are able and willing to take account of beliefs such as those discussed, and to the extent to which they can anticipate and hence circumvent, rather than override, objections and other expressions of unwillingness that arise from superstitions, magical beliefs, and ritual practices. In other words, the dealing with Indian workers requires competence that goes beyond the technical requirements of the job in hand. Not any foreman or engineer will do merely because of his technical qualifications. "Social skills," based on knowledge of Indian life, are a prerequisite for any large-scale industrialization in Ecuador.

Finally, we may cast a closer look at the Indians' alleged "conservatism," the tendency to adhere unchangingly, stubbornly, and blindly to old ways of doing things, to resist all and every innovation.

In the case of actions which seem to be guided by certain beliefs, such as those discussed above, it seems comparatively easy to deal with Indian workers, provided supervisory personnel has sufficient insight to unearth the reasons for apparently irrational behavior and, for instance, to enlist the co-operation of the local cura to give his blessing to the initiation of a piece of work which, from the point of view of the Indians, might be sinister or dangerous. By comparison, the "conservatism" of Indians would seem to be something far more difficult to deal with, quite apart from the difficulty arising from the obfuscating tendency to reduce inconvenient traits and attitudes to such general and vague characterizations and thus conveniently to sidestep real inquiries into reasons why some items or habits or institutions are inexplicably retained while others are accepted.

To take a few examples: that in the religious sphere conservatism is to be expected does not need much discussion. What does need study, however, are the precise circumstances under which something new in that sphere is accepted or rejected. Cases are cited of Indians who "worship a piece of wood /i.e., a saint's image/ and when some priest tries to replace it by a better shaped or better dressed image, he finds the Indians will not allow him to do so."[14] Yet what is one to conclude from cases recording the ready acceptance by Indians of a new saint's cult or of new forms of cult?[15]

"Conservatism" is the reason given for the relapse into their old dirt six months after they had been "taught" to bathe and had been given soap and additional clothes and had learned to use them after initial refusal.[16] This is the bare factual information. Yet we learn nothing of the climate, nor of any ready access to, or availability of, water, nor of the availability or price of soap, nor of the manner in which these Indians were "taught" such new habits of cleanliness, nor, finally, of any "estate" sentiments or group pressures by virtue of which other innovations are not accepted either (cf. Chapter X, B, and Chapter XI, note 18).

On the other hand, we have instances of the successful introduction of new ways and means of making a living, particularly where these tie in with existing skills and craft production. The comparatively high prosperity of many of the Indians of Otavalo canton is closely related to the introduction of the Spanish-style weaving loom some forty years ago by a hacendado who had one of his peons taught its use, gave him a loom, and set him up in business.[17]

"Conservatism" as a uniform characteristic of Indians is neither a valid nor a fair description. Apart from the external circumstances, the success in the acceptance of something new is also related to the character of the introducing agent, the manner of introduction, and the relative obviousness of the advantage or utility of the introduced item or habit. Some of these considerations are precisely those that lead into the question of what constitutes incentives for Indians to work, and their possible motivations for going into and making a living of industrial work. These questions will be touched upon in the summary assessment of the materials so far presented.

NOTES

1. I.e., a free-floating, universal principle that is relatively independent of a particular given social structure and/or composition of a population.

2. Rivet 1906; cf. Murra 1947:820. It has been shown previously that distinctions are nevertheless observed, although within the frame of these common facilities.

3. The use and concept of "Christian," as here discussed, is not, of course, a trait that is limited to the folk of Ecuador but is probably quite generally "folk," not only in Latin America (cf. Watkins, 1952:167) but among European "folk" of various tongues. To our modern ears that are attuned to other classificatory categories, it sounds quaint. But like so many other terms, this too is a clue to other peoples' "world views."

4. Rodríguez Sandoval (1949:32, 49, 92, 120) has verbatim examples of the use of this term in speech contexts and even explains its meaning.

5. See, e.g., various folk locutions, as is Gil Gilbert 1942.

6. Parsons 1945:44 (n. 3), 160-61, 151.

7. Franklin 1943:200-1; also Parsons 1945:13, 150-51, for observations on the very limited knowledge of the outside world among her comparatively wide-awake Indian informants. According to Santiana (1949:245), the Mojanda Indian does not know, or does not wish to know, that he is an Ecuadorean with rights and obligations.

8. See, e.g., Ferdon 1945; Parsons 1945:11, n. 17; Collier and Buitrón 1949:94.

9. Duendes are associated with any dark or subterranean place or with bodies of water, also with other natural features. See Parsons (1945: 135-36 and n. 56) for a tale concerning duendes and the places which they infest. The account following in the text above had been given Mrs. Parsons (p. 215) by one of her "school-bred young Indians" as illustrating general beliefs on the subject of sacrifices. The young peon figuring in the incident was a neighbor of this Indian informant. On the other hand, it may be recalled that, according to Rodríguez Sandoval (1949:64-65, 88), the building of socavones (subterranean, tunneled conduits) is one of the Indian trades. In his portrayal of one such master-socavonero, contempt of the professional engineer is distinct and unmistakable.

10. A similar belief regarding human blood and the necessity for a human sacrifice to insure completion of construction work seems to underlie the episode recounted by Flornoy (1945:33) and reproduced in quite a different context at the end of the introduction to Part II. The ingredients of the episode were: a landslide, timid behavior of Indians called to clear the road of debris, another landslide gravely injuring one of them and leaving him bleeding. See also Chapter VI, D, with an allusion to possible reasons for Indians to dissimulate or conceal wounds.
　　Human sacrifice as part of a contract entered into with a spirit or with the devil is, of course, a fairly universal European theme. Of

interest here are instances of the integration of such "superstitions" with aspects of industrial civilization. Machine and watery place (a canal) are linked in one "superstition" regarding a baleful and dangerous place where the unwary is likely to come to grief (Buitrón 1951c). Parsons (1945:136-37) has a tale associating the devil with a black automobile. See also Enock (1907 /1910/:147), on the belief of Peruvian Indians that the government requires human tallow for the lubrication of soldiers' carbines; that machinery is feared because inhabited by a demon and because it too requires human tallow for lubrication.

11. Rivet 1906. Mountains and bodies of water are deities behaving like human beings, according to Indian belief, on which see Parsons 1940 and Buitrón 1951c.

12. Cf. Hassaurek (1868:311), on the impression which the machinery of the new cotton factory near Otavalo made on the native weavers; its motion and the speed of work and output led them to believe it was of the devil. Today, la maquina (in this case, railway) figures quite naturally in Otavalo Indian songs (IEAG 1953, No. 3:266).

13. Certain days of the week are believed to be auspicious or inauspicious for specific undertakings: Thursdays and Fridays are considered good planting days in the Otavalo region; "bad days" to undertake anything are Mondays and Thursdays; Tuesdays, Wednesdays, Fridays, and Saturdays are accounted good days to make a trip or start anything. Tuesday is an inauspicious day for wedding in Cayambe, Sunday being the preferred day to celebrate this event. In the Riobamba region, Tuesdays and Fridays are reported as unlucky days, but they are good curing days in Cayambe (Parsons 1945:111-12, 193, 196; Collier and Buitrón 1949:52; Rivet 1903--some discrepancies in these data are noted).

14. Dale 1946:125 (quoting from La condición actual de la raza indígena en la Provincia del Tungurahua, by Nicolas G. Martinez /Ambato, 1916/). Cf. Bemelmans (1941:87-89) for a parallel account of the refusal of the Indians of Baños to be persuaded to change their allegiance from one church to a newer one despite all the appeals very cleverly made to their beliefs and concepts.

15. Parsons 1945:167 (n. 19), 165; Collier and Buitrón 1949:105-6.

16. Suárez (1934:33), discussing also the failure of Indians in Cotopaxi Province to build their own houses along the lines of a model house, specially set up, with windows and elevated bedsteads, although the costs for the old- and the new-type house were the same.

17. Parsons 1945:9, 25-26 (and n. 67); Collier and Buitrón (1949:160), on the beginnings of the tweed-weaving industry in the Valley of Otavalo some thirty years ago.
     Among the predisposing factors to the acceptance and spread of loom and industry: old hand-weaving center (on the basis of native horizontal belt-loom); colonial textile obrajes; old export of textiles as far as Popayan and Pasto (Colombia).

XIV / THE "LIMITED GOALS" AND INDUSTRIALIZATION

A. Some Considerations Concerning Motivations and Incentives: a Review

It has been the purpose of this study to raise, rather than to answer, questions relating to industrialization among nonindustrial people. Ecuador and its highland Indians have furnished the illustrations. This chapter raises one more question--the all-important one concerning the reasons for which Indians might enter industry as workers and the reasons, if any, for which they might stay in industry. This amounts to a consideration of motivations and incentives,[1] and their treatment will, at the same time, constitute a summary of many of the points presented throughout this study. In re-examining some of them from another angle, it will be possible to indicate something of the "dominant concerns," the "springs of action," the "interests," the goals and values which characterize Indian life and which guide it in its traditional, customary setting.

The import of such a consideration in the context of costly economic development projects is perhaps most briefly and effectively conveyed by Mr. Langewiesche's conversation with a young cab-driver in Bombay, an ex-India Navy man, who showed himself interested in flying and who began to seek information from the famous pilot on such a career. "What he really wanted, it turned out, was to earn money fast--30,000 Rupees. 'What do you want to do with 30,000 Rupees?' Well, by the time he had it, his mother would be dead. And he would then buy his sisters a farm. And then? 'I am going to be a saint!' 'I see,' I said. 'Yes, of course; but I mean what are you going to do after you buy the farm?' 'I am going to be a saint,' he said. 'You know, live in a lonely place, be a holy man'" (Langewiesche 1948).

The training of workers, the fitting of the "raw human material" for industry, is a form of investment which has to be borne by someone regardless under what system industry operates. The making of this investment is predicated upon the expectation that, once training is completed and the worker has attained full proficiency, such investment will bear a palpable return. In other words, industrialization, in order to succeed, must be able to count on the willingness of would-be workers to make a career of industrial work. How well or how nearly can Ecuadorean Indians be expected to fulfil this stipulation? What do they expect to derive from industrial work? What has industry to offer to them?

As must have become amply clear from the foregoing descriptions, Ecuadorean Indians are not, by and large, a spectacular piece of humanity. They constitute a peasantry, not much different from peasantries elsewhere, with certain details of its own, with conditions peculiar to itself, but with interests that are eminently peasant--and eminently "sober." Their actions are not informed by ends to which an individual elsewhere aspires: to become a warrior or raider, sage, saint or seer; they do not turn their energies toward the acquisition of supernatural powers to validate their existence. No struggles for independence, no crusades, no Indian risorgimientos carry them along. There is no trace of a specific set of "ethics" preoccupying them and apt to create a permanent set of attitudes as its residue, shaping action and acting as a constant prod thereto. Quite to the contrary, Ecuadorean Indians strike one as the most "down-to-earth" folk imaginable--how literally true this characterization is will be seen at once. Sedentary to the point of immobility, unventuresome, untrammeled by obsessive ideals, undistracted by single overriding interests transcending the very here-and-now, conditioned to the steady, plodding performance of the daily task--surely, once this specimen is pried loose from his own world, his staying power must assert itself also in industry. Or are there factors within the Indians' way of life on the basis of which to foresee not only a high degree of absenteeism but also a high degree of labor turnover? Once more, what has industry to offer them in terms of their own understanding, their own ends, their own values? Again, our answers consider matters sub specie momenti: the problems of industrialization at its first inception.

1. Money[2]

On several occasions we have suggested that manufacturing industry in Ecuador might have to provide certain services for its workers, among them educational and health services; as has also been indicated, such services are not necessarily expected or appreciated by Indians. In other matters, too, such as in providing food and drink, industry might have to meet its Indian workers halfway, as it were. Because it is likely that industry might find itself in competition for labor with agriculture and public works, it might have to offer wages at least equal to, if not higher than, those prevailing in nonindustrial sectors of the economy. Indeed, money wages are considered to be normally the primary rational incentive for work, industrial and otherwise, and up to a point to be the more effective as incentive the higher they are.

The question arises whether money wages as the form of reward for work rendered are sufficiently familiar to, and appreciated by, all Indians to constitute a realistic incentive for them to enter industrial work. While the Ecuadorean economy is, formally and officially, a money economy, "premonetary arrangements" persist to varying degrees, particularly among its Indian population. Among such "payments" that are at least in principle nonmonetary are the raciones (parts of the harvest given to harvest helpers), the diezmos (tithes given to the parish church), or the primicias of the tenant or share cropper that go to the landlord.[3]

Close examination of the literature here used shows that direct acquaintance with money and knowledge of money is differentially diffused among Indians. Not all alike are habituated to using money instrumentally; nor is money involved in all transactions among Indians; nor do all Indians bestow the same valuation on money or assign to a given unit a consistently identical value in all situations.

Two classes of Indian cannot be presupposed to appreciate money wages outright, since, in the nature of their situation, they fail to come into contact with money. Fully developed notions as to the true function of money cannot be expected from conciertos, debt-bound hacienda peons. In the typical situation, they do not, or barely, handle cash. The plot of land assigned them for their own use is supposed to provide them with the necessary food. With exceptions, they do not dispose of crop surpluses which would bring them into the market as buyers and sellers; such marketable surpluses might go to the hacienda and be booked against debts. Indeed, money is not likely to figure for them in any other form but in that of debts contracted at the start of the tenancy contract and continued and augmented by the contingencies of obtaining clothes and other unavoidable goods and services (baptisms, funerals, etc.). Money, for conciertos, are book entries the manipulation of which, needless to say, is beyond their understanding and control.[4] It is for this reason, as Stübel pointed out in his days, that he found it very difficult indeed to secure Indian pack-carriers, porters and guides from among huasipungeros, since these were not familiar with day-wages--a difficulty which he did not encounter in neighboring Colombia.

This is the background which makes it understandable that money does not by itself and immediately attract Indians who come from this situation. Such peons are attracted, according to Franklin, to mine work by reports that miners wear sandals. "These, among other things, attract them to the Mine. Since these Indios propios /"owned" Indians/ have very little idea of the value of money, that aspect of the Mine does not interest them very much at first...frequently, instead of attempting to draw their salary, they approach white people and ask them for money if they need it"[5]--a most faithful reproduction of the hacienda "advance" pattern.

There is no doubt that such Indians would learn readily to find money attractive and useful once they had come in contact with it. But in order that money constitute an incentive to work where it can be obtained, in industry, it would have first to have been acquired and effectively used. In the situation of the hacienda-bound peon there is little chance for that. Hence, initially, prospects other than that of acquiring money may prove far more efficient dislodgers from the hacienda and mobilizers into industry. Once again, mixed wages may prove to have an educational function. The translation of money into things that are wanted and pur- chasable--for instance, for wiping out debts, purchasing land of one's own, etc.--begins afterwards, and may not even then be very complete. At any rate, the appeal that money exercises for those who have not learned to handle it is bound to tax imagination, hence it is not primarily and initially an appeal on whose automatic effectiveness industry can rely.

While little is known of that other class of Indians, the purely sub- sistence independent farmers, the case is probably similar in effect to that just discussed for conciertos. There, however, distance from markets and isolation might be the decisive element that is responsible for deprecatory attitudes with regard to cash.[6] Again, no "money imagination" should be expected in their case.

Nearness to markets and subsistence farming in conjunction with a craft industry, as in the case of Otavalo Indians, do present very dif- ferent possibilities with regard to the attractiveness of money wages. Yet there are many segments of their "economy," objectively so con- ceived, that are not dependent on a money economy. Such cases shall be summarized presently.

Apart from these groups that are wholly or partially outside the money economy, there are, finally, the free Indian laborers. Yet in their case, too, remuneration in kind may play a role to a larger or smaller degree, depending on markets and isolation. On the whole, however, it is safe to say that by virtue of their economic situation they have full knowledge of money.

To round out this discussion, we may briefly stake out the seg- ments or areas in which money plays a role and those where money does not figure in transactions, as among farmer-craftsmen of Otavalo canton.

In the actual market, all transactions seem to involve money. A careful observer, like Mrs. Parsons, would not have failed to notice and to mention transactions made otherwise.' But outside the actual market there are many occasions where payments are made in kind, as payments, among Indians, be it to the curandera for services rendered, be it in the form of barter as when the hacienda milkmaid exchanges the milk which she has received for her services for soup at her Indian neighbor, or where salt is obtained by Indians in exchange for corn (Parsons 1945:68, 159; Buitrón 1947). Although moneyless, these are real business transactions in the eyes of the Indians. In other regions, as in Cotopaxi or Chimborazo, barter-transactions seem to play a more pervasive role: higher-altitude Indians will barter-trade cold-climate crops or totora articles for crops such as maize and for this purpose periodically go on more or less extended journeys to neighboring provinces (Bolívar, Tungurahua) or low-valley zones.[8] Barter-exhange also seems prominent between a Negro huasipungero group in the Chota Valley (Carchi Province) and the outside world, even via the regular market (IEAG 1953, No. 2:66).

On the other hand, there are exchanges of goods and services-- and their sphere is large--which are probably not, or not wholly, considered business transactions by Indians. Goods are exchanged as parts of fiestas and ceremoniously, and services are reciprocated, as in mingas. But these exchanges are interstitial to the "economic" and the "social," for money finds its way into such exchanges of gifts and is part of the contributions brought to a feast side by side with bought goods (alcohol, cigarettes, etc.) and with homegrown foods, building materials, and what not.

In sum, unlike those large numbers of Indians who are virtually excluded from the money economy on institutional grounds (hacienda peons) or those who, so to speak, exclude themselves because of spatial isolation and farming self-sufficiency, Indians in a situation such as Otavalo farmer-craftsmen can be deemed to have a fairly well-developed understanding of the money complex. And, despite the only partial penetration of money economy even in such cases, it is fair to assume that the prospect of getting money, such as in industry (and in addition to "payments" in kind), is attractive and is likely to be more attractive in proportion to the scale at which money wages are offered.

This observation leads immediately to the main question: To what uses are Indians likely to turn money earnings? And are the channels of Indian expenditures of such a kind as to be continuously operative in keeping Indians in industry?

The first question has practically been answered. The chief goals of Indian endeavor, both capable of being realized by means of money, are land and the celebration of fiestas. In addition, there are other contingencies in Indian life which require financing. These are surveyed in their order of importance in an attempt to gauge their strength as motivators for Indians to enter and to stay in industry.

2. Land

Before discussing land as a motivational force (an incentive for work) we may briefly recall the immobilizing function of land and the land complex, as well as of the Indian home. In Part I of this study it was pointed out that the hacienda tenant system constitutes a barrier toward geographical and occupational mobility. It was further suggested that "minifundism," small-scale landownership, also tends toward

immobilization of a potential industrial labor force, particularly since
the development toward minifundism seems to be aided and abetted by
agrarian reform pressure and attempts to stabilize the rural population.
The disinclination of Indians to leave their homes has found mention
elsewhere; their attachment to the familiar surroundings is a commonplace commentary on Indian "values."[9] The reciprocal, the tendency
toward self-immobilization, arises from Indian land hunger and thereby
suggests that land might, indeed, move them into industry.

The literature on Ecuadorean Indians presents an impressive degree
of unanimity on land as one of the two primary "interests" of Indians.[10]
A few statements may serve as samples.[11]

"The love of the Indians for the soil," says Saenz, "is traditional
and a fact sufficiently well known to need expatiating on. The land is for
the Indian the symbol of his right to live, the connecting link between the
material life with the divine existence. The plot of land that the Indian
possesses is protected by the title of century-old possession and his pure
love for it. It is almost impossible for a white to buy lands from the
Indian; when the white seeks to acquire lands he usually has recourse to
spoliation. If, on the other hand, the Indian could buy land, that is his
only passion." "He does everything to own, conserve and augment his
parcel." It is well known, says Monsalve Pozo with reference to the
Indians of Azuay Province, that they are capable of any sacrifice to acquire land, that they purchase land regardless of the price, with the result that the hacendado raises the price of land by 100 per cent and starts
molesting his Indian neighbors in order to drive them into purchase.
Suárez, on the basis of his investigations on budgets of the rural population of the central highland provinces, finds that the differences in incomes between conciertos and independent land workers go into savings
which are used to buy livestock or, "preferentially," more land (unless
such surpluses are spent on drinking, particularly at fairs). "Generally,"
says Garcés, "the Indian aspires throughout his life to being a land-owner,
a small-owner, a tiny owner." Cárdenas (1954:308-9) considers the
alternatives that are open to landless campesinos in general: they may
become estate-dependent workers (huasipungeros) or, as artisans or
day workers, go to the city to work and accumulate small savings,
return to the land intending to make themselves property-owners and
thus to combine farming with the exercise of their artisanry, profession
or office. Others emigrate seasonally to parallel economic zones
/Litoral or Oriente/ where productivity is greater, and some return with
their savings to buy land. This is the case of the Ecuadorean Sierra.
The minifundium is the result of this desire to return to the land...."

Mrs. Parsons has secured some statements from Indians directly
which give the half-romantic, half-political "Indian-loves-the-land"
theme a realistic ring. Speaking of the very few landless Indians who
work as tenants or peons for a hacienda in Peguche, she reports their
landed Indian neighbors as saying that these people work on the haciendas
"only because they are poor and landless," and, quoting her informant,
that "they would prefer to have their own land...; it is a more tranquil
life, a better life." On Mrs. Parsons' inquiry whether the Indian informant would sell land to a White, she says, "she could, but that she would
not; she and José wanted to leave it to their children."[12]

The attachment of Indians to land presents a motivational force
toward seeking remunerative work only when the matter is viewed in
terms of ownership, as has been done so far. The very strength of
Indian attachment to land has precisely the opposite effect in the case
of huasipungeros who are possessors of land. Mrs. Parsons, as well

as the Buitróns, has recognized that hacienda debt-bondage is not the only impediment to the immobility of so large a part of the Indian population. Thus the Buitróns observe: "In the hacienda, the great attraction for the peons is the piece of land constituting the huasipungo. The Indians adore the land. The love for the land is in their blood. The piece of land of the huasipungo keeps them tied to the hacienda, and it is this piece that makes them prefer 75 centavos a day that they earn as huasipungeros to the 6 sucres that the free peon earns."[13]

3. Fiestas and the Cargo

The extraordinary importance of fiestas in Indian life has been indicated in various contexts, especially in discussing the Indians' "use of time" and the significance of the priostes, the sponsors of fiestas, (Chapters VIII, B, and XII, B, 2). Looked at casually, it seems that "eating and drinking to excess" at fiestas are the main Indian interests (Chapter VII, B and C). Indeed, to participate in, or to finance and sponsor, fiestas constitutes the other major end toward which time, energy, and money are devoted. Thus merely to participate in a "popular" (not sponsored) fiesta, Indians of the Mojanda area are said to enroll two or three months before the fiesta of San Juan and San Pedro as peons in public works or seek other employment in order to obtain the necessary spending money and to buy new clothes for the occasion (Santiana 1949:260). More impressive, however, is the obligation for every adult male to sponsor a religious celebration for the local saint at least once in his lifetime, i.e., to undertake the cargo (literally, "the burden") of organizing and financing a costly service to his community and its saint as prioste (also mayordomo, capitán, alcalde). Again, there are many incisive statements on this matter.[14]

Thus Hassaurek comments on the Indians of Latacunga (Cotopaxi Province), who were famous for their mummeries and dances during Holy Week and who hired fancy dresses and jewels for the occasion "at an expense which not only swallows up a whole year's earnings, but generally increases the interminable debt for which they are held to labor." Saenz quotes Cevallos, according to whom all tastes and enjoyments of the Indians are limited to finding the wherewithal to drink and to celebrate their feasts with music, dances, fireworks, and processions, and who dwells on the heavy financial burden that falls on those who have to buy the costumes, the drinks, and the music.[15]

Here is an observation made at the turn of the century on the Indians of Riobamba: "For these feasts, the Indians designate one of them who pays for the expenses for the decoration of the church. This kind of organizer is called prioste." He gives a feast for his friends, "the only one that counts for the Indians, the function or obligation, as they say....To give this is a sacred duty for every Indian...he who fails to provide it is cursed even after death." The Indian works and scrapes the entire year, then becomes a prioste, and the savings of the entire year are gone in eight days' celebration.[16]

Saenz confirms these observations by his own, explaining the working of the cult of the saint: "...it is considered a really shameful thing not to have fulfilled this obligation. It is a sign of economic and social inability and a lack of communal solidarity [not to have done so]. The greatest insult that one can offer an Indian is to tell him...'he has not undertaken the cargo'." The cargo is a real economic burden: "I have been told that many individuals found themselves ruined as a consequence of the expense for the religious celebration," which, in Otavalo, was calculated in the early thirties to amount to 200 sucres or the equivalent of at least 400 work days.[17]

More recent observations among the Indians of Otavalo and elsewhere fully bear out the earlier ones. The minimum outlay involved in the financing of a fiesta by a capitán is no less than 2,000 sucres (early forties), and those borne by the paje ("page," junior cult official, the capitán's aide) are 1,500 sucres, for the first fiesta marking the first part of their service; the second part, calling for another fiesta after six months, involves similar expenditures.[18] These are sums that may well represent the savings of years even in this region of relatively high incomes from crafts and trading. To quote the Buitróns on these affairs: "At each of these fiestas, these Indians spend enormous sums of money. One could say that they work and save the whole year in order to spend it all during the fiestas. Above all, the priostes, the sponsors or godfathers of the fiesta, have to spend....There is so much social pressure obligating the Indians to take on the burden of sponsoring these fiestas and, furthermore, to take on this burden gives so much prestige to the individual, that the Indians could go as far as to rob in order to comply with this social obligation."[19] "The worst insult that one can inflict upon an Indian is to say of him he is poor and has not yet undertaken the obligation."[20] Similarly, the epithets applied to him who fails to serve as prioste on becoming head of a household and able to afford the expenditure is "inexperienced youth," "poor one," "savage,"[21] i.e., non-Christian.

This fiesta-sponsoring pattern seems to be fairly general. The host of a three-day celebration among the Indians of Saraguro incurs expenditures calculated to be between 800 and 1,000 sucres.[22] Fragmentary data on expenditures of "urban" Indians at the outskirts of Quito are comparable: 250 sucres for mass, 350 sucres for a small-size band, 350 to 500 sucres for a full-size music band per day, for a prioste fiesta lasting two to three days.[23] Finally, the case of the Cotopaxi ex-hacienda peon, who had worked at a mine and found himself with a slice of accumulated wages on his hands, is recalled. "Such an amount of money means only one thing to an Indian: a fiesta...So he takes his money home, gives everyone a big part...," and is promptly apprehended by his old hacienda employer for old debts (Franklin 1943:82).

Buitrón, summing up his studies on the relative economic position of low-income and high-income Otavalo Indians, arrives at the conclusion that "they are alike in their desire (afán), though not in ability to realize it, of saving money toward two principal ends: to buy land and to sponsor a fiesta."[24]

Land possession or ownership and the sponsoring of a fiesta are, then, the two dominant concerns of Indian life, the chief motivators to action, the first incentives to acquire and to save money.

But these two outstanding "interests" are not as isolated as they might seem in our presentation. To have and to hold land implies lawsuits. And the service of the saint by fiestas and cargos belongs in a whole context of efforts taken and expenditures made in the service of religion generally.

4. Legal and Religious Concerns

The role of litigations and lawyers in Indian life has been touched upon previously (Chapters VIII, C, and X, C, which see for documentation). The literature makes much of Indian involvement in costly and protracted litigations. "The Indian," reports Saenz, "litigates eternally over a few varas of land. More than sixty per cent of legal cases and controversies involving the Indians of Imbabura center generally on property and its legal titles." "It is one of the characteristics of the

Indians that they constantly bring suit and litigate. The questions concerned are largely disputes over land and property; but they also relate to all those petty and puerile differences with /the Indian's/ neighbors, and to his acts of restitution arising from the abuses of which he is a victim. The administration of justice is, for the Indian, a costly, complicated and inefficient affair,"[25] and a matter over which he is notoriously stubborn and tenacious.

Such cases, as Mrs. Parsons (1945:38, 186) and Rodríguez Sandoval (1949:24, 37) make clear, also arise very commonly over questions of inheritance and over disputes as to whether a presumed heir to parental land has forfeited his rights due to prolonged absence and failure to "serve" his parents (see Chapter XII, B, 3). Elsewhere cases are reported of the successful defense of their titles to land against outside encroachment by groups or communities of Indians by fighting the matter through the court (Monsalve Pozo 1942).

It is clear that lawsuits are very largely incidental to the ownership of land, but since their occurrence tends to be accidental, as it were, it is doubtful whether they constitute real motivators for the individual to extra efforts, i.e., in deliberate preparation against an expected contingency. However, the defense of land titles or other rights, when collectively undertaken, may furnish short-term incentives in so far as the need arises to raise funds for lawsuits and other steps by which to secure title deeds.[26]

More important, because more sustained, more generalized, and more pervasive, and less incidental, are all the activities that center on religious observances in general which entail money or other expenditures. Of such activities, the cargos and the fiestas just described are the most prominent. All of Indian life, however, is punctuated by religious observances, ceremonials, and other occasions implicating the realm of the religious.

That the church plays a prominent role in Indian life has been noted in various contexts. Much of Indian action is directly related to this ritual side of life, including efforts for the church, specifically, in support of the parish church or chapel. Many are the scathing comments on this form of "exploitation" of the Indians, and pro-Indian anticlericalism furnishes quite copious quotations on the amount of money spent (or "exacted") for masses, baptisms, funeral and wedding services, for tithes, first-fruits, and other fees rendered in cash or paid for in produce or in personal services.

Hassaurek notes these channels of expenditures at length, both generally and specifically. Of the former, a few examples may suffice. Noting the needs of Indians to be few, he points out that all their money goes to the church, the clericals, and "their greedy appetites." The Indians "will give to the Church more than they should, in justice to their own wants." "If /the Indian/ has enough to give some money to the priest, and to buy his raw food...and rum and chicha for what remains, he is perfectly satisfied."[27]

Mrs. Parsons, who herself has no anticlerical ax to grind, reports one informant as saying: "'Convinced by their priests,'...the Indians 'give primicia and diezmos as if it were a divine law and a way to conquer heaven'."[28] Her account, devoting particular attention to the Indians' religious life, contains sufficient data on expenditures in this realm[29] to warrant the conclusion that Indians spare no expense for their piety, formalistic and ritualistic as it may appear to be.

As may be expected, particularly among a peasantry, the various life events are of great importance not only subjectively, i.e., for the individual concerned, but also objectively when considered in terms of their financial involvements and effects. Weddings, baptisms, and funerals are, as has been pointed out before, festive, social affairs; they are, by themselves, not only time-consuming but also costly affairs.

In addition, these events have "budgetary" implications, and this is particularly true of weddings and marriage.[30] The Indian wedding now consists typically of two or three distinct ceremonies: the official regis- tration of marriage, a formal church wedding, and an Indian traditional ceremony, which may more or less coincide in point of time; more fre- quently, however, they are separated from each other by months or even years. The church, and certainly the traditional, wedding ceremonies are marked by extensive feasts, and even the act of registration may be fol- lowed by a feast of lesser dimension. At any rate, these affairs, including gifts exchanged among the parties involved, mean heavy and anticipated expenditures, particularly for the groom and his parents, but also for the bride's kin, and to some extent also for the wedding godparents, the padrinos de boda, a couple called upon to "sponsor" the marriage. The cheapest traditional-style wedding in Ilumán costs an estimated 300 sucres, and from there on costs may rise up to 1,500 sucres.[31]

But this is not all, of course. The setting up of a household--an event that does not necessarily coincide with any of the wedding cere- monies--is, in the first place, an incentive to the young couple to become economically independent of their parents. Ideally, the groom should have his own house and land on entering on married life. There appears to be considerable moral pressure on the groom to own house, land, and other appurtenances of an independent householder when he gets married. In practice, temporary residence in the home of the groom's parents and earning participation in that household, or in that of the bride's parents, seems to be the rule, though the latter appears to be less frequently the case.

Second, the marriage of children constitutes for the parents them- selves an anticipatory incentive to acquire the wherewithals, such as land, building materials, utensils, etc., with which to launch the young couple on the way toward household independence, not to mention the accumulation of funds with which to defray the expenses of the wedding ceremonies themselves.

It should be added that marriage is of the utmost importance to Indians--an obligation that should not be unduly deferred. Parents aim assiduously to marry their children off and derive considerable satis- faction from the number of kindred that result therefrom. The pressure is equally great on young people to get married, especially on men whose status in society and participation in festivity are contingent upon their married status. Marriage is the first step in the direction of economic independence, which is not acquired until the young couple is able to leave the parental home and fend for itself, a period that may last some years and which means, above all, work and saving.[32]

The death of their parents may or may not benefit offspring sub- stantially. Arrangements regarding inheritance or distribution of possessions even during the lifetime of the parents seem to vary (and are, furthermore, little described) between a traditional system accord- ing to which goods are distributed per testament or according to indicated wishes of the parent with special regard to the merit of the individual heir's case and individual child-parent relation, and the civil code's rules of inheritance which apply in the absence of such explicit testament and whereby children inherit in equal parts.[33] That questions of inheritance are a major source of lawsuits has been indicated before.

Since, in the majority of cases, Indians are not wealthy, the share of an individual in the patrimony is probably seldom large enough[34] to exempt him from further efforts of making a living. The share may nevertheless be important.

The incidence of death and succession to goods may, however, prod the heir to heightened economic activity, if a suggestion made by Rivet is considered as to its logical implications. In an investigation of the funeral customs of Ecuadorean Indians, Rivet notes that the wakes for the dead give rise to considerable consumption of his movable goods, in particular foodstuffs and livestock, either directly through banqueting or indirectly through a dice game (huayru, guayru) played on such occasions only, by persons not related to the deceased, and supposed to be of a divinatory character.[35] Economically, these wakes are, or tend to be, ruinous for the heir or heirs, in that the parent's goods go to the winners. The inference is clear: this "conspicuous consumption," which Rivet compares to that outstanding example of the potlatch of the Northwest Coast Indians of North America,[36] would, if substantiated, conceivably provide a constantly recurring incentive to economic activity to recoup the heir's losses. Rivet makes the following observation:

> The guayru game is not played if the deceased possesses nothing. It is considered obligatory that the dead leave a little money so that the widow can buy aguardiente for the guests /at the wake/. If there is no aguardiente, the feast is considered a flop. Sometimes the guests bring a little of the precious beverage themselves to drink before the guayru game. In that case it may happen that they insult the dead by calling him lazy and shameless and they reproach him for not having been willing to work, therefore leaving no money behind.[37]

It is possible that the game is still played in certain regions of Ecuador. However, there is nothing in the more recent literature on the northern parts of highland Ecuador[38] that would indicate a "cult of the dead" of this specific sort with economic consequences of this kind for the heir. What is indicated by Mrs. Parsons' account is that there are expenses arising on the occasion of death (1945:77-80, 199-205). And, in the thinking of Otavalo Indians, the dead (the "souls") play a very important role not much different from that of the saints (cf. Chapter X, C, and n. 61). Both are prayed to and given periodic offerings, and masses are read for them.[39] However, this "cult of the dead" is but one, though specialized, aspect of the "costs of religion," as they may be called.

6. The Interests and Virtues[40]

Whatever the economic significance of such death-focused customs may be, the observations just cited reveal a preoccupation with wealth and with economic standing and ability--attitudes which at first blush would seem congenial to the proposition of industrialization. It is certainly important to underline the fact that industry would be dealing with people who do not disdain material possessions for other values, such as acquiring wisdom or salvation through ascetic otherworldliness. The contents of Indian life, and the values of life are, as far as evidence is available, of this world, notwithstanding the apparently contradictory concern with matters that are on the religious plane, with ritual and ceremony and their entire social context. True, we do not directly "know"

of ultimate values Indians might cherish. All too little has been overheard by our various observers, all too much imputed by them to the
Indians, leaving us to infer goals and motives from overt and recurrent
behavior.

Yet, once in a while Indians become loud and loquacious enough
in the presence of an outsider to disclose more deepseated concerns,
aspirations, and attitudes ("values"). A case in point is what has been
reported on the occurrence of, and incidentally to, death: there ought
to be goods and evidences of prosperity and industriousness left behind;
the deceased ought to have given cause for being praised and well spoken
of for such virtues, and none for being blamed as lazy, incompetent, and
poor.

These reports of Rivet, Cevallos, and Rodríguez Sandoval (above,
and note 37) on this matter can perhaps be placed side by side with what
has been reportedly overheard in other conditions or situations which,
while they may not be crucial, are at least occasions for Indian self-
revelation, namely, the condition of inebriation. It is then that the Indian,
ordinarily reticent in earshot of outsiders, becomes boastful, as testi-
fied to by many observers (Chapter X, B, and notes 37 and 38, on Indian
aggressiveness and behavior at fiesta times and when drinking). And
what does he boast of? "Nobody is better than we, we are the strongest
men in the world; my farmstead is the best of all; there are no fields like
ours; we are powerful, we are rich, we can do anything..."[41] Even in
the condition of peonage, the content of drunken boasts and self-praise
is that of faithfulness and industriousness (Hassaurek 1868:298). In his
search for motives for the Indians' high consumption of drink, Rodríguez
Sandoval finds that the Indian "likes people to speak of him as rich,
industrious, generous and with plenty of friends," hence drinking is also,
whatever else it is, the outward symbol of a man's ability to spend for
himself, and particularly to spend for and with others. "With my own
money," he quotes an Indian as saying, "I can drink or not as I wish.
That is why I work from daybreak, to drink plenty of chicha with my
friends." It is for this reason too, as Rodríguez Sandoval comments,
that Indians are loud and boisterous in drink and that they often pretend
to be drunk and act drunkenly, showing off. In brief, drinking is a sign
of wealth, which in turn shows the drinker to be a good worker, in turn
permitting him to be generous and to display his good standing to and with
his fellowmen and friends.[42]

Apart from these instances of behavioral and verbal ostentatiousness that have a definite context in that they prove something about the
individual's worth or standing in an approved manner, ostentation for its
own sake is disapproved. Personal apparel--this being a good test--
"is not thought of ordinarily as indicative either of status or personal
taste. As a Cayambe man writes, 'People do not like to dress themselves
luxuriously even if they have the wherewithal'."[43] Excepted from this
negative evaluation of ostentatiousness are the jewelry worn by women
for display and the poncho of the man, in which some pride is taken.[44]
Some behavior and acts in the presence of non-Indians--callers, for
example--may be interpreted as "display" of savoir faire, of being
knowledgeable about White ways.[45] But these considerations would
lead us back to our discussion on imitation of White ways and acceptance
and nonacceptance of items felt to be not of the world of the Indians
(Chapter X, B, and note 34).

B. Indian Values and Industry: A Summary

There remains for consideration the bearing of Indian "values" on the question regarding incentives for the staying of Indians in industrial work. A psychological system, linking intangible "virtues" to wealth (possessions, earnings, wages), has just been presented. The "virtues"-- so defined in Indian terms (manifest and effective industriousness, generosity, lavishness toward one's friends)--contain motivations toward work, specifically toward continuous work; but it is obvious that these motivations are effective only if and as long as they can be translated into action among like-minded people, among social peers and cultural equals or, to phrase the matter differently, within a prestige system that corresponds to Indian "virtues" and the forms in which they are displayed. On the other hand, the incentives to work which industry offers primarily are merely the means, in the form of wages, toward "wealth" and thus toward that display of a man's worth which is understood and approved in Indian society. Moreover, industry does not, in principle, provide those "traditional" and "affectual incentives" to work which are here discussed.[46] It has no prestige system answering the Indian prestige system, which stands and falls with the validation of economic standing and ability among congeners. The good opinions of strangers and of out-siders, be they strange fellow-workers or strange foremen, are no spur to work, to acquire, or to spend.[47]

Hence the suggestions made earlier in a different light concerning the groupwise induction of Indians into industrial work against the piecemeal recruiting of individuals from here and there[48] acquire further importance: the functioning kin and neighborhood group not only provides for itself off the job, and furnishes its own disciplinary and supervisory mechanism on the job, but it also may constitute that stimulating social environment within which work and staying at work is worth while and where efforts and their fruits are appreciated. This means, in practice, that industry might have to provide for at least a partial reproduction of Indian group life and its setting.

These non-"rational" incentives to staying in industrial work cannot, of course, be expected to operate indefinitely and isolated from, and un-supported by, relatively more "rational" motivators. Certainly, these "psychological" incentives are related to, or represent the ultimate phase of, those Indian aims which have been elucidated by examining the channels of major expenditures or would-be expenditures. In evaluating the immediate and tangible uses to which earnings systematically tend to be turned we shall, in fact, be forced to the conclusion that they con-stitute most precarious motivators as far as permanence in industrial work is concerned, although they may be good motivators toward entering industry.

As has been shown, there are two goals pursued and attainable to varying degrees by means of accumulated money incomes: one consists of the preservation and acquisition of land, the other in the fulfilment of socially prescribed obligations, the cargo. Expenditures for lawsuits, fines, the church, religious rites related to life events, sickness, either may be referred to the two major ends or may be considered as more or less constant "prods" operating as the occasion arises. The motivational dynamics, if any, of the Indian pattern of consumption, i.e., the totality of things or services ordinarily purchased with money,[49] and of the traditional Indian standard of living had to be left out of consideration here. Only the implications of the urge for land and of the cargo institution will be considered.

The possession and use of land certainly have an objective importance for Indians and represent a definite need where no alternatives to making a living offer. Land has, however, an importance transcending its economic utility for its holders, as witness the case of Otavalo where farming is still the main occupation engaged in side by side with a flourishing part-time craft industry. There may be other good objective reasons for this continued reliance on farming. But from the point of meaningfulness for these Indians, it can only be suggested that farming is a preferential occupation rather than, or besides being, a need, and that what we are dealing with here is the outcome, above all, of a pure choice, a demonstrated preference, or a "taste"--that tertium quid as between "need" and "want." The "want" aspect, or the other subjective significance of the ownership of land, is present too. As a form of wealth, land stands for values and virtues: security, standing, ability to work and provide for one's self, one's kindred, and friends. (The case is simpler, but no less valid, for Indians in, or coming from, the concierto situation; for them, possession and use of land by tenancy are the decisive point.)

If the diagnosis of the significance of land for the Indian is correct, including the inference that the desire for land is a deeprooted and autonomous attitude, it follows that the prospect of acquiring the means toward obtaining it can act as an effective motivator for work, including industrial work, only where the acquisition of land is possible, and can be visualized and made the object of "rational" calculation by the Indian. In other words, the chances that Indians will enter industrial work to earn money with which to buy land are good. There the matter ends; thereafter industrial work would be purposeless.

The significance of the cargo, in the context of the question regarding its role in sustaining industrialization, is similar to that of land. But, in contrast to the motivator land, the cargo has a directly and purely social referent, whatever other meaning it may have as a religious ritual. It is not very relevant for our question to determine whether the cargo is undertaken voluntarily or under social pressure. It is relevant to state that it is a group affair, and that it is only in the group that it has a meaningful context. Hence it is the member of an intact, functioning Indian group who is likely to seek the means by which to undertake this expensive affair, and he might seek them in industry. Once this aim is realized, industrial work is likely to be terminated.

To recapitulate these matters and to spell out their consequences in detail in terms of recruiting for industry: land is likely to constitute an incentive for industrial work among the landless and land-poor Indian groups (free laborers and conciertos, tenants and very small owners) in regions where land is obtainable by purchase. Cargo is likely to furnish this incentive to seek industrial work where Indian groups are intact, as among landed farmers and, perhaps also, conciertos. Individuals who are further inclined to seek industrial employment in order to realize specific ends are young men who expect to marry or who have been recently married and wish to set up a household of their own; young men faced with the obligation of having to undertake their first cargo; men ambitious enough to want to sponsor more than the one obligatory fiesta; and men with half-grown children, for the purpose of equipping them with land or household goods in the near future.

NOTES

1. We abstain from stating explicitly the sense in which "motivations" and "incentives," as well as the subsequent concepts, are used here. The substance of the following discussion will make clear that we are dealing with actions not in terms of impersonal causes (historical, cultural, etc.), nor in terms of objective, functional reasons, but

primarily in terms of the actors' personal intentions and understanding of their own situation. The terms and concepts employed toward this end here are understood to be crude tools.

2. Cf. Chapter IX, C.

3. Cisneros Cisneros 1948:87. Some such traditional payments in kind may be converted into cash, or rights to them, as in the case of the diezmos, may be rented out to collecting agents. In Chimborazo, ración means the plot of land assigned to the huasipungero for his own use.

4. Gil Gilbert (1942:230 ff.) vividly describes an episode centering on this point. See particularly IEAG 1953, Nos. 10 and 11:19, 48-49 ff.

5. Franklin 1943:81; also pp. 82-83, where he points out that such Indians, once they had learned that they had to be paid wages and were not to be whipped, according to the law, came "to understand the matter of the lawyer's fee and pay him in full as soon as they can." See also his account (p. 77) of how a group of just such hacienda Indians refused to help move a stuck automobile when offered ten sucres but were persuaded to do so when offered 20 reales, which is two sucres.
    These observations may help to shed light on the fact that "increased pay does not offer the incentive to workers in Ecuador which might be expected from the standpoint of experience in the United States. Despite the higher levels of wages today, complaints of absenteeism are reported frequently. The emphasis placed on better working conditions and increased benefits in the demands advanced by Ecuadorean labor in recent months is of interest"(IRS V, 11 /Feb., 1948/:8).

6. Franklin (1943:199 ff.) has an example on this point in his encounter with a Cholo subsistence farmer who would not sell feed for the traveler's mule, since the money offered him had no (purchase) value for him.
    The points raised here and in the following may be compared with Antonio García's brilliantly conceived and informative essay (1948) in which he shows that contacts with money and with monetary matters were, and still are, so tenuous as to fail to "sophisticate" the Indian to the essential function of money. His case studies deal with various types of colonial economic activities (Nueva Granada) as well as with various types of tribal and marginal Indian groups of contemporary Colombia.
    Gill (1940:132-40) describes the case of a highly intelligent Oriente Indian curaca-trader whom "it took a full year or more to adjust his ideas of the value of currency to the flashing bulk" of the usual trade goods that up to then had been barter-traded.
    Cf. Herrnheiser (1946), who also emphasizes these points in relation to lowland Indian workers at estates and mines.

7. However, I consider it entirely likely that little "swaps" go on within the market setting, as when a woman will exchange a handful of corn for an equivalent amount of, say, barley with another woman--minute exchanges among acquaintances that happen to take place in the market, as can be observed in Indian markets in Peru as in Ayacucho or Puno.

8. Cisneros Cisneros 1948:218 and passim. IEAG (1953, Nos. 10 and 11: 35-36, 46) reports a number of such barter transactions among Chimborazo Indians, involving eggs, salt, and lard, and even identifies an entire group, called milines, which during the agriculturally slack seasons barter-trades textiles and household goods throughout the province with the Indians of the high páramos for their products.

9. See Garcés 1941:23, 24. The Indian, says Santiana (1949:245), tries to escape the tragedy of hiring himself out as peon to work in the city or the nearest hacienda by all means, and does so only under dire necessity. What the "dire necessity" might be, Santiana does not say; but see our succeeding text.

10. It is noticeable that none of the writers of the latter part of the nineteenth and the earlier twentieth centuries has anything to say on this point--a circumstance which leads one to think that the question of land did not become acute for Indians until the turn of the century at the earliest. Actually, it is not until the later twenties that comments appear regarding the efforts of Indians to acquire land, roughly the period when something like "bucolic romanticism" and agrarian reform pressure made their appearance in Latin America. The early twenties in Ecuador witnessed a heightened Sierra Indian unrest and the violent beginnings of a largely urban labor movement (cf. Chapter X, B, and note 42). Without having further inquired into this matter and without considering the obvious possibility of population increase having reached a point critical to this development, we may only speculatively suggest that a change in the inheritance system of Indians occurred with land coming to be divided in equal parts among children, and that the effects of such a new system did not come to be felt until about the turn of the century. Also to be considered in this light are the possible effects of the 1899 and 1918 legislations concerning regulation and formal abolition of the concertaje system.
     On the other hand, Parsons' observation (1945:183) on a village in the canton of Cayambe and its settlement about one hundred years ago by hacienda serfs who managed to acquire lands leads to the surmise that acquisition of land by Indians is not an entirely new phenomenon.

11. Saenz 1933a:116-17, 126, also p. 189; Monsalve Pozo 1942; Suárez 1934:39; Garcés 1941:25, 26; see also IEAG 1953, Nos. 10 and 11:36; Jaramillo Alvarado 1943, No. 12:52; Moomaw 1946:196; Rubio Orbe 1949 and 1953; Rodríguez Sandoval 1949:33-44, 79-80, 86. The acquisition of land as motive power for Indians to work in the coastal lowlands figures as one of the episodes in Gil Gilbert's novel (1942:202).

12. Parsons 1945:9 and 21 (the emphasis is Parsons'). On the reluctance of Indians to sell land, specifically to Whites, see also Santiana 1949:241; Buitrón and Buitrón 1945; Rodríguez Sandoval 1949:35-36.

13. Buitrón and Buitrón 1947:38 (emphasis mine). See Parsons 1945: 170-72. Saenz, incidentally, compares the Ecuadorean hacienda peon favorably with his Mexican counterpart because of the use of land which the former enjoys (1933a:126). See also Rodríguez Sandoval 1949:103-8 and CEPAL 1954:15 n. The dispossession of huasipungeros from their plots and their fierce resistance constitute the climax of Icaza's novel (1934).

14. In contrast to the problem "land," documentation for this "problem" is old.

15. Hassaurek 1868:72; see also p. 162 ff. on the money costs involved in the 1860's in the financing of a priostazgo or cargo including a mass, sermon, procession, evening sermon. Saenz 1933a:95; Cevallos 1873: 134 ff. on the danzantes, and pp. 128, 129 on danzantes, priostes, alcaldes.

16. Rivet 1903:75-76. He suggests that this institution is analogous to the potlatch of the Northwest Coast Indians of North America, in that these fiestas tend to become ever more "orgiastic," each prioste trying to outdo his predecessor in splendor.

17. Saenz 1933a:77-79, 155-56. Attempts by individual churchmen to curb or suppress these fiestas because of their high costs to the Indians were unavailing, as Saenz explains. The Indians kept on celebrating them. Sumptuary measures taken by municipalities, such as raising the license fee on the shooting of fireworks, did not stop the occasions for these expenditures; they simply increased the fiesta costs. (Cf. Chapter VII, C, 2, ii, and references.) See also Rodríguez Sandoval (1949:106-7) on the complaints of Indians that the suppression of the cargo, attempted by the government, will prevent them from telling henceforth who a "real man" is.

18. Buitrón 1947a; see also Collier and Buitrón 1949:124 ff. IEAG (1953, Nos. 10 and 11:82) asserts that the costs of a priostazgo in drink alone amount to 2,000 to 3,000 sucres.

19. Buitrón and Buitrón 1945. So great is the importance of having sponsored a fiesta that Indians will sell all they have; contract debts at usurious rates taking many years to pay; commit robberies; even sell their children. See Garcés 1941:32; Buitrón 1948b; Cisneros Cisneros 1948: 98-100; Santiana 1949:261.

20. Buitrón 1947a.

21. Parsons 1945:82; cf. Rodríguez Sandoval 1949:106-7.

22. J. Davis 1946:71. The Indians of this region are eminently farmers. No craft industries, like those of the Otavalo Indians, are reported for them.

23. Castro 1948. These Indians of the barrio of Magdalena (Quito) are makers of tiles, bricks, and adobe bricks and work as bricklayers and construction workers.

24. Buitrón 1947a. See also Rubio Orbe (1953:212), who notes that more sumptuous feasts, not higher levels of living, education, sanitation, are correlated with rising cash incomes in the Otavalo region. Also Rodríguez Sandoval (1949:125-26), who enumerates modern additions to fiestas, like printed souvenir cards of sponsoring priostes, which, inferentially, increase the costs of fiestas.

25. Saenz 1933a:117, 135. The "restitutions" probably refer to the custom of attaching articles of personal belongings of the Indians when they fail to render minga services for municipal public works.

26. See the case of the comuna de Chunazana (IEAG 1953, No. 4: 13-16).

27. Hassaurek 1868:187; see pp. 159-62 for information on rates for various church services for Indians and Negroes and fees for curates in the 1860's, and pp. 301 ff. on personal services to the priest. See also Rivet 1903:74; Buitrón 1948b; IEAG 1953, Nos. 10 and 11, passim.

28. Parsons 1945:81. The reference is to Cayambe. In Otavalo, Mrs. Parsons reports, the church sells its rights to tithes to Otavalo merchants who collect the produce--an interesting development away from "premonetary arrangements." Still, even hacendados send baskets of produce to the church as tithes, and Indian food offerings are brought to the church and deposited at the altars.

29. Parsons 1945: 47, 78, 81 (fees for burial service and mass), 85. See also Collier and Buitrón 1949:141 and 143, on services.

30. Major sources on betrothal, wedding, and connected ceremonies, and on marriage in general, are IEAG 1953, No. 3:202 ff., 210-16; Moomaw 1946:172; Parsons 1945:passim, esp. pp. 55 ff., 149, 193-95; Rivet 1903: 66-67; Rodríguez Sandoval 1949:97-99, 100-1, 19-22.

31. IEAG 1953, No. 3:101-2; data are for 1951-52. In order to make these estimated figures meaningful, a few comparative data from the same locality, applying to the same period, are here presented (ibid., passim). Three hundred sucres are the approximate equivalent of the total inversion (hired labor and ox-teams, seed, fertilizer) into a plot of land of one cuadra (1.727 acres) sown to corn and beans, up to and including harvesting. Fifteen hundred sucres are the equivalent of the cash value of its yield. Three hundred sucres represent approximately a six-weeks' food bill (market value of food items) for a family of five; or the total value of tools and implements owned by a farmer of a plot of land of one hectare (a little less than 2.5 acres). Wage-rates for free peons and huasipungeros are sucres 1.50 to 2 per day (whether food rations are given additionally is not known); hence three hundred sucres represent the approximate equivalent of 150 to 200 cash-paid working days. Fifteen hundred sucres represent approximately one-half the value of the total clothing of an Indian family of five; or, at the minimum, one-tenth of the appraisal value of land, according to registered title deeds, which in Ilumán ranges from 15,000 to 25,000 sucres per cuadra (three-quarters of a hectare).

32. Parsons 1945:33, 149. Her chief informants, both very competent people, lived for five years with the bride's parents until by weaving and spinning, in addition to contributing work to the parental household, they had saved enough to set up their own. Until then, they were "in the power of their father," i.e., the household head.

33. Parsons 1945:38, 129 (with a folk tale as model of unequal inheritance according to merit), 186; Rodríguez Sandoval 1949:20, 36-37.

34. See Beals (1952) for a drastic example of the rate of land-fractioning in the course of inheritance over three generations. Cf. n. 10 above.

35. Rivet 1926; see also 1903. This game is of a ceremonial nature, played only at wakes with a single die. From the Indian point of view it is not a game of hazard, but is played in honor of the deceased head of a family. The departed, or rather his soul, is thought to participate personally in the game in that he causes the die to fall in favor of those whom he liked during his lifetime. The players, only adult males and excluding all near relatives of the deceased, arrange themselves on both sides of the corpse and the die is tossed across it. The "stakes" consist in the livestock of the deceased, which are then distributed among the players according to the die-divined directions of the dead. Those who thus honor him by eating and drinking with him, waking for him, and interrogating him as to his wishes (through the game) will not lack thenceforth in food, and their crops will prosper.
    The ceremony is also described by Karsten in reference to the Indians of the Riobamba and Ambato regions where he, too, apparently witnessed these funeral rites and described them as one among the rites centering on the "cult of the dead." The above follows largely his description (1939, esp. pp. 42-44). See also the disucssion of the game by John M. Cooper (1949a:513-14, 516-22).
    In the version reported by Rodríguez Sandoval (1949:101) from eastern Tungurahua, it is the loser who has to collect chickens and guinea pigs from the house of the deceased for the meal of the day. Still another version on the same theme is reported from eastern Chimborazo (IEAG 1953, No. 11:145-46).

It is probably no accident that the games of partly European derivation played at wakes in Cayambe are forfeit games or are so understood.
See Parsons 1945:199 ff.; and Chapter VIII, C, and notes.

36. It is only fair to add that Rivet suggests this analogy regarding the
destruction of wealth with the greatest caution.
Huizinga's discussion on the sociological significance of gambling,
dicing, and squandering matches is most suggestive in this context
(1949:57-63).

37. The playing of the guayru game at wakes is also reported by Cevallos
(1873:137-38). The importance of possessions in the thinking of the dying
Indian is, however, presented differently: the Indians face death without
disquiet or fear. "If they see anything at all in death, it is apprehension
lest the priest try to take the pair of oxen or sheep from the inheriting
children as a fee for the burial rites. Thus the first sin of which they
accuse themselves when facing death is that they leave no goods behind
whatsoever" (Cevallos' emphasis, p. 139). Cf. Saenz 1933a:92-95. See
also statements by Indians on that matter recorded by Rodríguez Sandoval
1949:83-84. In all cases, death can be the occasion for prestige or de-
precation of the deceased.

38. Barring an obscure hint by Santiana (1949:256-58) in his discussion
of celebrations of life events, including wakes, funerals, and the rites
of the Day of the Dead.

39. Parsons 1945:86-87, 111, 113, 158, 180. See also Collier and Buitrón
1949:151 ff.; IEAG 1953, No. 3:221. On funeral customs specifically and
the so-called "cult of the dead," see Buitrón 1951a; 1951c; IEAG 1953, Nos.
10 and 11:73-75, 145-48; Rodríguez Sandoval 1949:101-3; Santiana 1952b.
For hacienda Indians these life events and their celebrations (births
and baptisms, weddings and marriage, death and funerals) mean primarily
contraction of new debts to the hacienda, in the form of "advances." Impressive figures on this matter are provided for indios propios of Chimborazo haciendas: with wage rates at 75 centavos a day or less than
150 sucres a year, church and registration fees for weddings and marriages
amount to 100 to 240 sucres; total costs for funerals to 200-470 sucres, and
up to 600 sucres for a funeral mass. Some of these figures are found in
the itemized lists of debts and advances kept by haciendas (IEAG 1953,
Nos. 10 and 11:21 ff., 50 ff., 74, 143 ff.).
Indian concern with the fulfilment of the very costly proprieties
toward the deceased and its consequences constitute one of the main
episodes in Icaza's novel (1934).

40. With this section see also Chapter VII, C, 2, on alcohol consumption,
and Chapter VIII, on drinking, fiestas, industriousness, and Indian attitudes toward work.

41. Saenz 1933a:86-87, and Parsons' version (1945:124). See also Santiana
(1949:252), where drunken affirmation of one's worth includes reference
to having fulfilled the cargo. Some such "boasting" or instances of self-
praise also occur in spontaneously arranged Indian children's games
imitating adult life (Parsons 1945:156).

42. Rodríguez Sandoval 1945. See also Rodríguez Sandoval 1949 (pp. 21,
38, 44, 82, 88, 89, 94-95), for a collection of such verbatim boasts which
refer to the boaster's personal accomplishments, abilities, and possessions, such as a large extended family with children married off, much
land, being a good worker and provider, honest and capable, with financial
ability to drink, having many friends and compadres. Boastful drinking

songs in the mouths of huasipungeros appear pathetic wishful dreamings (IEAG 1953, Nos. 10 and 11:81-82).

43. Parsons 1945:30. Elsewhere (p. 163), Mrs. Parsons mentions that her Indian informant seems to want to be thought of as charitable rather than rich (this woman keeps two servants, for their keep). She also notes, in Cayambe, outright depreciation and hostility toward the "rich" on the part of Indians (p. 187), but the context makes it clear that it is wealth, coupled with unneighborliness or oppression, that is so disparaged.

44. Parsons 1945:30. In Ilumán, women's jewelry is indicative of wealth; for example, each string of a woman's coral-bead collar represents 1,000 sucres, according to IEAG (1953, No. 3:249-52), discussing jewelry items. See also ibid., p. 140 ff. with comparative data on the value of Mestizo and Indian clothing outfits (male and female), and especially on prices of ponchos and hats, the two most important and prized items in Indian male attire. Market prices of Indian-made textiles, including ponchos, are also cited in Buitrón 1947a. For Chimborazo, see IEAG 1953, Nos. 10 and 11:31 (prices for dress and jewelry items).
   On the social, economic, and cultural significance of clothing items, in particular the poncho, see the very interesting observations of the Buitróns (1947:54-59); also Santiana 1949:251; our discussion, Chapter XI, B, on dress and its connotations.

45. Rodríguez Sandoval (1949:98-99) has an example.

46. These matters are discussed by Max Weber ("Conditions Underlying the Calculability of the Productivity of Labor") as one of the sociological categories of economic action. See Parsons and Henderson 1947:262-64.

47. This is a statement concerning the systematic aspect of the situation seen statically. Once the approval of outsiders is, or becomes, appealing, a very different situation calls for a different analysis and assessment. It probably signifies the point at which the Indian is ready to disassociate himself from his group, his social position, or his culture, or has done so already, and is set to enter another "estate," presenting an aspect of the dynamic process variously recognized as mestizaje, acculturation, modernization, etc.

48. See Chapter VIII (discussing the problem of Indian "leisure"), and Chapter XII, C, on Indian group organization and its possible integration into the industrial organization with reference to working teams and "associational discipline."

49. The determination of such a total pattern of consumption would require a separate and very detailed study. The raw data are scattered throughout much of the literature here used. An examination of descriptive materials on personal apparel (cf. above, n. 44 for some references), on house furnishings, inventories of goods (and prices) in markets, prices for medicines or fees for curanderos, information on fines and indirect and hidden taxes, fees for church services, etc.--all that exists and could be used to indicate traditional as well as possible new channels of expenditures. The observation, for instance, that a few women in Peguche own sewing machines, priced at that time (1940-41) at 3,000 sucres or more (Parsons 1945:179, n. 16) would tend to show that there is a potential and important "demand" for other things besides land and fiestas. In brief, the literature contains data with which to construct rough models of patterns of consumption or channels of expenditures, besides the main ones. Models of income-patterns would be more difficult to extract from existing materials.

Other topics which have not been treated here, but which of course relate intimately to the major problem, are those of "business" or "economic" or "money" behavior, of "calculation," of decision and initiative. On these topics, too, we have scattered materials, as on pricing and the institutional obstacles to rational, calculative pricing; and other data suggesting that "money sense" and business sense are differentially developed as between men and women, or that it is not the men who are novarum rerum cupidi, if at all, but, in many respects, the women.

All these questions relate, of course, much more to the dynamic, developmental, and long-range aspects of a question which we have sought to analyze mainly in terms of its static, momentary position.

XV / "INTERSTITIAL INDUSTRIALIZATION": A CONCLUSION

In considering the totality of the various findings and assessments resulting from the examination of the "case" of Ecuador and a distinct part of its population, it is evident that industrialization, as commonly and broadly understood, is not realistically practicable, although it might be technically feasible. Those among the discernible factors and aspects which have been reviewed which constitute difficulties if not obstacles seem to outweigh those favoring industrialization. However, ours is, to repeat, a "hypothetical" case, selected and treated mainly for the purpose of systematically pointing up those items which are, or should be, considered in deciding to industrialize.

Within these limitations, our findings in regard to existing conditions that would confront industrialization might still have practical significance for Ecuador for certain eventualities which, admittedly, are remote. For instance, industrialization might be instituted capriciously, as a gamble or sport; or for purposes of demonstration or experimentation; or in consideration of the particularly strategic situation of the country. In other words, the data furnished by this study may be of relevance in extremis.

I

In treating of industrialization, we are not committed to conceive of it as a process that is defined by mere vastness. Industrialization means a change by a sizable number of people from traditional to specifically industrial occupations. Hence it is not decisive whether such change occurs on a nationwide scale or whether it comprises the population of a single region, or even a locality of limited size. Nor do the areas to be industrialized need to be contiguous ones. In point of fact, the present study is apt to suggest strongly something which, for lack of a better term, may be called "interstitial industrialization," i.e., a pattern of implanting industrialism tailored to accommodate to Ecuadorean or similar preindustrial conditions and insinuated in betwixt other economic sectors. Such a pattern might be developed in response to scarcity of skilled as well as unskilled manpower and competition for manpower from other economic sectors, particularly the agricultural one; undeveloped transportation and communication system; small-scale markets and limited food supply; unconcentrated settlement patterns; relatively immobile manpower and inert labor supply due partly to traditional predilection for farming, partly to existing patterns of land tenure, and partly to trends by which the stabilization of the population on land is supported. "Interstitial industrialization" requires the creation of "external economies" on a modest scale, albeit in a repetitive and proliferated manner, and includes other provisions not directly related to, but affecting, industrial production, such as a variety of services. Its immediate purpose is comparable to that of a model farm or of an experimental or pioneering farming settlement, designed to stimulate a sluggish and technologically underdeveloped agriculture by precept and demonstration, and by priming consumption of goods, demands for services, and supply of labor beyond its confines.

Interstitial industrialism concentrates quantitatively limited factors of production in a nondissipatory, small-scale, but intensive effort. Diversification of production is probably a sine qua non of this type of industrialization; it may even have to include diversification of its worker's time, allocating it to industrial as well as to nonindustrial production, as, for instance, in cases where local farming production is insufficient to meet the food requirements of new, industrially concentrated, populations, or even as a measure to keep industrial recruits until they have sloughed off a traditional predilection for the cultivation of land. (Incidentally, the concept of "interstitial industrialization," as here developed,[1] may supply a partial answer to the problem of rapid versus slow industrialization.) With such premises, industrialization in Ecuador may be considered a realistic proposition.

II

It is evident from the foregoing chapter that the various motivating factors or incentives considered do not guarantee a stable Indian labor force for industry; rather they forbode a permanent tendency to labor turnover the rate of which may be slowed down if working and living conditions are, from the point of view and in the understanding of Indians, favorable and congenial. The tendency itself is likely to persist in that Indian workers will terminate industrial employment when they have attained their specific goals. And it will be the more pronounced the farther a given industrial plant is removed from centers of Indian habitation. Unless, therefore, industry is content with an ever-changing labor force recruited from among the Indian element of the population and is satisfied with workers who stay only "for the duration" (their duration), it will have to "appropriate" the set of Indian motivators for itself and offer those inducements by which the Indian career may become an industrial career. One of these inducements by which a relatively stable labor force could be attained has already been indicated: it consists of the groupwise rather than "piecemeal" individual recruiting of Indians so as to draw upon the staying power peculiar to in-groups.

The most effective single incentive, however, by which industry might motivate Indian workers into continuous, permanent staying consists of the provision to them of land by industry itself. Such provision might have to include other facilities, such as agricultural credits.

It is obvious that schemes of free land distribution or of land distribution for only nominal prices (cf. Chapter III) would deprive industry of the probably most effective single incentive by which to obtain workers-- most effective, that is, in the first period of operation. Once again, agrarian reform, if carried out as blueprinted, would nullify industrialization, precisely because the effects of agrarian reform directly answer Indian aims. But if industry were to take a hand in agrarian reform, as it were, it could insure for itself a labor force that stays. In other words, industry has a chance to stabilize its labor force on the premises, so to speak, by making land available to its workers either by purchase or under a tenancy contract, depending on whether it draws its labor from among "free" Indians or hacienda Indians; it would have to resign itself to having part-time farmers as workers rather than having full-time workers for a period of limited employment.[2] This is one aspect of the competition for labor which an incipient industry in Ecuador has to wage with the haciendas and, possibly, with public works (Chapter IV). And, disregarding for a moment the motivational intent of such an "industrial agrarian reform," the provision of land to its workers by industry might even be necessary as long as agricultural production in Ecuador fails to guarantee the food supply adequate to meet normal demands, not to mention those of an industrial sector.

Industrialization with the adjunct "land" (and a modicum of agricultural modernization) is comprised in the concept of "interstitial industrialization." The presentation of all the many and diverse questions raised in this study is based on the visualization of such a pattern. In the course of this study, increasing emphasis has been given for implanting industrialism in a nonindustrial country and among and with nonindustrial people in accommodation not only to existing "conditions" but also and eminently to the human element and in terms of its values; it was in terms of such accommodation that we have come to discuss gradually the problem of industrialization. To do this, we had to conceive of industry, specifically of manufacturing industry, as a far more elastic system, so far as details of organization are concerned, than is ordinarily believed and when considering only the very basic principles, the stringent "requirements" of that species of production-system which is called industry. The conception of industrialism which is capable (or finds it necessary) to insinuate itself at the first moment into the "interstices" of the given reality is derived from the "soft" aspects of industry rather than from its "hard" functional shell.

To revert once more to the inquiry into the distribution of total time typical to the Indian peasantry (Chapters VIII and IX), it was argued that the daily, weekly, monthly, or annual time schedules and arrangements of a modern factory are in principle vastly different from those observed by peasants and farmers in their work. Such differences extend to the various punctuations of all time units by specific events and specific activities. The problems resulting from bending one given system of time arrangements to another system affect given, but perhaps incompatible, regularities in the recurrence and alternation of activities. What is at stake are definite time arrangements specific to different "traditions"--arrangements which pervade all and every activity, whether annual, daily, or otherwise; in short, there are processes of differently experienced durée. Although this problem has been discussed in terms of the requirements of industry (Chapter IX, C), the question remains whether industry is entirely precluded from adapting to time regimens other than the orthodox one--whether it cannot unbend from its own "tradition."

III

The task of this study was not to prescribe for the salvation of a specific country by industrialization but to present a scheme of illustrated inquiry into the possibilities of industrialization with the human element as the hub. Such answers as we were able to give in implementation of our questions are necessarily schematic. On the basis of this case study, they happen to point to directions that seem to be the very opposite of industrialism and to attack the very underpinnings of rationally oriented action. In particular, the suggested interstitial industrialization implies the retention of a measure of "paternalism," even suggests an "industrial feudalism"[3]--the antithesis of rational order with calculable rules. In answer, no means-ends apologia is invoked, but only a reminder to the effect that the most perfect rational system as well as the most perfectly "paternalistic" order ultimately stands or falls with its men: its ethics and humaneness.

Perhaps this is what the Ecuadorean Delegate to the Conference of Commissions of Inter-American Development had in mind when he paid tribute to the North American engineer and builder of the Guayaquil-Quito Railway who came to learn that "there are three ways of doing things: the right way, the wrong way, and the Ecuadorean way." He represented the type of man whom the Delegate considered essential for the development of countries like his: "not the type of one-sided experts, ultra-scientific men who would try to investigate the Andes for investment purposes with microscopes and measure its potentialities by the amount of bullion in the ever-depleted government treasuries, but men of flexible minds and great hearts capable of understanding that in new lands the essential efforts of pioneers and drivers must consist for once in setting the people to work under cheerful conditions established through proper remuneration, sympathetic guidance for better forms of living, and social concern."[4]

NOTES

1. The concept has various precedents. For instance, recent development plans for French Morocco provided for "sectors of rural modernization" to lend impetus to development also beyond those sectors. The idea was to create a "psychological shock" directed against the old lethargy of the paysannat, the Moroccan fellahin, not only by employing the most modern mechanical methods in bringing new lands under cultivation, but also by the provision of schools, hospitals, houses, and technical assistance, "so that modernization should embrace all the most important social as well as economic aspects of life" ("France and Morocco," The World Today IV, No. 3 /March, 1948/ :125-36).
        The policies underlying the labor standards provisions in the wartime foreign procurement contracts of the United States government contain some of the elements of which the concept of interstitial industrialization has been built up here. These concern creating some of the "external" conditions conducive to stabilizing a labor force. See Mathews 1947.
        The idea of welfare, creating, on the one hand, a high-level working and living environment and designed, on the other hand, "to educate the people in the consumption of those articles which will raise the living standard," is at the basis of at least one unit of industrialization in Mexico. As planned, this unit was to offer services to workers "as a complement of their salaries" far beyond those which mature industrialism would consider essential for production. On the function and intended effects of this unit see Ruiz Galindo 1947.
        The mobile "cultural brigades" or "educational missions" employed in rural sectors of Mexico and other Indo-American countries operate on the same principle: to stimulate change and receptivity toward the new with maximal effect by concentrating means and spreading the effort.
        Interstitial industrialization also corresponds, of course, to such variants of industrialism as geographical decentralization, location of small plants in small communities, and similarly organized and localized ventures. Cf. Staley 1952:38. And technologically, "we are now in a position to return to cottage industry," due to fundamental innovations in the relaying and utilization of power (Wiener 1954, chap. ix).

2. Part industrial and part agricultural employment is apparently possible, witness artisan and industrial workers in Piedmont, Liguria and Campania (Italy) "who supplement their other incomes by working their small holdings" (Einaudi 1950:15). See also the informative and suggestive article by Aubrey (1951).

3. The term "industrial feudalism" is, of course, used in a very loose sense here. It is borrowed from what is--nota bene--already a current expression in Latin America to designate, equally loosely, features of modern plantation enterprises or of extractive industry (oil, mineral mining), often foreign-owned ("absentee lord"), frequently isolated, and, for the latter reason, having its own working conditions which may or may not be "good" from the point of view of labor's interests.

4. From the luncheon address of Mr. Manuel Adrian Navarro before the National Association of Manufacturers in New York, May 15, 1944, in Inter-American Development Commission n.d.:149.

APPENDIX

THE SOURCES: THEIR TREATMENT AND USE

This note intends to account for the sources used in our work and incidentally to suggest procedures for the study, by "indirection," of peoples and countries in the light of a given problem.

I

Our study is based on a considerable mass of scattered and heterogeneous materials. The "synthetic" character of the resulting picture of a slice of Ecuadorean reality is due, in great measure, to the character of these materials. Whether the inferences and conclusions drawn therefrom are "correct" or correctly weighed must remain an open question. Another question is whether a collective human situation, a culture, a society, a way of life, can be adequately and intelligibly depicted, first, at a high degree of specificity and, second, "at a distance," that is, without either firsthand, close and prolonged contact with the people that are to be dealt with, or without having recourse to such direct and systematic field work as is standard procedure of ethnologists, social anthropologists, or other social scientists and investigators. If nothing else, the foregoing study, in presenting an experimental model, may have succeeded in demonstrating the potential applicability of documentary materials (which, in part, rest on field work done by others) to the construction of a "case." Perhaps this study is able to suggest the utility and relevance which the exploitation of "secondary" materials can assume under certain conditions, namely, when related to a problem with which the used material itself is not concerned.

There is a tendency among social scientists, particularly anthropologists, to depreciate library research as an activity of the armchair devotee, in favor of field investigations. Our libraries are full of materials bearing on other "realities" or "universes," materials which to all intents and purposes are dead because they are not used; in other words, they represent wasted resources. This observation is addressed to designers of development projects, organizers of technical assistance, prospectors and blueprinters of industrialization, etc., and to others implicated in explorations of development projects in various countries. It applies equally to the professional social scientist who ventures into the "field" without more than a most general orientation. A few months of intensive and preparatory exploration of libraries going beyond the most recent and obvious items are apt to provide an ampler horizon--both as to space and time--and first clues and suggestions to further exploration in the field or to actual field work and developmental activities. Moreover, such materials lend themselves to the construction of "synthetic" or "constructed cases" such as the present one. To achieve comparable results, a comparable total over-all picture, by means of field research, would require many ethnographer-years, not to mention the years in the field of investigators in other areas of knowledge.

At any rate, the materials underlying the present study seem to suggest, first, that comparable materials for countries or regions other than Ecuador might be much more ample than would appear at first sight and, second, that the very inadequacy of such materials might, under critical analysis, be turned to excellent advantage.

The analyses that were undertaken here do not involve research in archives, private collections and other out-of-the-way depositories of documents. They are based mostly on published material, that is, material in principle accessible to the general public. Much of it is "fugitive," that is, published in obscure or nonspecialized periodicals or in specialized periodicals of which but a few numbers or volumes had been issued.[1] In general, the quantity of the materials here used might have partially succeeded in overcoming what it lacks in quality. Even so, our bibliography is of course not exhaustive. A number of items whose titles and general contents were known from paraphrases were not examined, mainly because they were not available in libraries or were out of print.[2] Time and patience, finally, set limits to further search. Hence the approximately 180 titles bearing directly, and the somewhat lesser number of titles bearing incidentally, on Ecuador represent a fairly solid sampling of information on that country and on distinct aspects and problems besetting it.

In retrospect, it is apparent that much less material might have sufficed for our purposes. But of this one cannot be sure unless and until available sources have been examined to the fullest extent possible.

II

Part I of this study is devoted to an assessment of the reality and potentialities of Ecuador, comprising not only an assessment of its present economy, resources and manpower, but also one of trends and tendencies. The conclusions, particularly those regarding the systemic drift, as it were, in certain directions, the over-all predisposition of the country, were arrived at on the basis of very diverse "hints."

The type, amount, and quality of literature which a literate society puts out about itself (as also the type and amount of literature which it draws upon itself) is not only symptomatic of its intellectual and other orientations and interests but is also apt to indicate fairly accurately in which respects a country is "developed" and in which it is "underdeveloped." By this token, Ecuador is a highly developed and rich country in considering, for instance, its belles-lettres. By the same token, Ecuador is not only poor but appears to be singularly unpromising of development in the economic sphere, to judge from the amount, type, and quality of economic and kindred literature pertaining to, or emanating from, that country. The space given over to Ecuador and to phases and aspects of its economic life in, for instance, current United States literature on Latin American countries is downright niggardly. Ecuadorean economic life receives a treatment that is most cavalier in comparison to that meted out to Latin American economic giants or would-be giants such as Argentina, Brazil, or Mexico, or even in comparison with its neighbors on the Pacific Coast. Even Guatemala, appreciably smaller in area and only slightly more populous than Ecuador, receives considerably more attention. The scant amount of descriptive information, not to mention detailed descriptive and reliable statistical data that Ecuador itself puts out and makes accessible, is another pointed reflection on the state of its economy and related aspects of its life. (It should be noted, however, that a certain improvement in that respect has become observable during most recent years; economic literature on the technical level is beginning to make an appearance, although it is still difficult to come by outside of Ecuador.)

By contrast, geographical descriptions for the country are ample. Ecuador, in fact, has been a classical scene or field for the study of the physical geography, geology, vulcanology, etc., of its Andean area since at least Humboldt's days. Consequently, we have dispensed with lengthy geographical descriptions and citations. There is scope and pressing need for studies in specialized geography: human geography, land use, and quantitative and qualitative inventories of land and resources.

Descriptions and analytical studies of the Ecuadorean economy as such or parts thereof are very scant and/or inaccessible. (See, however, the bibliography in Benites 1950.) Material especially on highland agricultural economy is virtually nonexistent. In recent years, the CEPAL study (1954) and the slim but useful volume by Linke (1954) have narrowed this gap somewhat by giving ampler coverage to the economy at large as well as to certain distinct aspects of it. Nevertheless, a comprehensive and detailed study of modern Ecuadorean economy, not only from the point of view of foreign trade, but also from that of the domestic market, and projected against longer-range historical developments, remains yet to be written.

Our presentation, then, had to rely very largely on chapter-length accounts or topical mentions in books devoted to Latin American economic matters (e.g., Hughlett 1946; Soule, Efron and Ness 1945; Whythe 1945); or on ad hoc reports (e.g., Ecuadorian Commission n.d.; OCIAA 1945), digests of materials prepared by Ecuadorean banking or other institutions and generally reproduced in other items or found in consular or foreign service sources (e.g., H. Davies 1945 and 1950; IRS; U. S. Tariff Commission 1940 and 1949; WTiC), or prepared by international agencies (e.g., CEPAL 1954; International Labour Organisation 1949; Pan American Union 1954; UN, ECLA 1951), and news notes found in daily and other periodical literature. In addition, a few articles of a technical nature figure among the materials (e.g., Jorge Andrade Marín 1951; McClure 1945 and 1946; Ruess 1951; Suárez D. 1950), some of which are published in little-circulated or short-lived periodicals put out by governmental bureaus or by other public or semipublic bodies.

Complete figures for the total population have become available for the first time in the history of Ecuador by virtue of the 1950 census, the first ever held in the Republic. Its scant coverage, deficiencies, and other limitations as regards the purpose of our study, have been indicated in Chapter II (text and notes). All other sets of statistical figures employed here are fragmentary and of varying and uncontrollable reliability. Some are derived from "guesses" and extrapolations. Others are based on sample studies made in the field, and in that respect the work of the Buitróns merits special mention. The compilations based on their studies do not intend to give more than an idea of the variability and range, for example, of rural occupational distribution (Table I) or of the proportion of huasipungero to other hacienda-employed farm labor (Table II).[3] In many other instances the shortcomings of the employed statistical material are compounded by the elusiveness and indistinctiveness of concepts and categories, such as "Indians," "Mestizos"; "urban," "rural"; "family," "household"; "number of children" and "births" per family, etc.

How "orders of magnitude" are nevertheless arrived at--on the basis of direct "informed guesses," estimates, partial enumerations, etc., and by the use of census and land-tenure figures--is shown in Chapter III. In view of such precarious "sources" the estimates arrived at regarding the Ecuadorean labor potential must seem audacious.

The picture such as presented was rounded out by a partial examination of materials pertaining to social and economic legislation (e.g., Lopez Arteta 1944; Meneses Pallares 1942; Alfredo Rubio Orbe 1954; Serrano Moscoso 1946), for trends and tendencies can also be constructed from a body of laws. Whether laws, decrees, and ordinances are effective at any one given moment or not is not pertinent in this context. Whatever else they are, laws are policy statements, and legislative proposals, together with articulate demands to call this, that, or the other arrangement into being, are equally indicative of the way the wind blows. Furthermore, actual and proposed laws provide a certain insight into existing social and economic conditions and into such states of affairs as in some quarters at least it is felt should be combatted. Quite frequently such materials reveal problems as well as "normal" situations not stated or not clearly stated elsewhere (the Code of Hammurabi told us a good deal about the social life, norms, and institutions of the ancient dwellers Between the Rivers). Again, the social history of Ecuador could very well be established from a history of its numerous constitutions, codes and other laws. They both pace its development and changes, and reflect them, just as any intellectual product is a projection and reflection of lived life.

"Reports to the People" or "to the Nation" by presidents and by ministers of the various governmental branches are invaluable sources both in what they say and in what they fail to say, for taciturnity can be quite eloquent. Very few such reports have been sampled, and of these none of the pre-World War II years (Alcivar Zevallos 1951; Plaza May 1949, June 1949, January 1950, May 1950; Tello 1949; Zevallos Menendez 1946). I believe, however, that more systematic, fuller examination of more such materials would not materially alter the findings as stated for the postwar years, nor shed substantially more light on developments during roughly the current decade. For the study of long-term "drifts," however, it would be very important to derive a history of the Ecuadorean economy on the basis of presidential and ministerial pronouncements and of those of other public functionaries. It is from the "slants" and omissions as well as from the objective inventories contained in such reports that most instructive information can be derived, and judgment formed, as to what are ephemeral and what are enduring aspects of an economy, especially if projected against a country's political and cultural history.

Expressions of "opinions," of course, are found throughout most of the sources; taken together, these provided in fact the main clues for the assessment of general drifts and potential developments.

III

All the foregoing comments apply in large measure to the materials used in Part II, which presented a descriptive and analytical account of a particular slice of Ecuadorean humanity for purposes of deriving an estimate of its "fitness" for industrialization. This portrayal, too, was built up from a mass of diverse materials, on the whole meager, uneven in quality, trustworthiness, and subject coverage. It is hoped that, as a byproduct of the present endeavor, the poverty of source materials, which in certain respects is great, may provoke Ecuadoreans and non-Ecuadoreans alike to inquire both more intensively and extensively, and more carefully, into the realities of the Ecuadorean social world. A number of open problems have been indicated in the text (and notes), and others are listed below (IV).

Comparatively little of the total material on Ecuadorean society and, particularly, on Ecuadorean highland Indians can be considered

"original" in the sense that it is based on firsthand, systematic and prolonged contact with, and independent findings on, these groups. In particular, descriptions of Ecuador and its "common people" tend to follow
conventional conceptions and patterns of thinking and/or expression.
Some of the formative elements of these "conventionalisms" are no doubt
to be sought in the colonial period, while others are accretions which
entered during republican times. They seem to be purveyed by the spoken
as well as by the written word. This conventionalizing tendency[4] also
mars the value of the factual information contained in such writings of
travelers and other casual observers which otherwise are apt to furnish
most revealing glimpses on matters which the professional observer is
more likely to pass by. The brotherhood of travelers is a congenial one.
It may be defined by the fact that they read each others' accounts, pay
each other the compliment of using their observations (and/or their
phrasings) and permitting them to slip into their own accounts, particularly in broad-brush sketches of the strange scene. It is partly in this
manner that conventional (stylized, standardized or mannered) observations, evaluations, and attitudes concerning the observed subjects are
perpetuated.[5] Such uncheckable "borrowings" occur apparently also
among professional scientists, although in these quarters this tendency
is of course less pronounced. Hence some of these materials, while
ostensibly original field studies or studies based on prolonged personal
contacts and observations, remain uncomfortably suspect as being built
up of hearsay, conventions, extraneous theories, and other secondary
and tertiary sources.

Field studies by professional anthropologists are very few in comparison to the scope which highland Ecuador offers. Those of the late
Mrs. Parsons (1940, 1945) take first place, of course. Beals' (1952) is
comparable in some respects, but more restricted in scope. The sheer
mass of materials furnished by Buitrón and his collaborators, including
the otherwise very uneven IEAG studies, does a great deal in bringing to
light the realities--and great diversities--of the Ecuadorean rural and/
or Indian populations. Among these important materials on Indians
should be named the studies by Father Leonidas Rodríguez Sandoval
(1945 and 1949), whose intimate knowledge particularly of central highland
Indians is evidently very great and who treats various otherwise neglected
topics with great care. Rivet's observations (1903, 1906, 1926) were made
some fifty years ago and are worth being repeated today and checked.
Disselhoff's almost accidental observations on witchcraft (1940) are very
valuable, particularly if set side by side with those of E. C. Parsons and
the beautiful pictorial record of Collier and Buitrón (1949). Santiana's
observations are certainly in part firsthand (1947, 1949, 1952b), as are
those of Monsalve Pozo (1942), whose main work (El indio, cuestiones
de su vida y de su pasión /Cuenca, 1943/) unfortunately was not available.
Field studies of restricted scope, that is, in public health or medicine,
are those by Pablo Arturo Suárez (1934, 1942) and León (1946, 1947); on
labor and other general conditions of life, by Victor Gabriel Garcés
(1941 ff.), Gonzalo Rubio Orbe (1946 ff.), Castro (1948), and perhaps one
or two others. As a general, over-all study of Ecuadorean Indians, that
by Saenz (1933a) is still unsurpassed. Despite their condensation, the
materials brought together by Murra (1947) are useful, while the data
assembled by Rycroft and his colleagues (Rycroft 1946), though valuable,
suffer from an all-too-frequent failure to identify specifically Bolivian,
Ecuadorean, and Peruvian Indians.

A reservation, similar to the one made with regard to the casual
observers' conventionalism, must be made with regard to much of the
otherwise useful and informative material emanating from Ecuadorean
writers interested in Indians qua Indians, their "defenders," in so far

as it has a polemical slant. For all its merits this material, too, tends
to be "conventional" in that it perpetuates a patterned interpretation of
Ecuadorean reality, that of "exploiter" and "underdog."

Both types of conventionalism in Ecuadorean literature and in literature dealing with Ecuador have been treated as facts just as opinions
have been treated as data in this study. They are the stuff from which
trends and tendencies, a "climate of opinion," an "intellectual atmosphere,"
explicit and implicit policies, and aspirations can be inferred. Moreover,
it is the very "tone" of much of these writings which constituted important
evidence for the construction of the type of society which here was termed
"estate" society. Certainly, tone and substance cannot always be clearly
distinguished: our evidence consists in the writings of those who inveigh
against "feudalism" and against the privileges of status (as over against
"earned" privileges), of references such as the one to the remnants of a
"quijotismo" de clase among the upper and middle and aspiring status
groups (García Ortiz 1951:30), and to the abuses committed with the sanc-
tion of the prevailing social order, the references to colonial conditions
as perpetuating themselves into the present, etc. There are innumerable
statements regarding the negative aspects of the relations between Indians
and non-Indians entailed, for example, by the roles of priests to their
parishioners, of lawyers to clients, of appointed administrative officials
to their charges, of hacendados and mayordomos to their workers, and
there is ample enumeration and documentation of the abuses to which
Indians are subjected. In discussing Indian-White relations and contacts,
however, we were concerned only with stating the existence of these relations as institutional and normal ones and, extricating these features from
beneath the laments and indictments as to how they function or mal-
function, to point out the nature of these relations and contacts. The
reader is invited to scour the same materials; the present writer doubts
whether a class, caste, or race formulation would make the interpretation
of these relations more intelligible.

Similarly, characterizations of the Indian provide a significant
social "image," doubly interesting when considered more diachronically
than was done here. This "image" not only is of diagnostic value in that
it bespeaks social distance between Indians and non-Indians. A composite
of impressions on which such an "image" rests is also of importance
so far as industry, through its managerial personnel, may start out with
such unqualified imagery of those to be managed. The theme "the Indian
in the estimation of the non-Indian" (Part II, Introductory; also Chapter X,
B) has been arranged in a roughly chronological order thus bringing home
the possibility that there has occurred some change in the evaluation of
the Indians from the merely contemptuous to one of some humane understanding and of both social and scientific interest, with overtones of
sympathy for the "underdog" and of admiration at least for the Indian
past. These changes do not necessarily touch the substance of the social
relations as they exist in actuality. But the change in "tone," approach,
and argumentation is of interest in that the newer, more optimistic
assessment of the Indian and the action-beckoning views themselves
might constitute an atmosphere favorable to the introduction of new ways.
Also diagnostic in this respect are attempts at what we may term "seman-
tic manipulation of the social situation" on the part of some pro-Indian
writers. These consist in advocating the elimination of such terms of
reference for Indians as peones, mitayos and similar ones on the ground
that such expressions tend to denigrate and depreciate the Indian and to
reinforce his humble and servile attitudes toward Whites. Conversely,
Indians should be discouraged from using such terms of address toward
Whites as patrón, amo ("master"), taita amo, taita cura ("father"...),
niño ("child", i.e., "young master"), and other terms which are typically
used by Indians to address their "betters" (e.g., Perez 1943).

In sum, a large part of our materials posed precisely the task of digging a substance out from under an overlay of national viewpoints, theories, schools of thought, ideologies, and policy-making statements which permeate so much of this type of sources; and to extrapolate such substances without being seduced into partisanship with a particular point of view and with, what is often to all intents and purposes, the primary intention of a book, pamphlet, or article.

There is one type of source material of which too little use has been made here: the fictional or semifictional account (Gil Gilbert 1942; Icaza 1934; also Bemelmans 1941 and 1944), especially the type of Hispano-American realistic tale which Salvador Bueno (1955) characterizes as "cuento criollista" and in which landscape, customs, idiom, the physical, political, and social circumstances not only are in the foreground but are directly pertinent to the plot. The few works here drawn upon for an occasional point partake of one characteristic frequent in the presentation of the human situation in the form of the novel or short story, namely, they fasten upon traits, recurrent situations, and decisive events so common or so well known that they are generally left without mention in other forms of writing, most of all scientific writing. This type of source contains that commonplace, taken-for-granted stuff, actual or bygone, which makes up the details of peoples' lives, their manner of living, and the circumstances within which they move and which move them. The Ecuadorean novel is a particularly rewarding source for the anthropologist and other "schooled and experienced observers," in that it contains the "primary particulars" and the "directly observed local color" which all but the rarest field account will studiously suppress.

None of the material here used is tailor-made for the purposes of our inquiry, and this circumstance is, on the whole, a real advantage. Some of the literature considers, of course, problems of culture change (as also, more specifically, of "acculturation") but does so mostly under a historical-reconstruction frame of reference. Hence ours is relatively "naïve," unreflective material which contains no hypotheses, theories, doctrines, or dogmas of direct relevance to the problem or problems posed here. We did not have to contend with any points to be proved, with views on theoretical aspects of industrialization, nor did we have to take into account practical aspects of Ecuadorean industrialization in so far as it affects Indians. The material could be taken as a body of raw data suitable by its very rawness for application to, and testing of, the specific questions on which this study revolves. All that had to be done was to disentangle these data from their own proper contexts and to build them into new contexts meaningful to the problem at hand.

In exploiting this material we have generally observed such rules and hints as are observed by the student of history in his work on documentary materials; in other words, the method observed is what is technically known as the "historical method" (cf. Gottschalk 1950, especially Part II) which, in this case, has very little to do with "history" but has very much to do with the evaluation of source materials and their use in treating of a given question.

Occasionally, a statement or a group of statements--such as a conclusion drawn from a piece of field investigation--has been subjected to more extensive scrutiny and critical examination. One case in point is the interpretation of the Indians' uncommunicativeness as advanced by the Buitróns on the basis of one of their excellent field studies (see Chapter X, B). It goes without saying that one can take issue with an interpretation or explanation only if and when substantial and substantive facts are available on the basis of which to debate or otherwise argue alternative interpretations.

In general, however, the material has been taken at its face value under one or all of the following assumptions. People commonly do not go out of their way to misrepresent facts deliberately. In stating goals (sometimes as though they were accomplished facts), people state them as they see them--hence, too, a writer or speaker can be placed in a "tradition." People who take the trouble to write on a given subject, whether they are pamphleteers or philosophers, consider with some degree of care what they commit to paper; hence they exercise some selectivity among the vast range of possible facts and considerations when they emit in print. Especially do public figures (and in a way every writer is a public figure) speak and write, if not the truth, at least a truth, a "truth" within a context that needs to be established by the analyst by considering such matters as intent and purpose, audience, period, antecedent events, etc. Finally, even an imitation, a forgery, a lie reveals something: a kernel of truth, a fragment of a fact, something probable, believable, or expectable. Hence even such statements (with which, in fact, we have had not much to do) are indices to an atmosphere that is propitious to such statement.

IV

Research Problems in Ecuador[6]

The Ecuadorean scene and the Ecuadorean humanity still offer many novel problems fit for field or other investigations. Some of these are here suggested in summary fashion.

The volume and character of urban migration, the nature of the "urban Indian" classes, and the process by and during which new urban dwellers, generally Indian, become citified (if at all, during a lifetime or less) and in what respects are entirely unexplored fields. Another problem, connected with the former, is mentioned with the greatest reservation. In the absence of systematic and reliable vital statistics, it is not possible to indicate rates of natural increase of the Ecuadorean population with any degree of accuracy. There are some figures at hand which suggest that high rates of natural increase are associated with urban-type populations or with dense-settlement populations partaking of an urban cast; the figures further suggest that such increases are due largely to a fertility rate that is higher in the urban than in the rural sectors, or higher among Whites and Mestizos than among Indians. This would yet further suggest that the fast growth of cities in Ecuador (a growth noted throughout Latin America) is by no means solely a matter of urbanward migration. The data which first suggested[7] this bold and thinly based hypothesis do not suffice for its elaboration. The question, nevertheless, remains and might find an answer through an investigation of the differences in ages at first and subsequent births as between largely urban-oriented groups (Whites and Mestizos) and Indians.

Information on income and consumption levels is very scant and scattered. Studies of actual as well as potential patterns of expenditures and consumption for differentiated groups appear feasible, and would be important not only in practical respects but also for an understanding of the "cultures" of the country. (See Chapter XIV, and especially note 49).

It seems of the utmost importance to have impartial, objective studies of highland hacienda economy and society. In making this suggestion, the difficulties besetting studies of this nature are fully appreciated.

In view of the comparatively heavy concentration of descriptive materials on the populations of the northern part of Ecuador, in particular of the Indians of Otavalo, intensive corrective and comparative studies of Indian groups other than those of Otavalo are urgently called for. Detailed descriptions especially of the often-mentioned Indians of Loja in the south, such as the Saraguro group, do not seem to exist.

There is no need further to harp on the paucity of materials on products, crafts, skills, techniques, styles, and manual operations in practically all studies relating to Indian groups. Statements on rounds of activities per unit of time and on "typical days" are equally conspicuous by their almost total absence. There is but one, and very sketchy, biographical study of an Indian, Mrs. Parsons' main informant, Rosita Lema of Peguche.

Other ethnographic endeavors, properly speaking, might concentrate with advantage on one or several of the following problems. The erstwhile and present character and role of the personage termed ñaupador remains undetermined. The existence, distribution, roles and functions of religious and secular leaders in highland Indian society, the functions of lay religious orders, the nature of witchcraft and its practitioners remain to be explored in much greater detail. The distribution and meanings of such activities as the "guayru" game, the "battle encounters" and their possible European ingredients, and similar culture-historical research still beckon. There is, finally, no systematic study of any of the supposedly mitimae-derived groups in Ecuador nor one attempting to link them up with their putative former habitats in Peru and Bolivia.

NOTES

1. The greater part of the materials, especially of those called "fugitive," were encountered in the New York Public Library and in the Library of the Wenner-Gren Foundation for Anthropological Research, Incorporated. Others were consulted at the University of Chicago Library. During my brief visit in Quito, I obtained three or four items in bookshops. Still others were sent me from Ecuador shortly after their publication, largely through the kind offices of Miss Lilo Linke. A few valuable items were put at my disposal by Dr. John Gillin.

2. See the following for bibliographies on Ecuador: Benites 1950; Linke 1954; Murra 1947; Rodríguez Sandoval 1949; Saenz 1933a.

3. Buitrón at one point warns not to consider any of these sample studies and their statistical data as representative for a larger whole.

4. Evident, for instance, in comparing Hassaurek 1868, Cevallos 1873, Orton 1875, Franklin 1943, Von Hagen 1949, whose descriptions and accounts include, or are based on, verbal information furnished by Ecuadoreans.

5. Lipschütz has two telling examples on these points. One (1950) compares two accounts of the seventeenth and eighteenth centuries on the inhabitants of Tierra del Fuego, the latter supposedly an eyewitness account but in reality simply an extract from the former. The other (1953, n. 27) brings home the conventionalism in the characterization of peasant peoples: a description of seventeenth century Letts parallels standard descriptions of Andean Indians today as yesterday, down to the very wording.

6. Cf. Gillin's review (1946) of E. C. Parsons' <u>Peguche</u> (1945).

7. Buitrón and Buitrón 1945, and 1947, Tables I-III; Parsons 1945: 34-37 and p. 138 (where note error of 7, instead of 8, as average number of persons per household); P. A. Suárez 1934:73-75.

BIBLIOGRAPHY*

Abbreviations Used in Text and in the Bibliography

AA	American Anthropologist (New Series)
AJS	The American Journal of Sociology
Am. Ind.	América Indígena
Am. Jn. Phys. Anthr.	American Journal of Physical Anthropology
Am. Soc. Rev.	American Sociological Review
BBAA	Boletín Bibliográfico de la Antropología Americana
Bol. Ind.	Boletín Indigenista
Bol. Inf. Cient. Nac.	Boletín de Informaciones Científicas Nacionales (Quito)
Bol. Min. Prev. Soc.	Boletín del Ministerio de Previsión Social (Quito)
Bol. Of. San. Panam.	Boletín de la Oficina Sanitaria Panamericana (Washington, D.C.)
Bol. Trim. Info. Econ.	Boletín Trimestral de Información Económica (Instituto de Investigaciones Económicas de la Facultad de Ciencias Económicas de la Universidad Central del Ecuador, Quito)
Brit. Med. Bull.	British Medical Bulletin
Brit. Med. Jn.	British Medical Journal
CEPAL	Comisión Económica para América Latina
CIAA	Coordinator of Inter-American Affairs
Dir. Gen. Est. Censos, Census 1950	Dirección General de Estadística y Censos...Censo National de Población de 1950
Dir. Nac. Est.	Dirección Nacional de Estadística

---

* Items marked (E) relate only to Ecuador. Items in square brackets are referred to in the text and notes but were not consulted directly.

HSAI	Handbook of South American Indians, edited by Julian H. Steward. Smithsonian institution, Bureau of American Ethnology, Bulletin 143. Washington, D.C. Vols. 1 (1946) to 6 (1950).
IEAG	Instituto Ecuatoriano de Antropología e Geografía. Informes Nos... Instituto Nacional de Previsión, Departamento de Información, Reclamaciones e Investigación Social. Quito.
ILO	International Labour Office
IRS	International Reference Service. U.S. Department of Commerce, Office of Foreign Trade, Washington, D.C. (Citations are by volume and number of that series.)
NRC	National Research Council
OCIAA	Office of the Coordinator of Inter-American Affairs
OIAA	Office of Inter-American Affairs
El Trimestre Estadístico	El Trimestre Estadístico del Ecuador (Quito)
29th ICA	Proceedings and Selected Papers of the XXIXth International Congress of Americanists (1949), edited by Sol Tax. Chicago: University of Chicago Press, 1952. (References are to volume entitled Acculturation in the Americas.
UN	United Nations
UN, ECLA	United Nations, Economic Commission for Latin America
UNESCO	United Nations Educational, Scientific, and Cultural Organization
Unión Panamericana, Noticias	Noticias de la Oficina de Información Obrera y Social, Unión Panamericana, Washington, D.C.
UNP	Unión Nacional de Periodistas /Ecuador7
WTiC	World Trade in Commodities. U.S. Department of Commerce, Office of International Trade, Washington, D.C. (Citations are by volume, series, and number of that series.)

Ackerknecht, Erwin H.
    1949   Medical practices. HSAI 5:621-43.

Acosta Solis, M.
1945   Las tierras agrícolas de la provincia de Tungurahua.
            Primera contribución al conocimiento agrológico de la
            provincia. Quito. (E)

1947   /Commerical possibilities of the forests of Ecuador,
            mainly Esmeraldas Province. Tropical Woods, No. 89
            (March 1)./ (E)

Albornoz, Miguel
1945   Alphabet in the Andes. The Inter-American 4, No. 3:
            14-16. (E)

Alcívar Zevallos, Clodoveo
1951   Informe a la nación, 1950-1951. Quito, Talleres Gráficos
            Nacionales. (E)

Alencastre G., Andrés and Dumézil Georges
1953   Fêtes et usages des Indiens de Langui (Province de
            Canas, Département du Cuzco). Journal de la Société
            des Américanistes, n.s. 42:1-118.

Andrade Marín, Carlos
1942   La sanidad y asistencia social en el Ecuador. Bol. Of.
            San. Panam. 21:639-43. (E)

1946   El indio y el seguro social campesino. In Cuestiones
            Indígenas del Ecuador, pp. 145-65. (E)

Andrade Marín, César
1941   El paludismo en la región interandina y en Valle de los
            Chillos. Previsión Social 8:133-36. (E)

Andrade Marín, Jorge
1951   Posibilidades reales e inmediatas de la industria
            química en el Ecuador. Bol. Inf. Cient. Nac. 4, No. 41
            (Ag.-Set.):206-13. (E)

Anonymous
1948   Derris in Ecuador. Foreign Agriculture 12:230-31. (E)

Aubrey, Henry G.
1951   Small industry in economic development. Social Re-
            search 18:269-312.

Bailey, Flora L.
1942   Navaho motor habits. AA 44:210-34.

Balchin, Nigel
1947   Satisfactions in work. Occupational Psychology 21:
            125-34. London.

Barrett, S.A.
1925   The Cayapa Indians of Ecuador. Indian Notes and
            Monographs. Miscellaneous No. 40. New York, Museum
            of the American Indian, Heye Foundation. (E)

Basile, David E.
Ms.   Panama hats from the Ecuadorean highlands. 1945. (E)

Baumgarten, Franziska
1947   Zur Psychologie des Maschinenarbeiters, eine Unter-
            suchung. Zürich, Rascher Verlag.

Beals, Ralph L.
1951   Urbanism, urbanization and acculturation. AA 53:1-10.

1952   Acculturation, economics, and social change in an Ecua-
            dorean village. 29th ICA, pp. 67-73. (E)

1953   Social stratification in Latin America. AJS 57:327-39.

Behrendt, Richard F.
1948   Inter-American economic relations: problems and pros-
            pects. The Committee on International Economic Policy
            in Cooperation with The Carnegie Endowment for Inter-
            national Peace, Paper No. 14. New York.

Bejarano, Jorge
1945   El cocaismo en Colombia. Am. Ind. 5:11-20.

Bemelmans, Ludwig
1941   The donkey inside. New York, The Viking Press. (E)

1944   Now I lay me down to sleep. New York, The Viking Press.

Benites, Leopoldo
1950   Ecuador, drama y paradoja. Colección Tierra Firme,
            48. Mexico, D.F., Fondo de Cultura Económica. (E)

Benjamin, A. Cornelius
1937   An introduction to the philosophy of science. New York,
            The Macmillan Company.

Bennett, Wendell C.
1946   Excavations in the Cuenca region, Ecuador. Yale Univer-
            sity Publications in Anthropology, No. 35. (E)

1947   The Andean highlands: an introduction. HSAI 2:1-59.

Bergson, Henri
1944   Creative evolution. New York, Modern Library.

Bernard, Jessie
1949   Sociological mirror for cultural anthropologists. AA
            51:671-77.

Blanksten, George I.
1954   Technical assistance and the political instability of
            Latin America. Economic Development and Cultural
            Change 2:350-56.

Borja-Cordero, Cesar
1924   Das Heutige Ecuador. In Zwei Vorträge gehalten an
            der Universität zu Hamburg vom Generalkonsul der
            Republik Ecuador, pp. 65-82. Hamburg. (E)

Brand, Donald D.
1948   The present Indian population of Latin America. In
            Some Educational and Anthropological Aspects of
            Latin America. Latin-American Studies V:48-55.
            Austin, Institute of Latin-American Studies, Univer-
            sity of Texas.

Bruzzone, Pedro
1946   Agricultura. In UNP, pp. 150-57. (E)

Bücher, Karl
1909   Arbeit und Rhythmus. 4th ed. Leipzig and Berlin,
            B. G. Teubner.

Bueno, Salvador
1955   El cuento en Hispano-America. Américas (Washington,
            D.C.) 7, No. 1 (Enero):3-6.

Buitrón, Aníbal
1946   La antropología y el problema del indio en América.
            In Cuestiones Indígenas del Ecuador, pp. 38-55.

1947a   Situación económica y social del Indio Otavaleño. Am.
            Ind. 7:45-62. (E)

1947b   Sobre el mejoramiento de las condiciones de trabajo
            en el campo (Projects for the improvement of working
            conditions in the rural sections). Bol. Ind. 7:210-19. (E)

1947c   Review of: Cuestiones Indígenas del Ecuador. BBAA
            IX (1946, México):140-42. (E)

1948a   Investigaciones etnológicas en el Ecuador. Bol. Inf.
            Cient. Nac. 2, No. 10:32-35. (E)

1948b   Vida y pasión del campesino Ecuatoriano. Am. Ind. 8:
            113-30. (E)

1949a   Missions for the social protection of the rural population
            of Ecuador. Am. Ind. 9:57-63. (E)

1949b   /Fiestas indígenas de Otavalo. Bol. Inf. Cient. Nac. 2,
            Nos. 18-19:36-41; 3, Nos. 20-21:62-66./ (E)

1949c   Sintesis de investigaciones sociales en la parroquía
            de Pomasquí. Boletín de Informaciones de Estudios
            Sociales y Económicos 12, Nos. 46-47:65-78. Quito,
            Instituto Nacional de Previsión, Departamento de
            Investigación Social y Propaganda. (E)

1951a   Review and Critique of Antonio Santiana's Los Indios
            Mojanda...(q.v.). BBAA 13 (1950, Part 2, México):150-
            53. (E)

1951b   El indio y el seguro social en el Ecuador. Am. Ind. 11:
            9-36. (E)

1951c   Leyendas, costumbres y supersticiones indígenas de
            Otavalo. Bol. Inf. Cient. Nac. 4, No. 40:56-62. (E)

1951d   Technological center for Indian textile industry. Bol.
Ind. 11:309, 311. (E)

1951e   Actividades antropológicas en Ecuador, 1950. BBAA
XIII (1950, Part 1, México):57. (E)

Buitrón, Aníbal and Barbara Salisbury Buitrón
1945   Indios, blancos y mestizos en Otavalo, Ecuador. Acta
Americana 3:190-216. (E)

1947   Condiciones de vida y trabajo del campesino de la
provincia de Pichincha. Quito, Instituto Nacional de
Previsión, Departamento de Propaganda. (E)

Buitrón, Barbara Salisbury
1947   Investigaciones etnológicas en el Ecuador. Bol. Inf.
Cient. Nac. 1, No. 3:35-39. (E)

Bustamante, Manuel
1942   ¿Conviene o no al país apresurar la industrialización
de sus materias primas? Revista de Derecho y Ciencias
Sociales, Epoca Segunda, 3, No. 17:75-81. Quito,
Facultad de Jurisprudencia, Universidad Central. (E)

Caluccio, Felix
1953   Contribución al diccionario folklorico americano.
Revista Colombiana de Folklore, 2ª época, No. 2
(Junio):17-31.

Cámara Barbachano, Fernando
1954   Aspectos sociales y culturales de la América indígena.
Am. Ind. 14:127-55.

Caplow, Theodore
1952   The modern Latin American city. 29th ICA, pp. 255-60.

Cárdenas, José C.
1954   Reforma agraria y desarollo económico en el Ecuador.
El Trimestre Económico 21:305-25. México.

Carlson, Fred. E.
1943   Geography of Latin America. Rev. ed. New York,
Prentice-Hall.

Carrera Andrade, César
1946   La reforma agraria en el Ecuador. Cuadernos Ameri-
canos, Año V, 26, No. 2:39-55. (E)

Castro, Víctor Manuel
1948   Sobre antecedentes y etnología de los indios Magdalena.
Revista de Filosofía y Letras, Año 1, No. 3:144-66.
Quito. (E)

Castro Pozo, Hildebrando
1947   Social and economico-political evolution of the communities of central Peru. HSAI 2:483-99.

Ceballos, Pedro Fermin; see Cevallos

Comisión Económica para América Latina
1954 El desarollo económico del Ecuador. México, Naciones Unidas. (E)

Cevallos, Pedro Fermin
1873 Jeografía de la República del Ecuador. Resumen de la historia del Ecuador desde su origen hasta 1845...Parte Jeográfica. Lima, Imprenta de Guzman i Ca. (Mss. concluded 1858, 1868). (E)

Coordinator of Inter-American Affairs
1944 Basic data on the other American republics. Washington, D.C.

Cisneros Cisneros, César
1948 Demografía y Estadística sobre el Indio Ecuatoriano. Quito, Talleres Gráficos Nacionales. (E)

1949 Comunidades indígenas del Ecuador. Am. Ind. 9:37-55. (E)

1950 Legislación cooperativista en el Ecuador. Previsión Social, No. 23 (May-Dec., 1949--Jan.-Feb. 1950):46-57. (E)

Cisneros Falconí, César
1951a Las cooperativas en el Ecuador. Primer Seminario Regional de Asuntos Sociales, Mayo 27 a 10 de Junio de 1950, pp. 203-17. Quito, Ministerio de Previsión Social y Trabajo. (E)

1951b Importancia y participación de las cooperativas en la vida de las comunidades urbanas y rurales. Primer Seminario Regional de Asuntos Sociales, Mayo 27 a 10 de Junio de 1950, pp. 218-25. Quito, Ministerio de Previsión Social y Trabajo. (E)

Clark, John M.
1943a Curtain-raiser in rehabilitation. Survey Graphic 33, No. 6:245-49, 267. (E)

1943b Revival in El Oro. Foreign Commerce Weekly 12, No. 8 (Aug. 21):5-8, 31. (E)

Clark, W. E. le Gros
1946 Physical anthropology applied to problems of war. /Brit. Med. Jn. 1 (Jan. 12):39./ Reprinted in Yearbook of Physical Anthropology 1946, pp. 18-21. New York, The Viking Fund, Inc., 1947.

Clothier, Walter J. K.
1946 Health. In Indians of the High Andes, ed. Stanley W. Rycroft, pp. 219-78.

Cohen, John
1949 Analysis of "psychological" fields. Science News 13 (Penguin Books, Harmondsworth, Middlesex, England): 145-58.

Collier, John, Jr. and Aníbal Buitrón
    1949   The awakening valley. Chicago, The University of
                     Chicago Press. (E)

Comité Central Nacional de Defensa Indígena
    1946   Segundo Congreso de indios Ecuatorianos...del 8 al 10
                     Febrero de 1946. Quito, Edit. Casa de la Cultura
                     Ecuatoriana. (E)

Cooper, John M.
    1949a   Games and gambling. HSAI 5:503-24.

    1949b   Stimulants and narcotics. HSAI 5:525-58.

Costales Samaniego, Alfredo
    1950   Puruhá. Filosofía, Letras y Ciencias de Educación 3,
                     No. 9:17-93. Quito, Universidad Central del Ecuador. (E)

Cuestiones Indígenas del Ecuador
    1946   Publicaciones del Instituto Indigenista Ecuatoriano,
                     Vol. I. Quito, Editorial Casa de la Cultura Ecuatoriana
                     (E)

Curle, Adam
    1949   Incentives to work: an anthropological appraisal.
                     Human Relations 2:41-47.

Dale, John T.
    1946   Anthropology. In Indians of the High Andes, ed. Stanley
                     W. Rycroft, pp. 97-153.

Daniels, Gilbert S. and H. T. E. Hertzberg
    1952   Applied anthropometry of the hand. Am. Jn. Phys.
                     Anthr. 10:209-15.

Darcus, H. D. and A. G. M. Weddell
    1947   Some anatomical and physiological principles concerned
                     in the design of seats for naval war weapons. /Brit.
                     Med. Jn. 5, No. 1:31-37./ Reprinted in Yearbook of
                     Physical Anthropology 1947, Vol. 3. New York, The
                     Viking Fund, Inc., 1948.

Davies, Howell (ed.)
    1945   Ecuador. In The South American Handbook 1945, pp.
                     543-59. 22d annual ed. London, Trade and Travel
                     Publications, Ltd. (E)

    1950   Ecuador. In The South American Handbook 1950, pp.
                     495-511. 27th annual ed. London, Trade and Travel
                     Publications, Ltd. (E)

Davis, J. Merle
    1946   The economic and social setting. In Indians of the High
                     Andes, ed. Stanley W. Rycroft, pp. 13-93.

Davis, Kingsley
    1946   Population trends and policies in Latin America. In
                     Some Economic Aspects of Postwar Inter-American
                     Relations, pp. 25-46. Latin-American Studies II.
                     Austin, Institute of Latin-American Studies, Univer-
                     sity of Texas.

Davis, William C.
    1944   Pearl Harbor sent quinine home. Agriculture in the
                    Americas 4, No. 3:43-45, 50.

De la Fuente, Julio
    1952   Ethnic and communal relations (and following discus-
                    sion). In Heritage of Conquest, by Sol Tax and others,
                    pp. 76-96.

Denney, Reuel and David Riesman
    1952   Leisure in industrial America. In Creating an Indus-
                    trial Civilization, ed. Eugene Staley, pp. 245-81.

De Quiros, Juan Bernaldo
    1945   El Seguro Social en Iberoamérica. Jornadas 44. México,
                    Centro de Estudios Sociales, El Colegio de México.

Dietze, Alfred G.
    1946   Psychology in work and efficiency. In Psychology in
                    Human Affairs, ed. Stanley J. Gray.

Digby, Adrian
    1949   Technique and the time factor in relation to economic
                    organization. Man 49, Art. 12:16-18.

Dirección General de Estadística y Censos, Ministerio de Economía,
República del Ecuador
    1952   Información censal. Resumen de los resultados defini-
                    tivos del Censo Nacional de Poblacíon de 1950 sobre:
                    sexo, edad, estado civil, alfabetismo y poblacíon económica-
                    mente activa e inactiva. Quito, Talleres Gráficos del
                    Censo. (E)

Dirección Nacional de Estadística
    1944   Ecuador en cifras de 1938 a 1942. Quito.

Disselhoff, H. D.
    1940   "Brujos" im Hochland von Ekuador. Zeitschrift für
                    Ethnologie 71:300-5. (E)

Dorfman, Adolfo
    1953   The role of development corporations financing economic
                    development in Latin America. Caribbean Economic
                    Review V, Nos. 1 and 2:109-17.

Drucker, Peter
    1946   The way to industrial peace, Part I. Harper's Maga-
                    zine 193, No. 1156 (Nov.):385-95.

Du Frane, Beatrice
    1945   Ecuador's Panama hat industry. Agriculture in the
                    Americas V, No. 4 (April):67-69, 75. (E)

Ebaugh, Cameron D.
    1947   Education in Ecuador. Federal Security Agency, U. S.
                    Office of Education, Bulletin 1947, No. 2. Washington,
                    D.C. (E)

Ecuadorian Commission of Inter-American Development
n.d.   Report presented to the conference of Commissions of Inter-American Development on Ecuador and Its Natural Resources. Washington, D.C., Inter-American Development Commission, 1944. (E)

Einaudi, Mario
1950   The Italian land: men, nature, and government. Social Research 17:8-34.

Enock, C. Reginald
1907   The Andes and the Amazon: life and travel in Peru. New York, Scribner's Sons. (4th impression 1910.)

1914   Ecuador, its ancient and modern history, topography and natural resources, industries and social development. London and Leipzig. (E)

Enriquez, Luis
1945   A Latin looks at Chapultepec. The Inter-American IV, No. 4 (April):16-17.

Erasmus, Charles John
1952   Changing folk beliefs and the relativity of empirical knowledge. Southwestern Journal of Anthropology 8: 411-28. (E)

Espinosa Bravo, Clodoaldo A.
1949   Coca addiction in Jauja, with reference to a book on coca /Gutiérrez-Noriega and Zapata Ortiz, Estudios sobre la Coca y Cocaína en el Perú/. Bol. Ind. 9:92-99.

Executive Committee on Post-War Problems of the Governing Board of the Pan American Union
1943   Recent trends in inter-American economic cooperation. Washington, D.C., Pan American Union.

Fejos, Paul
1943   Ethnography of the Yagua. Viking Fund Publications in Anthropology, No. 1. New York, The Viking Fund, Inc.

Ferdon, Edwin N., Jr.
1945   A mountain colony in Ecuador. El Palacio 52:129-37 (E)

1947   Notes to accompany a present day ethnic map of Ecuador. El Palacio 54:155-69. (E) (Reprinted in Ferdon 1950:1-7.)

1950   Studies in Ecuadorian Geography. Monographs of the School of American Research, No. 15. School of American Research and Museum of New Mexico, co-publishers. School of American Research, Santa Fe, and University of Southern California. (E)

Firth, Raymond
1946   Malay fishermen: their peasant economy. London, Kegan Paul, Trench, Trubner & Co., Ltd.

1948   Anthropological background to work. Occupational
Psychology 22:94-102. London.

Flornoy, Bertrand
 1945   Voyages en Haut-Amazone. Rio de Janeiro, Atlantica
Editora.

Formulation and Economic Appraisal of Development Projects
 1951   Lectures delivered at the Asian Centre on Agricultural
and Allied Projects. Training Institute on Economic
Appraisal of Development Projects, Lahore, Pakistan,
October-December 1950. United Nations.

Foster, George M.
 1942   A primitive Mexican economy. Monographs of the
American Ethnological Society, No. V. New York.

 1952   Relationships between theoretical and applied anthropology: a public health program analysis. Human
Organization 11, No. 3 (Fall):5-16.

Foster, George M. (ed.)
 1951   A cross-cultural anthropological analysis of a techni-
cal aid program, based on field analyses by Charles
Erasmus, Isobel Kelly, Kalervo Oberg, and Ozzie
Simmons of the Smithsonian Institution's Institute of
Social Anthropology, with the cooperation of the Health
and Sanitation Division of the Institute of Inter-American
Affairs, and the Ministry of Health Servicios of Brazil,
Colombia, Mexico and Peru. Washington, D.C., Smith-
sonian Institution. Mimeographed.

Franklin, Albert B.
 1943   Ecuador, portrait of a people. Garden City, N.Y.,
Doubleday Doran & Co. (E)

Galarza, Ernesto
 1943   Labor trends and social welfare in Latin America,
1941 and 1942. Washington, D.C., Pan American Union,
Division of Labor and Social Information.

Gamio, Manuel
 1945   Some considerations of Indianist policy. In The Science
of Man in the World Crisis, ed. Ralph Linton, pp. 399-
415. New York, Columbia University Press.

Garcés, Enrique
 1946   Defensa de la vida. In UNP, pp. 86-112. (E)

Garcés, Víctor Gabriel
 1941   Cuestionario de la Oficina Internacional del Trabajo
sobre la situación de la raza indígena. Previsión Social,
No. 8:12-44. (E)

 1942   La sociabilidad del indio. Am. Ind. 2:63-66. (E)

 1945   El indio Ecuatoriano y la coca. Am. Ind. 5:287-93. (E)

 1946a   Living conditions of the indigeneous populations in
American countries. Montreal, International Labour
Office.

1946b   La industria del indio. In UNP, pp. 87-95. (E)

1950   El indio y el Censo Nacional. Am. Ind. 10:321-26. (E)

García, Antonio
1939   Pasado y presente del indio. Bogotá.

1948   Regimenes indígenas de salariado: El salariado natural
               y el salariado capitalista en la historia de América.
               Am. Ind. 8:249-87.

García, Egberto
1950   El Servicio Nacional de Fiebre Amarilla en 1948.
               Previsión Social, No. 23 (May-Dec., 1949 to Jan.-Feb.,
               1950):123-31. (E)

García Ortiz, Humberto
1942   Consideraciones acerca de una legislación indígena en
               el Ecuador. Am. Ind. 2, No. 1:25-27. (E)

1946   Organización administrativa de los grupos indígenas.
               In Cuestiones Indígenas del Ecuador, pp. 166-78. (E)

1951   La clase media en el Ecuador. In Materiales para el
               estudio de la clase media en la América Latina, Pub-
               licaciones de la Oficina de Ciencias Sociales VI:15-
               35. Washington, D.C., Unión Panamericana. (E)

Garrett, Garet
1944   A time is born. New York, Pantheon Books, Inc.

Gerth, H. H. and C. Wright Mills (eds.)
1946   From Max Weber: Essays in sociology. New York,
               Oxford University Press.

Gibson, Charles
1948   The Inca concept of sovereignty and the Spanish admini-
               stration in Peru. Latin-American Studies IV. Austin,
               Institute of Latin American Studies, University of Texas.

Gil Gilbert, Enrique
1942   Nuestro pan. Guayaquil, Librería Vera & Cia. (E)

Gill, Richard C.
1940   White water and black magic. New York, H. Holt &
               Co., Inc. (E)

Gillin, John
1936   Quichua-speaking Indians of northern Ecuador. AA 38:
               548-53. (E)

1941   The Quichua-speaking Indians of the province of Imba-
               bura (Ecuador) and their anthropometric relations with
               the living populations of the Andean area. Smithsonian
               Institution, Bureau of American Ethnology, Bulletin
               128, No. 16:167-228. (E)

1946   Review of: Peguche, by Elsie Clews Parsons (q.v.). AA
               48:438-40. (E)

1947   Moche, a Peruvian coastal community. Smithsonian Institution, Institute of Social Anthropology, Publication No. 3.

1948a   Magical fright. Psychiatry 11:387-400.

1948b   The ways of men, an introduction to anthropology. New York, Appleton-Century-Crofts, Inc.

1949   Mestizo America. In Most of the World, ed. Ralph Linton, pp. 156-211. New York, Columbia University Press.

1952   Modern cultural development and synthesis in Latin America. 29th ICA, pp. 221-23.

Gomezjurado, Miguel Angel
1945   El latifundio en el Ecuador. Revista Económico-Social I, No. 1 (Nov.): 125-27. Quito. (E)

Gonzalez H., Cristobal
1941   Aparición y desarollo del tifus exantematico en Quito. Previsión Social, No. 8:130-32. (E)

Gottschalk, Luis
1950   Understanding history: a primer of historical method. New York, A. A. Knopf, Inc.

Gray, J. Stanley (ed.)
1946   Psychology in human affairs. New York and London, McGraw-Hill Book Co., Inc.

Greenberg, Clement
1953   Work and leisure under industrialism. Commentary 16, No. 1 (July):54-62.

Gutiérrez-Noriega, Carlos and Victor Wolfgang von Hagen
1950   The strange case of the coca leaf. Scientific Monthly 70, No. 2 (Feb.):81-89.

Hagen, Victor Wolfgang von
1940   Ecuador, the unknown. New York, Oxford University Press. (E)

1949   Ecuador and the Galapagos Islands. Norman, Okla., University of Oklahoma Press. (E)

Handbook on the Trust Territories of the Pacific Islands
1948   A handbook for use in training and administration, prepared at the School of Naval Administration, Hoover Institute, Stanford University. Washington, D.C., Navy Department, Office of the Chief of Naval Operations.

Hanke, Lewis
1946   Free speech in sixteenth-century Spanish America. The Hispanic-American Historical Review 26:135-49.

Hanson, Earl Parker and Raye R. Platt (eds.)
1945   Ecuador. In The New World Guides to the Latin American Republics, Vol. II, Andes and West Coast Countries. Rev. ed. New York, Duell, Sloan & Pearce. (E)

Hanson, Henry
1941   El paludismo en el Ecuador. Previsión Social, No. 9: 112-17. (E)

Hardy, Osgood
1919   The Indians of the Department of Cuzco. AA 21:1-27.

Hassaurek, F.
1868   Four years among Spanish-Americans. New York. (E)

Haudricourt, André G.
1948   Relations entre Gestes habituels, formes de vêtements et manière de porter les charges. La Révue de Géographie Humaine et d'Ethnologie 1-ère Année, No. 3 (July-Sept.):58-67. Paris.

Henry, Philip W.
1946   The technological future of the Latin American countries. In Some Aspects of Post-War Inter-American Relations. Latin American Studies II. Austin, Institute of Latin-American Studies, University of Texas.

Hernandez de Alba, Gregorio
1947   The highland tribes of southern Colombia. HSAI 2: 915-60.

Herrnheiser, Pavel
1946   El Indio como trabajador. Am. Ind. 6:149-55. (E)

Herskovits, Melville J.
1940   The economic life of primitive peoples. New York, A. A. Knopf.

1948   Man and his works: the science of cultural anthropology. New York, A. A. Knopf.

1952a   Some psychological implications of Afroamerican studies. 29th ICA, pp. 152-60.

1952b   The problem of adapting societies to new tasks. In The Progress of Underdeveloped Areas, ed. Bert F. Hoselitz.

Hertzberg, H. T. E.
1948   Post war anthropometry in the Air Force. Am. Jn. Phys. Anthr. 6, No. 3:363-71.

Hertzberg, H. T. E. and Gilbert S. Daniels
1952   Airforce anthropology in 1950. Am. Jn. Phys. Anthr. 10:201-8.

Hewett, Edgar L.
1939   Ancient Andean life. Indianapolis and New York, The Bobbs-Merrill Co.

Hitchcock, Charles B.
1953   Resources of the tropics: II--South America. Focus
              (American Geographical Society) 3, No. 8 (April).
              New York.

Hodge, William H.
1947   Coca. Natural History 56, No. 2 (Feb.):86-93. New
              York, American Museum of Natural History.

Hoffer, Charles R.
1947   Medical needs of the rural population in Michigan.
              Rural Sociology 12:162-68.

Hoijer, Harry
1953   The relation of language to culture. In Anthropology
              Today, by A. L. Kroeber and others, pp. 554-73.
              Chicago, University of Chicago Press.

Horn, Eugene F.
1947   Forest resources of western Ecuador. Agriculture in
              the Americas 7, No. 3 (March):46-49. (E)

Hoselitz, Bert F. (ed.)
1952   The progress of underdeveloped areas. Chicago, Uni-
              versity of Chicago Press.

Hughlett, Lloyd J. (ed.)
1946   Industrialization of Latin America. New York and
              London, McGraw-Hill Book Co., Inc.

Huizinga, J.
1949   Homo ludens: a study of the play-element in culture.
              International Library of Sociology and Social Recon-
              struction. London, Routledge & Kegan Paul, Ltd.

Icaza, Jorge
1934   Huasipungo. Buenos Aires, 1948. Penguin Books, Ltd.,
              Editorial Lautaro. (E)

Instituto Ecuatoriano de Antropología y Geografía
1953   Informe No. 2: Pusir: una comunidad de cultura negra
              en el Cañón de "El Chota." (E)

1953   Informe No. 3: Ilumán, una comunidad indígena acul-
              turada. (E)

1953   Informe No. 4: Chunazana, una comunidad juridica-
              mente organizada, sin antecedente histórico. (E)

1953   Informe Nos. 10 and 11: El campesino de la provincia
              de Chimborazo (No. 10, Hacienda "Gatazo Grande";
              No. 11, Hacienda "Gusutuz").

Inter-American Development Commission
n.d.   Proceedings of the conference of Commissions of Inter-
              American Development, New York, May 9-18, 1944,
              published by the Inter-American Development Commis-
              sion, Washington, D.C., 1944.

International Labour Office
1946   Public investment and full employment. Studies and
              Reports, n.s. No. 3. Montreal.

1951   Vocational training in Latin America. Studies and Reports, n.s. No. 28. Geneva.

International Labour Organisation
1949   Fourth conference of American states members, Montevideo, April 1949. Report II. Conditions of life and work of indigenous population of Latin American countries. Geneva, International Labour Office.

International Reference Service, U. S. Department of Commerce, Office of International Trade, Washington, D. C.

1947   IV, 52 (Oct.)--Economic situation in Ecuador, 1946. (E)

1948   V, 74 (Oct.)--Economic review of Ecuador, 1947. (E)

1949   VI (Aug.), Supplement No. 11--Economic review of Ecuador, 1948. (E)

1950   VII, 24 (May)--Ecuador, summary of basic economic information. (E)

Izquieta Pérez, Leopoldo
1944   La sanidad en el Ecuador. Bol. Of. San. Panam. 23: 1-5. (E)

James, Preston E.
1950   Ecuador. In Latin America, pp. 110-25. Rev. ed. New York, The Odyssey Press. (E)

Jaramillo Alvarado, Pío
1936   El indio ecuatoriano: Contribución al estudio de la sociología indo-americana. 3d ed. Quito. (E)

1943   Situación politica, económica y juridica del indio en el Ecuador. Previsión Social, No. 12 (Jan.-April): 35-58; No. 13 (May-Aug.):19-34. (E)

1946   El Indio, problema continental. In Cuestiones Indígenas del Ecuador, pp. 1-37. (E)

Johnson, Martin
1947   Time, knowledge, and the nebulae: an introduction to the meanings of time in physics, astronomy, and philosophy, and the relativities of Einstein and Milne. New York, Dover Publications.

Karsten, Rafael
1939   Überbleibsel der Inkareligion im heutigen Peru und Bolivien. Archiv für Anthropologie, Völkerforschung und kolonialen Kulturwandel (Neue Folge) 25, No. 1:36-46.

King, Barry G.
1948   Measurement of man for making machinery. Am. Jn. Phys. Anthr. 6, No. 3: 341-51.

King, P. H. M.
1947-48   Task perception and inter-personal relations in industrial training; the development of a training program in the hosiery trade. Human Relations 1:121-30, 373-412.

Kroeber, A. L.
1948   Anthropology. New rev. ed. New York, Harcourt,
               Brace & Co.

Kroeber, A. L. and others
1953   Anthropology today: an encyclopedic inventory. Chicago,
               University of Chicago Press.

Kubler, George
1947   The Quechua in the colonial world. HSAI 2:331-410.

1952   The Indian caste of Peru, 1795-1950: a population study
               based on tax records and census reports. Smith-
               sonian Institution, Institute of Social Anthropology,
               Publication No. 14. Washington, D.C.

Langewiesche, Wolfgang
1948   Look down, look down--flight over foreign parts.
               Harper's Magazine 197, No. 1182 (Nov.):64-69.

Laso, Luis Eduardo
1942-43   Breves consideraciones sobre el problema económico
               ecuatoriano. Revista de Derecho y Ciencias Sociales
               (Quito), Epoca Segunda, III, No. 17 (Oct., 1942):82-95;
               No. 18 (Sept., 1943):63-72. (E)

Lasso, Raphael V.
1944   The wonderland Ecuador. New York, Alpha-Ecuador
               Publications. (E)

Lear, John
1944   The lady pack mule rebels. The Saturday Evening
               Post 217, No. 26 (Dec.):17, 63-64. (E)

León, Luis A.
1946   Breves consideraciones sobre la patología del indio
               en el Ecuador. In Cuestiones Indígenas del Ecuador,
               pp. 241-62. (E)

1947   Paidometría indígena. Am. Ind. 7:249-60. (E)

1952   Historia y extinción del cocaismo en el Ecuador. Am.
               Ind. 12:7-32. (E)

Leonard, Olen E.
1947   Pichilingue, a study of rural life in coastal Ecuador.
               Foreign Agricultural Report No. 17. Washington, D.C.,
               U. S. Department of Agriculture, Office of Foreign
               Agricultural Relations. (E)

Linke, Lilo
1946   Scourge of the Andes. The Inter-American 5, No. 3:
               26-27, 45. (E)

1954   Ecuador, country of contrasts. London and New York,
               Royal Institute of International Affairs. (E)

Lipschütz, A.
1950   On the reliability of some written sources of the seven-
               teenth and eighteenth centuries. AA 52:123-26.

1953   El movimiento indigenista, y la reestructuración
            cultural americana. Am. Ind. 13:275-90.

Little, Elbert L., Jr.
1948   Trees in Ecuador. Foreign Agriculture 12, No. 3:
            54-59. (E)

Long, Boaz and Cristobal de Gangotena y Jijón
1946   The Long collection of Ecuadorean rugs. El Palacio
            53:338-47. (E)

Long, Lewis E.
1944   Hacienda Pichilingue. Agriculture in the Americas 4,
            No. 3:54-56. (E)

Loomis, Charles P.
1943   Applied anthropology in Latin America. Applied Anthro-
            pology 2, No. 2 (Jan.-March):33-34. (E)

Lopez Arteta, F. A.
1944   Social insurance reform in Ecuador. International
            Labour Review 49:19-37. (E)

McCain, Seward B. and George Loinaz
1946   The metalworking industries. In Industrialization of
            Latin America, ed. Lloyd J. Hughlett, pp. 191-201.

McCann, Lewis P.
1947   Ecuador's Naranjilla: a reluctant guest. Agriculture
            in the Americas 7, No. 12 (Dec.):146-49. (E)

McClure, F. A.
1945   Bamboo in Ecuador's lowlands. Agriculture in the
            Americas 5, No. 10 (Oct.):190-92, 194. (E)

1946   Bamboo in Ecuador's highlands. Agriculture in the
            Americas 6, No. 10 (Oct.):164-67. (E)

McIver, Robert M.
1937   Society: a textbook of sociology. New York, Farrar
            & Rinehart.

Mace, C. A.
1948   Satisfactions in work. Occupational Psychology 22:
            5-16. London.

Maes, Ernest E.
1941   Report on the Indian policies in Ecuador. Washington,
            D.C., Office of Indian Affairs, Division of Inter-American
            Cooperation. Mimeographed.

1942   Indian farming in South America. Agriculture in the
            Americas 2, No. 12 (Dec.):233-36.

Marquez, Javier
1946a   Conveniencia y peligro de la industrialización. Cuadernos
            Americanos (México), Ano V, 27, No. 3 (May-June):
            42-68.

1946b   Remarks on some aspects of the economic relations between the United States and the Latin American countries. In Some Economic Aspects of Post-War Inter-American Relations. Latin-American Studies II. Austin, Institute of Latin-American Studies, University of Texas.

Mathews, Robert E.
1947   Labor standards provisions in government foreign procurement contracts. Illinois Law Review of Northwestern University 42:141-68.

Mauss, Marcel
1936   Les techniques du corps. Journal de Psychologie 32; Nos. 2-3. Paris. (Reprinted in Sociologie et Antropologie, ed. Claude Lévi-Strauss, pp. 365-86. Paris, Presses Universitaires de France, 1950.)

Mayo, Elton
1945   The social problems of an industrial civilization. Boston, Division of Research, Graduate School of Business Administration, Harvard University.

Meadows, Paul
1950   The culture of industrial man. Lincoln, Neb., University of Nebraska Press.

Means, Philip Ainsworth
1925   A study of ancient Andean social institutions. Transactions of the Connecticut Academy of Arts and Sciences 27 (Sept.):407-69.

1931   Ancient civilizations of the Andes. New York and London, Scribner's Sons.

Meneses Pallares, Arturo
1942   La reforma de seguro social en el Ecuador. Noticias de la Oficina de Información Obrera y Social (Pan American Union), Nos. 9 and 10 (Nov.):7-12. (E)

Merton, Robert K.
1947   The machine, the worker, and the engineer. Science 105, No. 2712 (June 24):79-84.

Ministerio de Previsión Social y Trabajo
1951   Escuela Nacional de Servicio Social. Quito. (E)

Mishkin, Bernard
1947   The contemporary Quechua. HSAI 2:411-70.

Monsalve Pozo, Luis
1942   La figura social de los aborígines del Ecuador. Am. Ind. 2, No. 2 (April):35-42. (E)

1946   La industria de sombreros de paja toquilla. In Cuestiones Indígenas del Ecuador, pp. 96-125. (E)

Moomaw, Ira W.
1946   Agriculture. In Indians of the High Andes, ed. Stanley W. Rycroft, pp. 157-216.

Moore, Wilbert E.
1946   Industrial relations and the social order. New York,
             The Macmillan Co.

1951   Industrialization and labor: social aspects of economic
             development. Published for the Institute of World
             Affairs, New School for Social Research. Ithaca, New
             York, Cornell University Press.

Morant, G. M.
1947   Anthropometric problems in the Royal Air Force.
             Brit. Med. Bull. 5, No. 1:1017 ff. (Reprinted in Yearbook
             of Physical Anthropology 1947, Vol. 3, pp. 197-203.
             New York, The Viking Fund, Inc., 1948.)

1948   Applied physical anthropology in Great Britain in recent
             years. Am. Jn. Phys. Anthr. 6, No. 3: 329-39.

Moreno, Julio Enrique
1940   El sentido historico y la cultura: para una sociología
             ecuatoriana. Quito, Imp. Romero. (E)

Mosk, Sanford A.
1945   Main currents of economic thought. In Inter-American
             Affairs 1944, An Annual Survey, No. 4, ed. Arthur P.
             Whitaker, pp. 158-80. New York, Columbia University
             Press.

Mosquera C., Carlos Fernando
1952   Los yacimientos carboníferos de la provincia de Cañar.
             Criterios actuales del beneficio de su explotación y
             purificación. Anales de la Universidad Central del
             Ecuador 28, Nos. 329-30 (Enero de 1950--Diciembre
             de 1951):505-30. Quito. (E)

Mulliken, Otis E. and Sarah E. Roberts
1946   Labor and social welfare. In Inter-American Affairs
             1945, An Annual Survey, No. 5, ed. Arthur P. Whitaker,
             pp. 142-67. New York, Columbia University Press.

Mumford, Lewis
1934   Technics and civilization. New York, Harcourt, Brace
             & Co.

Murra, John
1947   The historic tribes of Ecuador. HSAI 2:785-821. (E)

National Research Council
1946   Survey of research on Latin America by United States
             scientists and institutions, prepared by The Committee
             on Latin American Anthropology, Division of Anthro-
             pology and Psychology, Washington, D.C.

Neumann, William L.
1948   Economic conflicts in inter-American relations. Inter-
             American Reports. Washington, D.C., No. 3.

Newman, Russell W.
1953   Applied anthropometry. In Anthropology Today, by A.
             L. Kroeber and others, pp. 741-49.

Northrop, F. S. C.
1946   The meeting of East and West: an inquiry concerning
               world understanding. New York, The Macmillan Co.

Office of the Coordinator of Inter-American Affairs
1943   Future forest vistas in American republics. Foreign
               Commerce Weekly 13 (Dec. 25):8-9, 31.

Office of the Coordinator of Inter-American Affairs, Research Division
1945   Latin-America as a market for machinery and equip-
               ment. Washington, D.C., Inter-American Development
               Commission.

Office of Inter-American Affairs
1945   Handbook of Latin American population data. Washing-
               ton, D.C.

Oficina de Estadística Regional
1949   Indice de morbilidad de la población asegurada a las
               Cajas de Previsión, en la ciudad de Guayaquil. Boletín
               de Informaciones y de Estudios Sociales y Económicos
               Año XII, Nos. 46-47 (Julio-Diciembre):54-59. Quito. (E)

Ojeda, Alejandro
1946   El Oriente y la colonización. In UNP, pp. 46-50. (E)

Oreamuno, J. Rafael
n.d.   Reports regarding the work of the Inter-American
               Development Commission presented to the Inter-
               American Economical /sic/ and Social Council during
               1946. Washington, D.C., Inter-American Development
               Commission, 1946.

Orton, James
1875   The Andes and the Amazon; or, across the continent of
               South America. 3d ed. New York.

Owen, Eugene Davis
1941   Recent Latin American labor codes. The Inter-American
               Quarterly 3:68-79.

Pan American Associates
1945   Ecuador. In The Pan American Yearbook 1945, pp. 247-
               91. New York. (E)

Pan American Union
n.d.   Tagua. American Commodities Booklet. Washington, D.C.

1944   Ecuador. Washington, D.C. (E)

1954   Ecuador. Washington, D.C. (E)

Paredes, Angel Modesto
1951   Estudio de la clase media en el Ecuador. In Materiales
               para el estudio de la clase media en la América Latina.
               Publicaciones de la Oficina de Ciencias Sociales VI:
               36-56. Washington, D.C., Unión Panamericana. (E)

Parsons, Elsie Clews
    1940   Cosmography of the Indians of Imbabura Province,
                Ecuador. The Journal of American Folklore 53:
                219-24. (E)

    1945   Peguche, canton of Otavalo, province of Imbabura,
                Ecuador: a study of Andean Indians. Chicago, Univer-
                sity of Chicago Press. (E)

Parsons, Talcott
    1937   The structure of social action. New York and London,
                McGraw-Hill Book Co., Inc.

Parsons, Talcott and A. M. Henderson (trans.)
    1947   Max Weber: the theory of social and economic organi-
                zation. New York, Oxford University Press.

Paviolo, Italo
    1927   /Apuntes numéricos sobre la actividad agropecuaria
                y forestal de la República del Ecuador. Revista de la
                Sociedad Nacional de Agricultura, Año IX, No. 63_7 (E)

Paz y Miño, Luis T.
    1936   La población del Ecuador. Quito, Talleres Gráficos
                Nacionales. (E)

    1942   /La población del Ecuador. Quito, Talleres Gráficos
                Nacionales._7 (E)

Pearl, Raymond
    1943   Un examen comparativo de ciertos aspectos de las
                poblaciones del Nuevo Mundo. Estadística (Journal
                of the Inter-American Statistical Institute) I, No. 4:
                29-66.

Perez, Aquiles R.
    1943   Así han vivido nuestros indios. Cuadernos de Divul-
                gación Cultural del Ecuador, No. 8. Quito, Ministerio
                de Previsión Social y Trabajo. (E)

Plaza, Galo
    May 1949   Economía y producción en el Ecuador. Exposición del
                Presidente Constitucional de la República, Excmo.
                Señor Galo Plaza, radiada en Guayaquil, el 7 de Mayo
                de 1949. (E)

    June 1949 Economía nacional, Junio 1949. El Gobierno del Sr.
                Galo Plaza, 1948-1952. Quito, Talleres Gráficos
                Nacionales. (A collection of addresses by the Presi-
                dent; by the Minister of Economy; and newspaper
                comments on the speech of May, 1949). (E)

    Jan. 1950 Mensaje al pais, enero 1 de 1950. Resumen de trabajo
                en 1949. Planes para 1950. Quito, Talleres Gráficos
                Nacionales. (E)

    May 1950   Mensaje económico del Presidente..., Guayaquil,
                Mayo 9, 1950. Quito, Talleres Gráficos Nacionales.
                (E)

(Plaza)--El Gobierno del Sr. Galo Plaza
1950   Plan de colonización italiana, Junio 1950. Quito, Talleres
            Gráficos Nacionales. (E)

Poblete Troncoso, Moisés
1942   El standard de vida de las poblaciones de América
            (Nivel de vida.) Santiago, Prensa de la Universidad de
            Chile.

1946   El movimiento obrero latinoamericano. Coleccion
            Tierra Firme 17. México, D.F., Fondo de Cultura
            Económica.

Polit, Gustavo
1946   La América Latina ante el momento económico.
            Cuadernos Américanos Año V, 25, No. 1:7-31. Mexico.

1947   Los minerales y la industrialización. Cuadernos
            Americanos Año VI, XXXI, No. 1:26-43. México.

Popenoe, Wilson
1924   Economic fruit-bearing plants of Ecuador. Contribu-
            tions from the United States Herbarium 24, Part 5:
            101-34. Washington, D.C., Smithsonian Institution,
            U. S. National Museum. (E)

Rainey, Froelich
1946   Quinine hunters in Ecuador. The National Geographical
            Magazine 89, No. 3:341-63. (E)

Randall, F. E.
1948   Anthropometry in the quartermaster corps. Am. Jn.
            Phys. Anthr. 6, No. 3:373-80.

Reichel-Dolmatoff, Gerardo
1953   Actitudes hacia el trabajo en una población mestiza de
            Colombia. Am. Ind. 13:165-74.

Richards, Audrey I.
1939   Land, labour and diet in Northern Rhodesia: an economic
            study of the Bemba tribe. International Institute of
            African Languages and Cultures. London, Oxford Uni-
            versity Press.

Ricketts, C. A.
1952   El cocaismo en el Perú. Am. Ind. 12:309-22.

Rivedeneira, Jaime
1942   Campaña antipalúdica en el Valle de los Chillos. Pre-
            visión Social, No. 11:76-88. (E)

Rivet, Paul
1903   Etude sur les Indiens de la Région de Riobamba.
            Journal de la Société des Américanistes de Paris, I,
            No. 1:58-80. (E)

1906   Le Christianisme et les Indiens de la République de
            l'Equateur. L'Anthropologie 17:81-101. Paris. (E)

1926   Coutumes funéraires des Indiens de l'Equateur. Congrès International de l'Histoire des Religions, Paris, 8-13 Octobre 1923, pp. 376-412. Paris. (E)

Robles, Gonzalo
1944   Obstaculos a la industrialización de los paises latino-americanos. In La Postguerra. El Colegio de México, Centro de Estudios Sociales, Jornadas 10. México.

Rodríguez Sandoval, Leonidas
1945   Drinking motivations among the Indians of the Ecuadorean Sierra. Primitive Man 18, Nos. 3 and 4:39-46. (E)

1949   Vida económico-social del indio libre de la sierra ecuatoriana. Universidad Catolica de America, Estudios en Ciencias Sociales No. 32. Washington, D.C., The Catholic University of America Press.

Roller, Jane W.
1947   Annatto. Agriculture in the Americas 7, Nos. 8-9:119. (E)

Romero, Emilio
1947   Geografía del Pacífico sudamericano. Colección Tierra Firme 32. México, Fondo de Cultura Económica.

Romero, Oscar A.
1945   Síntesis de estadística educacional. El Trimestre Estadístico del Ecuador I, No. 2:18-30. (E)

Rowe, John Howland
1947   Inca culture at the time of the Spanish conquest. HSAI 2:183-330.

Rubio Orbe, Alfredo
1954   Legislación indigenista del Ecuador. Ediciones Especiales del Institutio Indigenista Interamericano. México. (E)

Rubio Orbe, Gonzalo
1946   Organización escolar para grupos indígenas. In Cuestiones Indígenas del Ecuador, pp. 56-86. (E)

1949   El indio en el Ecuador (Síntesis histórica). Am. Ind. 9:205-35. (E)

1953   Aculturaciones de indígenas de los Andes. Am. Ind. 13:187-222.

Ruess, Gerardo L.
1951   El azufre de Tixán. Bol. Inf. Cient. Nac. 4, No. 41: 199-201. (E)

Ruiz Galindo, Antonio
1947   The basic idea of the industrial city "D. M. Nacional." The Social Sciences in Mexico and News about the Social Sciences in South and Central America 1, No. 2: 39-42.

Rycroft, W. Stanley
    1946   Government and Education. In Indians of the High
                Andes, ed. W. Stanley Rycroft, pp. 281-95.

Rycroft, W. Stanley (ed.)
    1946   Indians of the high Andes: report of the commission
                appointed by the Committee on Cooperation in Latin
                America to study the Indians of the Andean highlands,
                with a view to establishing a cooperative Christian
                enterprise. New York, Committee on Cooperation in
                Latin America.

Saenz, Moisés
    1933a   Sobre el indio ecuatoriano y su incorporación al medio
                nacional. México, Publicaciones de la Secretaria de
                Educación Pública. (E)

    1933b   Sobre el indio peruano y su incorporación al medio
                nacional. México, Publicaciones de la Secretaria de
                Educación Pública. (Translated by the Staff of the
                Strategic Index of the Americas, Coordinator of Inter-
                American Affairs, Research Division, as "The
                Peruvian Indian." Washington, D.C., 1944, Mimeo-
                graphed. /All page references are to this translation./

Saenz Vera, Cornelio
    1941   Estudio sobre la peste bubonica en el Ecuador. Pre-
                visión Social No. 9:67-92. (E)

    1949   La peste en el Ecuador durante el año 1948. Bol. Of.
                San. Panam. 28:906-9. (E)

Salinas, Raúl
    1954   Manual arts in Ecuador. Am. Ind. 14:315-26. (E)

Salz, Arthur
    1933   Occupation. Encyclopedia of the Social Sciences 11.

    1934   Specialization. Encyclopedia of the Social Sciences 14.

Salz, Beate
    1944   Indianismo. Social Research 11:441-69.

Samaniego, Juan José
    1942   Perfil demográfico sanitario de la provincia de Pichin-
                cha. Bol. Of. San. Panam. 21:132-38. (E)

    1943   /Bioestadística en el cosmos ecuatoriano. Quito,
                Talleres Gráficos de Educación./ (E)

Santiana, Antonio
    1947   Los grupos sanguineos de los indios del Ecuador.
                Comunicación definitiva. Anales de la Universidad
                Central del Ecuador 75, Nos. 325-26:5-50. Quito,
                1948. (E)

    1949   Los indios Mojanda--Etnografía y folklore. Filosofía
                y Letras, Año II, Nos. 4 and 5:238-74. Quito. (E)

1952a   Panorama ecuatoriano del indio (Síntesis de un
personaje olvidado y visión de su porvenir) (Con-
clusión). Anales de la Universidad Central del Ecuador
78, Nos. 329-39 (Enero de 1950-Diciembre de 1951):
7-149. Quito. (E)

1952b   Los indios Mojanda, etnografía y folklore--Comen-
tarios a una crítica. BBAA XIV (1951, Part 2, México):
159-62. (E)

Sauer, Carl O.
1950   Geography of South America. HSAI 6:319-44.

Schreiber, Walter R.
1946   Tagua. Agriculture in the Americas 6, No. 3:51-53,
58. (E)

Seashore, Stanley E.
1946   Psychology in industry, and Employment: training and
merit rating. In Psychology in Human Affairs, ed. J.
Stanley Gray.

Serrano Moscoso, Eduardo
1946   A statement of the laws of Ecuador in matters affecting
business in its various aspects and activities. Washington, D.C., Inter-American Development Commission.
(E)

Sewell, William H.
1949   Field techniques in social psychological study in a rural
community. Am. Soc. Rev. 14:718-26.

Shih, Kuo-Heng
1944   China enters the machine age: a study of labor in a
Chinese war industry. Cambridge, Mass., Harvard
University Press.

Sorokin, Pitirim, C. C. Zimmerman and C. J. Galpin
1930-32   A systematic source book in rural sociology. 3 vols.
Minneapolis, University of Minnesota Press.

Soule, George, David Efron and Norman T. Ness
1945   Latin America in the future world. New York and
Toronto, Farrar & Rinehart, Inc.

Spinden, H. J.
1948   Ecuadorian carpets--Indian or Spanish? El Palacio
55:3-8. (E)

Staley, Eugene
1944   World economic development: effects on advanced
industrial countries. International Labour Office,
Studies and Reports, Series B (Economic Conditions),
No. 36. Montreal.

Staley, Eugene, ed.
1952   Creating an industrial civilization: a report on the
Corning conference. New York, Harper & Bros.

Steward, Julian H.
1949   The native populations of South America. HSAI 5: 655-68.

Stirling, M. W.
1938   Historical and ethnographical material on the Jivaro Indians. Smithsonian Institution, Bureau of American Ethnology, Bulletin 117. Washington, D.C. (E)

Storm, Hans Otto
1948   Pity the tyrant. In Of Good Family. New York, Swallow Press and Wm. Morrow & Co. Originally published 1937.

Streich, Paul and Betty
1947   1946 Annual Report--Hacienda Picalqui, Tabacundo, Ecuador. New York, United Andean Indian Mission. Mimeographed. (E)

Stübel, Alphons
1897   Die Vulkanberge von Ecuador... Berlin, A. Asher & Co. (E)

Suárez, Pablo Arturo
1934   Contribución al estudio de las realidades entre las clases obreras y campesinas. Quito, Universidad Central del Ecuador. (E)

1942   La situación real del indio. Am. Ind. 2, No. 1:59-62. (E)

Suárez Dávila, Alberto
1950   Proyecto de una fábrica de cemento. Revista de la Asociación Escuela de Ciencias Económicas, Universidad Central, Año V, Nos. 4-5 (Junio):27-39. (E)

Tannenbaum, Frank
1944   Minorities in Latin America. In Group Relations and Group Antagonisms..., ed. R. M. McIver, pp. 171-82. Published by the Institute for Religious Studies; distributed by Harper & Bros., New York and London.

Tax, Sol
1953   Penny capitalism: a Guatemalan Indian economy. Smithsonian Institution, Institute of Social Anthropology, Publication No. 16. Washington, D.C.

Tax, Sol and others
1952   Heritage of conquest: the ethnology of Middle America. Glencoe, Ill., The Free Press.

Tello, Franklin
1949   Informe a la nación, 1948-1949. Quito, Talleres Gráficos Nacionales. (E)

Thurnwald, Richard
1932   Economics in primitive communities. International Institute of African Languages and Cultures. London, Oxford University Press.

Tiffin, Joseph
1944   Industrial psychology. New York, Prentice-Hall, Inc.

Trimborn, Hermann
1925   Der Kollektivismus der Inkas in Peru. Anthropos 20:
                978 ff.

Troncoso, Julio C.
1946   De Quito á Quevedo. In UNP, pp. 259-74. (E)

Tschopik, Harry, Jr.
1947a   The Aymara. HSAI 2:501-73.

1947b   Highland communites of central Peru, a regional survey.
                Smithsonian Institution, Institute of Social Anthropology,
                Publication No. 5. Washington, D.C.

1948   On the concept of Creole culture in Peru. Transactions
                of the New York Academy of Sciences, Ser. II, 10, No. 7
                (May):252-61.

1952   On the identification of the Indian in Peru. 29th ICA,
                pp. 261-66.

Tucker, Mitchell
1946   Petroleum Industry. In Industrialization of Latin Ameri-
                ca, ed. Lloyd J. Hughlett, pp. 273-99.

Tumin, Melvin
1945   Culture: genuine or spurious, a re-evaluation. Am.
                Soc. Rev. 10:199-207.

United Nations
1949   Yearbook of the United Nations, 1947-1948. Lake
                Success, New York, Department of Public Information.

United Nations, Economic Commission for Latin America
1949   Economic survey for Latin America, 1948. Lake
                Success, New York, U. N. Department of Economic
                Affairs.

1951   Labour productivity of the cotton textile industry in
                five Latin-American countries. New York, United
                Nations, Department of Economic Affairs.

United Nations Educational, Scientific, and Cultural Organization
1947   Fundamental education, common ground for all
                peoples. Report of a Special Committee to the Prepara-
                tory Commission of the United Nations Educational,
                Scientific, and Cultural Organization, Paris. New York,
                The Macmillan Co.

Unión Nacional de Periodistas
1946   Realidad y posibilidad del Ecuador. Contribución á
                la Orientación nacional por los periodistas ecua-
                torianos en el ciclo radial mantenido por la UNP
                durante el año de 1945 y en expediciones de conoci-
                miento periodistico del pais. Quito, Talleres Gráficos
                Nacionales. (E)

U. S. Tariff Commission
1940   The foreign trade of Latin America. Part II. Commer-
cial policies and trade relations of individual American
countries. Section 6--Ecuador. Washington, D.C. (E)

1949   Mining and manufacturing industries in Ecuador (one of
a series of reports on mining and manufacturing industries in the American republics). Washington, D.C.
First released 1945. (E)

Valcárcel, Luis E.
1945   Ruta cultural del Perú. Colección Tierra Firme 7.
México, Fondo de Cultura Económica.

Vallejo, Gustavo
1946   El analfabetismo. In UNP, pp. 75-85. (E)

Villavicencio, Manuel
1858   Geografía de la República del Ecuador. New York,
Imprenta de Robert Craighead.

Wagley, Charles
1941   Economics of a Guatemalan village. American
Anthropological Association Memoir No. 58.

Wandemberg, Benjamin and José Rivedeneira
1941   El paludismo del Valle de los Chillos. Previsión
Social, No. 8:138-65. (E)

Watkins, Mark Hanna
1952   Discussion /of a paper by Gonzalo Aguirre Beltran/.
In 29th ICA, pp. 166-68.

West, James
1945   Plainville, U.S.A. New York, Columbia University
Press.

White, Robert M.
1952   Applied physical anthropology. Am. Jn. Phys. Anthr.
10:193-99.

Whorf, Benjamin L.
1941   The relation of habitual thought and behavior to language.
In Language, Culture, and Personality: Essays in Memory
of Edward Sapir, ed. by Spier, Hallowell, and Newman,
pp. 75-93. Menasha, Wis.

Wiener, Norbert
1954   The human use of human beings: cybernetics and
society. 2d rev. ed. Garden City, Doubleday Anchor
Books. (Chapter IX, The First and Second Industrial
Revolution.)

Wolf, Teodoro
1892   Geografía y geología del Ecuador. Leipzig, F. A.
Brockhaus. (E)

Wolff, Raymond A.
1946   The Leather Industry. In Industrialization of Latin
America, ed. Lloyd J. Hughlett, pp. 180-90.

World Trade in Commodities, U.S. Department of Commerce, Office of
International Trade, Washington, D.C.

1948   VI, 1, 3 (Jan.)--Review of South American railroads
in 1947.

VI, 2, 6 (Feb.)--on tanning materials.

VI, 18, 8 (Sept.)--Glass containers: Cuba and Ecuador.

VI, 19, 22 (June)--On kapok and other fibers.

1949   VII, 1, 9 (July)--The Pan American highway system.

VII, 21, 19 (Aug.)--Large electric power projects in
selected American republics.

VII, 19, 9 (March)--Markets for wool carpets and rugs
in Colombia, Mexico, and Venezuela.

VII, 10, 1 (Jan.)--Pulp and paper market, Ecuador.

VII, 18, 2 (Jan.)--Flat glass: Dominican Republic and
Ecuador.

1950   VIII, 1, 4 (March)--Merchant shipping and shipbuilding--
Ecuador.

Wythe, George
1945   Industry in Latin America. New York, Columbia University Press.

Zambrano, Miguel Angel
1951   Las comunidades indígenas en el Ecuador y su posible
estructuración cooperativista. Primer Seminario
Regional de Asuntos Sociales, Mayo 27 a 10 de Junio
de 1950, pp. 175-202. Quito, Ministerio de Previsión
Social y Trabajo. (E)

Zevallos Menendez, Simon David
1946   Informe de labores realizadas el 19 de junio de 1945 al
15 de julio de 1946. Quito, República del Ecuador,
Ministerio de Economía. (E)

Abogado	Advocate; lawyer, solicitor
Aguardiente	Distilled cane liquor; "rum"
Alcalde	In Indian settlements, an Indian officer; headman; sheriff; "mayor"
Alcalde (de capilla)	Chapel alcalde, chapel officer; functionary within religious organization
Alguacil	Minor Indian functionary within religious organization; a kind of sheriff for the priest
Anejo, anexo	"Outlying section"; subdivision of a political-administrative unit; Indian settlement; hamlet; see parcialidad
Ayllu	(1) Rural population unit; settlement (general)
	(2) Bilaterally extended exogamous kinship group; husband's and wife's collaterals; large family group (modern Ecuadorean Indian)
	(3) "An association of families united by community, territorial, and genealogical links" which also may own lands in common ("classic" and modern Peruvian); community
Barrio	"Suburb," neighborhood; unit of generally urban settlement, section of a town or city
Blanco, Blancos	"White(s)"; upper social stratum, socially dominant group
Brujo	Sorcerer, magician, "shaman." See also curandero.
Cabecilla	"Little head" (lit.); subchief; Indian headman (see also alcalde); specifically hacienda Indian headman or foreman (see also mayoral)
Cabildo	Council, board
Campesino	Country man, rural dweller, peasant; farm worker
Canton	Administrative unit, "county," subdivision of province; the canton is divided into (secular) parishes (parroquias)
Capitán	See prioste

* Based in part on glossaries in HSAI (1946-50); Gillin 1947a; Rycroft 1946.

Cargador	One who takes on the cargo (q.v.); prioste
Cargo	"Burden" (lit.); "any civic or lay responsibility"; obligation to sponsor and finance a religious celebration
Caserío	Small, concentrated, compact type of settlement; hamlet
Cazique	Aboriginal Indian chieftain; "West Indian term used in the Andes to designate a chief, whether hereditary or appointed"; headman
Chicha	Fermented drink made of maize; "maize beer"
Chicha de jora	Maize beer made of sprouted corn
Chichería	Public drinking yard
Chichero	Maker and seller of chicha; tavern-keeper
Cholo, -a	Half-breed; Indianized Mestizo; also urbanized Indian, marginal Indian; in Ecuador, derogatory term to designate Mestizo; also poor, low-class rural White
Ciudadano	Urbanite; citizen
Coca	Erythroxylon coca; source of cocaine
Compadrazgo	Institution of compadreship
Compadre	One's son's or daughter's godfather, godparents (compadres), or godmother (comadre); "gossip" (god-sib); fictitious kin or kin by courtesy
Comuna	In Ecuador, "incorporated," legally established and formally organized community or settlement; rural settlement having legal powers to conduct its own affairs; a statutory body
Comunero	(1) Member of a comuna (q.v.) (2) Free Indian, i.e., Indian not subject to hacienda regime
Comunidad (pl. comunidades)	(1) Community (2) "Settlement of free Indians enjoying the communal use of land" (3) Communally owned lands
Concentración	Settlement, community (probably of colonial creation)
Concertado	Labor tenant; "serf"; see huasipungero
Concertaje	Labor-tenant contract; a tenant system; debt-peonage
Concierto	See huasipungero

Conquistadores	Spanish conquerors of the sixteenth century
Costa	Coast, coastal zone, the Pacific littoral, coastal lowlands
Criollo(s)	(1) Native American Spaniards, "creoles"
	(2) Mestizo population
	(3) Modern or emergent type of culture of western South America
Cura	Parish priest
Curandero, -a	Curer, witch doctor, medicine man, sorcerer, "shaman"
Diezmos	Tithes
Dotrina	Doctrine; catechism
Encomendero	Grantee; holder of an encomienda
Encomienda	Nonhereditary grant of land and its population to an encomendero for his and/or one other lifetime; grant under the Spanish-colonial system of land and/or tribute paying Indians thereon; "an assignment of Indian tribute to individuals or institutions" (monastery, church)
Faena	Work stint
Fiesta	Feast, celebration, religious holiday, saint's celebration
Gente decente	"Society," "proper folk," "gentlefolk," (white) upper social stratum
Gobernador	Governor; see also alcalde, cabecilla
Guarape	Fermented cane juice
Guayru, huayru	A kind of dice game
Hacendado	Owner of a hacienda (q.v.); landlord
Hacienda	Landed estate, farm, ranch
Hidalgo	Petty knight, military noble
Huasicama	Indian peon performing personal service in his master's home
Huasicamía	"System whereby a whole family performs personal services...in return for their food"; work for landlord's person, house service; part of obligations under concertaje (q.v.) or accruing to huasipungero (q.v.)
Huasipongo, huasipungo	Plot of land, allotment of huasipungero (q.v.)

Huasipungero	Debt-bound labor-tenant; worker on hacienda rendering work in return for use of plot of land with or without additional money or other remuneration; "serf"; also concierto
Impuesto	Tax; work obligation
Indígena	Native; Indian
Indios anejos	Hacienda Indians; conciertos, huasipungeros
Indios propios	"Owned" Indians; conciertos, huasipungeros
Junta	Board, council
Litoral	Littoral region; see costa
Llacta	Ecuadorean Indian term for parcialidad (q.v.); Indian community, settlement; also "country," "nation"
Maestro rezador	Prayer master; a lay religious personage
Mayoral	(1) Indian foreman (as of hacienda workers); cabecilla
	(2) Indian headman; alcalde
Mayordomo	(1) Steward, manager, overseer, superintendent of a hacienda.
	(2) Sponsor, financier, manager of a religious fiesta; see prioste
Mestizaje	Mestizohood; process of turning into Mestizo, or leading to Mestizohood
Minga	"A voluntary or semi-voluntary work group...involving recreational features as well as labor"; collective work party; "bee"; mutual help
Minguero	Participant in minga
Minifundium, minifundia	Fractional and small landholding(s); small-scale property usually worked only by the owner and his family
Mita	Forced or tribute labor; corvee
Mitayo	Laborer working under mita system; native forced labor of colonial times; also, term of depreciation for Indian laborer
Mitimaes	Colonists forcefully resettled under the Incaic system of population redistribution
Montuvio	Coastal lowlander
"Natoral," natural	Native; Indian
Ñaupador	Indian counselor; elder, ceremonial personage at wedding

Obraje — Colonial workshop, particularly textile factory employing draft labor

Oriente — Lowland regions east of the Andes; Amazonian headwater region

Padre — Priest; father

Padrino, padrino de boda — One's baptismal godfather; one's wedding godfather or sponsor

Panela — Unrefined brown sugar

Páramo — Cold, foggy, and rainy high-plateau grassland typical of the northern Andes (Ecuador and Colombia)

Parcialidad — Small community; Indian scatter-type settlement; tracts of land generally inhabited by Indians; unincorporated population nucleus; subdivision, with no offical standing, of a parish; also anejo, llacta

Patrón — Master, boss; landlord, hacienda owner; in address: sir

Pelota (guante) — Ecuadorean national ball game

Peon, peones — (Free, casual) worker; "hand"; day laborer

Peon concierto — See concierto

Peon suelto (also asalariado) — Free, wage-employed laborer

Predio — Farm, farm holding

Primicias — First fruits; contributions to the church

Priostazgo — Prioste system; organization centering on cult of a saint; system whereby a saint's fiesta is organized, financed, and sponsored by an individual; function of a prioste (q.v.)

Prioste — Sponsor, financier, and organizer of a religious feast or celebration of a saint's day; volunteer official in charge of local saint

Quechua, Quichua — Indian language spoken widely in the Andean area

Serrano — Highlander

Sierra — The Andean mountain area; the inter-Andine; highlands

Sindico — (1) Syndic; trustee; attorney

(2) Indian chapel trustee

Teniente político — Administrative political officer in charge of a parish

Tierras baldías	Idle, public lands; unclaimed lands; land of eminent domain
Tinterillo	Pettifogger, scribe, shyster lawyer (term of depreciation); often functions as "lawyer"; go-between
Totora	Reed
Yanape	A tenant system allowing for trespass and other rights (water, wood) in return for work
Yanapero	Renter of use-rights in lieu of labor

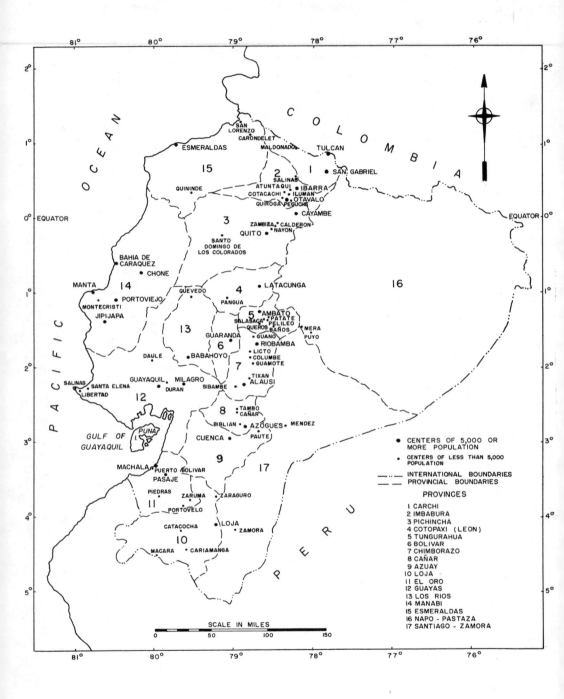

PROVINCES

1 CARCHI
2 IMBABURA
3 PICHINCHA
4 COTOPAXI (LEON)
5 TUNGURAHUA
6 BOLIVAR
7 CHIMBORAZO
8 CAÑAR
9 AZUAY
10 LOJA
11 EL ORO
12 GUAYAS
13 LOS RIOS
14 MANABI
15 ESMERALDAS
16 NAPO - PASTAZA
17 SANTIAGO - ZAMORA

• CENTERS OF 5,000 OR MORE POPULATION
• CENTERS OF LESS THAN 5,000 POPULATION
—·—·— INTERNATIONAL BOUNDARIES
— — — PROVINCIAL BOUNDARIES

SCALE IN MILES
0   50   100   150

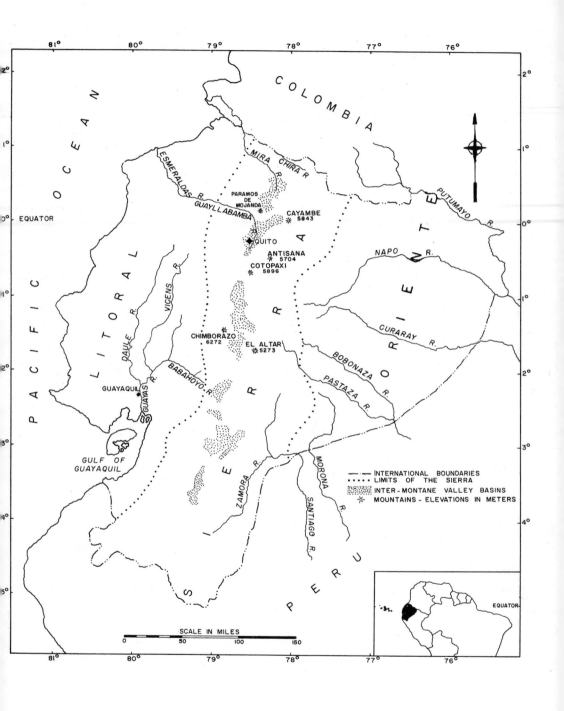

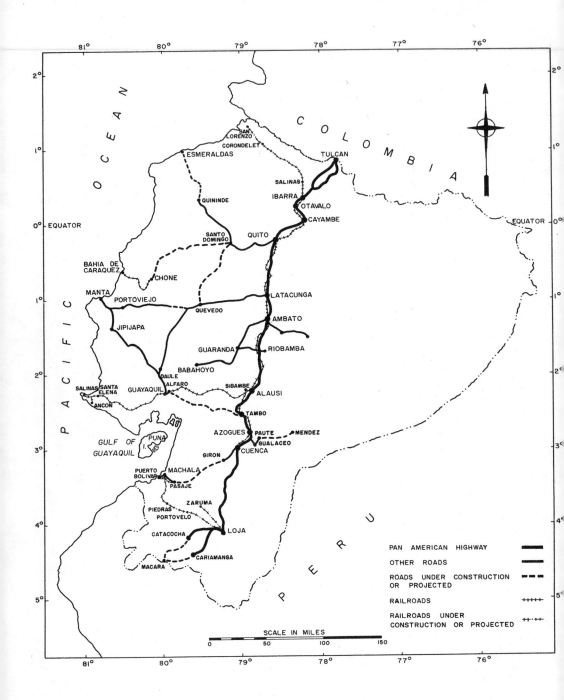

#26472304